Beer, Be...
and
Breakfast

'May not the darkness hide it from my face?'
'You cannot miss that inn.'
'Will there be beds for me and all who seek?'
'Yea, beds for all who come.'
– Christina Rossetti, Up Hill

BEER, BED
AND
BREAKFAST

Fourth Edition

Edited by Roger Protz

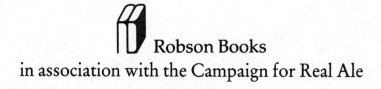

Robson Books

in association with the Campaign for Real Ale

Designed by Harold King

Maps by David Perrott

Cover picture of The Brocket Arms, Ayot St Lawrence, Herts, by the author

First published in Great Britain in 1992 by Robson Books Ltd, Bolsover House, 5-6 Clipstone Street, London W1P 7EB

British Library Cataloguing-in-Publication Data
A Catalogue record for this title is available
from the British Library

   ISBN 0 86051 785 3

Photoset in North Wales by
Derek Doyle & Associates, Mold, Clwyd
Printed and bound in Great Britain by
Biddles Ltd, Guildford and King's Lynn

CONTENTS

INTRODUCTION

'I have fed purely upon ale; I have eat my ale, drank
my ale, and I always sleep upon ale'
George Farquhar, The Beaux Stratagem

There has never been a better time to stay in a pub. If a recession
can have an 'upside' as well as a downside, it comes in the shape
of prices for accommodation in many pubs that have been
frozen for two years and in some cases even cut. That is good
news for users of this guide; it is not good news for publicans
who are attempting to weather the storm not only of economic
downturn but of fundamental changes in the brewing industry
and pub trade that are causing havoc, confusion and quite a lot
of pain.

You can ease that pain by enjoying one of the simple pleasures
of life: staying in a good, traditional and unspoilt British pub
where the landlord or landlady welcome you into their homes
and treat you not just as a valued customer but often as a friend.
In return for prices as low as £12 a head, you will drink, eat and
sleep well. You will rub shoulders with locals enjoying a pint
who will engage you in conversation and may invite you to join
them at darts, dominoes or crib. Pub accommodation allows
you to tour Britain on a limited budget and see a side of the
country rarely glimpsed from large and impersonal hotels.

From time to time there are disappointments. We try to
minimize them. This, the fourth edition of the guide, has been
rigorously overhauled. We take seriously complaints from
readers, investigate them and, when justified, remove the
offending pubs from the next edition. At the same time,
CAMRA members, branches and regional directors have
recommended new entries and have also critically scrutinized
every pub in the third edition. As a result there has been a
considerable change from the last edition. We welcome many
new entries and are glad to report that both London and the
adjacent counties of Kent, Surrey and Sussex now have better
representation.

There are many reasons why a pub is dropped. Complaints
usually concern a poor welcome or service and occasionally
guest rooms that fall below an acceptable standard of
cleanliness. CAMRA officials may not be satisfied with the

quality of beer served in a particular establishment. And readers may feel that a pub has changed out of all recognition and no longer merits an entry. A case in point is the pub described in the last edition as being 'as near idyllic as you can get'. Many readers wrote to say that if the pub was idyllic they would hate to stay in a real dump.

The reason for the fall from grace flowed from an expensive modernization of the bars that had caused prices throughout the pub to escalate. The result was that a comfortable old seaside local had been transformed into yet another identikit smart, brush-nylon bar with, upstairs, guest rooms that had missed out on the 'refurb'.

The recession has taken its toll. Some pubs have disappeared from the guide because they have closed or are no longer offering accommodation. If a pub's trade has fallen the licensees may no longer be able to afford the staff to look after guests and guest rooms. The astonishing turnover in licensees between editions three and four has resulted in many incomers to pubs deciding not to take on the additional burden of bed and breakfast accommodation until they have got their feet under the bar.

In every part of the country we have attempted to find new pubs to replace those that have fallen by the wayside. The Celtic fringe has been most badly hit: Cornwall, Scotland and Wales are always the first to feel any downturn in tourism. There is still a good choice in those areas in this edition though the numbers are slightly down on edition three.

Scotland, it must be emphasized, is a special case. The pub is a Borders phenomenon. Further north, bars and hotels take over; the former rarely offers accommodation, the latter rarely serves real ale.

Elsewhere other parts of the West Country – Devon, Dorset and Somerset – have survived the recession impressively well, as has East Anglia with the exception of Cambridgeshire where some pubs have disappeared not for economic reasons but as a result of Greene King's curious policy of offering pressurized beer through dinky fake 'handpumps'.

Standards of accommodation are now impressively high. Over the years that the guide has appeared, many publicans have beavered away to upgrade their guest rooms to offer first-class facilities. Not all pubs have the space to give each room its own shower or bathroom but the number is increasing. However, it is important to stress to first-time users of the guide that while a pub may have the word 'hotel' in its title it may not have the facilities of a modern neon-and-plastic emporium.

A pub will certainly not charge the same prices as a hotel and while en suite accoutrements are always welcome I, for one, have always found the two o'clock stagger down the corridor to the toilet to be one of the many pleasures and rituals of staying in an old country inn. You will find some modern hotels here, too: it is part of CAMRA's mission to encourage hotels to sell cask beer. The aim of the guide is to offer the widest range of pub and hotel accommodation possible and at prices to suit all pockets.

Other improvements include the high standard of pub food. One thing certain to raise my hackles is the sound of snooty foodies on television who claim they could never possibly eat in pubs because the offerings are so abysmal. Such attitudes are a mixture of snobbery and ignorance. The success of CAMRA's companion guide to Good Pub Food and even the conversion of the Good Food Guide are testimony to the fact that you can eat exceptionally well in many pubs. Chefs are forsaking restaurants to accept the challenge of preparing fine meals at affordable prices in pubs. A glimpse at some of the menus in the guide should prove the point and get even the most jaded tastebuds salivating.

No room for the innkeeper

Pubs have been dented by the recession and now rocked by changes in the way in which they are run. As a result of an investigation of the pub trade by the Monopolies and Mergers Commission, the government introduced two policies devised to bring more choice into outlets owned by the national brewers. The brewers were instructed to allow some of their tenants to buy in 'guest beers' from other producers and, second, to turn some of their pubs into fully-fledged free houses.

The brewers responded by offering their own 'in-house' list of guest beers to their tenants. The lists tended to offer beers from other large breweries with whom the nationals already had close trading links. In the extreme case of Whitbread, its list of so-called guest beers is made up mainly of beers owned by the combine itself, safe in the knowledge that most consumers and even many publicans are unaware that such famous 'independent' brands as Boddingtons, Chesters, Flowers and Higsons are now part of a national conglomerate.

Many national tenants have complained that brewery representatives have threatened rent reviews and other penalties if genuine guest beers are bought in against the wishes of the brewery. The anticipated choice has not materialized. Small brewers still struggle to find additional outlets for their beer.

The second stage of the government's changes – turning national brewers' pubs into free houses – has met with undisguised hostility by the pub owners. Rather than offering choice to consumers, the brewers prefer either to close pubs or sell or lease them in blocks to new independent pub-owning chains in return for an agreement for the brewery to supply the off-loaded pubs with its products. Early in 1992, for example, Allied Breweries leased 734 pubs to Brent Walker's Pubmaster chain with a seven-year beer supply deal. The names may change above the pub door but the beers inside do not.

At the same time the national brewers are busily changing the ground rules between themselves and their tenants. Ever since the 'tied house' system was introduced in the 19th century, brewers have traditionally charged low rents to tenants in return for high wholesale prices for beer. Now the brewers are switching many tenants from traditional three-year agreements to leases, running from ten years to as long as twenty. While beer sold to lessees remains dear, rents are often doubling or quadrupling and the lessees also find they are now responsible for all internal repairs and improvements to their pubs. The result has been that a number of publicans who accepted leases have quickly gone bankrupt and those that have refused to accept leases have been thrown on to the streets despite long years of dedication to both pub and owning landlord. Some tenants have little or no say in the changeover: one East Anglian licensee told the guide when he returned his survey forms: 'When I went on holiday last year I was a GrandMet tenant. When I came back I found I was a Brent Walker lessee.'

The fear is that Britain's pub stock will decline as lessees go bankrupt and that traditional pub tenants will be replaced by a new breed concerned not with the community role of the pub but making a fast buck.

Other changes are equally daunting. In spite of the MMC report and the government proposals for change, the big brewers have tightened their grip on the industry. Grand Metropolitan, Greenall Whitley and Boddingtons have got out of brewing.

GrandMet made the exit in style, selling its breweries to Courage in return for Courage's pubs. At a stroke, GrandMet became the biggest pub retailer in the country and it has a cosy seven-year supply deal with Courage. Both are now neatly excluded from the government's pub legislation, which applies only to breweries that own tied estates.

As CAMRA celebrated its 21st anniversary in 1992 it was clear that the Campaign still had many battles to tackle on behalf of pub consumers. Its burgeoning membership indicates that consumers are willing to be part of those battles.

A vigilant and powerful consumer movement will ensure that users of this guide will continue to enjoy the best of British pubs.

Opening times

Pubs in England and Wales may now open from 11am to 11pm Monday to Saturday but only around one third of publicans choose to do so. Most pubs close at 2.30 or 3pm and re-open at 6pm. However, guests can have access to pubs with residential licences at all times and may even be served with food and drink if staff are available. Children can stay in pubs when there are guest rooms. People under 18 cannot be served in bars and children under 16 cannot be served in pub dining rooms. But if a pub or hotel has a residential licence then children can be admitted to dining rooms and residents' lounges. Scottish pub hours are given at the start of the entries for that country; it also has new legislation making the admittance of children to pubs and hotels more relaxed and sensible.

Prices

The prices for accommodation are correct at the time of going to press and are based on information supplied by licensees. Please check tariffs when booking and also enquire whether any changes have been made to the information supplied. For example, new licensees may decide not to take children or dogs and may no longer have an arrangement to accept credit or charge cards.

Phone numbers

Telephone numbers are correct at the time of going to press but no doubt British Telecom will continue to tinker with thousands of STD codes, making life misery for guide book users and compilers.

The real thing

Real ale, also known as traditional draught beer or cask-conditioned beer, is a definition of a British beer style that is accepted by the Oxford English Dictionary. It means a top-fermented beer that undergoes a natural secondary fermentation in the cask and which is served without applied gas pressure. Most pubs in the guide serve real ale by a simple suction pump – a beer engine – which draws beer from the cask in the cellar when the handpump on the bar is pulled. Some pubs still serve the beer straight from the cask by gravity dispense while others, mainly in the Midlands and the North, use electric pumps. In Scotland, while handpumps are now widespread, the traditional method of serving cask beer is the tall fount primed by air pressure.

JOIN CAMRA!

If you want to join the growing movement to preserve Britain's unique beers and pubs, then £10 a year will bring you a monthly newspaper, What's Brewing, information concerning branch, regional and national activities, including beer festivals, and generous discounts on books published by CAMRA and Alma Books. Send a cheque made out to 'CAMRA Ltd' to CAMRA, (Dept BBB), 34 Alma Road, St Albans, Herts AL1 3BW. Further details, including direct debit and credit card payments, from the Membership Secretary on 0727 867201. To keep up to date with all changes in the brewing industry make sure you buy CAMRA's annual Good Beer Guide.

Roger Protz

ENGLAND

Bowl Inn, Bristol

BRISTOL

Bowl Inn
16 Church Road,
Lower Almondsbury, off M5 exit 16

Licensee: John Alley
Tel: 0454 612757/613717

The Bowl has been an inn since the
17th century and is a picturesque
whitewashed stone building on the
outskirts of Bristol and on the
south-eastern edge of the Severn
Valley. Its name derives from its
position in a dip in the flatlands of the
estuary. The inn stands opposite the
church of St Mary the Virgin and was
used by James I's sheriffs to try
supporters of the Duke of
Monmouth, leader of the failed
'pitchfork rebellion' against the
crown. The Bowl is a good base for
visiting Bristol and Bath, the
Wildfowl Reserve at Slimbridge, the
Wye Valley, Forest of Dean and
Tintern Abbey. Bar food, lunchtime
and evening, ranges from sandwiches
and soup to salads, grills, fish,
omelettes, curries and vegetarian
dishes. There is a separate restaurant
with an extensive menu.
Accommodation is in a cottage
annexe and the rooms have TV,
mini-bars and tea and coffee makers.

Beer: Courage BA, Best Bitter and
Directors, John Smith's Yorkshire
Bitter and Wadworth 6X on
handpumps.

Accommodation: 2 twins, 1 en suite, 1
with private bathroom. B&B £65 per
room, £45 per night Friday and
Saturday; £39.50 single occupancy,
£29.50 Friday and Saturday.
Breakfast served in the cottage. No
pets.
Cards: Access, Amex, Diners, Visa.

KEYNSHAM

Crown Inn
63 Bristol Road, ½ mile off A4

Licensee: G.P. Feltham
Tel: 0272 862150

The Crown is an unspoilt pub first
licensed in 1745. It has a large
collection of photographs and prints
of old Keynsham. Darts and cribbage
are played in the bar. Four miles from
Bristol and seven from Bath, the
Crown has graced more than ten
editions of the *Good Beer Guide* due
to the quality of its ale. A wide range
of good value, homemade food is
served lunchtime and evening.

Beer: Courage BA and Best Bitter,
John Smith's Yorkshire Bitter and
guest beers on handpumps.

Accommodation: 2 singles, 1 twin.
B&B £18.50 single, £29.50 twin.
Children welcome. No pets.

MONKTON COMBE

Wheelwrights Arms
1½ miles off A36, 3 miles south of
Bath

Proprietors: Marilyn & Roger
Howard
Tel: 0225 722287

The Wheelwrights Arms was built in
the middle of the 18th century and
first licensed in 1871. It stands in the
lovely Midford Valley and is quiet
and remote, yet it is just three miles
from Bath. The accommodation is in
a converted barn and stables block.
Each room has en suite facilities,
direct dial phone, shower, colour TV
and tea and coffee making facilities.
You can try your hand at darts and
cribbage with the locals and in winter
you can warm yourself by a roaring

log fire. There are bar snacks, lunches and evening grills.

Beer: Adnams Bitter, Butcombe Bitter, Wadworth 6X plus guest beers served straight from the cask.

Accommodation: 8 doubles/twins. B&B from £46 per person. Winter Break (Oct-March) any two days or more from £33 per day per person, includes B&B plus evening meal. Children 14 and over welcome, no reductions. No pets. Cards: Access and Visa.

TORMARTON

Compass Inn

Near Badminton. B4465 off A46; junction 18 M4

Proprietor: Mr P. Monyard
Tel: 0454 218242
Fax: 0454 218741

The ivy-clad Compass is a carefully modernized 18th-century coaching inn, so named because a former landlord decorated the building with chandlery from Bristol's shipyards. The four Cotswold stone bars maintain the sea-going flavour with beams and a pair of ship's lanterns in the Long Bar. The inn has a separate restaurant with à la carte menu, specializing in local game and produce. There is also a hot and cold buffet every lunchtime and evening. There are lawns, gardens and a charming orangery. All the guest rooms have private baths, TVs, tea and coffee making facilities and direct-dial phones. In the heart of the Cotswolds, the Compass is close to Tetbury and its annual Woolsack race, Badminton House with its horse trials, the ancient hilltop town of Malmesbury, and the old Roman town of Cirencester.

Beer: Archers Village Bitter, Draught Bass, Smiles Best Bitter on handpumps.

Accommodation: 31 rooms: 1 single, 25 doubles, 5 family. B&B £49.95-£63.50 single, £64.95-£77.50 double, £8.75 per child in family rooms. Winter Breaks £39.50 per person per day B&B plus evening meal. Family room. Pets accepted. Cards: Access, Amex, Diners, Visa.

BEDFORDSHIRE

CRANFIELD

Swan

2 Court Road. 4 miles from M1 exits 13 & 14; between Bedford and Milford Keynes

Licensees: Harry & Glenda Williams
Tel: 0234 750332/750772

The Swan is a spacious 1930s pub with facilities for all the family. The Sports Bar is for snooker and skittles enthusiasts while the lounge bar has a dining area. The enclosed garden has a play area for children. Food includes bar meals, evening meals and a traditional Sunday roast. There is a separate children's menu and a high chair is available for toddlers. Food includes fresh and toasted sandwiches, ploughman's, homemade beefburgers, steaks, chilli, croque monsieur, tikka pitta and vegetarian specials. The guest rooms have colour TVs and tea and coffee makers. The Swan is close to a flying school that was formerly a wartime bomber base. It now offers flying lessons and hot-air ballooning. A nearby lake has a boating club and water sports, and Woburn Safari Park is nearby.

Beer: Greene King IPA, Rayments Special Bitter and Abbot Ale on handpump.

Accommodation: 3 doubles/twins, 1 family room, 3 rooms with en suite facilities. Double/twin £35 per room, £45 en suite, £25/£35 single occupancy. Family room £45. No pets. Cards: Access, Visa.

LOWER STONDON

Bird in Hand
A600 4 miles north of Hitchin, 9 miles south of Bedford

Licensees: Brian & June Cullen
Tel: 0462 850385

The Bird in Hand is on the Beds/Herts border and the nearest town is Hitchin. It is a large and welcoming pub that specializes in home-cooked food, which is available seven days a week, lunchtime and evening and has a range that covers everything from sandwiches to steaks. The Greene King beers include the delectable dark mild.

Beer: Greene King XX, IPA, Abbot Ale on handpumps.

Accommodation: 14 rooms: 8 singles, 5 twin, 1 family room. £17 single, £34 double. Children's rates negotiable. No pets.

SALFORD

Red Lion Country Hotel
Wavendon Road: unclassified road 2 miles NW of M1 exit 13; off A421 & A507

Licensee: Bob Sapsford
Tel: 0908 583117

The Red Lion is a 16th-century inn in extensive grounds in a rural village

that is only 10 minutes from Milton Keynes. There are exposed beams and cottage decor, bric-à-brac and a roaring log fire in winter. For couples keen on nuptials as well as real ale there are six suites with four-poster beds. All the guest rooms have TVs and direct-dial telephones. The hotel is a good base for Woburn Sands, Aspley Heath, Milton Keynes shopping centre and Silverstone motor racing circuit. The Red Lion offers bar snacks with a separate restaurant for lunch and dinner.

Beer: Charles Wells Eagle Bitter and Bombardier on handpumps.

Accommodation: 6 doubles with en suite facilities £42; 1 twin £42; 2 singles £32. Ground-floor facilities for the disabled.

SHEFFORD

White Hart
2 Northbridge Street, junction of A600 & A507; close to M1 & A1

Licensee: Charles Fraser
Tel/fax: 0462 811144

The White Hart is an old coaching inn in the centre of Shefford. Extensive bar meals and evening restaurant meals are available; no bar meals Sunday evening, restaurant closed Sunday and Monday. The pub was a runner-up in the 1991 Guinness Pub Food awards. Coarse and trout fishing are available locally. The area is good for golf and Woburn Abbey, Rutland Water, the RSPB bird sanctuary at Sandy and the Shuttleworth Collection are all close by. All guest rooms have colour TVs and tea and coffee makers. One room can be converted to a family room. The beers come from the micro-brewery in Shefford.

Beer: Banks and Taylor Shefford Mild, Shefford Bitter, Black Bat, Edwin Taylor's Stout and Shefford Old Strong on handpump and direct from the cask.

Accommodation: 4 twins, 2 with private showers. £30 single, £50 double. Children welcome, rates negotiable. No pets. Cards: Access, Visa.

SILSOE

Old George Hotel
High Street, just off A6; 9 miles from Bedford, 11 miles from Luton

Licensees: John & Elaine Bridge
Tel: 0525 60218

The George is a handsome old coaching inn shaded by trees with a full range of hotel facilities, including family rooms, a restaurant that can cater for up to 50 people and two bars. It is well placed for visitors to Woburn Abbey and Wrest Park. As well as a full English breakfast, packed lunches can be arranged for guests. All the guest rooms have hot and cold water, colour TVs and tea and coffee makers. Full meals and bar meals are available every day. Cots and high chairs are available for children. There is a large enclosed beer garden with caravan facilities and an animal farm.

Beer: Greene King IPA and Abbot Ale on handpumps.

Accommodation: 7 rooms: 3 singles, 2 doubles, 1 twin, 1 family room. Single £28, double £48. 10% reductions for CAMRA members. Pets by prior arrangement. Cards: Access and Visa.

STEVINGTON

Red Lion
1 Park Road. 1½ miles north of A428, signposted five miles from Bedford

Licensees: George & Hilary Lee
Tel: 02302 4138

The Red Lion is a friendly local next to a medieval stone cross in an attractive village. The lounge bar serves snacks, lunches and evening meals plus a traditional Sunday lunch. The emphasis is on homemade food and includes tempting pies and pasties and an award-winning lamb and apricot pie. The cheerful public bar has darts, dominoes and crib and there is a garden with a children's play area that includes a rabbit. Stevington has John Bunyan connections and a restored 18th-century windmill and a holy well. Bromham, two miles away, has a water mill and museum on the river Ouse.

Beer: Greene King IPA and Abbot Ale on handpumps.

Accommodation: 2 double rooms. B&B £22 single, £34 double. Children welcome, terms negotiable.

BERKSHIRE

EAST ILSLEY

Swan
High Street. A34 Oxford road, 5 minutes from M4, exit 13.

Licensee: Michael Connolly
Tel: 063 528 238 Fax: 063 528 791

The Swan is a 16th-century coaching inn nestling in the peaceful downlands village of East Ilsley and decked out with colourful hanging baskets and window boxes. It is within easy reach of Newbury and its racecourse and the Ridgeway path, which passes through many famous pre-historic sites. Oxford is close by. Bar meals include steak and kidney pie, steak and onions braised in ale, chicken curry, macaroni au gratin, a range of burgers (including vegan), ploughman's and sandwiches. Full restaurant meals (Tuesday to Saturday) include prawn bisque, marinated fish, seafood vol au vents, roast lamb, breast of chicken, duck, salmon and fillet of sole. All the guest rooms have colour TVs and direct-dial phones.

Beer: Morland Original and Old Masters on handpumps.

Accommodation: 3 singles, 5 doubles, 1 family room, 8 rooms with en suite facilities. £21 single, £32 en suite; £40 double, £49 en suite; £55 family room, £60 en suite. Pets accepted. Cards: Access and Visa.

GORING-ON-THAMES

Queens Arms
Gatehampton Road. A329 Reading to Oxford road. M4 exit 13

Licensees: Steve & Bridget Carter
Tel: 0491 872825

The Queens Arms has been a licensed house since 1859 and new licensees have tastefully modernized it to meet today's requirements. It has a large garden, car park, public and lounge bars and serves full meals every day except Sunday. Goring village, on the borders of Berkshire and Oxfordshire, is one of the loveliest places in the Thames valley and is handy for the Ridgeway Walk, Thames footpath and the Chilterns.

Beer: Morrell Dark Mild and Best Bitter with occasional guest beers, all on handpumps.

Accommodation: 2 singles, 1 twin. £18 per person. Children and dogs welcome by arrangement.

HURLEY

Black Boy Inn
A423 between Hewley and Maidenhead

Licensees: Alan & Hazel Wymark
Tel: 0628 824212

The Black Boy is a 16th-century beamed rural inn just 400 yards from the Thames, with log fires in winter and hanging baskets in summer. The inn has a large beer garden and has superb views over the Thames valley. It is a fine base for country and river walks, with Windsor just 12 miles away. The Black Boy was reputed to have been a safe house for the followers of Charles II who met to plot his return from France to the throne. There is wide range of snacks and bar meals, with the emphasis on home cooking. A traditional roast is available on Sundays and there are always three or four dishes for vegetarians.

Beer: Brakspear Bitter and Old on handpumps.

Accommodation: 1 single, 1 twin. £25 single, £40 twin. Children welcome, no reductions. No pets.

KNOWL HILL

Seven Stars
Bath Road. On A4 between Maidenhead & Reading, 5 miles from Maidenhead, 2½ miles from exits 8/9 of M4

Licensees: Robin & Lyn Jones
Tel: 0628 822967
Fax: 0628 823697

The Seven Stars is a 17th-century coaching inn with a Georgian frontage and comfortable panelled rooms with log fires in winter. The large gardens have tree houses and swings for children and the pub has a children's room. The splendid home-cooked food is served until 9pm every day. The pub has a skittles alley and there are limited facilities for the disabled. Knowl Hill is a good base for Henley-on-Thames, home of Brakspear's traditional brewery, Windsor, Marlow – no longer the home of Wethered's traditional brewery, closed by Whitbread – and the Shire Horse Centre.

Beer: Brakspear XXX Mild, Bitter, Special and Old on handpumps.

Accommodation: 2 double rooms. B&B £18 single, £40 double. Children welcome.

LAMBOURN

George Hotel
High Street, B4000, M4 exit 14

Licensee: Maureen Naylor
Tel: 0488 71889

The George is less than an hour's drive from Heathrow airport yet it offers superb accommodation in tranquil countryside. It dates back to the 16th century and serves bar meals every lunchtime and early evening; there is a separate restaurant. The emphasis is on traditional English cooking and guests can enjoy both splendid cask ale and a fine range of crusted ports, too.

Beer: Arkell BBB on handpump

Accommodation: 1 single, 3 doubles/twins, 1 family room, 2 rooms with en suite facilities. Single £22.50, double £38, family room rates negotiable. Winter weekends negotiable. Pets accepted. Cards: Access and Visa.

REMENHAM

Two Brewers
Wargrave Road, junction of A321 & A423

Licensees: Graham & Deana Godmon
Tel: 0491 574375

A warm welcome is waiting in this cosy part-panelled pub with a roaring log fire in winter and hanging baskets in summer. An excellent bar menu is served every day with additional daily specials. Nearby you can enjoy riverside walks or stroll across the attractive 18th-century bridge with five arches into Henley, home of Brakspear's brewery and the annual Royal regatta.

Beer: Brakspear Bitter, Special and Old on handpumps.

Accommodation: 1 single, 2 twins, 1 double with en suite facilities. B&B £20 single, £42 twin and double. Children welcome.

WARGRAVE

Bull Hotel
High Street, A321, 1 mile from A4, between Maidenhead and Reading

Licensee: Noel Harman
Tel: 0734 403120

The Bull is a 16th-century listed building with exposed beams and unusually decorated brick walls in the bars and dining area, and two enormous fireplaces with blazing log fires in winter. Wargrave is an attractive Thames-side village four miles from Henley. The pub has a garden and patio. Guest rooms have central heating and colour TVs. The restaurant, known as Mo's Kitchen, has a good local reputation for the quality of its meals, and features such dishes as chicken filled with smoked salmon mousseline, roast duck with Calvados apple purée, lemon sole with wild mushroom and prawn sauce, rack of lamb with garlic and rosemary and scampi with tomato and basil.

Beer: Brakspear Bitter and Special on handpumps.

Accommodation: 2 singles. 3 doubles. B&B £20 single, £35 double. Evening meals available. No children.

WOOLHAMPTON

Rowbarge Inn
Station Road, off A4.

Licensees: Roger & Lyn Jarvis
Tel: 0734 712213

The Rowbarge is a delightful old-world pub on the river Kennet where it meets the Kennet and Avon canal. A canal lock is next to the pub garden and is a good watering hole for canal users. Accommodation is in a separate building in the village owned by the Jarvises, who supply it with their food from the pub. They have decorated the pub with fascinating bric-à-brac, including a collection of 80 blow lamps. A large conservatory has fine views of an ornamental pond, the garden and the river and can be used for small-scale conferences. Bar food is based on home-cooked recipes.

Beer: Brakspear Bitter, Courage Directors, Morland Bitter, John Smith's Yorkshire Bitter, Wadworth 6X on handpumps.

Accommodation: 4 singles, 1 double, all with private showers. £23 single, £33 double for bed and continental breakfast; cooked breakfast £3.50 extra. Cards: Access, Amex, Diners, Visa.

BUCKINGHAMSHIRE

BENNETT END

Three Horseshoes
Bennett End, Radnage, Nr High Wycombe. Off A40, follow Radnage signs. 3 miles from M40 exit 5

Licensee: Tim Ashby
Tel: 0494 483273

The Three Horseshoes is an 18th-century country inn in the secluded Hughenden Valley, nestling down narrow lanes. It has old beams and open fires and a fine garden with splendid views over the rolling Chilterns. Woodstock, Windsor and Oxford are close by. The pub offers lunchtime snacks, a full evening menu and a traditional roast lunch on Sundays (no food Mondays). The guest rooms all have en suite facilities, colour TVs and tea and coffee makers, and one room has a king-size waterbed.

Beer: Brakspear Bitter and Flowers Original on handpumps.

Accommodation: 2 doubles, 1 twin. B&B £38 single, £48 double. Children and pets welcome.

CUDDINGTON

Crown
Aylesbury Road, 1 mile off A418,
between Aylesbury and Thame

Licensee: Barry Jones
Tel: 0844 292222

A fine old thatched building dating
from the 13th century, the Crown has
low beams and inglenooks plus such
20th-century attributes as central
heating and tea and coffee making
facilities in the guest rooms. The
excellent pub food is all home made
and the bar has a wealth of traditional
pub games. Cuddington won the
coveted Best Kept Village in Bucks
award in 1989 and 1990. Aylesbury is
six miles away and nearby attractions
include Waddesdon Manor, and
Wotton House in Wotton
Underwood, which is almost
identical to the original Buckingham
House before it became Buckingham
Palace. To the north, steam trains run
to Aylesbury in the summer from
Quainton Railway Centre. The pub
offers lunches Monday to Saturday,
evening meals Wednesday to
Saturday.

Beer: Fullers Chiswick Bitter,
London Pride and ESB on
handpumps.

Accommodation: 1 twin. B&B £19.25
per person.

HIGH WYCOMBE

Bell
Frogmore, town centre, rear of
Sainsbury's; off M40 & A40

Licensee: Mr H.W.J. Lacey
Tel: 0494 521317

The Bell is a 17th-century heavily
timbered pub that has retained its
charm and character. Food is served
in a carvery and is available lunchtime
every day and Monday to Thursday
in the evening. West Wycombe caves
are a short drive away.

Beer: Fullers Chiswick Bitter,
London Pride and ESB on
handpumps.

Accommodation: 2 singles, 3 doubles.
B&B £17.50 per person. No
reductions, no children. Cards:
Access, Visa.

LONGWICK

Red Lion
Thame Road, B4129 1 mile from
Princes Risborough

Licensees: Anthony & June Goss
Tel: 08444 4980

The Red Lion is some 200 years old, a
listed building that is thought to have
once been a chapel. Some leaded
windows remain. It serves as a centre
for the village but a warm and
informal welcome is extended to
visitors. Bar meals – soup,
ploughman's, pâté, burgers, scampi
and various homemade pies – are
available as well as grills in the
restaurant. The pub is a splendid base
for walkers in the Chiltern hills and
Blenheim Palace and the Hell Fire
Caves at West Wycombe are close by.

Beer: Fullers London Pride and
Hook Norton Best Bitter on
handpumps.

Accommodation: 4 singles, 4 doubles,
all with en suite facilities. B&B £38
single, £49.50 double. Children over
12 welcome, no reductions. Cards:
Access and Visa.

WENDOVER

Red Lion
High Street. A413, 5 miles south of
Aylesbury

Licensee: Mr B Hickin
Tel: 0296 622266
Fax: 0296 625077

The Red Lion Hotel is a coaching inn
that was built in 1619 and combines
the best of the old world and the new:
log fires in the inglenook in winter
back up the central heating. The fine
exterior has dormer windows and
impressive tall chimneys. Wendover
nestles at the foot of the Chiltern
Hills and is close to Blenheim,
Chequers, Woburn, Luton Hoo and
Hughenden. There are facilities
within the area for fishing, riding,
walking and golf. The hotel has a
cheery lounge bar with a buttery
section where children can sit and
enjoy informal meals with their
parents. There is an oak-panelled
dining room too. Bar and buttery
meals include crab soup, smoked
salmon, steaks, burgers, chicken
surprise, devilled kidneys, smoked
haddock, omelettes, Welsh rarebit,
ploughman's, filled jacket potatoes,
vegetable pie and a separate children's
menu. All the guest rooms have
private baths or showers en suite.

Beer: Brakspear Bitter, Cains Bitter,
Marston Pedigree Bitter, Morland
Bitter and occasional guest beers, all
on handpumps.

Accommodation: 3 singles, 16
doubles/twins, 7 family rooms. B&B
£44 single, £54 double/twin, £64
family room. Weekend rates
available. Well-behaved pets
accepted. Cards: Access, Amex,
Diners, Switch, Visa.

WESTON TURVILLE

Chandos Arms
1 Main Street, B4043, 1 mile from
A413, 2 miles from A41: take Aston
Clinton turn

Licensee: Kenneth Nickels
Tel: 0296 61 3532

The Chandos is more than 200 years
old with a great range of traditional
games, including dominoes, darts,
crib, bar billiards and Aunt Sally. The
large garden has 20 picnic tables and a
children's corner with swings and a
climbing frame. Zena Nickels
specializes in homemade, traditional
English food; lunch and dinner are
available every day. Morris Men
perform in the summer, there are
golf, riding, flying and fishing
facilities close by as well as the Prime
Minister's residence at Chequers.

Beer: Benskins Best Bitter, Ind
Coope Burton Ale and Tetley Bitter
on handpumps.

Accommodation: 2 singles, 2 doubles.
B&B £15 per person. Children
welcome, no reductions.

WEST WYCOMBE

George & Dragon
On A40

Licensee: Philip Todd
Tel: 0494 464414
Fax: 0494 462432

The George and Dragon, in a
delightful National Trust village, is a
500-year-old coaching inn, renovated
and restored in 1720. An archway
leads to an attractive cobbled

courtyard, large walled garden, play area and parking space. The inn retains some half-timbers and has ancient pigeon lofts: pigeons used to carry messages when bad weather delayed coaches. Two bedrooms have four-poster beds. The George & Dragon is also reputed to have the ghost of a 'White Lady', thought to be a young girl named Sukie who came to an unfortunate end in the Hell Fire Caves. The caves are close by, as are West Wycombe Park and the Church Mausoleum, all open to the public. Bar meals are available lunchtime and evening and the extensive menu includes homemade soup, ploughman's, smoked mackerel, savoury mushrooms and courgettes, Cumberland lamb, steak and kidney pudding, beef Wellington, spinach and blue cheese pancakes, and sandwiches.

Beer: Courage Best Bitter and Directors plus a guest ale on handpumps.

Accommodation: 1 single, 7 doubles, 1 family room all with en suite facilities. B&B £40 single, £55 double, £62 family. Weekend £75 double for 2 nights. Children's room; children sharing a guest room are charged £7 per night. Pets accepted. Cards: Access, Amex, Diners, Visa.

WINSLOW

Bell Hotel
Market Square. A413 between Aylesbury and Buckingham

Licensee: Rachel Watts
Tel: 0296 71 2741/4091

The 16th-century coaching inn dominates Winslow market square. An inn has stood on the site since Tudor times and has always been the focal point of the town. It was once used as the local magistrates' court and petty sessions were held there on alternate Wednesdays; stage coaches to and from London stopped at the Bell every day except Sunday. The bar has log fires in winter and has a welcoming atmosphere with its ancient oak beams and comfortable seats. The Verney bar has some wattle and daub panels and an open fire. It is named after the Verney family of Claydon House, which is a few miles from Winslow and has Florence Nightingale connections. The Claydon Restaurant offers modern English cuisine and bar meals are also available daily. Winslow is handy for Silverstone motor racing circuit, Towcester racecourse and Buckingham golf course.

Beer: Bateman XXXB, Courage Best Bitter and Directors and Marston Pedigree Bitter on handpumps.

Accommodation: 6 singles, 11 doubles/twins, 1 family room, all with en suite facilities, colour TVs, telephones, trouser presses and tea and coffee makers. £50 single, £60 double/twin (per room), £75 family room. Children's and weekend rates on application. Pets accepted. Cards: Access, Amex, Diners, Visa.

CAMBRIDGESHIRE

CAMBRIDGE

Clarendon Arms
35 Clarendon Street

Licensee: Pauline Milton
Tel: 0223 313937

The Clarendon is a bright and cheery local with a tasteful colour scheme of chocolate and cream and complementary blue curtains, light shades and a collection of dinner plates. There is a sun-trap patio at the back. The splendid, uncomplicated barfood ranges from massive crusty sandwiches to salads and ploughman's, with a daily hot special (hot food 11-3pm; 6-8.45pm). The pub, run with enormous verve and enthusiasm by Mrs Milton, is close to the great open greensward of Parker's Piece.

Beer: Greene King IPA, Rayments Special Bitter and Abbot Ale on handpumps.

Accommodation: 1 double, 2 twins. B&B £18 single, £30 double. No pets.

ELY

Lamb Hotel
Lynn Road, city centre, off A10 & A142

Manager: David Highfield
Tel: 0353 663574
Fax: 0353 666350

In the shadow of the magnificent and historic cathedral, The Lamb is an old coaching inn with high standards of accommodation. The Fenman Bar in the old stable block has been developed for ale lovers but draught beer is also available in the cocktail bar. The 32 beautifully appointed rooms all have private bathrooms, colour TVs and tea and coffee making facilities. The spacious Octagon Restaurant offers à la carte and table d'hôte lunches and dinners and there are tasty snacks in all the bars.

Beer: Greene King IPA and guest beers on handpumps.

Accommodation: 6 singles, 22 doubles, 2 triples, 4 rooms with four-poster beds. B&B £55 single,

£72 double, £75 triple, four-poster room £90. Weekend Breaks from £37.50. Details of antiques appreciation weekends and luxury weekend breaks on application. Children welcome; stay free if under 14 and sharing with parents.

HOLYWELL

Olde Ferry Boat Inn
Near St Ives; signposted from A1123 at Needingworth; off A604

Licensee: Richard Jeffrey
Tel: 0480 63227

This historic thatched and whitewashed inn is one of the country's oldest pubs, standing on the banks of the Great Ouse, and was recorded as selling ale in 1068. The rambling beamed bar of the inn has panelled and timbered walls with ancient settles and rush seats. No fewer than four fires belt out welcome heat in the winter. A stone in the centre of the inn marks a 900-year-old grave and it is haunted by the ghost of Juliette Tewsley, who hanged herself in 1050 when she was rejected by the local woodcutter. There is a large beer garden outside and a terrace; both have fine views of the river. Mr Jeffrey gets his produce fresh from London markets and offers all homemade dishes such as chicken liver pâté, ploughman's, omelettes, lasagne, venison burgers, smoked boar in red wine sauce, salmon, steaks and trout.

Beer: Adnams Bitter and Broadside, Draught Bass, Greene King IPA and Abbot Ale on handpumps plus up to four guest beers in summer.

Accommodation: 6 doubles, 1 twin, all en suite. B&B £39.99–£49.50 single, £44.50-£68 double. No charge for children under 4. Nov-Feb: 2

nights for the price of 1 – must include Saturday. Cards: Access and Visa.

KENNETT

Bell
Bury Road; junction of B1506 & B1085; off A45 Bury St Edmunds-Cambridge road

Licensee: Colin Hayling
Tel: 0638 750286

The Bell is a superb 16th-century timbered inn with heavy oak beams, a brick inglenook, free-standing fireplace and stripped tables with Windsor armchairs and cushioned dining chairs. A tiled room leads off the bar and is used as an evening seafood bar. Bar food includes soup, brunch and steak and stout pie. Accommodation is in a cottage in the grounds: 'It's only 200 years old,' says Mrs Hayling. 'It's a bit recent!'

Beer: Adnams Bitter, Nethergate Bitter and a rotating series of guest ales, including Courage Directors, Mansfield Bitter, Marston Pedigree Bitter and Whitbread Flowers Original on handpumps.

Accommodation: 7 twins, all with en suite facilities. £27.50 single, £35 double. Children from 5 years. No pets. Cards: Access and Visa.

MOLESWORTH

Cross Keys
100 yards off A604

Licensee: Frances Bettsworth
Tel: 080 14 283

The Cross Keys is a handsome inn in a quiet village midway between Huntingdon and Kettering. The wide range of home-cooked food – pies, curries, grills, fish dishes and vegetarian selection – is served informally in the bar and there is a traditional Sunday roast lunch for £5, £3.50 for children. The modern guest rooms have tea and coffee making facilities and central heating and all have their own bathrooms. The welcome is warm and genuine and visitors are encouraged to try their hand at darts and skittles with the locals. Molesworth is just three miles from Kimbolton Castle, while Grafham Water is five miles away. The pub is a good resting place for travellers from the North to the East Coast.

Beer: Adnams Bitter on handpump.

Accommodation: 1 single, 7 doubles, 1 family room, all en suite. Room £18 single, £28 double, £12.50 per person in family room. Breakfast extra: £2.50 English, £1.50 continental. Children welcome; rates by arrangement. No pets. Cards: Access and Visa.

STILTON

Bell
High Street. Off A1 south of Peterborough

Licensees: John & Liam McGivern
Tel: 0733 241066

A certain blue cheese is on the menu and can be bought at the inn, though it was never made in the village. Stilton cheese was originally known as Quenby cheese and came from villages around Melton Mowbray, but coaches taking supplies to London stopped at the Bell in Stilton. The rest is history. The inn has a cobbled back courtyard that is believed to date from Roman times. The gantry inn sign has the distances to cities carved on it. Inside the

CAMBRIDGESHIRE

rambling building there are log fires, flagstones, bow windows, wooden seats and sailing and coaching prints on the partly-stripped walls. Bar food includes terrine of Stilton and hazelnut pâté, soups, filled baguettes, curried lamb's kidneys, liver and bacon in onion sauce and traditional Stilton with plum bread.

Beer: Adnams Bitter, Marstons Pedigree Bitter, Ruddles County, Tetley Bitter and regular guest ales on handpumps.

Accommodation: 19 rooms, all en suite. 2 four-posters, 5 de luxe doubles, 8 doubles, 2 singles, 2 family rooms. Rates £57 single, £62 double. Weekend: £40 for two people per day, £25 single. Children sharing £10. No pets. Cards: Access, Amex, Diners, Visa.

WISBECH

White Lion Hotel
5 South Brink. A47, Peterborough-King's Lynn road.

Licensee: Michael Gregory
Tel: 0945 584813
Fax: 0945 583221

The White Lion is a family-run hotel on the banks of the River Nene: North and South Brink have some of the finest Georgian houses in the country, including the National Trust's Peckover House, built by a local banker. The White Lion was named the Queen's Head until 1773 when it changed to its present name. Extensive renovations and improvements were made in the middle of the 19th century. Food is available every day and ranges from sandwiches, salads, fish dishes and steaks at the bar to table d'hôte and à la carte menus in the restaurant.

CAMBRIDGESHIRE

Beer: Ruddles County on handpump.

Accommodation: 4 singles, 14 doubles, all with en suite facilities. B&B £43.50 single, £28.38 double. Extra child in room: £12.50. Weekend: £45.40 per night for 2 people. Cards: Access, Amex, Diners, Visa.

CHESHIRE

CHESTER

Pied Bull
Northgate Street

Licensee: C. McIntyre
Tel: 0244 325829
Fax: 0244 350322

The Pied Bull is an old coaching inn in the heart of the historic city and on the former London to Holyhead route. There is a plaque on an exterior pillar indicating the number of miles to such coaching destinations as London, Worcester, Ludlow, Bristol and Bath. The façade is Georgian, the interior much older, opened into one room but with many smaller sections. The striking fireplace has the painted coats of arms of city companies. The hot pub lunches are a feature of this welcoming old inn, where the accommodation has been thoroughly renovated.

Beer: Greenall Bitter and Thomas Greenall Original on handpumps.

Accommodation: 12 rooms, 1 single, 9 doubles, 2 family rooms, all with en suite facilities. B&B £39.90 single, £49 double, £69 family room. Four-poster room and premier suite available. Children no charge under 12 sharing family room. Weekend Break £17.50 per person per night.

3-day winter break £123 B&B plus evening meal. 'Weekend of Romance' £95. Pets accepted. Cards: Access, Amex, Diners, Visa.

COTEBROOK

Alvanley Arms
A49 near Tarporley

Licensee: Doreen White
Tel: 0829 760200

The red brick and creeper-clad 17th-century inn is located in tranquil countryside close to Chester and the M6. Nearby attractions include Delamere Forest, Beeston Castle and Oulton Park motor racing circuit, and there are facilities for golf, fishing and riding in the surrounding area. Visitors are guaranteed a genuine welcome in the bars and in the Cobbles restaurant where steak pie and fresh fish are popular.

Beer: Robinson Best Mild, Best Bitter and Old Tom (winter) on handpumps.

Accommodation: 1 single, 2 doubles. B&B £25 per person. A cot is available in one room: children's rates on application. Cards: Access and Visa.

FARNDON

Greyhound Hotel
High Street, on B5130, off A534; M6 exit 17

Licensees: Christopher & Wendy Gray
Tel: 0829 270244

The Greyhound is close to the River Dee: cross the river by the 14th century bridge and you are in Wales. Farndon is a picturesque village,

Greyhound Hotel, Farndon

popular with fishermen. Local salmon is a speciality of the pub where Chris and Wendy Gray run a popular and welcoming local with a pottery attached. There are traditional games in the bar and a family garden where children can play with the donkeys, Henry and Guinness, and three goats. Farndon is a good base for Chester, Beeston and Cholmondeley castles, Oulton Park, Stretton Water Mill and Snowdonia. Shooting can be arranged at a new and nearby clay shooting range. The guest rooms have colour TVs and tea and coffee making facilities.

Beer: Greenall Mild, Bitter and Thomas Greenall Original on handpumps.

Accommodation: 1 single, 1 double, 1 twin. B&B £22 single, £27 double, £30 twin plus VAT. There are also self-catering cottages: terms on application. Children welcome, terms negotiable.

GEE CROSS

Grapes Hotel
Stockport Road (A560), near Hyde; 3 miles from exit 15 of M63 & 30 minutes from exit 35 of M1

Licensees: Brian & Hilary Samuels
Tel: 061-368 2614
Fax: 061-368 6508

The Grapes is an old coaching inn first licensed in 1778 and modernized in Victorian times and again in 1985. It has its own bowling green and is the centre of life in the village and has stables for guests who bring horses or ponies. It is a good base for the Peak District, the Cheshire plains and Manchester and its international airport. For walkers, the hotel is close to the Tame Valley, Werneth Low and Etherow country parks and both Lyme Hall and Satton Hall and their

parks are close by. Bar snacks are available and the guest rooms have colour TVs, tea and coffee makers, wash-hand basins and central heating.

Beer: Robinson Best Mild and Best Bitter on electric pumps.

Accommodation: 1 single, 2 doubles. B&B £21.50 single, £35 double, £45 family in converted double. Children's rates on application. Horses by arrangement.

HAZEL GROVE

Woodman
60 London Road. A6, 7 miles from Manchester, 2 miles from Stockport

Licensee: Mrs L. Birtwistle
Tel: 061-483 7186

The Woodman was once a home-brew house run by the Simpson family. It was bought by Robinson of Stockport in the 1930s and was the company's first pub in the Hazel Grove area. The pub has recently been thoroughly renovated in a traditional style and has a games room with darts, pool and TV (with satellite as well as terrestrial programmes), and a comfortable lounge and bar, together with a separate restaurant. The pub is close to Lyme Park, the Peaks, Etherow Park and Bramhall Hall. Bar food includes chilli and garlic bread, beefburgers, hot beef barm, sandwiches and a children's menu. The restaurant offers curries, chilli, moussaka, deep-fried chicken, plaice, scampi, roast beef, and lasagne verde. Food is available at lunchtime seven days a week.

Beer: Robinson Best Mild and Best Bitter on handpumps.

Accommodation: 1 double, 3 twins. £18 per person, £20 with full breakfast. All rooms have TVs. No pets.

MALPAS

Red Lion Hotel
Old Hall Street, on B5069 off A41
Whitchurch to Chester road

Licensee: Shelagh Lever
Tel: 0948 860368

The Red Lion is an hospitable and historic brick-and-timber frame building, one of the oldest hostelries in south Cheshire, with wood-panelled walls and several rambling rooms. It was host to James I in 1624 when Malpas was a major stopping place for traffic between London, Shrewsbury and Liverpool. A relic of the king's visit remains in the bar – a chair known as the King's Chair. Customers must pay a penny to sit in it or stand drinks for everybody in the bar. In the heyday of coaches, the famous London to Liverpool coach known as the Albion used to stop here. Guest rooms are furnished to a high standard. Each room is individually named and the exposed timbers point up the antiquity of the inn. There is a solarium and sauna for visitors.

Beer: Draught Bass and guest beer on handpumps.

Accommodation: 8 rooms all with en suite facilities, one suitable as family room. B&B £21.95 per person. Half and full board available. Some of the accommodation is in the attached Tudor Cottage, which has won a civic conservation award.

HARTBURN

Stockton Arms Hotel
Darlington Road, ½ mile off A66,
1½ miles from junction of A66 & A19

Licensee: Derek Bramley
Tel: 0642 580104

A friendly, welcoming pub on the outskirts of Stockton, with open fires, and brasswork on the walls. There are excellent, good value bar snacks and separate dining facilities, including Sunday roast lunch, plus summer barbecues in the garden. The guest rooms have en suite facilities, colour TVs, tea and coffee makers and trouser presses. Hartburn is in easy reach of the coast and the North Yorkshire Moors while Yarm and Darlington are close by.

Beer: Draught Bass on handpump.

Accommodation: 1 single, 2 doubles, 1 twin, 2 rooms with en suite facilities. B&B £22.50 single, £30 double and twin. Family room. Pets accepted. Cards: Access and Visa.

MIDDLESBROUGH

Eston Hotel
Fabian Road, Teesville, 1 mile off
A66 Middlesbrough to Redcar road

Licensees: C. Burns & C. Hunt
Tel: 0642 453256

An early-1960s pub of unusual design, with three attic peaks at the front and large bay windows. There are three bars – lounge, cocktail and public – with darts and pool in the public. Bar food, lunchtime and evening, includes pizzas and sandwiches. Places of interest to visit include the National Trust Ormesby Hall, the Captain Cook Museum in

Stewarts Park and the North Yorkshire Moors. To reach the pub, turn right at Eston Baths traffic lights, then first left.

Beer: Samuel Smith Old Brewery Bitter on handpump.

Accommodation: 3 singles, 2 doubles, 1 family room. B&B from £12 per person. Evening meals available. Children welcome; residents' lounge with colour TV. No pets.

STOCKTON-ON-TEES

Parkwood Hotel
64-66 Darlington Road. ½ mile off A66 on old Darlington to Stockton road

Licensees: Bob & Evelyn Smith
Tel: 0642 580800/580172

The Parkwood is a friendly and inviting pub converted from the former mansion of the local ship-owning Ropner family. The hotel has a large garden with a children's play area. The bar features a large range of liqueurs and whiskies and a renowned variety of sandwiches and bar meals. There is a separate dining room for private lunches and dinners. The pub is next to Ropner Park and a mile from Stockton town centre.

Beer: Lorimer Best Scotch, Vaux Extra Special Bitter and Double Maxim, Ward Sheffield Best Bitter on handpumps.

Accommodation: 4 singles, 7 doubles, 3 rooms with en suite facilities. B&B £24 single (£35 en suite), £35 double (£45 en suite). Weekend rates on application. Children welcome, no reductions. No pets. Cards: Access and Visa.

ALTARNUN

Rising Sun
1 mile north of village on Five Lanes to Camelford road; 7 miles west of Launceston off A30

Licensee: Les Humphreys
Tel: 0566 86636

The Rising Sun is a popular 16th-century inn built with granite from Bodmin Moor. The large bar, often packed with local farmers, has fire-places at both ends. There are pub games and a family room, and the locality offers pony-trekking and sea and reservoir fishing opportunities. You can visit the Altar of St Nonna church with 79 richly carved bench ends. St Clether Church, with its holy well, is two miles to the north-east. You can tramp over the raw beauty of Bodmin Moor and the famous tourist pub, the Jamaica Inn, made famous by Daphne du Maurier's novel, is just a few miles away along the A30. The Rising Sun serves hot and cold food every day with roast lunch on Sundays. Don't miss the homemade pasties; there is a separate children's menu. There is a beer garden and facilities for camping and caravans.

Beer: Butcombe Bitter, Cotleigh Harrier SPA, Flowers IPA and Original, Marston Pedigree Bitter and regular guest beers, all on handpumps.

Accommodation: 1 twin, 2 doubles, 2 family rooms. B&B £11.50 per person. Reductions for long weekends or weeks. Children welcome, rates by arrangement.

BUDE

Brendon Arms
Inner Harbour

Licensees: Jen Wade & Desmond
Gregory
Tel: 0288 354542/352713

The Brendon is a charming old
country pub overlooking the
harbour. A warm welcome is
guaranteed – the 'warmest in the
West' claims landlord Desmond
Gregory. The pub is a few minutes
from a spacious beach and is within
easy distance of Bude's boating canal,
which has some of the finest coarse
fishing in the south-west. Sea fishing
trips can be arranged. The pub serves
breakfast and dinner in the
restaurant, plus pub lunches. Fresh
seafood, including local crab and
lobster, are regular specialities.

Beer: Draught Bass, St Austell
Tinners Bitter on handpump.

Accommodation: 3 twins, 3 doubles,
1 with private bathroom. B&B £14
per person. Pets welcome.

CAMBORNE

Old Shire Inn
Pendarves Road, B3303 Camborne
to Helston road

Licensee: Chris Smith
Tel: 0209 712691

The Old Shire is a tastefully
converted lodge in beautiful
countryside outside Camborne. The
inn stands in large grounds with its
own car park. The guest rooms are
spacious and well-furnished and have
colour TVs and tea and coffee making
facilities. The pub is pleasingly quiet,
without electronic distractions. There
are log fires and excellent meals

lunchtime and evening, including a
carvery serving roast beef, turkey,
pork and gammon as well as steaks.

Beer: Ind Coope Burton Ale and
Tetley Bitter on handpumps.

Accommodation: 1 single, 5 doubles,
all with en suite bath or shower. £25
single, £35 double including full
English breakfast. Children welcome,
terms by arrangement. No pets.
Cards: Access and Visa.

CAMELFORD

Darlington Hotel
Fore Street. A39 N of Wadebridge

Licensee: Mr & Mrs P. Richards
Tel: 0840 213314

The 15th-century coaching inn gets
its rather grandiose name from its
former owner, Lord Darlington, in
the time of the infamous 'Rotten
Boroughs' – parliamentary seats that
were bought by the wealthy instead
of being part of the democratic
process. The pub is a striking black
and white building in the centre of
Camelford. It has two ghosts, one of
a young soldier who appears on the
first-floor landing, and one of an old
lady who occupies the top floor. The
home-cooked menu, chalked on a
blackboard in the bar, is available
lunchtimes and evenings except
Monday lunch and Thursday evening
in winter. A traditional Sunday roast
lunch is served all year round. Guest
rooms have colour TVs and tea and
coffee makers.

Beer: St Austell Tinners on
handpump.

Accommodation: 1 double, 1 family
room. B&B £13.50 per person.
Reductions for children.

Mason's Arms
Town centre. A39, 25 yards from
free car park

Licensee: Terry Nicholls
Tel: 0840 213309

The Mason's Arms is a cheery old
three-storey pub that is mercifully
unchanged and still has old beams,
low ceilings and open fires in its two
bars. The lounge bar is a haven of
peace and quiet while the more
boisterous public has darts, pool and
games machines. Food, lunchtime
and evening, ranges from filled jacket
potatoes to fresh homemade dishes
and there is always a good-value daily
lunchtime special for around £3. A
beer garden leads down to the river.

Beer: St Austell Tinners and HSD on
handpumps.

Accommodation: 3 doubles. B&B
from £18 per person.

CONSTANTINE

Trengilly Wartha
Nancenoy, 1 mile from Constantine,
off B3291, 4 miles off A394

Licensees: Nigel Logan & Michael
Maguire
Tel: 0326 40332

This lovely old inn was built in the
18th century as a farmhouse and has
evolved over the years into a hotel
and restaurant. It has extensive
grounds set in a peaceful valley close
to the Helford river and is well-
placed for Helston and Falmouth.
The inn, whose name means
'settlement above the trees', offers a
comfortable bar with meals available
lunchtime and evening. There is a
good range of locally made sausages,
fresh Cornish fish, salads and
numerous specials, such as hake and
prawn strudel, cassoulet, and grilled
polenta. The restaurant has a separate

Trengilly Wartha, Constantine

menu. The owners have a passion for food and drink which is reflected in the wide range of beers, spirits and wines; there are more than 100 bins on the wine list and tutored tastings are held in winter and spring while more than 100 cask beers have featured in the past three years. Other special events include a sausage festival, which has attracted many European varieties. The guest rooms have central heating, colour TVs, direct dial phones and tea and coffee making facilities and there is a separate lounge for visitors.

Beer: Courage Directors, Draught Bass, Exmoor Gold, Theakston XB and guest beers, all straight from the cask, plus 'Really Fowl Cider' from Bodmin.

Accommodation: 6 doubles, 5 with en suite facilities. B&B £32-£48 single, £19.50-£26.50 double, per person. Winter Weekend from £30 B&B plus evening meal per person per night. Children's room. Pets accepted. Cards: Access, Amex, Diners, Visa.

CRIPPLESEASE

Engine Inn
Nancledra. B3311 St Ives-Penzance road

Licensee: Bob Knight
Tel: 0736 740204

The Engine Inn is a true Cornish pub, a magnificent granite building in the heart of the moorland that once served as the counting house for the local tin mine. Locals tend to burst into song and visitors enjoy the meat roasted on the pub fire. There are stunning views of the Atlantic coast to St Ives and beyond. The guest rooms have private showers, TVs and tea and coffee making facilities. The Engine Inn is the ideal base for

walking holidays and free camping is available.

Beer: Marston Pedigree Bitter and Whitbread Boddingtons Bitter on handpumps.

Accommodation: 3 doubles, 1 family room. B&B from £12.50 per person. Evening meal available. Children's room. Cards: Visa.

LISKEARD

Fountain Hotel
The Parade. A390

Licensees: Mr & Mrs T. Boneham
Tel: 0579 42154

The Fountain is a comfortable and welcoming old Cornish pub with wood panels and oak beams. It is the centre of a busy market town, and is popular with town folk and people from the surrounding rural areas. There is splendid homemade grub including generous portions of steak and kidney pie, plus full restaurant facilities.

Beer: Courage Best Bitter and Wadworth 6X on handpumps.

Accommodation: 1 single, 3 doubles, 2 family rooms. B&B £16 per person. Children welcome, terms by arrangement.

LOSTWITHIEL

Royal Oak
Duke Street off A390

Licensees: Malcolm & Eileen Hine
Tel: 0208 872552

The Royal Oak is a 13th-century inn in a Cornish town that claims once to have been the county capital. The

Royal Oak's interior has been sympathetically renovated in keeping with the pub's age and character. The back bar is popular with younger people while the lounge and dining room are quieter. An underground tunnel from the pub is reputed to connect the cellar to the dungeons in the courtyard of Restormel Castle. The pub is a cask-beer lover's paradise with up to seven ales on tap. The food is equally renowned for its quality and its quantity; bar food includes soup, pâté, ploughman's, scallops in cheese and white wine sauce, curries and salads in summer. The guest rooms have TVs, tea and coffee makers and en suite facilities. Close by you can enjoy strolls along the banks of the River Fowey and visit Lanhydrock House and the 14th-century church of St Bartholomew. Fishing, sailing and golfing are all within easy reach of the inn.

Beer: Draught Bass, Eldridge Pope Royal Oak, Flowers IPA and Original, Fullers London Pride and ESB, Marston Pedigree Bitter plus guest beers, all on handpumps.

Accommodation: 6 doubles, all en suite. B&B £26 single, £46 double. Children's room. Pets accepted. Cards: Access, Amex, Diners, Visa.

MEVAGISSEY

Fountain Inn
Cliff Street, 5 miles south of A390

Licensees: Bill & Trudy Moore
Tel: 0726 842320

The Fountain has been licensed for 500 years and the unspoilt interior includes a slate floor and open fire. It is well placed to enjoy the tumbling cliffs and streets of this charming and historic old fishing town. The inn is just a few yards from the harbour and

trips for mackerel and shark fishing can be booked. The Fountain is an unspoilt local with darts in the bar. There is a piano singalong at weekends. The bar food is generous and includes homemade pasties while a separate restaurant specializes in steaks and local fish dishes. Bar food is available Monday to Saturday; the restaurant is open every night in summer, Thursday to Saturday in winter. Car parking is difficult: use the main public car park as you enter the village.

Beer: St Austell Tinners on handpump.

Accommodation: 1 double, 1 twin. B&B £15 per person. TV available. Children's and weekend rates on application. Well-behaved pets welcome.

MULLION

Old Inn
Churchtown, off A3083 & B3296

Licensee: Andrew Kent
Tel: 0326 240240

A whitewashed and partially thatched inn with parts dating back to the 11th century, the Old Inn has one bar with a lounge area. A restaurant, open all year, serves buffet lunches and full à la carte dinners with local fresh seafood as a speciality; there are bar snacks all the year round. The inn is on the Lizard Peninsula and you can visit the spectacular cliffs and harbour of Porth Mellin, Mullion and Polurrian beach. Surf-riding and even surf-fishing are available. The attractive and comfortable guest rooms all have tea and coffee making facilities.

Beer: Cornish Original and guest beer on handpumps.

Accommodation: 5 rooms, 3 with private bathrooms. B&B from £14 per person. Families welcome in summer. There is also 1 self-catering cottage.

PADSTOW

London Inn
Lanadwell Street. Take Padstow sign from A30 after Bodmin bypass and Victoria Inn

Licensee: Clive Lean
Tel: 0841 532554

The London Inn has been a pub since 1802. It was formerly three fishermen's cottages and a recent facelift has carefully pointed up the original features. Nautical memorabilia and brass decorate every available area. Mr Lean says: 'We have attracted mature drinkers of all ages over the years and, apart from the cask-conditioned beers and White Shield Worthington, have a large collection of malt whiskies. Most international and selected club Rugby Union matches are discussed and re-played too often!' The White Shield Fan Club meets there daily. Bar and restaurant food is available lunchtime and evening, with a roast lunch only on Sunday.

Beer: St Austell XXXX Mild, Bosun's Bitter, Tinners and HSD on handpumps.

Accommodation: 2 doubles, 1 family room. B&B £15 per person, £5 single supplement. B&B plus evening meal £25 per person per day, reducing to £22 for stays of more than 3 days. Children over 14: rates by negotiation. B&B only in summer months; B&B plus evening meal 1 Nov-31 March.

PENZANCE

Fountain Tavern
St Clare Street, off town centre. A30

Licensee: David Pryor
Tel: 0736 62673

Mr Pryor's heartening message is the same every time he writes to the guide: 'NO juke box!' – underlining the tranquil and traditional atmosphere in this friendly town pub, a fine centre to enjoy the local beaches, coves, Land's End, the cathedral town of Truro, and St Michael's Mount reached by a causeway at low tide from Marazion. Lunchtime bar food includes pasties and sandwiches. 'There's no food in the evening – we're too busy drinking,' Mr Pryor says. 'It doesn't matter where you come from, you will soon feel at home.' Guest rooms have central heating, colour TVs and tea and coffee makers.

Beer: St Austell Bosun's Bitter and HSD on handpumps.

Accommodation: 1 double, 1 family room. B&B £12 per person. Children welcome, terms by arrangement. Pets by arrangement.

PORT GAVERNE

Port Gaverne Hotel
Off A39 & B3267/3314, 5 miles north of Wadebridge

Licensees: Freddie & Midge Ross
Tel: 0208 880244
Fax: 0208 880151

The Rosses have been running the 380 year-old hotel for 23 years and have a deserved reputation for the quality of the welcome, the food and the ale. Port Gaverne is a tiny, isolated cove near Port Isaac. The hotel's front bar is decorated by old photographs and paintings that are sometimes for sale. There are two tiny snug bars at the back and all the floors have ancient and worn Delabole slate floors. The bar meals are seafood-based and feature lobster and crab in season from Port Isaac. The restaurant offers à la carte and daily specials menus plus a separate vegetarian menu. There is seating outside in the summer and facilities for golf, fishing, pony trekking, sailing and surfing within easy reach. As well as the hotel accommodation, the 18th-century Green Door cottages offer self-catering in restored fishermen's houses.

Beer: St Austell HSD and Flowers IPA on handpumps.

Accommodation: 19 rooms all with private baths, colour TVs and direct dial phones. B&B £38-40. Special weekly and short breaks: rates on application. Phone for details of self-catering rates (most cottages sleep 4).

PORTHLEVEN

Harbour Inn
Overlooking Inner Harbour. B3304, 2 miles from Helston

Licensees: Dave & Wendy Morton
Tel: 0326 573876

The inn is 300 years old. It was known first as the Commercial and offered victuals and accommodation in a small fishing village known as Port Elvan until the 19th century. The village grew with the building of a harbour that encouraged a thriving fishing industry to develop. The Mortons have renovated the inn but they have sensibly retained all its old charm. It is an excellent base for visiting Land's End, Goonhilly, the

Lizard, St Ives and Truro. Bar food includes homemade soup, garlic mushrooms, crab pâté, smoked mackerel, tuna and prawn pasties, filled jacket potatoes, ploughman's, Dover sole, lemon sole, fillet of plaice and steaks. 'Sprats Corner' has a children's menu. There is a separate restaurant.

Beer: St Austell Bosun's Bitter and HSD on handpumps.

Accommodation: 1 single, 8 doubles/twins, 1 family room, 8 rooms with en suite facilities. B&B £29 single, £26 double/twin per person, £80 family room per family of 4. Children half price sharing. Weekend rates on application. No pets. Cards: Access, Amex, Visa.

PROBUS

Hawkins Arms
Fore Street. A390 between St Austell and Truro

Licensee: Peter Cotterill
Tel: 0726 882208

The Hawkins Arms takes its name from the Hawkins family that once lived in Trewithen House a mile away. It is a delightful and unspoilt old one-bar pub with a coal fire in winter and a large garden with a children's play area. There is also an indoor children's room. Bar meals are served lunchtime and evening and are mainly home-cooked with such dishes as ham, beef, lasagne and pizzas. Probus is famous for its church, which has the highest tower in Cornwall, and for the village's two lovely gardens.

Beer: St Austell XXXX Mild, Tinners and HSD on handpumps.

Accommodation: 1 double. B&B £12.50 per person. Children by arrangement. Pets welcome.

ST AGNES

Driftwood Spars Hotel

Trevaunance Cove, ½ mile off
B3285 St Agnes to Perranporth road

Licensees: Gordon & Jill Treleaven
Tel: 0872 552428/553323

Built in 1660, the Driftwood Spars over the years has been a tin mining store, chandlery, sail makers' loft and fish cellar. The old beams come from driftwood washed up on the beach from the many ships wrecked off the rugged coast. The hotel has log fires, guest ales, an extensive range of malt whiskies, three bars and live music at weekends. Food ranges from bar snacks, including real pasties, steak and kidney pie and fisherman's pie, to four-course meals or an à la carte menu in the restaurant. Breakfast can

be taken as late as noon. There are fine cliff walks to be enjoyed, mine workings, a model village, surfing, sea fishing, swimming, good rock pools and nearby Truro. Most of the guest rooms have en suite facilities, sea views, TVs, tea and coffee making facilities, hair dryers and telephones.

Beer: Ind Coope Burton Ale and Tetley Bitter on handpumps plus a wide range of guest beers.

Accommodation: 1 single, 8 doubles, 1 family room, 7 with en suite facilities. B&B £25 low season to £27 high season per person. Pro rata reductions e.g. 2 days low season £46, 3 days £69. Children sharing bunk-bedded rooms half price. Dogs £1 a night. Cards: Access, Amex, Diners, Visa.

Driftwood Spars Hotel, St Agnes

ST AUSTELL

Duke of Cornwall
98 Victoria Road, Mount Charles.
A390.

Licensees: Wendy & Geoff Billing
Tel: 0726 72031

The Duke has been open since 1868;
in Geoff Billing's words, 'it's just an
old pub, full of character.' The public
bar has no less than three darts boards
and two pool tables. The large lounge
has a blazing log fire in winter. Bar
meals range from sandwiches to
steaks while the restaurant offers a
range of home-cooked specials,
including steak and fish.

Beer: St Austell Tinners and HSD on
handpumps.

Accommodation: 6 doubles. B&B £15
per person. Pets welcome.

ST EWE

Crown Inn
Nr Mevagissey. 5 miles south-east
of St Austell between B3287 &
B3273

Licensee: Norman Jeffery
Tel: 0726 84 3322

The Crown is a superb old inn
bedecked with hanging basket,
flowering tubs and window boxes
outside. The small main bar has an
ancient fireplace with a wood
surround, and a high-back settle on a
slate floor. A 40-seater restaurant has
been added since the last edition and a
small adjacent dining area specializing
in homemade pies and also offering
steaks, scampi and chicken has been
retained. Both full meals and bar
meals are served every day, lunchtime
and evening. You can eat in the
pleasant garden in good weather. The
pub is a good base for visiting
Mevagissey and the nearby beaches.

Crown Inn, St Ewe

Beer: St Austell Bosun's Bitter on handpump.

Accommodation: 2 doubles. £14 per person. No children.

ST JUST-IN-PENWITH

Star Inn
Fore Street, town centre, A3071

Licensees: Peter & Rosie Angwin
Tel: 0736 788767

The Star is St Just's oldest hostelry. A former coaching inn, it is a traditional Cornish building of mellow stone with a spacious bar and cosy snug. There is a large stepped mounting block outside, used by horse-borne travellers in earlier times. One of the guest rooms is in the converted stables and has its own bathroom, TV and tea and coffee making facilities. Bar food ('absolutely no chips!') is available at all times and includes homemade soups, casseroles, real Cornish pasties, ploughman's and local crab and prawns. St Just is close to Cape Cornwall, Land's End airport and the skybus to the Scillies and is a fine base for a walking holiday with Sennen close at hand. There is a room for children with toys and games in the pub.

Beer: St Austell Tinners and HSD straight from the cask.

Accommodation: 1 single, 2 doubles, 1 with private bath. B&B £15 single for 1 night, reducing to £12.50 for additional days, £12.50 per person in double, £17.50 per person in room with shower. No pets.

Star Inn, St Just-in-Penwith

Wellington Hotel
Market Square. 6 miles from
Penzance on B3306.

Licensee R.D.S. Gray
Tel: 0736 787319

The Wellington is an imposing
granite building overlooking the main
square of St Just. It has a cosy,
character-filled bar with attractive
brass fittings and paintings on the
wall. There is a separate pool room
and a picturesque garden at the rear
with a children's play area. Families
are welcome and the hotel has a
deserved reputation for the quality of
its bar meals, including locally caught
fish, crab, steaks and light snacks.
There is a roast lunch on Sundays.
Food is served every day, lunchtime
and evening. All the guest rooms have
colour TVs and tea and coffee making
facilities. En suite rooms have direct
dial telephones. St Just is close to
Land's End and Cape Cornwall and
the beaches at Sennen Cove,
Porthcurno and St Ives with golf and
water sports. Cliff walks, hiking and
climbing are all available locally.

Beer: St Austell Tinners and HSD on
handpumps.

Accommodation: 9 doubles, 6 en
suite, 4 family rooms. B&B £15
single, £25 double. Rates for children
and weekend breaks on request.
Family room. Pets welcome. Cards:
Access and Visa.

ST MERRYN

Farmer's Arms
B3276 Newquay to Padstow road,
2½ miles south of Padstow

Manager: Bob Mann
Tel: 0841 520303

The Farmer's Arms is some 250 years
old and was formerly three cottages.

It is a charming old Cornish inn with
a large public bar and a lounge with a
low beamed ceiling, log-burning
stone fireplaces and a Delabole slate
floor. St Merryn takes its name from a
religious figure, the Patroness Sancta
Merina. The village is famous for St
Merryn Church which has the lovely
font rescued from the ruined church
at Constantine. Near the shore at
Harlyn Bay is an ancient burial site,
discovered in 1900 when more than
2,000 tons of sand were removed to
reveal 130 slate coffins. It is thought,
from tools and ornaments found in
the coffins, that the people buried
there lived some 300 years before
Julius Caesar. Food in the carefully
renovated Farmer's Arms includes a
hot and cold carvery and the
emphasis is on homemade dishes.
You may find soup, garlic
mushrooms, farmer's pâté,
fisherman's pâté, smoked mackerel,
ploughman's, burgers, filled jacket
potatoes, salads, seafood platter and
steaks. A separate dining room is
open from September to July.

Beer: St Austell Tinners and HSD on
handpumps.

Accommodation: 3 doubles, 1 family
room, all with en suite facilities. B&B
£20 per person. Children half price.
Children's room. Pets welcome.
Cards: Access, Amex, Visa.

TREBARWITH

Mill House Inn
Off Tintagel-Camelford road; A39
near Camelford, A3295 to Tintagel,
pick up signs for Trebarwith Sands

Licensee: Kevin Howard
Tel: 0840 770200
Fax: 0840 770355

The Mill House is a former corn mill
in the dramatic scenery of the
Trebarwith Valley. The mill is

surrounded by sycamores and a small trout stream, which once provided the power for the mill, runs outside. The mill wheel has been restored. The main bar has massive beams, a Delabole stone-flagged floor, oak tables and settles. There are food and terrace bars, a pool and boules in the garden. The beach is a few minutes' walk. Bar food includes homemade soup, sandwiches, pâté, ploughman's, fish platter, salads, steaks, lasagne, curries, vegetable bake and beef in beer. The separate evening restaurant specializes in local produce. The inn is a superb base for visiting Tintagel, Port Isaac, Boscastle and Wadebridge. There is a children's play area in the garden.

Beer: Draught Bass, Flowers IPA and Flowers Original, Ind Coope Burton Ale, Marston Pedigree Bitter, St Austell Tinners and HSD and Wadworth 6X on handpumps or straight from the cask.

Accommodation: 1 single, 7 doubles, 1 twin, 1 family room. Most rooms are en suite. B&B £26 single high season, £22.50 low season; double/family room £24 high season, £19.50 low season per person. Midweek Break £16.50 per person per day, minimum 3 days. Weekend Break £17.50 per person per day minimum 2 days. Children two-thirds of adult rate if sharing. Pets welcome. Cards: Access and Visa.

VERYAN

New Inn
Off A3078

Licensee: Melville Grigg
Tel: 0872 501362

The New Inn is a small, unspoilt one-bar granite pub in the heart of a picturesque village famous for its

roundhouses, with a warm welcome from the landlord and the locals. Veryan is close to some superb beaches at Pendower and Carne and the breathtaking scenery of the Roseland peninsula. Falmouth and Trelissick Gardens can be reached by the King Harry Ferry, and Truro and St Austell are just 11 miles away. There is good home-cooked pub grub in the inn – liver and bacon is popular – served lunchtime and evening.

Beer: St Austell Bosun's Bitter and Tinners Bitter from the cask.

Accommodation: 2 doubles, 1 twin. Tea and coffee makers in all rooms. B&B £15 per person.

ZELAH

Hawkins Arms
Just off A30 (New Zelah bypass)

Licensees: David & Jackie Eyre
Tel: 0872 540339

The Hawkins Arms is an old coaching inn set in a peaceful Cornish village thankfully bypassed by a new road. Zelah is just a few minutes from the cathedral city of Truro and the beaches of Perranporth and Newquay. The homely pub has just one bar with two open log fires, many nooks and crannies, cob granite walls and original beams. It plays host to a local choir and a good pub sing-song is a frequent event. An organist plays most Saturday nights, too. Pub games include darts and euchre; CAMRA member David Eyre will allow no juke box in the inn. Jackie Eyre has 18 years' catering experience and her pub food, including a hearty breakfast that can be taken up to midday, is highly regarded.

Beer: Ind Coope Burton Ale and

Tetley Bitter with a wide range of guest beers on handpumps, plus farmhouse cider in summer.

Accommodation: 1 single, 1 double, 2 family rooms. £15 single, £12 double/ family room per person. Children half-price sharing. No pets except goldfish and budgies.

CUMBRIA

BARNGATES

Drunken Duck
Nr Hawkshead. From Ambleside take the B5286 to Hawkshead; turn left at Outgate and the inn is 1 mile along the road at crossroads

Licensees: Peter & Stephanie Barton
Tel: 05394 36347

This famous old lakelands pub is flourishing under the energetic tutelage of the Bartons. There are additional guest rooms with en suite facilities, a residents' breakfast and dining room and a modern kitchen to cope with the demand for food. But the idyllic old inn remains, with its oak beams, thick stone walls, old oak settles and log fires. The original name of this superb pub, set in stunning scenery of mountains and lakes, was for 300 years the Barngates Inn. Its Victorian nickname stems from a legend that a landlady in the late 19th century found her pet ducks stretched out in the road. She thought they were dead but they had been drinking from a leaking cask in the cellar. She began to pluck them in preparation for the oven which roused them from their stupor in time to be saved. The landlady knitted them jerseys until their feathers grew

again and the pub nickname quickly took over from the original one.

Duck features on the bar menu in the shape of half Cressingham duck deep fried with chips or baked potato, along with such dishes as walnut and Stilton and venison pâtés, ploughman's, soup, boeuf bourguignon, Spanish pork with olives, chicken in green chilli sauce, ravioli in basil and bacon, broccoli and gruyère quiche, fennel, orange and butterbean bake, game pie, Dijon lamb casserole, lasagne, spinach and mushroom tortellini, beef curry and a wide range of old-fashioned nursery puds such as jam roly-poly. Residents can have dinner in their own lounge for £18. The Duck is a splendid base for visiting Ambleside, Coniston, Hawkshead and Tarn Hows.

Beer: Jennings Bitter, Marston Pedigree Bitter, Tetley Bitter, Theakston XB and Old Peculier and Whitbread Castle Eden on handpumps.

Accommodation: 1 single, 9 doubles/ twins. All rooms en suite with colour TVs, tea and coffee makers and direct dial phones. B&B £40 per person single, £30 in double/twin. Children welcome, rates on application. Pets welcome. Cards: Access and Visa.

BECKERMET

Royal Oak Inn
Off A595 from Egremont and Thornhill

Licensees: Bob & Pat Chapman
Tel: 0946 841551

The Royal Oak is a delightful and homely inn, popular with anglers who enjoy access to one of Cumbria's finest salmon rivers or sea angling from boat and shore. The inn is set in superb and rugged countryside, ideal for walkers and hikers. The bars and dining room were renovated in 1991. Excellent bar meals are supplemented by a barbecue when the weather allows. The separate restaurant seats 28 and there is also a beer garden. The eight guest rooms are in a well-appointed annexe. All have en suite facilities, colour TVs and tea and coffee makers and were being upgraded as the guide was completed.

Beer: Jennings Bitter and Cumberland Ale on handpumps.

Accommodation: 6 doubles, 2 singles, all en suite. B&B £27.50 single, £35 double. Cards: Access, Mastercard, Visa.

BOTHEL

Greyhound Inn
A595 Carlisle to Cockermouth road, near junction of A591

Licensee: Ian Taylor
Tel: 06973 20601

The Greyhound is a busy local that serves several surrounding Cumbrian villages. The warmth of the welcome from Mr Taylor and his staff attracts visitors en route between the Lakes, Carlisle and Scotland. Bar meals are available every day, lunchtime and evening. The pub has a wealth of old beams and an open fire in the lounge and there is live entertainment every Wednesday and Saturday. Bothel is a short distance from the market town of Cockermouth, birthplace of Fletcher Christian, leader of the mutiny on the Bounty, and the home of Jennings' brewery. It is also a good base for the northern Lakes and the Solway coast.

Beer: Jennings Bitter on handpump.

Accommodation: 1 twin, 1 double. B&B £12.50 per person.

Royal Oak Inn, Beckermet

BOWNESS-ON-WINDERMERE

Albert Hotel
Queen's Square. Off A592

Licensee: Peter A. Steen
Tel: 05394 43241
Fax: 05394 88067

The Albert is a Victorian hotel in the heart of the delightful village of Bowness. It is guarded by a chestnut tree in the middle of the road and is just 300 yards from Windermere's steamer pier and next to the Beatrix Potter exhibition. The Regency Bar, open all day, has a roaring fire in winter months and a darts board. The Victoria Bistro is open for lunch and dinner all year and opens all day Sunday. It serves steaks, fish and salad meals. Bar meals are served in the Regency. The six guest rooms include a honeymoon suite and all have en suite baths or showers, colour TVs and Teasmaids.

Beer: Hartley XB and Robinson Old Tom on handpumps.

Accommodation: 5 doubles, 1 family room. B&B from £45 double; rates depend on length of stay. Weekend Breaks, autumn, winter and spring: from £110 per couple, 2 nights, including evening meals. Cheaper rates mid-week. Children under 16 with 2 adults charged only for meals. Children's room. Pets welcome. Cards: Access and Visa.

BROUGHTON-IN-FURNESS

Black Cock Inn
Princess Street, A595

Licensee: Mr K. Howarth
Tel: 0229 716529

The Black Cock is a popular 16th-century country inn in a charter town in southern Lakeland, with a fascinating collection of vintage motor bikes in the town square. The Black Cock, with striking black and white façade and heavily beamed bar with an open fire, has comfortable modern guest rooms with TVs and tea and coffee making facilities. Tuesday is market day; the pub is open all day and local farmers flock into Broughton with their animals.

Beer: Ruddles Best Bitter and County, Websters Choice on handpumps.

Accommodation: 1 double, 2 twins, 1 family room. B&B £14 per night per person. Children welcome, half price under 12.

Eccle Rigg Manor Hotel
Foxfield Road, south-west of village, off A595

Proprietors: Howard & Susan Loxley
Tel: 0229 716398

The Manor Hotel is an imposing 19th-century mansion in 35 acres of gardens and woodland, with stunning views of Coniston Old Man and the Duddon estuary. Eccle Rigg was built by Lord Cross, whose varied parliamentary career encompassed Home Secretary, Secretary of State for India, and Lord Privy Seal (one later holder of the third office observed 'I am neither a lord, a privy nor a seal'). Lord Cross used Eccle Rigg as his summer retreat and brought parts of the demolished Ashton Old Hall at Ashton under Lyme to Broughton: the old dungeon towers from Ashton now stand at the entrance to Eccle Rigg. The lounges and restaurant are elegantly furnished

and the 12 guest rooms have colour
TVs, in-house video, and tea and
coffee making facilities. Bar food
includes Morecambe Bay shrimps,
Cumberland sausage, jacket spuds
with a variety of fillings, chilli, and
homemade steak and kidney pie. The
hotel has a heated swimming pool,
sauna and solarium.

Beer: Ind Coope Burton Ale,
Jennings Cumberland Ale on
handpumps.

Accommodation: 12 rooms, all en
suite. Single £44; double/twin/family
room £72. Children sharing charged
only for meals. Weekend rates on
request. Cards: Access, Amex, Visa.

CARTMEL FELL

Masons Arms
Strawberry Bank off A5047

Licensees: Helen & Nigel Stevenson
Tel: 044 88 486

This delightful and welcoming old
pub is devoted to good beer and good
food. The seriousness with which
Nigel Stevenson takes his beer is
measured by the fact that the pub has
a beer menu as well as a food one and
since the last edition he has built his
own micro brewery. In homage to
Arthur Ransome of *Swallows and
Amazons* fame, Nigel brews Amazon
Bitter and Great Northern? on
draught and Big Six in bottle and,
with a Belgian touch, has added a
damson fruit beer. There is also a vast
range of foreign bottled beers to try.
The pub got its name in the 18th
century when Kendal freemasons met
there in secret. The Masons Arms is
set in lovely countryside close to the
heart of Lakeland. Excellent pub grub
includes homemade curries,
hoummous and coachman's

casserole, washed down with a
Belgian Trappist beer, a Czech
Pilsner Urquell or a straightforward
pint of ale. The extension to the pub
means there is no longer bed and
breakfast accommodation; guests
now use self-catering flats.

Beer: Amazon Bitter, Great
Northern?, Bateman XB, Thwaites
Bitter and Yates Bitter on
handpumps, with James White and
Westons cider.
Accommodation: 4 self-catering flats;
rates on application.

CONISTON

Ship Inn
Bowmanstead. A593, ¼ mile from
village on Torver road

Licensees: Derrick & Linda
Freedman
Tel: 05394 41224

The Ship is a traditional old pub with
beams, a stone fireplace and a log
blaze in winter, close to Coniston
Hall camp site and Park Coppice
caravan park. The inn is a popular
venue for campers, hikers and sailors.
Pub food is served lunchtime and
evening and offers soup, grills,
burgers, prawn and meat salads,
sandwiches and ploughman's, plus
daily specials and a children's menu.
There are summer barbecues. A
separate games room has darts, shove
ha'penny and pool.

Beer: Hartley XB on handpump.

Accommodation: 1 twin, 2 doubles, 1
family room. B&B £14 per person, £3
supplement for single occupancy.
Children 2-12 years £8; under 2 years
free if using own cot. Dogs welcome;
kennel and pen also available.

DOVENBY

Ship Inn
A594 Maryport to Cockermouth
road; 2 miles from Cockermouth

Licensees: Sheila & Alan Darvill
Tel: 0900 828097

The Ship is a true Cumbrian pub with a welcoming atmosphere. It has been sensitively updated to provide all the modern comforts but its original features have been left intact. There is an open fireplace and 130 horse brasses. The menu is based on homemade dishes and there is always a vegetarian choice; meals and bar snacks are served every day, lunchtime and evening. Children have their own menu and from Monday to Thursday there is a free child's meal for each adult meal bought. There is a beer garden with a children's play area, located behind the pub away from the road. The guest rooms have colour TVs, tea and coffee making facilities and hot and cold water. Dovenby is just 10 minutes from Cockermouth and close to the Solway Firth and Maryport.

Beer: Jennings Bitter and Cumberland Ale on handpumps.

Accommodation: 2 doubles, 1 twin; 1 room has a third bed if required. B&B £12.50 per person. Children half price, free under 4 if sharing. Weekly rates on application.

DRIGG

Victoria Hotel
Off A595 west of Holmrook

Licensees: George & Christine Richardson
Tel: 09404 231

The hotel dates from 1850 and was for a time renamed the Station Hotel when the iron way reached the area. It is close to the delightful Furness line that links Carlisle and Lancaster. Its many original features include an open fire, beams and a framed collection of knots, jugs and maps. Children are welcome and bar meals are served lunchtime and evening. There is a separate dining room for residents and a beer garden. All the guest rooms have central heating, colour TVs (including satellite) and hot and cold water. There is salmon fishing on the River Irt and an 18-hole golf course close by. Drigg is on the fringe of the Lake District and within easy reach of England's highest mountain, deepest lake and smallest church. There is a fine sandy beach a mile away and the hotel is also close to the La'al Ratty railway that runs between Ravenglass and Eskdale. If you send a postcard home you can pop it into one of the few remaining Victorian pillar boxes just outside the hotel.

Beer: Jennings Bitter on handpump.

Accommodation: 1 single, 3 twins (2 en suite), 1 family room. B&B plus evening meal £17 per person.

ELTERWATER

Britannia Inn
From Ambleside take A593 to Langdale & Coniston, then B5343

Licensee: David Fry
Tel: 09667 382/210
Fax: 09667 311

The Britannia is a 400-year-old inn, originally built as a small farm which became an alehouse in the late 19th century. Much of the original building remains, with oak beams and three-feet thick walls. The bars were once living areas or parlours and part of the kitchen is thought to have been a milking parlour. One group of bedrooms was the village 'ballroom' or meeting place. Set in the great beauty of the Langdale Valley, the Britannia is a popular centre for keen walkers and specializes in superb four-course dinners – you must book well in advance as there is a long waiting list. A typical menu may include avocado pear stuffed with crab meat, chicken in a mild curry salad, leek and bacon soup, grapefruit sorbet, fresh Scottish salmon, roast ribs of beef, sirloin steak, fresh fruit Pavolva, homemade blackcurrant ice cream, and Athol Brose. Children are made welcome and can choose from the bar menu if they join their parents in the dining room. Bar meals include homemade soup, ploughman's, rainbow trout and daily hot specials. There is a residents' lounge and walkers are welcome, even with muddy boots, in the bar. The cheery front bar has an open coal fire, oak benches and settles.

Beer: Bass Special Bitter, Mitchells Best Bitter, Jennings Bitter, Marston Pedigree Bitter plus draught cider on handpumps.

Accommodation: 8 doubles, 1 family room. B&B £20.25 per person, £23-£29 with private shower, dinner £15.50 extra. Week £129.50-£192.50. Children half price when sharing. Cards: Access, Switch, Visa.

FAR SAWREY

Sawrey Hotel
B5285 towards Windermere Ferry on Hawkshead road

Licensee: David Brayshaw
Tel: 05394 43425

The hotel is an attractive whitewashed early 18th-century inn made up of three separate buildings. The old stables now form the bar, with the guest rooms above. The pub's original name is thought to have been the Angler's Rest and later was called the New Inn. The stables were converted in 1971 and named the Claife Crier bar after the ghost of a monk in Furness Abbey whose mission in medieval times was to save 'fallen' women. But it was the monk who fell: he proposed to one of the women, was rejected, went mad and died. The hotel has beams in the bar that are thought to have come from wrecks of the Spanish armada, many of which perished off the Cumberland coast. The bar has old stable stalls for seating, harnesses on the walls and a variety of traditional games. There are full restaurant meals every evening, while lunchtime bar meals offer ploughman's, Cumberland sausage and local Esthwaite trout. The guest rooms have colour TVs and telephones and most have private baths.

Beer: Jennings Bitter, Theakston Best Bitter and Old Peculier on handpumps.

Accommodation: 3 singles, 12 doubles, 2 family rooms, 13 rooms with private bathrooms. B&B £28.50 per person, £32.50 with bath. Reduced rates November-March. Children half price under 13, £5 per night under 3.

KESWICK

Bank Tavern
Main Street. Off A591 & A66

Licensees: Jack & Olive Hobbs
Tel: 07687 72663

The Bank Tavern is in the centre of one of Lakeland's most popular and picturesque towns. The pub has been carefully updated to meet modern demands but retains such original features as beams, open fires and old church pews. Bar food is served from 11.30am to 9pm in the friendly lounge bar or in good weather in the beer garden to the side of the pub and away from the main street. The guest rooms are all heated and have hot and cold water and tea and coffee making facilities. A residents' lounge has a colour TV and is used for breakfast.

Beer: Jennings Mild and selection of three bitters on handpumps.

Accommodation: 1 twin, 2 doubles, 1 triple, 1 double with single beds. B&B from £11 per person.

Pheasant Inn
Off A66 towards Keswick on Crossthwaite road

Licensees: David & Marion Wright
Tel: 07687 72219

The Pheasant, a traditional old Cumbrian local, was a a 'Jerry House' in the early 19th century, when short-lived parliamentary legislation allowed anyone to run a pub on payment of two guineas for a licence. The Pheasant today does not have a rough, ale-house reputation though it has retained such original features as open fires in stone hearths and wood panelling. The walls are decorated with cartoons by a local artist. Bar food is served lunchtime and evening and is based on home-cooked Cumbrian dishes, using fresh local ingredients, from Cumbrian farm recipes and served in farm-size portions. A separate dining room for residents has an à la carte menu. The Pheasant is host to the Blencathra Foxhounds, which meet there twice a year. There is outside seating for families in the summer months.

Guest rooms are heated and have tea, coffee and chocolate making equipment. Dogs up to labrador size are accepted.

Beer: Jennings Bitter on handpump.

Accommodation: 1 single, 3 doubles/twins, 2 family rooms. B&B £18 single, £30 double. Children half price in family rooms. Dogs welcome.

Twa Dogs Inn
Penrith Road

Licensee: Gordon Hallatt
Tel: 07687 72599

Rebuilt in 1967 on the site of a traditional 17th-century Cumbrian inn, the Twa Dogs is home to the only captured specimen of the legendary Bogart Vulgaris, a cross between a fox and a badger. The bogart pole used in the capture now hangs above the bar in the spacious lounge. Gordon Hallatt boasts a certificate to prove his runaway success in the 1981 'Biggest Liar in the World' competition, which means you can take the fox-cum-badger tale with an outsize pinch of white condiment. Bar meals are served lunchtime and evening and there is a pleasant beer garden. The pub takes its name from a poem by Robert Burns, the 'Twa Dogs', which is a discussion between two dogs about their differing lifestyles. A photograph in the pub was taken at the Burns Museum in Alloway, Ayrshire, and shows the original Burns's chair with the two dogs carved as the arms. The finest collection in Keswick of caricatures of locals by artist Billy Wilkinson decorates the pub. All in all, a lively sort of place. The guest rooms have colour TVs, hot and cold water and tea and coffee making equipment.

Beer: Jennings Mild, Bitter and Cumberland Ale on handpumps.

Accommodation: 3 doubles, 2 family rooms. B&B from £18 per person.

LANGDALE

Old Dungeon Ghyll Hotel
B5343 at end of Langdale Valley. Off A593 & A591

Licensees: Neil & Jane Walmsley
Tel: 096 67 272

The Old Dungeon Ghyll is a famous rock climbers' inn in a breathtaking setting at the heart of the Great Langdale Valley. The inn takes its name from the nearby Dungeon Ghyll Force waterfall. It is a simple and homely pub with great thick walls to keep out the winter blasts, sing-songs in the bar and generous home-cooked meals, including hot soup, curries and Cumberland sausage ... and a choice of snuff.

Beer: Marston Pedigree Bitter and Merrie Monk, Theakston Best Bitter, XB (summer) and Old Peculier, Yates Bitter, Bulmer medium cider and a regular guest beer, all on handpumps.

Accommodation: 3 singles, 4 doubles, 1 twin, 2 family rooms, 4 rooms with showers. B&B from £22.50 per person, evening meal £14 extra. Reduced rates for minimum of 2 nights. Winter Breaks (from Oct) 4 nights mid-week £123 per person B&B plus dinner. Reduced rates for children under 12.

MUNGRISDALE

Mill Inn
Off A66 Penrith to Keswick road; signposted midway between the two towns. Leave M6 exit 40

Licensee: Margaret Roper
Tel: 07687 79632

The Mill was built in the 16th century and the two-storey buildings stand on the banks of the river Glenderamackin in the northern lakeland fells. It is a splendid base for walking and climbing: Souther Fell, Bannerdale Crags, Bowscale Fell and Blencathra lie in the range behind the inn. The inn has been sensitively modernized but retains old oak beams and open fires. It has played host to both Charles Dickens and Wilkie Collins as well as the legendary huntsman, John Peel, buried in nearby Caldbeck village. Bar meals are served lunchtime and evening and there is a separate dining room with grills, daily specials and a three-course Sunday lunch. Most of the guest rooms have private facilities and all have tea and coffee makers, hot and cold water and electric blankets.

Beer: Theakston Best Bitter and XB on handpumps.

Accommodation: 6 doubles, 4 en suite. £20 per person per night. Dogs accepted.

OUSBY

Fox Inn
Off A686 Penrith to Melmerby road
Licensees: Richard & Susan Thomas
Tel: 0768 881374

Ousby is a quiet village at the foot of Cross Fell, the highest point on the Pennines. The Fox is in the centre of the village. It began life as a hunting lodge and farmhouse and was known as the Fox and Hounds when it was first licensed. It is a genuine

local, as there is little passing trade at the foot of the fell. The area is popular with fell walkers and horse riders and the inn offers stabling for guests arriving on horseback; there are also two donkeys at the inn. The Thomases promise a warm welcome in every way: they light the pub fires when it gets chilly at any time of the year. Bar food includes gammon, haddock, steak and scampi and one homemade special such as chilli, curry or quiche; homemade soups and apple pie are always available. Guests can choose an evening meal from the bar menu and there is a residents' lounge.
Beer: Theakston Best Bitter and XB on handpumps.

Accommodation: 2 twins. £14 per person per night. Children's rates negotiable. No pets.

ROWRAH

Stork Hotel
7 miles from Whitehaven. M6 exit 40, A66, then A5086 Cockermouth to Egremont road

Licensees: Mrs E.L. & Mr D. Heydon
Tel: 0946 861 213

The Stork dates from 1864 and is a welcoming Cumbrian village local with blazing fires in winter, hunting memorabilia and active darts and dominoes teams. Regulars are active participants in the area's pub quiz league. Rowrah is at the northern end of the Lake District, close to Ennerdale, and offers clay pigeon shooting, a scrambling track, an international go-kart track and the famous Melbreak foxhounds. Coast-to-coast walkers can be transported to and from Ennerdale village or St Bees. Breakfast is the only meal available.

Fox Inn, Ousby

Beer: Jennings Mild and Bitter, Cumberland Ale and Sneck Lifter on handpumps.

Accommodation: 4 twins, 1 family room. B&B £12.50 per person. Children under 5 free. Pets accepted.

Near SAWREY

Tower Bank Arms
B5285 Hawkshead road near Windermere Ferry

Licensee: Philip J. Broadley
Tel: 05394 36334

The Tower Bank is a charming cottage pub next to Hilltop, the home of Beatrix Potter, which is open to the public. The pub is known to generations of children as the small country inn featured in *The Tale of Jemima Puddleduck*. There is a kitchen range, stone-flagged floors, high-back settles and a grandfather clock. A good range of bar meals includes Cumberland sausage, game pie, local trout and home-roast ham. Dinner is served in a separate dining room. You can enjoy good ale and food in the beer garden in summer. The guest rooms have showers and toilets en suite, colour TVs, central heating and tea and coffee making facilities.

Beer: Matthew Brown Mild, Theakston Best Bitter, XB and Old Peculier, Younger Scotch Bitter on handpumps.

Accommodation: 2 doubles, 1 twin. B&B £30 single, £38 double room. Weekly £120 per person sharing a room.

Near STAVELEY

Watermill Inn
Ings, 2 miles from Staveley. Leave M6 exit 36, take A590/A591 via Windermere; 1½ miles past Staveley take Ings turning

Watermill Inn, near Staveley

Partners: Alan, Barbara & Brian
Coulthwaite
Tel: 0539 821309

The Watermill is a 250-year-old wood mill that has twice before been owned by the Coulthwaite family. Among other items, the mill made shuttles for the Lancashire cotton mills and coffins for undertakers. The river Gowan that flows through the grounds provided the power via a water shoot for the mill. The river banks are now a beer and pub food garden in spring, summer and autumn. The Coulthwaites have turned the ground floor of the mill into a locals' bar and an extension has been added as a games room. The bar has a counter front built from old church pews and a wood and coal-burning fire. All the guest rooms have en suite facilities, colour TVs and tea and coffee makers. Bar food, lunchtime and evening, includes homemade soup, vegetarian dishes, fish, steaks, gammon, cold ham grill, salads, sandwiches, Cumberland sausage, sweets and a children's menu. After just 12 months' operation, the inn was named South Lakes Pub of the Year in 1991 by CAMRA.

Beer: Marston Pedigree Bitter, Moorhouse Black Cat Mild and Pendle Witches Brew, Theakston Best Bitter and Old Peculier, plus local and national guest beers, all on handpumps.

Accommodation: 6 doubles/twins. 4 rooms suitable for parents and 2 children. B&B £18.50 per person. Children £7-£12, depending on age; cot service charge £2. Winter Breaks (Nov-Feb) £17 per person per night. Pets accepted; £3 per night for dogs.

SWINSIDE

Swinside Inn
Newlands Valley. Off A66 & A591, 2½ miles from Keswick

Manager: Jane Fletcher
Tel: 07687 78253

Swinside Inn has breathtaking views across the Newlands Valley to Barraside, Causey Pike and Cat Bells. It is a superb 17th-century Cumbrian inn with open fires and low beams, an ideal spot for fell walking, climbing, fishing, sailing and windsurfing, with Keswick close at hand. Homemade soups are a speciality at the inn and the bar menu also offers fresh haddock, Borrowdale trout, gammon steak pies, chicken and mushroom pies as well as vegetarian dishes and a children's menu. All the food is home-cooked. The bar is open for morning coffee and afternoon tea. There are two lounge bars, often packed with locals who play darts and pool and participate in the winter quiz teams. There is a residents' dining room and the beamed guest rooms have heating, colour TVs, hot and cold water, and tea and coffee making equipment.

Beer: Jennings Bitter and Cumberland Ale on handpumps.

Accommodation: 1 single, 3 doubles, 1 twin, 4 family rooms. B&B from £17.50 per person. Reductions for children. Cards: Access, Amex, Diners, Visa.

TALKIN

Blacksmiths Arms
Nr Brampton, off A69 & B6413. 6 miles east of M6 exit 43

Licensees: Mr & Mrs Tom Bagshaw
Tel: 069 77 3452

The pub was once the village smithy in this delightful village close to the tranquil beauty of Talkin tarn. It is the ideal base for visiting the ancient city of Carlisle, Hadrian's Wall, Lanacost Priory and Gretna Green. The surrounding fells are good walking country and there are facilities for golf, fishing and pony trekking. The guest rooms in the pub are all en suite. Food is available lunchtime and evening in the bar and restaurant and offers homemade soup, salads, sandwiches, Cumberland sausage, haddock in beer batter, local trout, steaks, beef Stroganoff, chicken Kiev, vegetable lasagne, tagliatelle niçoise and sweets.

Beer: Theakston Best Bitter, Whitbread Boddingtons Bitter on handpumps.

Accommodation: 5 rooms: can be used as singles, doubles or twins. £27 single, £40 double. 10% winter discount if you mention this guide. No pets. Cards: Access and Visa.

ULVERSTON

Armadale Hotel
Aradd Foot, Greenodd. A590, 2 miles north of Ulverston

Licensee: Stephanie Gibson
Tel: 0229 861 257

A convivial village welcome is guaranteed in this 19th-century hotel, once a doctor's house, that now serves the communities of Aradd Foot and Greenodd on the outskirts of the town. It is the ideal base for touring the southern lakes and it overlooks the grand sweep of Morecambe Bay. Bar meals, lunch and evening (not Mondays) include pasta dishes, a vegetarian selection, cold platters, homemade pies and grills. The guest rooms are all en suite

and have tea and coffee making facilities; cots for children are available.

Beer: Theakston Best Bitter on handpumps.

Accommodation: 1 single, 2 doubles, 1 family room. B&B £25 single, £40 double, £50 family room. Children two-thirds of adult rate. Cards: Access and Visa.

Canal Tavern
Canal Street. Take A590 Kendal road; follow signs for Barrow; pub is 200 yards on left past lighthouse on hill

Licensees: Mr & Mrs Bardell
Tel: 0229 57093

The Canal Tavern is 200 years old and has been sensitively modernized to win a two-crown rating from the tourist board. It is close to Ulverston's market town and offers coarse fishing in the canal at the rear. Home-cooked food is available lunchtimes and evening.

Beer: Hartley XB and Robinson Best Bitter on handpumps.

Accommodation: 2 doubles, 2 family rooms. B&B £18 single, £12 per person double, £30 family room. Children's rates on application. Pets welcome.

Kings Head Hotel
Queen Street, just off A590

Licensee: Jack Lowther
Tel: 0229 52892

The Kings Head is a cosy old oak-beamed, low-ceilinged pub in the centre of Ulverston, with two blazing fires in winter and crown green bowling at the back – woods are available for hire. Drinks and food can be enjoyed on the terrace in warm weather. Children are welcome in the beer garden. The pub is open all day except Tuesday.

Beer: Theakston Best Bitter plus guest beers on handpumps.

Accommodation: 3 twins, 1 double. B&B £17 per person. No pets.

DERBYSHIRE

ASHBOURNE

White Lion Hotel
Buxton Road. A515, 50 yards from market place

Licensee: Richard Gregory
Tel: 0335 46158

The White Lion is a small 300-year-old coaching inn in a market town that is a fine base for touring the peaks and dales and is within easy reach of Chatsworth House, Haddon, Hardwick Hall and Kedleston Hall. The hotel has ancient beams and log fires, and is the venue for enthusiastic darts and dominoes teams. The guest rooms have TVs, hot and cold water, controlled heaters and tea and coffee making equipment; most rooms have private showers or baths. Cask beer is served in two bars, the restaurant offers an à la carte menu and there is also an extensive range of bar meals, available lunchtime and evening. Trout fishing can be arranged on the River Dove, once fished by that Compleat Angler, Isaak Walton. Buxton is close at hand and there are family pleasures at Alton Towers and the American Adventure Park. Ashbourne is home

to the famous Shrovetide football match, which is played on the streets with the goals three miles apart.

Beer: Ind Coope Burton Ale, Marston Pedigree Bitter and Tetley Bitter on handpumps.

Accommodation: 1 single, 3 doubles, 1 family room, 4 rooms with en suite facilities. B&B £24 single, £40 double, £55 family room. Children half price sharing. No pets. Cards: Access and Visa.

BAMFORD

Derwent Hotel
Main Road. A6013, 2 miles off A57 at Ladybower

Licensees: Angela & David Ryan
Tel: 0433 51395

The Derwent is a superbly situated hotel in the heart of the Peak District, close to the spectacular Ladybower reservoirs. The hotel lounges have old sewing machines, harnesses, copper, brass and fascinating pictures and prints. The emphasis is on home-cooked food and the guest rooms all have TVs, tea and coffee making facilities and fine views of the Derbyshire hills. Bar food includes soup, sandwiches, lasagne, steak and kidney pie, fish dishes, vegetarian specials and homemade desserts. There is a separate dining room and seats in the garden. Boat and tackle can be hired for fishing in the reservoirs. Places of interest nearby include Chatsworth House, Haddon Hall and Little John's grave.

Beer: Stones Best Bitter, Wards Sheffield Best Bitter and Whitbread Boddingtons Bitter on handpumps with regular guest beers.

Accommodation: 1 single, 9 doubles,

2 with private baths. B&B £25 single, £27 with bath, £35/£40 double. Children welcome, babies and toddlers free, small charge under 10. Short Breaks throughout the year, minimum of 2 days: £24.50 per person per day B&B plus evening meal. Pets accepted. Cards: Access and Visa.

BRADWELL

Valley Lodge
B6049 near Castleton

Licensees: Reg & Angie Davies
Tel: 0433 620427

Valley Lodge is beautifully situated in the heart of the Peak District and is a fine base for a range of outdoor pursuits such as fishing, shooting, climbing and potholing with facilities for mountain bike hire, pony trekking, hang gliding and gliding, all of which can be arranged by the Davieses. The lodge has an an excellent choice of food from a varied menu including vegetarian dishes. There is a beer garden for the summer months and 13 picnic benches at the front. The Davieses keep budgerigars and more than 70 of them come home to roost at night.

Beer: Stones Best Bitter, Wards Sheffield Best Bitter, Younger IPA and regular guest beers on handpumps.

Accommodation: 1 twin, 1 double, 2 family rooms. £15 per person per night, £18 with breakfast. Children welcome. Dogs by arrangement.

Derwent Hotel, Bamford

BUXTON

Grove Hotel
Grove Parade

Proprietors: Paul & Mary Kershaw
Tel: 0298 23804

This commanding 18th-century listed building in the centre of the famous spa town, close to the Opera House, The Crescent and Pavilion Gardens, offers great comfort, bar meals lunch and evening and the perfect base for visiting Chatsworth House, Bakewell and Dovedale and the Goyt and Manifold valleys. The guest rooms have TVs and tea and coffee making facilities. Bar food is available in Charlie's Bar and the Rowan Room has both à la carte and table d'hôte menus.

Beer: Robinson Best Mild and Best Bitter on electric pump.

Accommodation: 20 rooms including 12 doubles/twins and 8 family rooms, 7 rooms with en suite facilities. B&B £18 single, £22.50 en suite, £36 double, £45 with bath. Children and pets welcome. Cards: Access, Amex, Diners, Visa.

GLOSSOP

Manor Inn
77 High Street East. A57

Licensee: Eric Cooper
Tel: 0457 855605

The Manor is a 17th-century coaching inn on the main road between Sheffield and Manchester, a mile from Snake Pass and a short drive to the heart of the Peak District. It is a fiercely traditional pub with a separate lounge, dining room and games room. Good homemade food is served every lunchtime and

Monday-Friday evenings, 5-8pm.

Beer: Theakston Best Bitter, Whitbread Boddingtons Bitter and OB Bitter on handpumps.

Accommodation: 1 double, 1 family room. B&B £15 single, £27 double, £42 family room. Children half price under 10. Pets accepted.

HAYFIELD

Royal Hotel
Market Square. A6, follow signs through New Mills to Hayfield

Tel: 0663 742721
Licensee: Bob Hadfield

The stone-built hotel dominates the square of this picturesque village bounded by the River Sett. Built in 1755 as a vicarage, the Royal has retained some of its old atmosphere. It has well-appointed rooms and a restaurant serving à la carte meals. Home-cooked bar meals are also available and parties are a speciality. Food is available lunchtime and evening except Saturday; there is a table d'hôte Sunday lunch. Hayfield stands on the highest part of the Peak and is the natural gateway to Kinder Scout, where a 'mass trespass' in 1932 struck a major blow for ramblers' rights.

Beer: Ruddles County, Whitbread Boddingtons Bitter, Wilsons Original Mild and Bitter on handpumps.

Accommodation: 1 single, 4 doubles, 1 family room. B&B £19.75 single, £17.50 per person in double/family room. Children half price under 12, babies free; children's room. Pets accepted. Cards: Access, Amex, Visa.

HURDLOW

Bull I'Th' Thorn
Nr Buxton. A515, Ashbourne-Buxton
road

Licensee: Bob Haywood
Tel: 0298 83348

This famous hostelry on the old
Roman road between Chester and
Buxton has acted as a coaching inn
and resting place for travellers for
more than 500 years. There was a
farmhouse on the site nearly 700
years ago and in 1472 it became an
inn called the Bull. The name changed
to Hurdlow House in the 17th
century and documents of the time
refer to it as Hurdlow Thorn. The
present name is a combination of its
two main associations. At the height
of the horse-drawn coaching period it
was a major stopping place for
coaches on the Derby to Manchester
route. All this fascinating history is
caught by the rich atmosphere of
Tudor panelling, period carvings and
stone-flagged floors. Bar meals –
soup, ploughman's, fish and chips,
steaks, salads, sandwiches, children's
meals plus Sunday roast – are served
lunchtime and evening. A large
function room and dining room
caters for large parties and coaches.
As well as the accommodation in the
inn there is also a self-catering flat.

Beer: Robinsons Best Bitter on
handpump.

Accommodation: 1 single, 1 double.
Bathroom and toilet serves both
rooms. B&B £13 per person. Self-
catering flat sleeps 4, £150 a week.
Children's room; children's terms on
application. Pets accepted.

ILKESTON

Durham Ox
Durham Street. Off B6096, M1 exit
26

Licensee: Frank Barton
Tel: 0602 324570

An old-fashioned (in the best sense)
backstreet pub where beer, grub,
accommodation and companionship
are all marvellous value. The pub is a
real community centre, hosting
cricket, football and quiz teams as
well as offering such games as darts,
skittles and pool. Durham Street is a
back road and you will find this
splendid boozer, the oldest pub in the
town, from either Station Road or
Bath Street. The pub fare is simple
and nourishing: sausage, egg, chips
and beans, fish, chips and peas and
chicken, chips and peas.

Beer: Wards Mild, Sheffield Best
Bitter and a guest beer on hand and
electric pumps.

Accommodation: 1 single, 1 double.
B&B £10 per person.

KIRK IRETON

Barley Mow
Off B5023 Wirksworth to Derby road

Licensee: Mary Short
Tel: 0335 370306

The Barley Mow is a splendidly
unspoilt 17th-century village inn.
From the outside it looks like a
private house, set behind stone walls,
standing three storeys high and with
two dormer windows. Inside it is a
ramble of small, interconnecting
rooms with a plethora of wood-
panelling and a wide range of ales that
come straight from the casks. The
guest rooms have en suite facilities,

colour TVs and tea and coffee making equipment. There is a residents' lounge and guests can have a three-course evening meal. Lunchtime bar meals consist of soup and sandwiches. The High Peak Trail is two miles away, there is trout fishing in a nearby lake and Alton Towers, the Derbyshire dales and the many stately homes in the area are all close at hand.

Beer: Hook Norton Best Bitter and Old Hooky, Marston Pedigree Bitter, Timothy Taylor Landlord, regular guest beers and Thatcher's Cider straight from the cask.

Accommodation: 5 doubles/twins, all en suite. B&B £20.50 single, £35.75 double. Evening meal £8.50. One room has a double and single bed, suitable for families. Pets welcome.

TADDINGTON

Waterloo
On A6 midway between Buxton and Bakewell

Licensee: Tony Heathcote
Tel: 0298 85230

The Waterloo, high in the Peak National Park, has superb views of the dales and is within easy reach of the old market towns of Buxton and Bakewell, and is a short drive to Chatsworth House, home of the Duke and Duchess of Devonshire. The Waterloo Bar has open log fires and a beamed ceiling, a small and cosy dining room seats 22, and a larger room with seats for 120 acts as function room and larger dining room. There are singalongs on Sunday evenings with a regular pub pianist. Bar meals (not Wednesday evenings) include such homemade dishes as steak and kidney pie, chilli

Barley Mow, Kirk Ireton

con carne, cheese and asparagus flan and beef curry, with steaks, fish and chips and ploughman's. The dining room offers soup, garlic mushrooms, whitebait, steaks, fresh trout, grilled salmon and boeuf bourguignon. All the guest rooms have colour TVs and tea and coffee making equipment.

Beer: Robinson Best Bitter on handpump.

Accommodation: 2 singles, 2 doubles. B&B £17.50 per person. Children's room. No pets. Cards: Access and Visa.

TIDESWELL

George Hotel
Commercial Road, ¼ mile off A619
Chesterfield-Stockport road

Licensee: Dale Norris
Tel: 0298 871382

The George is a much-photographed 18th-century coaching inn in a medieval market town and next to the soaring Cathedral of the Peak. The friendly atmosphere of the George is underscored by a log fire in winter and a cheerful informality that happily allows guests to choose to eat in either the separate dining room or by the fire in the lounge. The menu, lunch and evening, includes daily specials chalked on a board, soup, old ale and mushroom pâté, homemade pie, lasagne, mixed grills, and a wide variety of fillings for wholemeal rolls. Within a 10-mile radius of the hotel you can visit Chatsworth, Castleton, the Derwent Valley, Buxton, Bakewell and Hathersage, the legendary burial place of Little John. The guest rooms have colour TVs and tea and coffee makers.

Beer: Hardys & Hansons Kimberley Best Mild, Best Bitter and Classic on handpumps.

George Hotel, Tideswell

Accommodation: 4 doubles, 1 family room. B&B £17.50 per person. £16.50 per day for a stay of 2-3 days. Half board available. Children's room; children 20% reduction. Pets accepted. Cards: Access and Visa.

WHITEHOUGH

Old Hall Inn
Chinley, ¼ mile off B6062

Proprietors: Michael & Rita Harper
Tel: 0663 750529
Fax: 0663 751900

The inn, a grade two listed building and part of Whitehough Hall, is in a quiet hamlet with panoramic views of the Peak District. The hall dates back to the 16th century and for generations it was the home of the Kirke family. Sir David Kirke's sister, Mary, was maid of honour to Queen Catherine of Braganza. George Kirke was groom to the royal bedchamber of Charles I and was present when the monarch lost his head on the block. Colonel Percy Kirke put down the Monmouth Rebellion with terrible severity after the battle of Sedgemoor in 1685. The inn retains splendid beamed ceilings and mullioned windows. Comprehensive bar food is available.
Accommodation includes private baths and showers, colour TVs, central heating, telephones and tea and coffee making facilities.

Beer: Marston Burton Bitter, Pedigree Bitter, Thwaites Bitter and Whitbread Boddingtons Bitter on handpumps.

Accommodation: 3 doubles, 1 family room. B&B £35 single, £40.50 double/family. Reductions for longer stays. Pets accepted. Cards: Access and Visa.

BLACKAWTON

Normandy Arms
1 mile off A3122 Totnes to Dartmouth road

Licensees: Jonathan & Mark Gibson
Tel: 080 421 316

Parts of the Normandy date back to the 16th century and it has been licensed since 1836. It has been called the Bay Horse and the Commercial Inn before acquiring its present name in the 1950s to commemorate the Normandy landings in World War II which left from nearby Slapton Sands. The pub is close to Totnes, Kingsbridge and the beaches of the South Hams. There are facilities for sailing, boating, windsurfing, golfing, riding and sea and trout fishing. The Normandy Arms has a small comfortable bar, a separate restaurant and a children's room upstairs with toys, games and books. It plays up the Normandy theme with photos of General Montgomery and other World War II memorabilia. Bar snacks offer homemade soup, steak and kidney pie, Atlantic prawns, vegetable pancake, ploughman's and sandwiches while the restaurant (open lunch and dinner) menu includes such house specials as pork fillet cooked with local cider, and gamekeeper's casserole. There is a beer garden for warmer days and the brews include ales from the local Blackawton Brewery.

Beer: Blackawton Bitter, Gold (summer only) and 44 (winter), Draught Bass and Ruddles County on handpumps.

Accommodation: 4 doubles, all en suite. 1 room has extra bed and a cot is available. B&B £32 single, £26 double per person. Children £6 up to 5, £12 6-12 years. Autumn & Winter Breaks: £70 B&B 2 people for 2 nights. Pets accepted. Cards: Access and Visa.

BOVEY TRACEY

Riverside Inn
Fore Street. 1 ½ miles off A38

Licensees: David & Susan Grey
Tel: 0626 832293

The Riverside Inn, with its striking gabled, dormered and whitewashed façade, is in a small town of great historical interest. Bovey Tracey takes its name from the de Tracey family, one of whom, Sir William, helped murder Thomas à Becket in Canterbury Cathedral in 1170; he paid penance by building the parish church. In 1645, during the Civil War, Oliver Cromwell defeated a party of Royalists in a tavern in the town, the old Riverside House. A sword from the battle was discovered 300 years later. The inn has a heavily beamed de Tracey bar, bar food lunchtime and evening, an à la carte evening restaurant and beautifully appointed guest rooms, all with en suite facilities, colour TVs, hair dryers, direct-dial phones and tea and coffee makers.

Beer: Draught Bass, Marston Pedigree Bitter and Whitbread West Country Pale Ale on handpumps with a weekly guest beer.

Accommodation: 6 doubles, 4 family rooms. £30 single, £25 double per person, £20 family room per person. No charge for children in cots. Weekend rates on application. Pets accepted. Cards: Access and Visa.

BRANSCOMBE

Masons Arms
In village centre. Off A3052

Licensee: Janet Inglis
Tel: 029 780 300

The Masons is a delightful 14th-century creeper-clad inn with beamed ceilings and stone-flagged floors. In winter joints are occasionally spit-roasted over the great open hearth in the main bar, which has wall benches and old settles as well as a casement clock. Outside there are seats on a terrace that leads into a small garden. Lunchtime bar food includes soup, ploughman's, demidoff potatoes, pan-fried lamb cutlets and homemade steak and kidney pie. Evening dishes usually include chicken with curry mayonnaise, duck and bacon pie, moules marinière and homemade fish cakes. There is a Sunday roast lunch. Darts, shove ha'penny and dominoes are played in the bar and the sea is just a mile away. Some of the guest rooms are in a cottage across the road.

Beer: Dartmoor Best Bitter, Draught Bass and Wadworth 6X on handpumps, plus Luscombe cider.

Accommodation: 19 rooms. 1 single, 6 twins, 10 doubles, 2 family rooms, 13 rooms with private bath. B&B £22 single, £22-£40 double, £32-£37 family room. Children under 2 free, 2-10 years £10. Winter Breaks: rates on application. Dogs welcome. Cards: Access and Visa.

BUTTERLEIGH

Butterleigh Inn
From Cullompton take turning between Manor House Hotel and Midland Bank: follow signs to Butterleigh. 3 miles from M5

Licensees: Mike & Penny Wolter
Tel: 0884 855407

The Butterleigh is a small 16th-century mid-Devon pub in a tiny hamlet between Tiverton and Cullompton, set in delightful countryside. Both the lounge and main bars have open fires. Food ranges from homemade soups and chilli sausages to fillet steak and vegetarian specials. The modern guest rooms have tea and coffee making facilities. The main bar is divided into two areas: one part is a standard lounge bar while the other is for locals (and guests) dedicated to such pastimes as darts, shove ha'penny and dominoes. There is also a small snug. Bickleigh Castle is close at hand.

Beer: Cotleigh Harrier SPA, Tawny and Old Buzzard, plus guest beers on handpumps.

Accommodation: 2 twin rooms, sharing a bathroom. B&B £20 single, £15 per person sharing. Children over 14 years welcome. No pets.

CHILLINGTON

Chillington Inn
4 miles east of Kingsbridge on A379 Dartmouth road

Licensees: Mr & Mrs D.R. Mooney
Tel: 0548 580 244

The Chillington Inn's origins date back to the 17th century and while it serves high-class food in its restaurant it still retains the atmosphere and attitudes of a traditional country ale house. The two comfortable bars have many original furnishings and other artefacts and welcoming open fires. It is just two miles from some of the area's finest beaches. The beautifully appointed guest rooms have private bathrooms, are centrally heated and have colour TVs and tea and coffee making equipment. Bar snacks are available, while the restaurant food is based on fresh ingredients and home-cooking, with such dishes as salade niçoise, crab and lobster in season, local fish and steaks.

Beer: Flowers IPA and Palmer IPA on handpumps.

Accommodation: 3 doubles, 1 family room, all en suite. B&B £17.50 per person, £18 single occupancy. Children half price. Special Breaks: from £26 per person per night B&B plus evening meal. Family room. Pets welcome. Cards: Access, Amex, Visa.

COLEFORD

New Inn
2½ miles from A377, near Crediton

Licensee: Paul S. Butt
Tel: 0363 84242

The New Inn is a very old inn, built in the 13th century, with a thatched roof and cob and granite walls. It was formerly a monks' retreat and was later a staging post for coaches on the Exeter to Plymouth road. The bars have oak beams, stone walls and large log fires with a profusion of gleaming brass and copper and old prints. A small stream runs by the inn with resident ducks, and the village has many other old and attractive houses. The bar menu is chalked on a blackboard and based on home-cooked meals, including chilli, curry, steak and kidney pie, grills, fish dishes and a good vegetarian choice, Hungarian mushrooms, avocado and Stilton, beef and walnuts and such good old nursery puds as spotted dick and bread pudding. There is a separate restaurant. Fishing and golf are available nearby.

Beer: Flowers Original and IPA, Wadworth 6X plus a a regular guest beer, all on handpumps.

Accommodation: 3 doubles, 1 room with en suite facilities. B&B £20-£27 single, £18-£22 double per person. Children welcome; under 10 years charged £10 when sharing with parents. A self-contained holiday flat with 1 bedroom is also available. Pets accepted. Cards: Access, Amex, Visa.

DODDISCOMBSLEIGH

Nobody Inn
2½ miles from A38 at Haldon Hill (signposted Dunchideock & Doddiscombsleigh)

Licensees: N.F. Borst-Smith & P.W. Bolton
Tel: 0647 52394

A famous old 16th century inn six miles from Exeter and close to Dartmoor and the coast, its name, according to local legend, stems from an unknown buyer who locked the doors and refused hospitality to travellers seeking bed and refreshment. They went wearily on their way, reporting that 'nobody

was in the inn'. You are assured of a welcome today, backed by fine food, ale, 250 whiskies and 700 wines, ports and brandies. The restaurant is open Tuesday to Saturday evenings and offers dishes made from local produce; local trout cooked in pastry is a speciality. Bar meals, served lunchtime and evening every day, include homemade soup, sandwiches, hot smoked mackerel, butter bean casserole, sausage and mash, vegetable or lamb casserole. The inn has old beams and carriage lamps, and high-back settles. You can eat in the lovely garden in good weather. Guest rooms have tea and coffee making facilities; breakfast is served in the rooms.

Beer: Draught Bass, Flowers IPA, Wadworth Farmer's Glory and Grays farm cider on handpumps and straight from the cask.

Accommodation: 1 single, 6 doubles,

Nobody Inn, Doddiscombsleigh

5 with en suite facilities. B&B
£23-£32 single, £33-£55 double. £2
reduction per person for stays of 4
days or more. No children. No pets.
Cards: Access and Visa.

ERMINGTON

Crooked Spire Inn
B3211, 2 miles off A38 near
Ivybridge

Licensee: Jim Shield
Tel: 0548 830202

A cosy and welcoming village inn
with such traditional games as darts
and euchre in the bar and excellent
pub food. Bar snacks include pasties,
ploughman's and sandwiches. The
separate restaurant has local trout,
moussaka, steak and kidney pie,
grills, salads, lasagne and curries.

Beer: Flowers Original and Marston
Pedigree Bitter on handpumps.

Accommodation: 3 doubles. B&B
£22.50 single occupancy, £40 double.
Half and full board available. Cards:
Access and Visa.

HATHERLEIGH

George Hotel
Market Street. A387. A30 from
Okehampton (6 miles)

Licensees: John Dunbar-Ainley &
Veronica Devereux
Tel: 0837 810454

The George is an old coaching inn
with a thatched roof, timbered cob
walls and an impressive balcony
overhanging the street. It was built as
long ago as 1450 as a retreat for
monks. The inn has retained its
period charm with a cobbled
courtyard and low beamed ceilings.

The small front bar, used mainly by
residents, has a vast fireplace and
thick stone walls. A second lounge
has a wood-burning stove and old
settles. A third bar is open only on
market days for local farmers and
other market folk. Bar food, available
every day, includes ploughman's,
sandwiches, soup, spinach and
mushroom roulade, and steak and
kidney pie. A separate restaurant
(evenings except Sunday) offers à la
carte meals with such dishes as
scallops in Chablis, skate with black
butter and lamb with raspberries.
There are seats outside in the
courtyard and the hotel also has a
heated swimming pool. Some of the
guest rooms have four-poster beds
and all have colour TVs and
telephones.

Beer: Draught Bass is permanently
on handpump with a rotating guest
beer list including Greene King
Abbot Ale, Wadworth 6X and
Whitbread Boddingtons Bitter on
handpumps.

Accommodation: 1 single, 10 doubles,
3 family rooms, 9 rooms with en suite
facilities. B&B £29 single, £42 en
suite, double £40.50 per room, £54 en
suite, four-poster with bath £62. 3
nights or more out of season: 10%
discount. Children's rates on
application. Pets welcome. Cards:
Access and Visa.

Tally Ho
14 Market Street

Licensees: Gianni & Annamaria
Scoz
Tel: 0837 810306

The Scozes have installed a 3½-barrel
micro-brewery and have added a
range of home-brewed beers to the

general delights of their hotel. Signor Scoz, from Milan, fell in love with Devon on a holiday, decided to stay and runs a highly traditional English pub. The inn is 15th century, with wood-burning stoves in large stone fireplaces. There is a separate restaurant and all the rooms have antique furnishings. Annamaria Scoz is the power behind the kitchen and supplies the bar with homemade pasta and pizzas, chicken diavola, fritto misto, lasagna and grilled trout while the restaurant offers an à la carte menu with onion soup, Parma ham with melon, smoked salmon, filetto al carpaccio, châteaubriand, valdostana, scaloppine alla Romagnola, anatra alla Medici, scampi Provençale and sogliola alla mugnaia. Signor Scoz has a good Milanese attitude to enjoyment: a leaflet in the guest rooms says: 'As the Tally Ho is above all a country inn, the locals are likely to become a little boisterous at times, especially on darts night. If you are finding it difficult to sleep, then why not come downstairs and join in the fun.' *Salute!*

Beer: Tally Ho Dark Mild, Potboilers Brew, Tarka Tipple, Nutters and a winter brew all on handpumps.

Acccommodation: 3 doubles, all with en suite facilities. B&B £20 per person; £25 single occupancy. Children over 8 only, special rates on application. Cards: Access and Visa.

HAYTOR VALE

Rock Inn
Moorland road to Widecombe; signposted from B3344 west of Bovey Tracey; 6 miles from Newton Abbot

Licensee: Christopher Graves
Tel: 0364 661305
Fax: 0364 661242

The Rock has a long and fascinating history. Down the centuries it has been an alehouse for Haytor granite quarrymen and iron miners, a meeting place for farmers and landowners, and a coaching inn. It has an unspectacular façade but the interior is a delight with half-panelled walls and high-back settles. Other rooms have log fires in handsome fireplaces and many old prints and paintings on the walls. The inn is set in a small village nestling in Dartmoor National Park below the stark beauty of Haytor Rocks. The wide-ranging bar food includes sandwiches, homemade soup, filled jacket potatoes, ploughman's, lasagne, curries, vegetarian dishes, rabbit and cider casserole, fish casserole, local trout and good desserts such as apple cheesecake, treacle tart and bread and butter pudding. There is a separate restaurant with such dishes as venison marinated in real ale, duck à l'orange and local salmon. The inn has a pleasant garden and there are nearby facilities for golf, horse riding and fishing.

Beer: Draught Bass, Eldridge Pope, Thomas Hardy Country Bitter and Royal Oak plus regular guest beers on handpumps.

Accommodation: 1 single, 9 doubles, seven rooms with en suite facilities. 1 four-poster bedroom; all rooms have colour TVs, direct dial phones and tea and coffee makers. B&B £37.50 single en suite, £25.50-£27.50 double, £30.50 de luxe double per person. Four-poster £35.50 per person. Children's room. No pets. Cards: Access, Amex, Visa.

HORNS CROSS

Hoops Inn
A39 midway between Bideford and
Clovelly

Licensees: Derek & Marjorie
Sargent
Tel: 0237 451 222/247

The Hoops dates from the 13th
century and has a reed thatched roof,
thatched porches and great white cob
walls. It stands 500 feet above sea
level on the main road to Cornwall
and is less than a mile from the coast.
The atmosphere and antiquity of the
inn is caught by the stone fireplace
and period furniture, while some of
the guest rooms have four-poster and
half-tester beds. The Hoops has been
a smugglers' inn and a home-brew
house and was used by such famous
old sea dogs as Sir Richard Grenville,
Drake, Raleigh and Hawkins. They
all sponsored the parliamentary bill
of 1566 to build a quay at nearby
Hartland where potatoes and tobacco
were first imported to Britain. The
picturesque village of Clovelly is just
four miles away. The restaurant
offers French and English cuisine
while the bar food includes steaks,
fish, salads, ploughman's, homemade
soup and filled jacket potatoes.

Beer: Whitbread Flowers IPA,
Original and Boddingtons Bitter,
Marston Pedigree Bitter on
handpumps.

Accommodation: 1 single, 13 doubles,
3 family rooms, 8 rooms with en suite
facilities. B&B single £25, double
£22-£30 per person, family room £17
per person. Weekend (Nov-March)
£50 per person for 2 nights B&B plus
dinner. Children's room. Small dogs
welcome. Cards: Access, Amex,
Diners, Visa.

Hoops Inn, Horns Cross

KNOWSTONE

Masons Arms Inn
1½ miles north-east of A361
between South Molton & Tiverton

Licensees: David & Elizabeth Todd
Tel: 03984 231/582

The Masons is an unspoilt thatched
13th-century rural inn opposite the
village church and close to Exmoor.
The bar has a stone floor, settles and
old farm implements on the walls,
with a beamed ceiling and a large
open log fire. A smaller room is used
mainly for games, including bar
billiards and table skittles. Bar food
includes homemade soup, smoked
mackerel pâté, salade niçoise,
ploughman's, homemade pies, fritto
misto, curry and rice and steaks.
There is a separate restaurant for
evening meals. All the guest rooms
have colour TVs, direct-dial
telephones and tea and coffee making
facilities.

Beer: Cotleigh Tawny Bitter and Hall
& Woodhouse Badger Best Bitter
from the cask.

Accommodation: 1 single, 4 doubles,
2 rooms with private facilities. B&B
£21.95 per person, £26 in en suite
room. Children under 5 free. Pets by
arrangement.

LIFTON

Lifton Cottage Hotel
A30 between Okehampton and
Launceston

Licensees: N.H. & F.P. Beer
Tel: 0556 84439

The small hotel is a 350-year-old
Gothic building that is grade two
listed. It has a cosy bar with a cheery
open log fire in winter. Lifton is on

the edge of Dartmoor and Bodmin
Moor, while Roadford reservoir is
some five miles away. Facilities for
fishing and golf are available locally.
Bar food and restaurant meals are
served lunchtime and evening.

Beer: St Austell HSD on handpump.

Accommodation: 4 singles, 6 doubles,
3 family rooms, 9 rooms with en suite
facilities. B&B £25 per person, £29.95
en suite. Family room £29.95 per
person, children half price under 11.
10% discount for stays of 3 days or
more. Children's room. Pets
welcome. Cards: Access, Amex,
Diners, Visa.

LYDFORD

Dartmoor Inn
On A386

Licensees: Paul & Margaret Hyde
Tel: 0822 82221

The Dartmoor Inn is a 16th-century
pack-horse inn on an old route from
north to south Devon, an excellent
base for walking and riding holidays,
with access to Dartmoor via a bridle
path that runs by the side of the inn.
There are two welcoming bars with
low ceilings, wood-panelling, open
fires and comfortable furnishings.
Darts and dominoes are played in one
bar. An extensive bar menu ranges
from snacks to three-course meals,
including local trout, steaks and the
popular Dartmoor tipsy pie – steak
and kidney pie made with real ale. All
the guest rooms are en suite and have
colour TVs, central heating and tea
and coffee making facilities.

Beer: Draught Bass, St Austell
Tinners, HSD and Winter Warmer
on handpumps.

Accommodation: 1 twin, 2 doubles, B&B £20 per person. Children welcome.
Cards: Access, Diners, Visa.

Near LYNTON

Hunter's Inn
Heddon's Mouth near Parracombe. Signposted on A39 Lynton to Barnstaple road.

Licensee: Chris Moate
Tel: 05983 ?30

Hunter's Inn, well signposted in the area, is set in one of the loveliest and most spectacular parts of Exmoor National Park. Several inns have stood on the spot over the centuries and some of them were the haunts of smugglers. The present building is turn-of-the-century Edwardian, designed like a Swiss chalet after the previous inn had been destroyed by fire. The large bars are partitioned to give a cosy atmosphere while outside there is no less than five acres of garden with a wide variety of wildlife. The guest rooms are sumptuous, three have four-poster beds and most have en suite facilities, colour TVs and hospitality trays. Bar food, served lunchtime and evening, includes cold platters (cheese, honey roast ham, smoked mackerel, trout, salmon served with salad), steaks, fried chicken, spicy sausage, haddock or plaice, homemade lasagne, chilli con carne, vegetarian dishes and a children's menu. There is a separate restaurant with à la carte menu.

Beer: Exmoor Ale, Flowers Original, Wadworth IPA and 6X on handpumps and regular guest beers.

Accommodation: 7 doubles/twins, most with en suite facilities. B&B from £24.50 per person. Children under 12 half price sharing; infants

free of charge. Children's room. Pets welcome. Cards: Access and Visa.

MORETON-HAMPSTEAD

White Hart Hotel
The Square. Leave A38 at Newton Abbot/Bovey Tracey junction; take A382 to Moretonhampstead

Licensee: Peter Morgan
Tel: 0647 40406
Fax: 0647 40565

The White Hart is based in a small former wool town with the longest single-word name in England. The hotel was built in the reign of George II and was a coaching inn on the Exeter to Plymouth run; coaches stopped there to change horses. During the Napoleonic Wars it was a meeting place for captured French officers on parole from Princetown prison on Dartmoor. The hallway has a vast road map of Devon, some 160 years old. The back bar has rough whitewashed walls, beams and horsebrasses and serves bar food, lunchtime and evening, that includes renowned ploughman's with great generous chunks of Cheddar, along with curry, steak and kidney pie, king prawns, local trout and quail. The restaurant has full à la carte meals and the impressive breakfasts offer kippers as well as fried food. Moretonhampstead is in the heart of Dartmoor National Park and has 16th-century alms houses, a 14th-century church and offers facilities for fishing and riding nearby. All the hotel guest rooms have en suite facilities and are furnished to a high standard.

Beer: Draught Bass and Furgusons Dartmoor Best Bitter on handpumps with regular guest beers and ciders.

Accommodation: 1 single, 16 doubles/twins, 3 family rooms, all en suite. B&B £37.50 single, £57.50 double/twin, £67.50 family room. Special Rates any 2 days from £76 per person B&B plus dinner. Pets welcome. Cards: Access, Amex, Diners, Visa.

NORTH BOVEY

Ring of Bells
Off A382, 1½ miles from Moretonhampstead

Licensees: Tony & Brenda Rix
Tel: 0647 40375

The Ring of Bells is a 13th-century inn in a stunning village of whitewalled, thatched and slated cottages. It was built originally by stonemasons as their lodging place while building the parish church. The Ring of Bells has great oak beams and in the dining room there is an old oven, next to the vast inglenook, where the village baker used to make his bread. The small bar has another large inglenook and a brass-faced grandfather clock built into the three-foot thick wall. The guest rooms all have en suite facilities, and four-poster beds are available. A full menu is available lunchtime and evening in the bar and restaurant, and daily specials include local fish and game pies.

Beer: Ind Coope Burton Ale, Furgusons Dartmoor Best Bitter, Wadworth 6X, regular guest beers and a winter warmer on handpumps.

Accommodation: 3 doubles, 1 family room, all rooms with en suite facilities. B&B from £20 per person. Half board from £30. Outdoor swimming pool. Children and pets welcome.

Near PLYMOUTH

Boringdon Arms
13 Boringdon Terrace, Boringdon Road, Turnchapel. Follow roadsigns to Turnchapel and RAF Mountbatten from A379 Plymouth-Kingsbridge road at Plymstock. Pub is in centre of village

Licensee: Janet Rayne
Tel/fax: 0752 402053

Turnchapel was once a fishing village with a quarry and the Boringdon Arms was built as the quarrymaster's house in the early 18th century. The pub takes its name from the Boringdon family; it was Baron Boringdon who transformed the quiet village in 1797 when he built a dry dock there, which for some time was the busiest shipyard in the Plymouth area. The pub's ales are stored in the original stone cellar of the building. It has an extensive bar menu (lunchtime and evening) featuring homemade chilli, cottage pie and 'seriously hot' Bori-burner curries. Fish suppers, summer barbecues and folk evenings are organized and the pub can arrange deep-sea fishing trips and sub-aqua diving. Turnchapel is at the western end of the South Devon Coastal Path which runs some 110 miles east to Lyme Regis and the pub is the first and last port of call for many walkers.

Beer: Butcombe Bitter, Draught Bass, Summerskills Best Bitter, Whistlebelly and Vengeance, Tetley Bitter and other guest beers, all on handpumps.

Accommodation: 2 doubles, 4 family rooms, 1 room with en suite facilities. B&B £12 per person. Children under 2 free, half price 2-10 sharing. Winter Break: 4 nights for price of 3. Pets accepted.

PRINCETOWN

Plume of Feathers Inn
The Square. A3212 Plymouth to
Moretonhampstead road

Licensee: James Langton
Tel: 082 289 240

In a village famous for the Dartmoor
prison – completed in 1809, once the
jail of renowned villains but now just
the local lock-up – the inn is
Princetown's oldest building, dating
from 1785. It has slate floors, granite
walls, copper bars, exposed beams
and log fires. The large garden is a
delight for children, with rabbits and
domestic animals. Bar food is served
lunchtime and evening all week and
includes ploughman's, curry, scampi,
lasagne, chilli, filled jacket potatoes,
homemade soup, and burgers.

Beer: Draught Bass and Worthington
Best Bitter, St Austell Tinners on
handpumps.

Accommodation: 2 twins, 1 double.
B&B £10 per person per night.
Children under 5 sharing free.
Children's room. Pets welcome.

SHEEPWASH

Half Moon Inn
5 miles west of Hatherleigh off
A3072

Licensees: Benjamin & Charles
Inniss
Tel: 040 923 376

This fine old inn, commanding one
side of the village square, has been
run by the Inniss family for more
than 30 years. The exterior has
steeply sloping roofs, porches,
creeper and plants. Inside there are
ancient oak beams, an open log fire
and slate floors. Riding and pony

trekking are available in the area. The
guest rooms all have private
bathrooms, heating, colour TVs,
direct-dial phones and tea and coffee
making facilities. Three of the rooms
are on the ground floor. Lunchtime
bar food includes snacks, sandwiches
and salads, and there is a separate
evening restaurant.

Beer: Courage Best Bitter, Draught
Bass and a guest beer on handpumps.

Accommodation: 2 singles, 11
doubles, 2 family rooms. B&B
£30-£50 single, £26.50 per person in a
double; family room and children's
rates on request. Children's room
until 9pm. Pets welcome. Cards:
Access and Visa.

SIDFORD

Blue Ball Inn
On A3052 between Exeter and
Lyme Regis

Licensee: Roger Newton
Tel: 0395 514062

The Blue Ball is a cob and flint inn
dating from 1385, with a thatched
roof, large inglenook fireplaces in
both bars and low beamed ceilings.
The public bar has a stone-flagged
floor and there are carpets and
comfortable furnishings in the
lounge. Food ranges from chunky
sandwiches, through a ploughman's
that will satisfy the most ravenous
appetite, to salads and hot dishes that
include steak and kidney pie, chicken
Mornay, chilli con carne, steaks,
locally made sausages and vegetable
moussaka or lasagne. There are
summer barbecues in the attractive
garden. Farway Countryside Park
and Salcombe Donkey Sanctuary are
close by, as are Honiton and
Sidmouth, the stately Regency
seaside town. Guest rooms have tea

and coffee making facilities and there is a residents' TV lounge.

Beer: Cornish Royal Wessex, Marston Pedigree Bitter, Whitbread West Country Pale Ale and Boddingtons Bitter on handpumps.

Accommodation: 3 twins. B&B £16 per person, single room supplement £4. Children welcome, no reductions. Residents' lounge. Dogs by arrangement.
Cards: Access and Visa.

SILVERTON

Three Tuns
14 Exeter Road. Off A396, 7 miles south of Tiverton

Licensees: Lyn & Nick Radmore
Tel: 0392 860352

Among Silverton's attractions is its own small brewery, Exe Valley, and the oldest row of cottages in the county. The Three Tuns is a 15th-century inn that has carefully retained much of its original atmosphere with all the modern comforts. There is a cheerful locals' bar and a separate restaurant. Bar food (lunchtime and evening) includes homemade soup, smoked mackerel pâté, homemade lasagne and cottage pie, lemon sole and monkfish, venison steak, several vegetarian options including vegetable and lentil lasagne, and puddings that include homemade fruit crumble. There is a separate restaurant and a traditional Sunday lunch. The guest rooms all have private bathrooms, colour TVs, telephones, hair dryers and tea and coffee makers. One room is designed for use by disabled people.

Beer: Courage Best Bitter, Directors and John Smith's Bitter, Fullers London Pride and Ruddles County on handpumps.

Accommodation: 4 twins, 1 double, 1 family room all with en suite facilities. B&B £30 single, £40 double. Winter Break: 3 nights for the price of 2. Family room. Pets welcome. Cards: Access, Amex, Visa.

SLAPTON

Tower Inn
Off A379 between Dartmouth & Kingsbridge; in village lane opposite church gate

Licensees: Keith & Kim Romp, Jan Khan & Carlo Cascianelli
Tel: 0548 580216

The Tower is a 14th-century inn up a narrow lane opposite the village church. The inn was originally cottages for the monks who built the local monastery, of which the chantry tower still stands. The collegiate chantry of St Mary was founded in 1373 by Sir Guy de Brian, standard bearer to Edward II at the Battle of Calais in 1349. The inn was first licensed in 1382. It has stone walls and the flag-stoned bar has settles, a wood-burning stove, chairs made from old beer casks and an inglenook log fire. The rear garden has picnic tables and overlooks the chantry. Slapton Sands are close at hand. Food, including a separate restaurant, is served lunchtime and evening every day. As one of the partner's names suggests, there is a strong Italian bias in the cooking, which features seafood pasta, whole sole cooked with dill, scallops en croute, a selection of vegetarian dishes and a children's menu.

Beer: Blackawton Bitter, Eldridge Pope Royal Oak, Exmoor Ale, Gibbs Mew Bishop's Tipple, Hall & Woodhouse Tanglefoot and Wadworth 6X on handpumps.

Accommodation: 2 doubles, 1 family room. B&B £17.50 per person. Children half price. Pets welcome.

SOUTH ZEAL

Oxenham Arms
19 miles west of Exeter; village signposted from A30

Licensee: James Henry
Tel: 0837 840244

This ancient inn has been licensed since 1552 and its creeper-clad granite exterior is testimony to its age. Inside there are original beams and half-panelled walls, mullioned windows and old fireplaces. The walls are thick stone and fine stone steps lead up to the garden at the back. Bar food has won wide acclaim in the area and is served lunchtime and evening every day; there is a separate restaurant. Food in the bar includes soup, ploughman's, fish and chips, homemade steak and kidney pie cooked in Guinness, and daily specials such as coq au vin. All the guest rooms have colour TVs, direct-dial phones and tea and coffee making facilities.

Beer: Draught Bass and St Austell Tinners from the cask.

Accommodation: 6 doubles, 4 family rooms (including 2 in cottage across the road), 9 rooms with en suite facilities. B&B £32.50 single, £50 double room, £55 family room. Children £5.50 sharing with 2 adults. Winter Break (Nov-March): £140 for 2 people, 2 nights, B&B plus dinner. Children's room. Dogs welcome, 50p per day. Cards: Access, Amex, Diners, Visa.

SPREYTON

Tom Cobley Tavern
Leave A30 at Merrymeet roundabout (12 miles west of Exeter); follow B3219 and pick up signs for Spreyton

Licensees: John & Holly Filor
Tel: 064 723 314

The tavern was where Uncle Tom and his assorted topers set off on their ill-fated journey to Widdecombe Fair in 1802. An inn is reputed to have stood on the site since 1589. The exterior of the tavern has a striking porch and a riot of flowers in season from tubs and pots. There is a simple and cheerful bar, popular with locals – and with a portrait of Tom Cobley above the fireplace – and a plusher restaurant in a back bar where homemade food is served every day except Monday. Bar food includes pies, lasagne, moussaka and toasties. A traditional roast is served on Sundays and there are barbecues in summer.

Beer: Cotleigh Tawny Bitter and Marston Pedigree Bitter straight from the cask, with regular guest beers.

Accommodation: 2 singles, 2 doubles. B&B £16.50 per person. Pets welcome.

TRUSHAM

Cridford Inn
Off A38. Take B3193 Christow & Trusham road; signposted after quarry

Licensees: Mike Shepherd
Tel: 0626 853 694

The inn is based in the lovely Teign valley, just one mile from Dartmoor. The building dates back to the 14th century and has a wealth of old beams. It has been a pub for just a few years; it was a farmhouse before that and many old farming implements have been retained and you can buy free-range eggs from the bar. There are two spacious and homely bars and the beer is stillaged behind them. The guest rooms all have en suite facilities, colour TVs and tea and coffee making facilities. Bar snacks are served every day, lunchtime and evening, and the restaurant is open Friday and Saturday evenings with an à la carte menu, and for Sunday lunch.

Beer: Cotleigh Old Buzzard, Draught Bass, Exmoor Ale and weekly guest beer on handpumps and straight from the cask.

Accommodation: 3 doubles, all en suite. B&B £20 per person. Pets welcome. Cards: Access and Visa.

UPLYME

Black Dog Hotel
Lyme Road, A3051

Licensee: John Govier
Tel: 0297 442634

The postal address is Dorset but the Black Dog is just over the border, the first and last pub in Devon. It has an imposing roadside exterior with tall chimneys and a large free-standing inn sign. It is an excellent base for visiting Lyme Regis and the Abbotsbury swannery. The hotel runs a courtesy service for guests arriving by train at Axminster. It is a cheerful and genuine local and the piano in the long and comfortably furnished bar is often used for impromptu sing-songs. Bar meals are served lunchtime and evening and there is a traditional Sunday lunch. There is a separate restaurant and beer garden, and the guest rooms

have colour TVs, tea and coffee making facilities and bowls of fresh fruit.

Beer: Palmer IPA on handpump.

Accommodation: 1 single, 2 doubles, 3 family rooms. B&B £12.50–£16 per person, children £9; infants free. Reductions for stays of more than 4 nights and low season. Dogs welcome.

Near BEAMINSTER

New Inn
Stoke Abbott. A3066 from Beaminster; village signposted. From Broadwinsor take Bridport road, turn left at Stoke Knapp farm

Licensee: Graham Gibbs
Tel: 0308 68333

The New Inn belies its name. It is ancient, with thatched roofs and cobbled walls outside and a bar sporting old beams decorated with horse brasses, tables and wheelback chairs. There is a separate dining room which children can use and the pub has a large enclosed garden with swings for children. Stoke Abbott is a secluded village set among rolling Dorset hills and with picturesque thatched houses and a 12th-century church. Local places of interest include Parnham House at Beaminster, Forde Abbey and Clapton Court Gardens. Bar meals in the inn are available lunchtime and evening Tuesday to Sunday and include homemade steak and kidney pie, lasagne, Stilton flan, quiche, pizza, curries, steaks, salads, ploughman's, fish and vegetarian meals plus a daily hot special. A traditional Sunday lunch is served from October to April.

Beer: Palmer Bridport Bitter, IPA and Tally Ho on handpumps.

Accommodation: 3 doubles. Rooms can be let as singles, and 1 double is large enough for a family. B&B £17.50 single, £15 per person sharing. Family rates by negotiation. Children's room. No pets. Cards: Access and Visa.

BRIDPORT

Tiger Inn
Barrack Street. Off A35

Licensee: Geoffrey Scott Kenyon
Tel: 0308 27543

The Tiger is a modernized and redecorated free house 1½ miles from the coast. At West Bay you can take the coast path over the cliffs as far as Lyme Regis, following in the steps of the French Lieutenant's Woman. The Tiger offers a warm welcome, with full meals and bar snacks in the restaurant or garden patio. Local trout and steaks are a speciality and there are always vegetarian dishes and daily specials. There is a good-value Sunday roast lunch. There are facilities for golf and fishing close by along with a sports centre. The double guest rooms have colour TV and tea and coffee makers.

Beer: Draught Bass, Wadworth 6X and Bulmer Dry Cider on handpumps or from the cask.

Accommodation: 1 single, 2 doubles. B&B from £12.50 per person. Winter Break: Oct-Easter £70 for 2 people for 2 nights B&B plus dinner. No pets.

Near BRIDPORT

Loders Arms
Loders. Off A35 north-east of Bridport. Leave main road at signpost for Loders and Uploders

Licensee: Mrs C. Jennings
Tel: 0308 22431

The Loders Arms has a delightful position in the heart of a small village of stone-built and thatched cottages. The bar is popular with locals and in summer the terrace and garden, both bright with flowers and with fine views of the sheltering hills, attract many visitors. It is a good base for exploring the west Dorset coast stretching from Weymouth along the Chesil Beach to Lyme Regis, while Hardy country is all around. An 18-hole golf course is nearby. Lunchtime bar snacks are available every day and include ploughman's, sandwiches, pasties, soups and scampi. The evening restaurant serves steaks cooked in creamy Stilton sauce or peppercorn sauce, along with local fish, all served with fresh vegetables and followed by such tempting puddings as walnut pie and profiteroles. The guest rooms all have showers or baths en suite and tea and coffee making equipment. A cosy residents' lounge has a colour TV.

Beer: Palmer Bridport Bitter and IPA on handpumps.

Accommodation: 3 doubles. B&B £25 single occupancy, £17.50-£20 per person sharing. Children's room. Pets welcome. Cards: Access and Visa.

Marquis of Lorne

Nettlecombe. From Bridport take A3066 towards Beaminster; turn right at crossroads, signposted Powerstock; from Powerstock follow Nettlecombe sign

Licensee: Robert Bone
Tel: 030885 236

The Marquis is a 16th-century stone inn in a remote location beneath the old Roman hill fort of Eggardon. It has two bars with open fires, large gardens and a children's play area. The main bar has settles and many photographs of Dobermanns and Rottweilers. Bar food is available every day lunchtime and evening and includes sandwiches, homemade lemon and lentil or onion soup, ploughman's, daily specials such as rabbit pie or lobster and a roast Sunday lunch. The intimate, 40-seater restaurant offers game, salmon, lobster, mussels, Dover sole and a special vegetarian section.

Beer: Palmer Bridport Bitter and IPA on handpumps.

Accommodation: 6 doubles, including 2 rooms suitable for families, 4 rooms with en suite facilities. B&B £21 per person, £22 en suite. Dinner B&B £30, £32 en suite. Children under 8 half price. Nov-March B&B £10 per person eating dinner from à la carte menu. No pets.

BROADSTONE

Broadstone Hotel

Station Approach, off A349; from M27 take A31 to Wimborne, follow Poole signs and turn right at Dunyeats roundabout

Licensees: Keith & Trish Leech
Tel: 0202 694220

The Broadstone is a cheery, traditional local with an emphasis on entertainment. There are live music evenings, and a separate skittles alley. The beer garden has a patio and a

Marquis of Lorne, near Bridport

barbecue. Broadstone is handily placed for Wimborne, Bournemouth and Poole. The hotel offers hot and cold bar food, and the guest rooms all have showers, TVs, central heating, and tea and coffee making equipment.

Beer: Whitbread Boddingtons Bitter, Strong Country Bitter and guest beers on handpumps.

Accommodation: 5 doubles, 1 family room. B&B £18.50 per person, £31.50 double. Reduced rates for 3 days or more. Bargain breaks: details on request.

BURTON BRADSTOCK

Three Horseshoes
Mill Street. B3157, off A35

Licensee: W.H. Attrill
Tel: 0308 897259

The Three Horseshoes is a long and low-slung thatched pub with attractive thatched porches, in a village close to Chesil Beach on the Bridport to Weymouth coast road. West Bay is near at hand with its fleet of fishing boats and a golf course. The low-beamed lounge has an open fire and the separate dining room and bar seats 40 people. Food (served every day) includes curry, crab and lobster salads, lasagne, moussaka and vegetarian dishes, served in the lounge, the dining room or the fine walled garden at the rear. There is a large children's room with activities to the side of the garden. The guest rooms have hot and cold running water, colour TVs and tea and coffeee making facilities.

Beer: Palmer Bridport Bitter, IPA and Tally Ho on handpumps.

Accommodation: 3 doubles. B&B from £14.50 per person. No children or pets. .

MILTON ABBAS

Hambro Arms
3 miles off A354, near Milton Abbey (OS 018812)

Licensee: K.A. Baines
Tel: 0258 880233

The Hambro is a delightful 18th-century thatched inn in a picturesque village. Milton Abbas was the first purpose-built village in England and all the cottages are in the same thatched style. The Hambro Arms has two charming guest rooms, one with a four-poster bed, both with en suite facilities. There is splendid pub food, plus a separate restaurant and a Sunday carvery.

Beer: Cornish Royal Wessex, Flowers IPA on handpumps.

Accommodation: 2 doubles. B&B from £25 per person. No pets. Cards: Access and Visa.

POOLE

Inn in the Park
6 Poole Road, Branksome Park. From A338 at Frizzel House roundabout follow Branksome Chines sign into The Avenue; turn left at signpost for Branksome Dene Chine on Westminster Road which leads to Pinewood Road

Licensees: Paula & Alan Potter
Tel: 0202 761318

This is a comfortable inn converted from a handsome Victorian house, with a log fire in a bar decorated with postage stamps and old cigarette cards. In pleasant weather you can enjoy drink and food on a patio. There is an extensive hot and cold menu lunchtime and evening. All the guest rooms have colour TVs and tea and coffee making facilities. The inn is a good base for visiting Bournemouth and Poole and is near the beaches of Branksome Chines.

Beer: Adnams Bitter, Draught Bass and Wadworth 6X on handpumps.

Accommodation: 4 doubles, 1 family room, all with private bath. B&B from £21.50 per person in double rooms, plus £7.50 for single occupancy. Rates for children on application.

POWERSTOCK

Three Horseshoes
Take Askerswell turn from A35 and drive round Eggardon Hill; or take West Milton turning from A3066 and follow Powerstock signs

Licensees: Pat & Diana Ferguson
Tel: 030 885 328/229

The 'Shoes' is a remote Victorian stone-built pub, well worth the effort of finding. The village has a Norman church and cows wander down the main street. There are fine views and country walks, and trout and sea fishing facilities. The pub has a separate restaurant built with local stone and with pine-clad walls. Two of the guest rooms have en suite facilities. There are good bar meals such as fish soup, mussels, Lyme Bay plaice, squid, baked red gurnard and scallops. The restaurant specializes in local sea food as well as steaks and venison and a Sunday roast.

Beer: Palmer Bridport Bitter, IPA and Tally Ho (winter) on handpumps and Taunton traditional cider from the cask.

Accommodation: 2 doubles. B&B £27.50 per person. Single occupancy of double room £30. Bargain Breaks: 3 days half-board £210 for 2.

SHAFTESBURY

Royal Chase Hotel
Royal Chase roundabout off A30/A350

Licensee: George Hunt
Tel: 0747 53355
Fax: 0747 51969

The Royal Chase is a small, beautifully-appointed 3 star hotel in the old Saxon hill town in the heart of Wessex, with its tumbling cobbled streets, thatched cottages and breath-catching views over Dorset. The hotel was a monastery until 1922 and it still enjoys a wonderful serenity and seclusion. It has an indoor swimming pool. There is a genuine locals' bar with an open fire and a fine old-fashioned cash register. The Country restaurant offers fine food based on local produce. It is a good base for visiting the Fox Talbot Museum of Photography, Montacute House Tropical Bird Garden, Wookey Hole, Thomas Hardy's cottage and Stonehenge.

Beer: Eldridge Pope Royal Oak (usually in winter) and Ushers Best Bitter on handpumps with regular guest beers including Ringwood Best Bitter and Wadworth 6X.

Accommodation: 3 singles, 18 doubles, 10 family rooms, all with private bath or shower. B&B from £32.25 per person. Weekend (2 nights B&B plus evening meal) £106-116. Real ale breaks from £106. Children's room; children free if sharing. Dogs welcome. Cards: Access, Amex, Diners, Visa.

STURMINSTER NEWTON

White Hart
Market Cross. A30 to East Stour then B3092 or A357 Blandford to Wincanton road then B3092

Licensee: D.G. Rice
Tel: 0258 72593

The White Hart is an early 18th-century thatched coaching inn in the heart of the Blackmore Vale and Hardy country. Coarse fishing is available in the picturesque River Stour nearby. The lovely old pub is free from noisy music, it has a small and pleasant garden, fires in winter and such traditional games as skittles, crib and darts. An extensive menu of hot and cold bar meals and snacks is available every day lunchtime and evening.

Beer: Hall & Woodhouse Badger Best Bitter on handpump.

Accommodation: 1 twin, 2 doubles, 1 family room. B&B £17 per person. Children's rates on application. Pets by arrangement.

WEST LULWORTH

Castle Inn
Main Road, B3070, off A352 & A351

Proprietors: Patricia & Graham Halliday
Tel: 092941 311
Fax: 092941 415

A picturesque thatched cottage pub near Lulworth Cove, the Castle is some 450 years old and takes its present name from the castle at East Lulworth designed by Inigo Jones and destroyed by fire in 1929. The inn, first known as the Jolly Sailor, has two bars, rolling gardens and outdoor seats at the front. The bar has a flag-stoned floor and leatherette seats round the tables while the lounge has tankards hanging from a beam and rural prints on the walls. Bar food is served whenever the pub is open and includes soup, tuna cocktail, egg mayonnaise, spaghetti bolognese, plaice or cod and chips,

White Hart, Sturminster Newton

steak and kidney pie, crofters pie, rabbit and pork casserole, curry and rice, salads, ploughman's and filled jacket potatoes. There is a separate restaurant; children can eat in the restaurant or part of the bar reserved for diners. The guest rooms have central heating, colour TVs and tea and coffee makers. There are facilities for fishing, shooting, riding, windsurfing and golf in the area.

Beer: Cornish Royal Wessex, Flowers IPA and Marston Pedigree Bitter on handpumps.

Accommodation: 1 single, 4 twins, 1 family room, 1 four-poster room, 5 doubles, plus 2 ground floor double rooms (no stairs). 9 rooms with en suite facilities. B&B £20-£26 single, twin £33 (£39 en suite), family room £46, four-poster £42, double £39. Winter Breaks: terms on application. Cards: Access, Amex, Diners, Visa.

WIMBORNE

Albion
19 High Street, town square A31

Licensee: Marion Edmonds
Tel: 0202 882492

The Albion is the oldest licensed premises in Wimborne, the last surviving part of an ancient coaching inn with an original inglenook fireplace. This is very much a locals' pub, with a warm, friendly atmosphere, where dominoes, crib and darts are played. Marion Edmonds specializes in traditional food such as beef cobbler and Minster pie, jacket potatoes and ploughman's. There is a large garden with a swing and barbecues. The pub is a fine base for Wimborne Minster and Kingston Lacy House (NT).

Beer: Hall & Woodhouse Badger Best Bitter on handpump.

Accommodation: 1 double or family room with bath, shower, colour TV and tea and coffee maker. B&B £16.50 per person.

DURHAM AND TYNE & WEAR

BARNARD CASTLE (CO DURHAM)

Morritt Arms
Greta Bridge. Signposted from A66; 10 miles from Scotch Corner

Licensees: David & John Mulley
Tel: 0833 27232/27392
Fax: 0833 27570

The Morritt Arms is close to a bridge by the imposing gates of Rokeby Park. The lounges have high ceilings, oak settles, Windsor armchairs, and there is a model traction engine in one of them. One bar is named after Charles Dickens who stayed there while researching *Nicholas Nickleby*. The bar has a Pickwickian mural all round the room, drawn by J.V. Gilray who also drew the famous pre-war Guinness posters – there are six in the hotel. Bar food and a restaurant supply excellent food, restricted to soup and sandwiches in the evening in the bar in the busy summer months. In the public bar you will find darts, dominoes, shove ha'penny and a juke box – the only canned music in the hotel. The Mulleys do just one cask beer because they believe in serving it in tip-top condition: 'We fly a flag from the flagpole when we run out!'

Beer: Butterknowle Conciliation Bitter on handpump.

Accommodation: 3 singles, 14 doubles, all with en suite facilities.

B&B £48 single, £72 double. Children under 6 free, £10 a night 6-15 years if sharing. Breaks: £50-£86 dinner B&B minimum 2 days. Pets welcome. Cards: Access, Diners, Visa.

FELLING (TYNE & WEAR)

Old Fox
Carlisle Street, Gateshead. Off Sunderland and Durham roads (A6127): look for Felling bypass

Licensee: David White
Tel: 091 4380073

The Old Fox is a cheery, one-roomed local with an open coal fire and an area for darts and pool. It is a good base for Newcastle city centre and the new Metro Centre at Dunston; the splendid and cheap Metro light railway makes sightseeing and shopping in the area a pleasure. Gateshead is also a handy base for visiting the Tyneside coast at Whitley Bay, South Shields and Tynemouth, and for touring 'Cookson Country'. Bar meals are available in the pub lunchtimes, and the guest rooms have central heating, colour TVs and tea and coffee making facilities.

Beer: Ruddles Best Bitter, Websters Yorkshire Bitter and Websters Choice on handpumps.

Accommodation: 2 doubles. B&B £12 per person sharing. £15 single occupancy. Children half price. No dogs.

NEASHAM (CO DURHAM)

Newbus Arms
Hurworth Road. Off A1 and A67

Licensee: John Abel
Tel: 0325 721071
Fax: 0325 721770

A fine old country house hotel approached along an avenue of trees, the Newbus Arms is a 17th-century listed building with 19th-century embellishments. It has an ornate Victorian bar and first-class bistro and restaurant. The beautifully appointed guest rooms all have bathrooms, and some have showers, too; they all have direct-dial phones, colour TVs, trouser presses, baby-listening service and tea and coffee makers. The management can arrange fishing rights on the Tees and the hotel is a good base for visiting North Yorkshire, Co Durham and the Beamish Museum.

Beer: Cameron Traditional Bitter and Strongarm, Tolly Original on handpumps (beer range liable to change).

Accommodation: 3 singles, 12 doubles, 4 family rooms. B&B £45 single, £65 double. Children under 16 sharing charged only for meals. Facilities for the disabled. Special Rates: £48 per person per night sharing double, dinner B&B minimum 2 nights. Pets accepted. Cards: Access, Amex, Diners, Visa.

PIERCEBRIDGE (CO DURHAM)

George
B6275 south of village

Licensees: Jennifer & John Wain
Tel: 0325 374576
Fax: 0325 374577

A warm welcome is guaranteed in every way in the George, which has no fewer than five open fires in its bars and lounges. It is well sited on the old coaching route between Scotch Corner and Edinburgh. The bars have old farming implements on the walls as well as plates and prints, and the furniture is solid wood. The lounge has good views over the Tees and a splendid garden runs down to the river. Bar food, some available all day, includes soup, filo nests, curries, nine special vegetarian dishes including vegetable Stroganoff, tomato and onion risotto or mushrooms in Stilton, plus all-day breakfast, steaks, chicken in mushroom sauce and a range of puddings. Piercebridge was an important Roman military fort, Morbium, controlling a crossing of the River Tees. Remains of the fort have been restored and are open to visitors.

Beer: John Smiths Bitter on handpump.

Accommodation: 25 double rooms, all en suite. B&B single £35, double £45. Cards: Access, Amex, Visa.

ROMALDKIRK (CO DURHAM)

Rose & Crown
Village green, B6277 Middleton to Teesdale road, 6 miles north-west of Barnard Castle

Licensees: Christopher & Alison Davy
Tel: 0833 50213
Fax: 0833 50828

The Rose & Crown has a lovely setting on the village green which still has a water pump and the original village stocks. The bar has cream-painted walls, a large clock, photos of old Romaldkirk and an open fire. Locals play dominoes. Bar food offers homemade vegetable soup, ploughman's, steak, mushroom and Old Peculier pie, fresh pasta and salad, chicken breast stuffed with garlic butter, steaks and sweets as well as daily specials and fresh fish. The pub is well-placed for High Force waterfall and the Bowes Museum.

Beer: Theakston Best Bitter and Old Peculier, Younger Scotch Bitter on handpumps.

Accommodation: 1 single, 11 doubles, 1 family room, all en suite. B&B £48 single, £68 double. Children sharing £10. Weekends: 2 nights dinner B&B £87 per person. Pets welcome. Cards: Access and Visa.

WOLSINGHAM (CO DURHAM)

Bay Horse Hotel
59 Upper Town. B6296 Tow Law road.

Licensees: Mandy & Jan Ellila
Tel: 0388 527220

The Bay Horse is a traditional two-bar pub with old oak beams in a peaceful Weardale village close to the Beamish Museum and within easy reach of High Force, Durham and Kilhope Wheel. Bar food is served every day, lunchtime and evening, and includes fish, chicken, steaks and homemade pies; there is a traditional Sunday roast. All the guest rooms have colour TVs and tea making facilities.

Beer: Tetley Bitter on handpump.

Accommodation: 1 double, 7 singles, 5 with en suite facilities. B&B from £18 per person. Weekend: 2 nights' break dinner B&B £40 per person. Pets welcome. Cards: Access and Visa.

BRAINTREE

Hare & Hounds
High Garrett, 1½ miles outside town on A131 Halstead to Sudbury road.

Licensee: Barry Auitabile
Tel: 0376 24430

The 17th-century Hare & Hounds is fine stopping place if you are en route for Bury St Edmunds, Lavenham, Cambridge, Newmarket or Stansted airport. It is close to Finchingfield, the most attractive village in Essex, and Gosfield sporting lake. The inn is just a few minutes from Braintree town centre but is in lovely countryside and there are steam train rides close by. The inn has been sensitively updated by the Auitabiles to provide both modern facilities and a charming period atmosphere. A restaurant has been incorporated in the design, and the inn opens all day. You can enjoy table d'hôte meals or hot and cold bar snacks, and morning coffee, sandwiches and afternoon tea are also available. There is a traditional Sunday lunch and a large patio has garden tables and chairs and a children's play area with a tree house. All the guest rooms have colour TVs and tea and coffee makers.

Beer: Greene King IPA and Abbot Ale on handpumps.

Accommodation: 5 doubles/twins, 1 family room, 2 rooms with en suite facilities. B&B £12.50 per person in double, £30 for en suite room. Family room £40. Children's room. No pets. Cards: Access and Visa.

Olde White Harte Hotel, Burnham-on-Crouch

BURNHAM-ON-CROUCH

Olde White Harte Hotel
The Quay, B1010, off A12

Licensee: G. John Lewis
Tel: 0621 782106

A good pull-up for yachtsmen on the River Crouch is this fine old waterside inn that is popular with landlubbers too. The front bar has comfortable seats, oak tables and parquet floors. There are several other rooms, some with bare brick walls covered with emotive seascapes. Excellent bar snacks include lasagne, fish pie and lamb chops while the restaurant – open for lunch and dinner – has à la carte and table d'hôte menus. There are riding, fishing and golf facilities available.

Beer: Adnams Bitter and Tolly Cobbold Bitter on handpumps.

Accommodation: 13 doubles/twins, 2 family rooms, 11 rooms with private bath. B&B £19.50 single, £31-£35 with shower or bath, £16 double per person, £25-£30 double with bath or shower. Family room rates on application. Residents' lounge. Pets welcome.

COLCHESTER

Rose & Crown Hotel
East Gates, off A12 & A133

Manager: Shahrokh Bagherzadeh
Tel: 0206 866677/867676
Fax: 0206 866616

The Rose & Crown bills itself as the oldest inn in England's oldest recorded town. It is an imposing old building with an impressive half-timbered edifice and a sumptuous interior with low beams, wooden

pillars, log fires and beautifully appointed guest rooms, including some with four-poster beds. Built in the 15th century, the hotel has stood at the corner of the old Ipswich and Harwich roads and was once a leading coaching inn. Food is available every day of the year: the restaurant offers fresh turbot, Dover sole, lobster, steaks, roast duckling, veal Madeira and pheasant and venison in season, while there are bar meals in the Prison Bar – the present building incorporates the site of an old jail.

Beer: Tolly Cobbold Original and Old Strong (winter) on handpumps.

Accommodation: 5 singles, 18 doubles/twins, 3 rooms with four-poster beds. All rooms have en suite facilities with colour TVs, trouser presses, hair dryers and tea and coffee makers. The four-posters have jacuzzis. £58 single, £71 double/twin. Four-posters: £68 single occupancy, £88 double. Weekend Break: £25 per person per night (not four-posters). Children welcome. Cards: Access, Amex, Diners, Visa.

DEDHAM

Marlborough Head Hotel
Off A12, midway between
Colchester and Ipswich

Licensee: Brian Wills
Tel: 0206 323250/323124

An impressive 500-year-old inn in the heart of Constable Country with, inevitably, a Constable Bar with alcove seating, beams and timbers, and a comfortable lounge. Constable went to school over the road. The hotel is thought originally to have been the Master Weaver's House when Dedham was an important wool town; the Royal Square room

ESSEX

ESSEX

still has the large diagonal beam in the ceiling from which bales of wool were weighed; old weavers' cottages are nearby. The building was converted into a coaching inn some 300 years ago. Homemade bar food includes mussel chowder, beef carbonade, steak and kidney pie and cashew nut and pumpkin seed risotto.

Beer: Adnams Bitter and Benskins Best Bitter on handpumps.

Accommodation: 1 single, 2 doubles, all with en suite facilities. B&B £32.50 single, £50 double with continental breakfast, cooked breakfast £3.50 extra. Family room for residents. Cards: Visa.

EARLS COLNE

Castle Inn
77 High Street. A604 between Halstead and Colchester

Licensee: Ron Davis
Tel: 0787 222694

The Castle is a splendid and ancient inn with exposed beams and inglenook fireplaces with welcoming fires in winter. The east wing was built before the 12th century and is thought to have been a priest's house. Other parts date back to the 16th century. The saloon bar is a popular meeting place for locals, and the pub is close to Constable Country and the steam railways in the Colne Valley. Bar meals and home-cooked specials are served lunchtime except Sundays. Guests have a TV lounge.

Beer: Greene King XX Mild, IPA and Abbot Ale on handpumps.

Accommodation: 1 single, 1 double, 1 twin. B&B £15 single, £12.50 per person sharing. Children's rates negotiable. No pets.

ELMDON

Kings Head
Heydon Lane, near Saffron Walden, just off B1039, 4 miles from M11 at Duxford

Licensees: Jenny Hughes & Bill Lovell
Tel: 0763 838358

A delightful 350-year-old Essex inn with tables on the lawn, a beer garden and clay pigeon shooting. It has two bars, a separate dining room and accommodation in a modern adjoining building. The Kings Head has a wide range of pub games, including darts, pool and a quiz league. Bar snacks are served every day and the restaurant (Tuesday-Saturday) has an à la carte menu. The pub is a good base for visiting Duxford air museum, Linton Zoo, Audley End and Saffron Walden.

Beer: Greene King IPA and Tetley Bitter on handpumps.

Accommodation: 1 twin, 1 double, both en suite. B&B £30 per chalet. Children and well-behaved dogs welcome.

MANNINGTREE

Crown & Trinity House
47/51 High Street. A137 between Colchester and Ipswich

Licensee: E.J.W. Chapman
Tel: 0206 392620

Trinity House was a rectory until 1985 and is now a small private hotel. With the George pub next door, it faces Manningtree's charming Georgian high street while at the rear of the buildings is a quayside with fine views of the Suffolk countryside across the Stour estuary. It is a good base for visiting Dedham, Constable Country and Colchester, and is a useful stopping place for people en route to Harwich and the continent. Bar snacks and full lunches are served and private parties are catered for by arrangement in the evening.

Beer: Greene King XX Mild, IPA and Abbot Ale on handpumps.

Accommodation: 2 singles, 2 doubles, 2 family rooms. B&B £18.50 per person. Pets welcome. Cards: Access.

TILLINGHAM

Cap & Feathers
South Street, B1021 between Southminster and Bradwell

Licensee: Brian Warrens
Tel: 0621 779212

The Cap & Feathers is a superb weather-boarded, listed building in a remote part of Essex, close to the coast, Dengie Marshes and St Peter's on the Wall, England's oldest church. The pub is the first tied house owned by the tiny Crouch Vale brewery and the landlord's aim is to keep it as a firmly traditional pub with blazing fires, pub games and 'no flashing lights'. It has a resident ghost of an old sea dog. The pub has its own smokery and you can tuck into smoked fish, trout, eels, ham and other meat. There are also such daily specials as venison in ale, lamb and cider pie, pork in orange and cream, and fish and prawn pie. Vegetarian dishes include homemade vegetable burgers, savoury sausages mixing hazelnuts and peas, and leek and lentil slice. The only bought in food comes from a local butcher, Tillingham Pie cooked with Willie Warmer ale. Not surprisingly, the pub features in CAMRA's guide to Good Pub Food.

The pub has won many awards, including CAMRA's East Anglian Pub of the Year and the Campaign's National Pub of the Year. It has no canned music and has live folk music on the first and third Sundays of the month. There is a garden at the back and one small room acts as a family room, meeting room and tea room for the local cricket team, which was soundly defeated by the Guild of Beer Writers XI in 1991.

Beer: Crouch Vale Best Mild, Woodham IPA, Best Bitter, Strong Anglian Special, Willie Warmer and Essex Porter on handpumps (the last two beers are seasonal).

Accommodation: 3 twin rooms (including 1 family room). B&B £15 single, £28 twin.

GLOUCESTERSHIRE

AMPNEY CRUCIS

Crown of Crucis
A417, 2½ miles east of Cirencester.

Licensee: R.K. Mills
Tel: 0285 851806
Fax: 0285 851735

The Crown is a 16th-century Cotswold stone building which has been thoughtfully refurbished as a pub and restaurant. Old oak beams and open log fires have been retained in the large bar. The inn stands beside Ampney Brook and is close to Cotswold Water Park, Cotswold Farm Park, Slimbridge wild fowl sanctuary (founded by the late Sir Peter Scott), Cirencester's Corinium Museum, craft workshops and golf course. Bar food in the inn is available lunchtime and evening and includes sandwiches and ploughman's, homemade lasagne verde and steak and kidney pie, a dish of the day and a children's menu. There is a separate evening menu. A lawn at the back runs down to the brook with tables on the grass. All the guest rooms have private bathrooms, colour TVs and tea and coffee making facilities. Most of the rooms overlook the brook and village cricket ground.

Beer: Archers Village Bitter, Greene King Abbot Ale and Tetley Bitter on handpumps.

Accommodation: 26 doubles/twins, 2 family rooms, 26 rooms with en suite facilities. B&B £47 single, £58 double. Children's room. Pets welcome. Cards: Access, Amex, Visa.

BROCKWEIR

Brockweir Country Inn
30 yards over Brockweir Bridge off A466, 6 miles from Severn Bridge (M4)

Licensee: Howard Shields
Tel: 029 689548

A 17th-century inn standing on Offa's Dyke in the Lower Wye Valley, a few yards from the river and close to Tintern Abbey, the Forest of Dean and Chepstow and its race course. Fishing, riding and walking can be enjoyed in the area. The inn has oak beams, an open fire, two bars and a dining room with excellent food. Outside there is a covered courtyard, a walled beer garden, and beyond there are beautiful forests and pastures. Brockweir is a fascinating village with a rather shady past: it was a port in the 19th century, feeding the Severn, had all the usual port-side associations and was chosen by Lord Nelson as the place to court Lady Hamilton.

Beer: Draught Bass, Hook Norton Best Bitter, Wye Valley HPA plus guest beers and Bulmers traditional cider, all on handpumps.

Accommodation: 2 doubles, 1 family room. B&B £20 single, £35 double. Half board available.

Near CHELTENHAM

High Roost
Cleeve Hill, B4632 between Cheltenham and Winchcombe

Licensee: John English
Tel: 0242 672010

The High Roost gets its name from its commanding position overlooking the Cotswolds and the Severn Valley towards Wales, with one of the finest views in the county. It is a welcoming family-run free house close to a golf course, Sudeley Castle and the ancient town of Winchcombe. There is always a choice of 20 meals or more on the lunchtime menu, with homemade pies and baps with a variety of fillings.

Beer: Hook Norton Best Bitter and Old Hooky and a guest beer all on handpumps.

Accommodation: 2 singles, 2 doubles, 1 room with en suite facilities. B&B £15 single, £30 for 2 in en suite room. No children.

FAIRFORD

Bull Hotel
Market Place. Junction of M4 (exit 15) and A361; towards Lechlade, turn left at traffic lights, A419 to Fairford. M5 25 miles

Licensees: Keith & Judy Dudley
Tel: 0285 712535
Fax: 0285 713782

The Bull has an impressive stone exterior with bowed windows, a handsome porched entrance and many dormers in the roof. Much of the building dates from the 15th century when it was a monks' chanting house; during recent improvements a secret tunnel was discovered leading from the hotel to the 500-year-old St Mary's Church. A more 'modern' part of the hotel is thought to have been a 16th-century hall for a merchant or trade guild. By 1792 the building, sited on the London to Gloucester turnpike road, became a famous posting house, with stables for 30 horses. Today it is a good base for Cirencester, Cheltenham, Gloucester and Swindon. Such famous Cotswold villages as Bibury and Lechlade are close at hand. The hotel offers bar food and a separate restaurant. The guest rooms have oak beams and sloping floors and include a George Suite with a four-poster bed and a double room with sunken bath. Two ground floor rooms are suitable for disabled people. All the rooms have colour TVs.

Beer: Arkells Bitter and BBB from the cask.

Accommodation: 3 singles, 10 doubles, 5 twins, 2 four-posters, 18 rooms en suite. B&B £29 single, £39 en suite, £35 double, £49 en suite, bridal suite £67.50. Children under 5 free. Dogs accepted. Cards: Access, Amex, Diners, Visa.

GREAT BARRINGTON

Fox
Signposted from A40; pub between Little and Great Barrington

Licensees: Pat & Bill Mayer
Tel: 045 14 385

The Fox is a low-ceilinged inn with stone walls, rustic seats and welcoming fires in winter. There is a skittles alley and seats by the River Windrush; the pub was originally called the Wharf Inn when locally quarried stone was taken down the river to build St Paul's Cathedral. Bar food (lunchtime and evening) includes sandwiches and toasties, steak and kidney pie, chicken and mushroom pie, ploughman's and soup (cold food only on Sunday). The Mayers are the longest-serving tenants of Donnington's brewery and have been running the pub since 1967. The Fox has been in every edition of CAMRA's Good Beer Guide.

Beer: Donnington XXX, BB and SBA on handpumps.

Accommodation: 1 single, 4 doubles. B&B £18 single, £32 double. Children's rates according to age. No pets.

GREAT RISSINGTON

LAMB INN
6 miles off A40 near Bourton-on-the-Water; 5 miles from Burford

Licensees: Richard & Kate Cleverly
Tel: 0451 20388

The Lamb is a Cotswold stone inn with parts dating back to the 17th century but offering such modern accoutrements as an indoor swimming pool and central heating. It has fine views over the surrounding countryside from its delightful garden. The bar is comfortably carpeted, with wheel-back chairs, round tables and wall decorations of plates, pictures and old cigarette tins. Bar food, all home-cooked, lunch and evening, includes soup, seafood platter, curry, local trout, chicken breast with cheese and smoked ham filling, and steaks. There is a roast lunch on Sunday and the inn has a separate restaurant. There is a resident ghost. The inn offers a residents' lounge with colour TV and there are several golf courses nearby.

Beer: Flowers Original, Hook Norton Best Bitter, Wadworth 6X and regular guest beers, all on handpumps.

Accommodation: 12 doubles, inc 1 four-poster room. 10 rooms with en suite facilities. B&B £21 per person, £25 en suite, double £34, £42 with private bath. Four-poster room, en suite, £48. New Rissington Suite with king-size four-poster and own sitting room and bathroom £68. Winter Breaks: details on application. Pets accepted. Cards: Access and Visa.

LECHLADE

Red Lion Hotel
High Street. A417

Licensees: Keith, Judy & Mark Dudley
Tel: 0367 52373

The Red Lion offers a cheery oak-beamed atmosphere in an old Costwold building busily regenerated by the Dudley family since 1985. It is just 100 yards from the river and offers fine food and comfort. Meals, lunchtime and evening, include soup, pâté, filled jacket potatoes, ploughman's, chicken, scampi, steaks, lemon sole, plaice, haddock, and local trout. There is a traditional roast lunch on Sunday. The hotel is a fine base for visiting the Cotswolds, Oxford, Cheltenham and Gloucester. Fishing and boating facilities are close by, and you can follow in the poet's footsteps along Shelley Walk. There is yet another pub ghost: this one is

claimed to pop out of the wardrobe in the family room to say goodnight and turn back the bed covers: Arkell's ale does have that effect on some people. The rooms, with or without ghost, have colour TVs and tea and coffee making facilities.

Beer: Arkell Bitter and BBB straight from the cask.

Accommodation: 1 double, 1 family room. B&B £14.50 per person, £38 for family room (sleeps 4). Reductions for children under 12. Special rates all year for 3 nights or more. Pets welcome.

LOWER SWELL

Golden Ball Inn
B4068, 1 mile from Stow-on-the-Wold

Licensees: Stephen & Vanessa Aldridge
Tel: 0451 30247

The Golden Ball, in keeping with its beer supplier, Donnington, the most picturesque of all Britain's country breweries, is a delightful old building of mellow Cotswold stone, dating back to the 17th century. There is a log fire in winter, a range of pub games – darts, shove ha'penny, dominoes and cribbage – and a garden with a stream where Aunt Sally is played. Bar snacks (lunchtime and evening) include homemade · soups and pies, filled jacket potatoes, salads and sandwiches, with steaks and fish dishes in the evening. You can visit Broadway, Stratford, Warwick or Donnington's brewery, 20 minutes' walk away.

Beer: Donnington BB and SBA on handpumps.

Accommodation: 2 doubles. B&B £32-£36 per room; rates depend on time of year. No pets. No smoking in guest rooms.

NAUNTON

Black Horse Inn
1 mile from B4068 Andoversford to
Stow road, near Guiting Power

Licensees: Adrian & Jennie Bowen-
Jones
Tel: 0451 850378

The Black Horse is a 17th-century
inn in a lovely old Cotswold village
by the River Windrush and close to
the unnervingly named hamlets of
Upper and Lower Slaughter. The inn
is a superb base for walking through
the Cotswolds and visiting such
famed beauty spots as Bourton-on-
the-Water. Excellent pub food is
served lunchtime and evening and
includes homemade soups, salads,
daily specials on a blackboard,
lasagne, scampi, ploughman's, fresh
salmon in season, steaks, chops and
duck.

Beer: Donnington BB and SBA on
handpumps.

Accommodation: 2 doubles. B&B £15
per person. No children.

NYMPSFIELD

Rose & Crown Inn
Take Nympsfield turning from A46 at
Nailsworth; single track for 3 miles.

Licensees: Bob & Linda Woodman
Tel: 0453 860240
Fax: 0453 860900

The Rose & Crown is a 300-year-old
coaching inn in an unspoilt village
close to the Cotswold Way and with
easy access to the M4 and M5. The
Woodmans run the Rose & Crown as
'a real pub – we don't worry too
much about muddy boots – and we
don't have a restaurant, just
extremely good value bar food'. Food

Rose & Crown Inn, Nympsfield

ranges from a choice of more than 40 bar meals, including faggots, salads, steaks, fish, curries, stews, sandwiches and sticky puddings. There is also a children's menu. Local attractions include Berkeley Castle and Slimbridge Wildfowl Trust, and Bristol and Gloucester Gliding Club is just down the road.

Beer: Draught Bass, Theakston Best Bitter, Uley Bitter, Old Spot and Wadworth 6X on handpumps.

Accommodation: 1 double, 3 family rooms, 1 en suite. B&B £22 single, £30 double, family room from £39. Children from £5. Children allowed in restricted bar area. Pets welcome. Cards: Access, Amex, Visa.

Near TETBURY

Hunters Hall Inn
Kingscote. A4135 4 miles west of Tetbury

Licensee: David Barnett-Roberts
Tel: 0453 860393

Hunters Hall is a superb, unspoilt 16th-century creeper-clad Tudor coaching inn, a maze of rambling rooms with old beams and open fires. It is one of the finest family pubs in the country with an enormous and beautifully kept garden with climbing frames and a children's walk-way linked by old wooden casks with thatched roofs. There is a garden barbecue in summer. Inside, the lounge that opens on to the garden is set aside for customers who are eating: the buffet menu is chalked on a board and includes mussels in white wine, steak and kidney pie, seafood pancakes, steaks, turkey and ham pie, and smoked trout. Children can eat in this room, the separate restaurant and an upstairs gallery. Buffet food is available every day, lunchtime and

evening; the separate evening restaurant is open Tuesday to Saturday. Other rooms are like small parlours with comfortable chairs and sofas. The public bar is large and atmospheric with a flag-stoned floor, settles and heavy wooden tables. Guest rooms are in a converted building next to the inn. Mr Barnett-Roberts and his staff run a smoothly efficient and friendly inn and support the local micro-brewery, Uley, which brews wonderfully tart and fruity ales.

Beer: Bass, Hook Norton Best Bitter, Uley Bitter and Wadworth 6X on handpumps.

Accommodation: 11 doubles/twins, 1 family room, all with en suite facilities. B&B £41 single, £49 double, £64 family room. 2-day breaks £49 per person, £75 with dinner. Children's room. Pets by arrangement. Cards: Access, Amex, Diners, Visa.

TEWKESBURY

Berkeley Arms
Church Street, A38

Licensee: Ruby Jones
Tel: 0684 293034

The Berkeley Arms dates from 1467 and has a fine timbered exterior and original interior beams in this famous and historic old abbey town. The pub has darts and cribbage but, says Mrs Jones, 'no place for a pool table': Bacchus be praised. There are lounge and public bars and excellent pub grub.

Beer: Wadworth Devizes Bitter, 6X, Farmer's Glory and Old Timer on handpumps.

Accommodation: 1 single, 1 double, 1

family room, all with colour TVs. B&B £12.50-£15 per person. Evening meals available. Children welcome, up to half price, according to age. Pets accepted.

UPPER ODDINGTON

Horse & Groom Inn

Off A436 Chipping Norton road, 2½ miles from Stow-on-the-Wold
Managers: Paul & Carol Sutcliffe
Tel: 0451 30584

The Horse and Groom is a 16th-century inn built of Cotswold stone with original beams and timbers in the bars and some of the guest rooms. The delightful village of Upper Oddington has an ancient church, St Nicholas, dating back to the 12th century. The inn has a splendid beer garden with a stream, fishponds, an aviary and a children's area with swings and a climbing frame. Inside, the bars have wood panelling, masses of brass on the beams and fireplaces and a dining room where local produce abounds. Bar and restaurant meals are available lunchtime and evening; bar food includes homemade pies, sandwiches, ploughman's and vegetarian options, while the restaurant offers medallion of pork with orange, peppercorn and cream sauce, pork, beef and lamb fillets glazed with brie and red wine sauce, and fish dishes. The guest rooms all have en suite facilities and tea and coffee makers. The inn is a fine base for touring the Cotswolds and visiting Broadway and Chipping Campden.

Beer: Cotleigh Tawny Bitter, Hook Norton Best Bitter, Timothy Taylor Landlord and Old Timer, Wadworth 6X on handpumps.

Accommodation: 2 twins, 4 doubles, 2 family rooms, all with en suite

Horse & Groom Inn, Upper Oddington

facilities. B&B £29-£31.50 single, £42-£47 double. Family room rates on application. Children under 1 £4, under 2 £8, 2-10 years £13. Breaks: Nov-March 2 nights dinner, B&B £60-£62 per person. Jan-Feb mid-week £15 per person B&B. No pets. Cards: Access and Visa.

WATERLEY BOTTOM

New Inn
North Nibley, Dursley. Off B4058, B4060 and A4134. (OS ST758963)

Licensee: Ruby Sainty
Tel: 0453 543659

Ruby Sainty is the kind of character that makes finding this remote old pub in a lovely wooded valley worth the effort. 'There are two golf courses two miles from the pub, where you can work off excess ale,' she says. As for the accommodation: 'Although I only let two bedrooms I have in the past put up a cricket team, and a party of six lads who bring their own sleeping bags – they're only here for the beer!' The inn has every modern comfort, with central heating, colour TVs and tea and coffee making facilities in the guest rooms. Part of the building was a cider house more than 200 years ago, and the old cider press stands in the garden. The lounge bar has a magnificent beer engine, 160 years old, rescued from the New Cut market in London where it was being used to dispense paraffin! There are many other old beer engines on display in the bar, including one called the 'Barmaid's Delight'. Darts, dominoes, draughts, chess and crib are played in the bar. If you tear yourself away, Berkeley Castle is just four miles distant. The pub has a fine range of pub food, including homemade soups, pâté, ploughman's, salads, steak and onion pie, toasted sandwiches and brown

baps with a choice of fillings.

Beer: Cotleigh Tawny and a house brew, Waterley Bottom, Greene King Abbot Ale, Smiles Best Bitter and Exhibition, Theakston Old Peculier, guest beers and Inch cider.

Accommodation: 1 twin, 1 double with children's beds if required. B&B £20 single, £35 double. Half price for children under 12. No pets.

CHERITON

Flower Pots
Off A272, on B3046

Licensees: Joanna & Patricia Bartlett
Tel: 096 279 318

The Flower Pots is an unspoilt village pub in an award-winning village near Tichborne and Alresford and the Watercress Steam Railway. The pub has two bars with striped wallpaper, hunting scenes and old copper distilling equipment. Mrs Bartlett offers a homely welcome and excellent bar snacks such as ploughman's and toasted sandwiches as well as jacket potatoes, beef stew, or chilli with crusty bread. There are seats at the front of the pub and, inside, locals join in darts, crib, dominoes and shove ha'penny. The beer is tapped from casks on a stillage behind the bar. The guest rooms are in a converted barn, separate from the pub.

Beer: Archers Village Bitter and Hopback Summer Lightning, Ringwood Bitter and a guest beer from the cask.

Accommodation: 2 doubles, 3 twins, all with en suite showers, TVs and tea and coffee makers. B&B £18 per person in double, £20 in larger twin room.

DAMERHAM

Compasses Inn
3 miles west of Fordingbridge on B3078

Licensees: James & Monica Kidd
Tel: 07253 231

The Compasses is a fine old inn in a delightful rural setting, overlooking the village cricket green and with an antique brewhouse complete with brew tower. The pub has an extensive menu with daily specials, served lunchtime and evening every day, prepared by the chef and proprietor, James Kidd. It is a good family pub with a large garden and children's play equipment. There are blazing fires in winter in both bars. Two of the guest rooms have private bathrooms and they all have wash basins and tea and coffee makers. Damerham is close to the New Forest, Salisbury Plain and the south coast, and there is good fishing in the area, including trout lakes in Damerham and Rockbourne.

Beer: Ringwood Bitter and Wadworth 6X, plus a guest beer on handpumps.

Accommodation: 5 doubles/twins, 2 can be used as family rooms. B&B £19.50 single, £17.50 per person in double room. Children half price, cot available. 10% reduction for 3 nights or more. Well-behaved children welcome in lounge area.

EAST STRATTON

Plough Inn
Nr Winchester; just off A33 near Micheldever

Licensees: Richard & Trudy Duke
Tel: 0962 774241

A former 17th-century farmhouse, the Plough is set amid pretty thatched cottages in a tiny hamlet surrounded by farmland. The pub has its own green with swings, a seesaw, an ancient tractor and a fine cottage garden. The public bar has darts and a quiet juke box, while there is a cosy lounge and seats in a courtyard. The thriving skittles alley also has a bar. Food is available lunchtime and evening (not Monday) and ranges from snacks, including homemade soups, to three-course meals. Children's portions are available. The restaurant (Tues-Sat) seats 28. The guest rooms have tea and coffee making facilities and are large enough to accommodate two adults and two children.

Beer: Gales BBB and HSB, Ringwood Fortyniner on handpumps.

Accommodation: 3 twins. B&B £37.50 per room with colour TV; single occupancy £24.50. Children under 8 £7.50.

FACCOMBE

Jack Russell
Near Hurstbourne and Andover; signposted from A343 Andover-Newbury road

Licensee: Paul Foster
Tel: 0264 87 315

The Jack Russell is a remote but comfortable and carefully renovated inn overlooking the village pond, on a private estate midway between

Andover and Newbury. The pub is quiet and free from electronic devices. There are fires in winter, a garden for summer drinking and eating, and good pub food is served lunchtime and evening. Don't miss such delights as Jill Foster's steak and kidney pudding with freshly steamed vegetables. It is a splendid base for the Wayfarers' Walk, which begins three miles north at Inkpen Beacon, and the site of the Combe gibbet. The Bourne Valley, with its painted railway viaduct, is close at hand, and Newbury and Andover are both a short drive away. The guest rooms have TVs and tea and coffee making facilities.

Beer: Ringwood Bitter and Fortyniner and regular guest beers all on handpumps.

Accommodation: 2 doubles, 1 twin with en suite facilities. B&B £25 single, £40 double. Half board available. Dogs (including Jack Russells) welcome by prior arrangement. Cards: Access and Visa.

GRATELEY

Plough Inn
On main road through village, 1½ miles south of A306, near Andover

Licensees: Chris & Joy Marchant
Tel: 0264 88221

The Plough is a splendid old country inn run by an enthusiastic couple, with darts, crib, pool and ring the bull played in the bar, while a restaurant leads off the comfortable lounge. Pub food ranges from snacks to full meals, served every day, lunchtime and evening, except Sunday evenings in winter; there is a children's menu. Both Grateley and nearby Quarley have 13th-century churches, while the flying museum at Nether Wallop and the Hawk

Conservancy at Weyhill are just short journeys. The guest rooms have tea and coffee making facilities.

Beer: Gibbs Mew Wiltshire Traditional Bitter, Salisbury Best Bitter and Bishop's Tipple from the cask.

Accommodation: 2 twins, 2 doubles, 3 rooms with en suite facilities. £45 double, £25 single occupancy; £35 and £20 for room without private facilities. Cards: Access and Visa.

HAVANT

Bear Hotel
East Street, off A27

Licensees: J. Carruthers & I. Todhunter
Tel: 0705 486501

The Bear is a handsome old coaching inn that combines the comfort of an AA three-star hotel with the genuine cheer of a country town pub, with a large public bar. The restaurant has à la carte and set meals, with quick lunches such as a platter of mackerel, pâté, prawns and avocado, lasagne, seafood risotto, and tagliatelle. There is a Sunday lunch and a separate children's menu. The guest rooms all have en suite showers and baths, colour TVs and tea and coffee making facilities. Havant is a good base for the New Forest, Portsmouth and Chichester.

Beer: Whitbread Flowers Original and Boddingtons Bitter on handpumps.

Accommodation: 10 singles, 8 twins, 24 doubles. B&B £55 single, £67 double. Weekend terms on application. Children welcome, terms by arrangement. Cards: Access, Amex, Diners, Visa.

HORNDEAN

Ship & Bell Hotel
London Road. 5 miles from
Portsmouth; signposted from A3(M)

Licensees: Mr & Mrs R.W. Pearce
Tel: 0705 592107
Fax: 0705 598641

The Ship & Bell is the original site of
Gale's sturdily independent brewery.
It is the brewery tap now and is
owned by Horndean Hotels, a
subsidiary of the brewery. The pub is
18th century and is reputed to have a
lady ghost in a blue dress who is seen
from time to time descending the
back stairs. There is an excellent
range of reasonably priced food in the
bar and restaurant, lunchtime and
evening, while pub games are played
with great enthusiasm. The brewery
is next door and guests can go on
tours if arranged in advance.

Beer: Gales XXX, BBB, HSB and 5X
(in winter) on handpumps.

Accommodation: 1 single, 13 twins,
all with en suite facilities. B&B £32
single, £40 twin. No pets. Cards:
Access and Visa.

HURSTBOURNE PRIORS

Hurstbourne
On B3400 between Whitchurch and
Andover, off M3, A34 & A303

Licensees: Dave & Joy Houghton
Tel: 0256 892000

The Hurstbourne is a century-old
inn, renovated to a high standard but
retaining the atmopshere of an old
country inn. Food is served seven
days a week and ranges from a light
bar snack to full à la carte restaurant,
with steaks, fish and homemade
vegetarian dishes. The inn is close to

Ship & Bell Hotel, Horndean

the River Test walk, Apsley shooting school and trout fishing rivers, and the village church and cricket ground form a picturesque backdrop. The guest rooms have central heating and tea and coffee making facilities.

Beer: Fullers London Pride, Gales Best Bitter and Wadworth 6X and regular guest beers on handpumps.

Accommodation: 4 twin rooms, 1 family room. B&B £23 single, £36 twin, family room £15 per person when 3 or more people sharing. Children welcome, terms by arrangement. No dogs. Cards: Access and Visa.

LYMINGTON

King's Arms
St Thomas Street. Off A337; M27 exit 1

Licensees: Steve & Sandra Poingdestre
Tel: 0590 672594

The King's Arms is a half-timbered 16th-century coaching inn in an historic old town mentioned in the Domesday Book, in a street leading down to the quay. Lymington today is a thriving market and sailing town and both the town and the pub are popular with yachting people. The pub has no juke box or noisy games and, according to the Poingdestres, 'no designer lagers or poseur potions'. Food is available seven days a week, lunchtime and evening and includes homemade soups, sandwiches, steaks, pies and daily specials. The guest rooms have TVs and tea and coffee making facilities. Lymington is close to the New Forest and has rail links via Brockenhurst to Southampton and the Isle of Wight.

Beer: Brakspear Bitter, Flowers

Original and Pompey Royal, Fullers Chiswick Bitter, Gales HSB and Marston Pedigree Bitter straight from the cask (four beers available at any one time).

Accommodation: 1 double, 1 family room with 3 beds. B&B from £26 single occupancy, £18 double per person. Children under 12 half price. No pets.

NORTH WARNBOROUGH

Jolly Miller
Hook Road. A32 towards Alton. M3 exit 5

Licensees: David & Stephanie Metcalfe
Tel: 0256 702085
Fax: 0256 704030

The Jolly Miller is a half-timbered inn just a minute or two from the M3. It has a large garden where summer barbecues are held, a skittles bar that can hold up to 80 people and is used for parties and club meetings, and pleasant bars and a restaurant with 20 covers. Bar food ranges from snacks and toasted sandwiches to steaks, with daily specials on a board, and is available lunchtime and evening.

Beer: Hall & Woodhouse Badger Best Bitter, Marston Pedigree Bitter and Ruddles County on handpumps.

Accommodation: 2 singles, 3 doubles/ twins, 2 family rooms, 1 luxury double. B&B £29 single, £39 en suite, £39/£49 double, £51/£59 family room. All rooms have colour TVs and tea and coffee making facilities. Reductions on application for children sharing. Pets by arrangement. Cards: Access and Visa.

PETERSFIELD

Old Drum
16 Chapel Street, off A3

Licensee: Brian Barnes
Tel: 0730 64159

The Old Drum, dating back to at least 1796, is a friendly pub with a relaxing atmosphere, just north of the market square in a bustling and prosperous town. Mr Barnes has a singular approach to pub music: 'There is recorded jazz played on tapes at a reasonable level, from Erroll Garner to Grover Washington. This frightens the morons in this town to death so they stay away, leaving the pub to the regulars and music lovers.' There are pub games and excellent bar food at lunchtimes. The large back garden, once a bowling green but now laid with lawns and fishponds, is a past winner of the Friary Meux Best Garden award. The guest rooms have colour TVs.

Beer: Charrington IPA and Ind Coope Burton Ale on handpumps.

Accommodation: 3 doubles. B&B £10-£15.

PORTSMOUTH

Sally Port
57/58 High Street, opposite cathedral; M275 to city centre, follow signs to Old Portsmouth

Manager: A. Poulton
Tel: 0705 821860

The Sally Port is ideally placed in historic Old Portsmouth with its Round Tower, the Cathedral of Thomas of Canterbury and the gate in the old fortified sea wall known as the sally port: naval officers 'sallied forth' from there to the ships. The original tavern dates back to the 17th century and was rebuilt in the 1970s from a bomb-damaged site. The present imposing four-storey hotel includes many of the original beams and more 'modern' ones from the early 19th century. The bars and guest rooms have beams and sloping floors and there is a magnificent cantilever staircase, the hub of the fine Georgian building. Most of the delightful guest rooms have en suite showers and all have colour TVs and tea and coffee making equipment. There is excellent bar food and an à la carte restaurant.

Beer: Gales HSB, Marston Pedigree Bitter, Whitbread Flowers Original and Boddingtons Bitter plus guest ales on handpumps.

Accommodation: 10 rooms including 3 singles. B&B £39 single, £59 double. Cards: Access and Visa.

Surrey Arms
1-3 Surrey Street

Licensee: Mrs E. Sinclair
Tel: 0705 827120

The Surrey Arms, in Portsmouth's city centre and close to the railway station, was originally a free house and was bought by the former Brickwoods Brewery in 1924: the bar on the right-hand side of the pub was once the bar from the brewery itself, while the fireplace came from another defunct brewery, Mews Langton on the Isle of Wight. To add to the nostalgia and breweriana, two doors leading into the bar were rescued from the George & Dragon at Cosham. The Surrey Arms, rich in pub and brewing history, is sumptuously done out with wood panels and etched glass mirrors. Pub food is served at lunchtime; evening meals are available for residents. The guest rooms have tea and coffee making facilities.

Beer: Flowers Original and Wadworth 6X on handpumps.

Accommodation: 5 singles, 2 twins, 3 doubles. B&B £15 single, £28 double.

SOUTHAMPTON

Royal Albert
Albert Road; follow signs to Ocean Village

Licensee: Ron Ousby
Tel: 0703 229697

The Royal Albert is a solid, unpretentious town pub dating back to the 1830s and extensively modernized a few years ago. There is one large room with a horseshoe bar, and pool and darts are played. The Royal Albert is in a side street in the shadow of Itchen toll bridge and close to the Ocean Village marina and Michel Air Museum. The pub has facilities for families and lunchtime food.

Beer: Gale BBB, HSB and 5X (winter) on handpumps.

Accommodation: 7 singles, 2 twins, 1 double. B&B £16 per person.

TITCHFIELD

Queen's Head Hotel
High Street, ¼ mile off A27; M27 exit 9

Licensee: Keith Blackmore
Tel: 0329 42154

There is a wealth of oak beams, open fires and history in this 17th- century inn in the centre of a small and historic village. The hotel is named after Catherine of Braganza, the second wife of Charles II, who built Titchfield Abbey. Bar food is available lunchtime and evening and offers soup, ploughman's, jacket potatoes, burgers, plain and toasted sandwiches, steak and kidney pie, salads and fish. There is a separate à la carte restaurant. The hotel is handy for Portsmouth, Southampton and the cross-Channel ferries.

Beer: Strong Country Bitter and Marston Pedigree Bitter on handpumps.

Accommodation: 2 singles, 3 doubles, 1 family room. B&B £26 single, £36 double. Children welcome, reductions under 4. Dogs welcome. Cards: Access, Amex, Diners, Visa.

WINCHESTER

Rising Sun
14 Bridge Street, B3404

Licensees: Alfie Morrison & Steve Sankey
Tel: 0962 862564

The Rising Sun is a superb timber-framed Tudor town inn just a minute's walk from King Alfred's statue in this stunning old city that was once the capital of England, with architecture so ancient and remarkable that even Barclays Bank and Boots look like listed buildings. The Rising Sun is one pub where you may hesitate before asking to see the cellar: it was once a prison. The pub has hot and cold food, including vegetarian dishes.

Beer: Courage Best Bitter and Directors, John Smith's Bitter on handpumps.

Accommodation: 2 twins, 1 double. B&B £15 per person.

BROADWAY

Crown & Trumpet
Church Street, off A44

Licensees: Andrew & Stella Scott
Tel: 0386 853202

A fine 16th-century inn behind the village green in the famous and lovely village of Broadway, the Crown and Trumpet has oak beams, log fires and first-class food lunchtime and evening. The menu includes soups, steak and kidney pie, lamb and aubergine pie, beef and Guinness pie, vegetable gratin, ploughman's, steaks and salads. The inn is an excellent base for visiting Warwick, Stratford, Worcester, Tewkesbury and the Malvern Hills. The guest rooms have colour TVs and tea and coffee making facilities.

Beer: Whitbread Flowers Original, IPA and Boddingtons Bitter, guest beers and Bulmer traditional cider, all on handpumps.

Accommodation: 2 doubles, 1 family room. B&B from £22.50 per person. Weekend £18.50 with evening meals, Week £154 with evening meals. Off-season rates on application. Children's room; children's terms on application.

BROMYARD

Bay Horse Hotel
High Street, A44

Licensee: Derek Hiles
Tel: 0885 482635

Derek Hiles is a former partner at the Talbot in Knightwick who wanted to run his own pub. He has taken over the 16th-century Bay Horse, a heavily timbered listed building where the staircase, priesthole and bar counter are also listed. There is a large lounge, a small cosy snug and a separate restaurant for 24. Food is served lunchtime and evening every day. Bar food may include steamed bacon pudding, smoked haddock and poached eggs and vegetarian roly-poly, while the restaurant offers scrambled egg and smoked salmon, avocado with crab and cheese, kidneys with smoked bacon, duck with blackcurrant and brandy sauce, pork loin with mustard and mushroom sauce, venison, steaks and vegetarian options.

Beer: M&B Brew XI on handpump with such guests as Banks Bitter and Woods Parish Bitter.

Accommodation: 1 twin, 3 doubles with bath. B&B £18 twin, £20 double per person. Dogs welcome. Cards: Access and Visa.

Crown & Sceptre
Sherford Street. A44; M5 exit 7

Licensee: Gavin Trumper
Tel: 0885 482441

The pub, in the centre of the market town, is a former timber-framed building refashioned some 150 years ago, but its original cottage atmosphere and old beams have been retained. Snacks and full meals are available lunchtime and evening in the bar and separate restaurant; fresh ingredients are brought from Birmingham and vegetarians are catered for. There are fine lawns at the rear of the pub. Bromyard is a good base for visiting both Hereford and Worcester and the many border area black-and-white villages.

Beer: Banks Bitter, Bass Highgate Mild, Hook Norton Best Bitter and Woods Special plus many guest beers on handpumps.

Accommodation: 2 singles, 2 doubles, 3 rooms en suite. B&B £18.50 per person. Children sharing room £10. Dogs accepted.

CAREY

Cottage of Content
Off A49 1½ miles north-east of Hoarwithy. (OS 0565110)

Licensee: Michael Wainford
Tel: 043 270 242

The Cottage is a beautiful country pub in a remote area of idyllic scenery. The timber-framed building was originally three labourers' cottages built in 1485. One of the conditions of tenancy was that one labourer should keep an ale and cider parlour and the cottage has been licensed ever since. The bars have wooden benches and high-back settles, darts, dominoes and cribbage are played in the public bar and they are decorated with bines of fresh hops. Two other rooms are set aside for eating; pub meals include a regular 'pie of the day' and main meals include fillet and rump steak, pork tenderloin, lasagne, shepherd's pie, fresh salmon fish cakes, stuffed aubergine and beef Stroganoff. In summer there are tables at the front of the pub and on a back terrace.

Beer: Draught Bass, Hook Norton Best Bitter and Old Hooky on handpumps plus Old Rosie scrumpy cider.

Accommodation: 3 doubles en suite, 1 twin with own private bathroom next door. B&B £30 single, £45 double. Children welcome, terms on application. Cards: Access and Visa.

Near EVESHAM

Norton Grange Hotel
A435, Norton hamlet outside Evesham

Licensee: M. Smith
Tel: 0386 870215

There is lots of old world charm in this spacious building with a large bar and intimate restaurant. A separate function room can be booked for parties and is also used as a skittles alley. Bar snacks include sandwiches, salads, steak and kidney pie, fish and chips, seafood platter, steaks, mixed grills and grilled trout. There is a large play area for children. Stratford and Worcester are nearby and the hotel is popular with people visiting local racecourses. Fishermen will find the hotel a good base for the Avon.

Beer: Marston Burton Bitter and Pedigree Bitter on handpumps.

Accommodation: 4 singles, 3 doubles, 1 family room, 1 room with en suite facilities. B&B £17 single, £36 double. Children welcome. Cards: Access and Visa.

FOWNHOPE

Green Man Inn
B4224 midway between Ross & Hereford

Licensees: Arthur & Margaret Williams
Tel: 0432 860243
Fax: 0432 860207

The Green Man, first known as the Naked Boy, dates from 1485, and in coaching days it was on the main Hereford to Gloucester road. Petty sessions were held in the inn in the 18th and 19th centuries. Relics of those times include the iron bars to which prisoners were chained, the cell, the visiting judge's bedroom and a notice dated 1820 showing the scale of costs of prisoners' subsistence: accommodation is a little more expensive today. One former landlord was Tom Spring, bare-knuckle prize fighter and Champion of All England. This fine timbered and brick building has two bars – one with beams, exposed timbers and settles, and a smaller one where darts and dominoes are played – log fires in winter, good hot and cold bar food, a separate restaurant and Sunday roasts. Bar food includes soup, sandwiches, ploughman's, lasagne verde, trout and steaks, with children's portions available. The spacious back garden has a children's play area and bench tables; afternoon teas are served in good weather.

Beer: Hook Norton Best Bitter, Marston Pedigree Bitter and Sam Smith's Old Brewery Bitter on handpumps, with Westons farmhouse cider from the cask.

Accommodation: 1 single, 11 doubles, 3 family rooms, all with private bath. B&B £31.75 single, £44.50 double. Winter Breaks £60.50 per day for 2 people with evening meal allowance of £19.50. £5 reduction for third night. Reduced rates for children. Well-behaved dogs welcome, £2.50 per night. Self-catering cottage also available.

HEREFORD

Castle Pool Hotel
Castle Street

Licensees: John & Lisa Richardson
Tel: 0432 356321

The Castle Pool is an imposing city-centre hotel; the pool in its

grounds is the remains of the moat of Hereford Castle. The castle, once 'high and strong and full of great towers', has sadly all but disappeared. The hotel was built in 1850 and was once the residence of the Bishop of Hereford. The handsomely appointed hotel has guest rooms with en suite facilities, colour TVs and tea and coffee makers. There are good bar snacks, while the separate restaurant offers an imaginative range of dishes on a menu where a three-course meal costs £16. In summer there are barbecues on the lawn overlooking the moat.

Beer: Courage Directors, Hook Norton Best Bitter, Wye Valley Hereford Supreme and guest beers on handpumps.

Accommodation: 8 singles, 7 doubles, 8 twins and 3 family rooms. B&B £49 single, £68 double. Children's terms by agreement. Weekend Breaks: £57 single, £89 double/twin, minimum 2 days, includes dinner, B&B. Dogs welcome. Cards: Access, Amex, Diners, Visa.

KINGSLAND

Angel Inn
B4360, 4 miles W of Leominster off A44 Kington road

Licensees: J.S. Tonry & S. Nugent
Tel: 056 881 355

The Angel is a fine roadside inn with 16th-century origins and plenty of remaining beams in the lounge bar, where there is an open log fire. A smaller beamed restaurant is open seven days a week and specializes in local game and fish. The extensive bar meals (lunch and evening, except Monday lunch) have an international flavour with rogan josh, paella and chicken Biarritz. There is a menu for children, too, and the garden has a play area. Steve Nugent is a CAMRA member who keeps his ale in impeccable condition and has a wide range of guest beers.

Beer: Draught Bass, Marston Pedigree Bitter, Wadworth 6X and Whitbread Castle Eden Ale with guest beers on handpumps and Weston cider in summer.

Accommodation: 2 doubles. B&B £18 single, £30 double. 30% reduction for children under 14. No pets. Cards: Access and Visa.

KINGTON

Burton Hotel
Mill Street, centre of town (A44)

Licensees: John & Lisa Richardson
Tel/fax: 0544 230323

This attractively modernized coaching inn with log fires is in the centre of a small market town near the Welsh border, and is run by the Richardsons who also own the Castle Pool in Hereford. There is a comprehensive snack menu in the two bars and a separate restaurant. The highest golf course in the country is close by and Kington is a natural stage on Offa's Dyke footpath. All guest rooms have private facilities, colour TVs, direct-dial phones and tea and coffee makers.

Beer: Courage Directors and Hook Norton Best Bitter with guest beers on handpumps.

Accommodation: 1 single, 8 doubles, 6 family rooms. £40 single, £53 double, £60 family room (1 child), £65 (2 children). Weekend Break:

£49.50 single per night, £73 double, dinner B&B, minimum 2 days. Pets welcome. Cards: Access, Amex, Diners, Visa.

KNIGHTWICK

Talbot Hotel
Knightsford Bridge. B4197, just off A44 Worcester to Bromyard road.

Licensee: J.P.P. Clift
Tel: 0886 21235
Fax: 0886 21060

The Talbot is a 14th-century inn in a lovely setting by a bridge over the Teme. The spacious lounge has comfortable seats including settles in the bow windows, coaching prints and Jorrocks paintings on the walls, and a great wood-burning stove in the fireplace. Thoughtful food (with the same menu for both the bar and the small restaurant) includes local snails in pastry, stir-fried pigeon, ink caps with aubergines and spinach, lamb noisettes and steaks, plus a tempting range of hot and cold puddings. You can walk that off in the Malvern Hills and visit Edward Elgar's birthplace or sit in the gardens at the front and the back of the pub. The small public bar is popular with locals who play darts, dominoes and cribbage.

Beer: Banks Bitter, Draught Bass, Flowers IPA and Wadworth 6X on handpumps.

Accommodation: 3 singles, 3 doubles, 1 family room, all with private baths. B&B £25 single, £23 en suite. £43 double, £58 en suite. 4 nights 10% reduction, Friday-Sunday 15% reduction. Well-behaved children and dogs welcome. Cards: Access and Visa.

Near ROSS-ON-WYE

Kerne Bridge Inn
Bishopswood. B4228, 4 miles south
of Ross towards Colesford and
Forest of Dean

Licensee: John Martin-Slater
Tel: 0600 890495

The inn was built of stone at the turn
of the century and overlooks the
River Wye in beautiful surroundings.
It once had close connections with
the Ross-to-Monmouth railway: the
old station stands nearby. The inn has
a children's play area, and Morris
Dancers perform in summer. There
are extensive bar meals from
sandwiches to ploughman's,
casseroles and daily specials. Food is
available every day lunchtime and
evening and all day on Saturday;
roast lunch on Sunday.

Beer: Adnams Bitter and Greene
King Abbot Ale with a weekly guest
beer, special winter beers on
handpumps and a traditional cider.

Accommodation: 2 doubles, 1 family
room, all en suite. B&B £21.50 single,
£33.50 double and family room.
Children free under 5, charged for
breakfast only up to 12, half price
13-16. Breaks: minimum 2 nights £47
per person; 10% reduction for 3
nights or more. Special rates for
CAMRA members and groups. No
pets.

Near WHITNEY-ON-WYE

Rhydspence Inn
A438 Brecon to Hereford road; pub
signposted 1½ miles west of
Whitney

Licensees: Peter & Pamela Glover
Tel: 04973 262

The Rhydspence is a justly famous
16th-century timber-framed inn on a
hill overlooking the Wye valley and
the Black Mountains. It is either the
first or the last inn in England,
depending on whether you are
coming to or from Wales: the border
is a stream running through the pub's
garden. The inn has been lovingly and
carefully restored. Centuries ago it
offered ale, food and accommodation
to Welsh drovers on their way to
English markets, and it was
mentioned several times in Kilvert's
Diary. There is a large stone fireplace
in the central bar, seats built into the
timbered walls and a profusion of
beams. Food is served in the bar and
in a pleasant dining room. The bar
menu is changed frequently but may
include homemade soup, Devon farm
sausages, Rhydspence pastie, pizza,
baked aubergine parmesan, spinach
and mozzarella crunch, lasagne,
grilled sardines, burgers, filled jacket
potatoes and a range of ploughman's.
Dominoes, crib and quoits are played
in the bar. Cwmnau Farmhouse, a
17th-century working Herefordshire
farmhouse owned by the National
Trust (open 2-6 weekends and some
bank holidays) is three miles to the
north.

Beer: Draught Bass, Marston
Pedigree Bitter and Robinson Best
Bitter on handpump, Dunkertons
organic cider from the cask and
occasional guest beers.

Accommodation: 1 single, 1 twin, 3
doubles all with en suite facilities and
colour TVs and tea and coffee making
facilities. B&B £27–£35 per person.
Winter Weekend £88 per person for 2
nights.

WOOLHOPE

Butchers Arms
Off B4224, signposted from
Fownhope. (OS 618358)

Licensees: Charles Power &
Lucinda Matthews
Tel: 0432 860 281

The Butchers Arms, found down a
country lane, is a delightful 14th-
century half-timbered inn with low
beams in the bars and a terrace with
flowers, a rockery and a small stream.
In winter there are cheerful log fires.
Bar food (lunchtime and evening)
offers homemade soups, Woolhope
Pie (rabbit and bacon cooked in local
cider), steak, kidney and mushroom
pie, mushroom biriani, salads and
ploughman's. A separate restaurant is
open Wednesday to Saturday
evenings. Beer is not only impeccably
kept but is remarkably good value.
Guest rooms have TVs, tea and coffee
making facilities and baskets of fresh
fruit. Woolhope got its name from
Wulviva's Hope or valley: she was
the sister of the better-known Lady
Godiva. In the 11th century Wulviva
gave the manor of Woolhope to
Hereford Cathedral.

Beer: Hook Norton Best Bitter and
Old Hooky, Marston Pedigree Bitter
and regular guest beers on
handpumps.

Accommodation: 2 doubles, 1 twin.
B&B £25 single, £39 double.
Children welcome; terms by
arrangement.

WORCESTER

Kings Head
67 Sidbury, The Commandary. Near
town centre. M5 exit 7

Licensee: Alfred James Thomas
Tel: 0905 26204

The Kings Head is a picturesque old
black and white pub that dates back
to the Civil War. It is just a few
minutes from the town centre, the
cathedral, the Commandary Museum
and the Tudor Museum in Friary
Street. Lunchtime bar food (not
Sundays) includes filled rolls and a
daily platter.

Beer: Banks Mild and Bitter on
electric pumps.

Accommodation: 2 doubles, 3 twins.
B&B £15 per person. Children under
12 years £10. Guests staying 7 days
charged for 6. No pets.

HERTFORDSHIRE

AYOT ST LAWRENCE

Brocket Arms
Shaw's Corner, near Welwyn. Off
A1 & B652

Licensee: Toby Wingfield-Digby
Tel: 0438 820250

The Brocket Arms, a rugged 14th-
century building with a walled
garden, forms part of the surrounding
Brocket Hall estate. The hamlet of
Ayot St Lawrence nestles down
narrow lanes and is yet only a few
minutes from the A1. There are
timbered cottages, the ruins of a
12th-century church and its restored
18th-century Palladian successor.
George Bernard Shaw lived down the
road and his house, now owned by
the National Trust, is open to the
public in the summer. Henry VIII is
supposed to have wooed Catherine
Parr at the manor opposite the pub,
which gets very busy at weekends
with visitors arriving on horse as well

as car, foot and cycle. During the week, though, it has the atmosphere of a quiet country pub with its two small bars and a vast inglenook in the back room. Bar food, with a buffet in summer, includes soup, ploughman's, game pie, fish pie, shepherd's pie, coq au vin, tagliatelle and a roast lunch on Sundays. A separate candle-lit à la carte restaurant is open Monday to Saturday evenings and for lunch every day and specializes in game dishes.

Beer: Adnams Bitter, Cains Bitter, Greene King IPA and Abbot Ale, Marston Pedigree Bitter and Wadworth 6X on handpumps with guest beers in winter.

Accommodation: 3 singles, 2 doubles, 1 family room. B&B £40 single/double, family room £55, double en suite £60. Cards: Access and Visa.

LILLEY

Lilley Arms
West Street. Off A505

Licensee: Peter Brown
Tel: 046 276 371

The Lilley Arms, close to the church and a farm shop in this picturesque Herts-Beds border area, dates from the early 18th century. It has two bars, including a traditional and atmospheric public, and a separate games room used for live music on some Friday nights. The lounge bar has a dining area. The pub, a listed building, has its own stables for the Brown family's ponies and there is a hitching rail on the green in front of the pub for customers who arrive on horseback. The beer garden has several pets and is popular with children. Food is served every day and includes soup, garlic mushrooms, steak stuffed with Stilton, mixed grill,

Brocket Arms, Ayot St Lawrence

chicken Kiev, coq au vin, scampi, fillet of plaice or cod, rainbow trout, lemon sole, salads, omelettes, vegetarian spicy burger and pancake rolls, and a wide range of sandwiches. There is a roast lunch on Sundays and a special children's menu.

Beer: Greene King IPA, Rayments Special Bitter and Abbot Ale on handpumps.

Accommodation: 1 double, 1 family room. B&B £18.50 single, £32.50 double/family. Children's rates depend on age. Families allowed in pool room and dining room. No pets. Cards: Access, Amex, Visa.

ODSEY

Jester Inn
Ashwell Station, near Baldock, 300 yards from A505

Licensee: Pam Mildenhall-Clarke
Tel: 046 274 2011

The Jester is a 300 year-old pub with oak beams, and blazing log fires in winter. It is just off the Baldock-Royston road and two minutes from the Cambridge to London railway. There is a large and attractive garden for families. The inn offers both bar snacks and full meals in a separate restaurant, with a traditional roast on Sundays. All the guest rooms have en suite facilities and TVs, and there is a four-poster bedroom as well as two honeymoon suites.

Beer: Hook Norton Best Bitter, Marston Pedigree Bitter, Morland Old Speckled Hen, Whitbread Boddingtons Bitter and Flowers IPA and Original all on handpumps.

Accommodation: 3 singles, 1 twin, 7 doubles. B&B £40 single, £52 double. Weekend double charged at single rate. Honeymoon suite/four-poster £65. Cards: Access, Amex, Visa.

ROYSTON

Jockey
31-33 Baldock Street. A505

Licensee: J.C. Booth
Tel: 0763 243377

The Jockey is a cheerful town pub with a red tiles on the roof and over the two bow windows at the front. Inside the theme is aviation, not equestrian; Duxford and Old Warden air museums are close by and the pub has many old aircraft prints and memorabilia. The Jockey has a large garden with summer barbecues. Bar food is served lunchtime and evening (not Sundays). There is a daily special and such regular favourites as beef Wellington, coq au vin, beef Stroganoff, venison and rabbit pie, cod steaks in cider or chicken in brandy and cream, plus ploughman's and omelettes. Curries, seafood lasagne and macaroni cheese appear in the evenings. Royston has a challenging golf course, and Royston Cave with its wall paintings.

Beer: Elgoods EB, Whitbread Flowers IPA and Boddingtons Bitter on handpumps with occasional guest beers.

Accommodation: 2 singles, 2 twins. B&B £18 single, £34 double.

ST ALBANS

Lower Red Lion
34-36 Fishpool Street. Off A1 & A405

Licensee: J.S. Turner
Tel: 0727 55669

The Lower Red is a 17th-century pub in the heart of St Albans' conservation area and in a winding street of fine houses and artisans' cottages that leads to Verulam Park, an old water mill, the site of Roman Verulamium and the great abbey cathedral. There is a cheery welcome in the pub with its blazing fires in winter. Both bars have comfortable red seating and brick and half-timbered walls. The pub's name distinguishes it from the now defunct Great Red Lion by the historic Clock Tower. The Lower Red prides itself on the lack of juke box, background music, fruit machines and video games. It serves lunchtime meals from a set menu with daily special dishes.

Beer: Adnams Bitter, Fullers London Pride, Greene King IPA and Abbot Ale on handpumps plus a regular guest beer.

Accommodation: 3 singles, 4 doubles, 1 family room. B&B £25-£30 single, £40 double, £50-£55 family room. Pets accepted.

White Hart Hotel
Holywell Hill

Licensee: Julian Tann
Tel: 0727 53624
Fax: 0727 40237

A late 15th-century inn first known as the Harts Horn and built for pilgrims to the abbey, the White Hart became a major coaching inn, the first stop on the road north from London. It is immediately opposite the great abbey and cathedral with its Norman tower and ancient shrine to Alban, the first Christian martyr. The inn, with its striking half-timbered exterior, has two comfortable pubby bars, a conference room with a minstrels' gallery on the first floor, reached by a barley-twist staircase, and a separate restaurant. Bar meals are served every day lunchtime and evening. The White Hart is a good base for visiting the abbey, French

Row – where French troops were garrisoned in 1217 during the struggle with King John – the street market on Wednesdays and Saturdays, and the Clock Tower.

Beer: Benskins Best Bitter, Greene King Abbot Ale, Ind Coope Burton Ale and Tetley Bitter on handpumps.

Accommodation: 11 rooms, 8 with full en suite facilities, 3 with showers, all with direct dial phones, colour TVs and tea and coffee making facilities. B&B £50 single, £60 double. Friday/Saturday nights £35 single per day, £45 double. Children welcome. Cards: Access, Amex, Visa.

HUMBERSIDE

BARTON UPON HUMBER

George Hotel
George Street, Market Place. A1077

Manager: Lee Terry Syrett
Tel: 0652 32433

The George has nine guests' rooms and all have private baths or showers, TVs and tea and coffee making facilities. There is a 50-cover restaurant, a coffee lounge, a lounge bar, and a bar with TV area and pool room. Bar meals and restaurant meals are served every day, lunchtime and evening (not Sunday evenings) and include homemade soup, vegetable delight, peppered mackerel, taramasalata, steaks, chicken Mexican, duckling cooked in Grand Marnier, halibut steak, sole, vegetable lasagne and sweet and sour vegetables. Barton was once an important port and shipbuilding centre and has two ancient churches, including a restored Saxon one. The Humber Bridge has magnificent views and provides access to Hull and East Yorkshire. North of the town, strung along the banks of the Humber, there are a number of meres of great interest to naturalists and with facilities for anglers and weekend sailors.

Beer: Draught Bass and Stones Best Bitter on handpumps.

Accommodation: 3 singles, 5 twins, 1 family room. B&B £30 single, £50 double/family room. No pets. Cards: Access, Diners, Visa.

CLEETHORPES

Crows Nest
Balmoral Road. From M180 follow Cleethorpes sign, right at roundabout, along Clee Road, third left into Davenport Road, first left at roundabout

Licensees: Bill & Sheila Hayward
Tel: 0472 698867

The Crows Nest is a substantial, friendly estate pub in a quiet residential area, with a large car park and separate residents' entrance. There is a public bar and a comfortable lounge. The welcome is warm and the pub is deservedly popular with locals. Bar food is available both lunchtime and evening. There is a television lounge for residents and the guest rooms have tea and coffee making facilities.

Beer: Sam Smith's Old Brewery Bitter on handpump.

Accommodation: 2 singles, 1 twin, 2 doubles, 1 family room. B&B £12 per person.

DRIFFIELD

Bell in Driffield
Market Place. Off A163 & A166

Licensee: George Riggs
Tel: 0377 46661
Fax: 0377 43228

The Bell is an 18th-century coaching inn in an area of outstanding beauty and historical interest. Driffield is a market town close to York and Beverley and the country houses of Castle Howard, Sledmere and Burton Agnes. Kings Mill garden, just 800 yards from the Bell, is a 20-acre site that includes a watermill dating from Domesday times, and is also home to many migratory birds and animals, including kingfishers, voles and wild deer. The hotel reflects its period with some four-poster and half-tester bedrooms. All the guest rooms have private baths or showers, direct-dial phones, colour TVs, radios, and tea and coffee making facilities. The Bell also offers a swimming pool, sauna and squash court. Bar food is available every lunchtime and evening except Sunday. The dining room is open for Sunday lunch and evenings the rest of the week.

Beer: John Smith's Magnet Bitter, Younger Scotch and IPA on handpumps.

Accommodation: 2 singles, 12 doubles. B&B £63 single, £43 per person in double room. Children's rates on application. Pets by arrangement. Cards: Access, Amex, Diners, Visa.

GRIMSBY

County Hotel
Brighowgate, A180

Licensee: Michael Kearney
Tel: 0472 354422/344449

The County is a large and bustling pub with a lounge and restaurant decorated in Victorian style. There is always something happening in the hotel – quiz nights, discos, live music and fund-raising events, but there is a secluded area for those who want to rest or read. Extensive bar meals, available lunchtime and evening, include chilli, filled jacket potatoes, large Yorkshire puddings with various fillings, and sandwiches. There is a separate restaurant with table d'hôte menu. All the guest rooms have en suite facilities, colour TVs, direct-dial phones and tea and coffee making equipment. The hotel is close to the main railway station.

Beer: Younger Scotch Bitter, IPA and No 3 on handpumps with Theakstons Best Bitter as an occasional guest beer.

Accommodation: 3 singles, 3 doubles, 3 twins. B&B £35 single, £45 double/twin. Weekend £22.50 single, £32.50 double/twin. Special rates on request. Cards: Access, Amex, Visa.

ISLE OF WIGHT

CARISBROOKE

Shute Inn
Clatterford Shute off B3323
Carisbrooke to Shurwell road

Licensee: Tony Simmons
Tel: 0983 523393

The Shute is a delightful old inn in a lovely rural setting a mile from Newport. There are fine views from the inn of Carisbrooke Castle, where Charles I was imprisoned, and over the Bowcombe Valley. A few yards from the inn a ford crosses Lukeley

Brook, a tributary of the River Medina. The Shute's guest rooms all have colour TVs and tea and coffee making facilities. Bar food is served lunchtime and evening (not Sunday evening) and there is a family room.

Beer: Draught Bass and Charrington IPA, Wadworth 6X on handpumps.

Accommodation: 1 single, 1 twin, 1 double. Room £13.50 single, £24 twin, £28 double en suite. Choice of breakfast from £3. 10% reduction for 4 nights or more. Cards: Access and Visa.

CHALE

Clarendon Hotel & Wight Mouse Inn
B3399, off B3055

Licensees: John & Jean Bradshaw
Tel: 0983 730431

Two for the price of one in this 17th-century hotel with attached inn where there is live music every night of the week, winter and summer – jazz, country and western, and singing guitarists. The stone-built buildings have wood-panelling from a 19th-century shipwreck. There is a strong family emphasis: children are welcomed warmly and there is a garden with swings, slides and menagerie and no fewer than three children's rooms. Generous bar food, leaning on local produce and home-cooking, includes soups, ploughman's, burgers, steaks, salads, crabs, prawns, cockles, sandwiches and sweets. There is a separate restaurant. The pub is open all day, every day for drinks and food (no hot food on Sundays between 3 and 7pm).

Beer: Marston Pedigree Bitter, Wadworth 6X and Whitbread

Boddingtons Bitter and Strong Country Bitter on handpumps.

Accommodation: 14 doubles, 8 family rooms, 8 rooms with private bath and 1 de luxe suite. B&B £23-£26 per person. Full board £32-£35. Weekend £64-£70, Week £175-£195. Top prices are for rooms with baths. Off-season: 17½% reductions. Children 0-2 years £2 per day, 3-5 £5, half price 6-12 years. Pets accepted. Cards: Access.

NEWPORT

Wheatsheaf Hotel
St Thomas Square

Licensees: David & Sally Rudge
Tel: 0983 523865

The Wheatsheaf is a 17th-century coaching inn in the centre of the old market town. The inn has

Cromwellian connections – the leader of the republic held a parliamentary meeting here. The guest rooms have all been thoughtfully modernized and refurbished, with colour TVs, tea and coffee makers and most with en suite facilities. The public rooms have beamed ceilings and the comfortable bar has a casement clock and a fireplace, with chairs placed round circular tables. There is a family room and a separate function room overlooking the square. The bar is open all day Monday to Saturday and food is served from 11am to 9pm daily. The extensive menu includes homemade soup, ham and asparagus, steaks, chicken breast in a mushroom and celery sauce, steak peppercorn, plaice or cod, steak and kidney or cottage pie, stir fried vegetables, cauliflower cheese, filled jacket potatoes, ploughman's and sandwiches. A separate children's menu offers soup, steak and kidney pie, burgers, sausage, or fish fingers.

Clarendon Hotel & Wight Mouse Inn, Chale

Beer: Flowers Original and Strong Country Bitter on handpumps.

Accommodation: 6 singles, 9 doubles/twins. B&B £25 single, £34 with shower, £43 twin/double, £53 with shower. Children: £5 for extra bed in room. Pets accepted. Cards: Access, Amex, Visa.

SEAVIEW

Seaview Hotel
High Street

Licensees: Nicola & Nicholas Hayward
Tel: 0983 612711
Fax: 0983 613729

The Seaview is an imposing and elegant three-storey hotel in a pleasant Edwardian seaside setting. The Haywards, with their own young family, welcome other families, including well-behaved dogs, and provide cots and children's menus. There are two bars, a plush cocktail bar with many naval photos, and the Pump Bar with an open fire in winter, popular with locals and yachtsmen. Elegance is everywhere, with antique clocks, watercolours and French cuisine in the acclaimed restaurant (closed Sunday evening). Bar food includes homemade soup, whitebait, ploughman's, pizzas, toasted sandwiches, fresh crab cocktail, hot crab ramekin and smoked haddock pasta.

Beer: Flowers IPA and Original on handpumps.

Accommodation: 16 rooms, all with private bathrooms or showers and including 1 family suite. B&B £43.50 single, £32.50 per person in twin/double. Breakaway: 2 nights or more, dinner, B&B £56.50 single, £45 twin/double. Children's terms

according to age and season. Cards: Access, Amex, Visa.

ASH

Volunteer Inn
43 Guilton, A257, 3 miles from Sandwich

Licensees: Vic & Jan Simmons
Tel: 0304 812506

The Volunteer is an attractive Victorian pub built in 1834 on the Sandwich to Canterbury road, handy for Sandwich golf course, Richborough Castle, Howletts Zoo, Canterbury and the cross-Channel ferries: the Simmons provide dawn breakfasts for Channel hoppers. The inn has a public bar and lounge, and bar billiards is played as well as darts. Good bar snacks and meals include provision for special diets and are served lunchtime and evening.

Beer: Adnams Bitter, Arkells BBB and Shepherd Neame Master Brew Bitter on handpumps.

Accommodation: 1 double, 1 family room. B&B £28 double, £30 family room. Children welcome, half price. Reductions for stays of 3 days or more. No pets.

BOUGHTON

Queens Head Hotel
111 The Street. Near Faversham and Canterbury. End of M2 take A2 Dover road to Boughton and Dunkirk

Licensee: Elizabeth Sabey
Tel: 0227 751369

The Queens Head is an historic, 400-year-old beamed inn with gardens overlooking the apple orchards and hop gardens of Kent. The hospitality is warm and locals will invite guests to join them in games of chess, cribbage, dominoes and shove ha'penny. The hotel has a small and cosy restaurant with 18 covers; bar meals and restaurant meals are served lunchtime and evening every day (not Sunday lunch). Mrs Sabey concentrates on good home-cooking and offers pies, puddings, chicken with prawns, beef in red wine, sandwiches, burgers, jacket potatoes and desserts. There are vegetarian and children's menus. The guest rooms all have colour TVs, central heating and tea and coffee making facilities. The Queens Head is a fine base for visiting Canterbury and the Kent coast, Mount Ephraim, Bossingham Woods, Brogdale, Syndale Vineyards or as a stopover for the cross-Channel ferries. There are facilities for disabled people in the bar areas.

Beer: Shepherd Neame Mild, Master Brew Bitter and Spitfire Ale on handpumps.

Accommodation: 4 doubles/twins, 1 family room. Single occupancy available. B&B £15-£20 per person. Children welcome. Special rates for stays of 3 days or more. Closed Xmas Day.

BROADSTAIRS

Royal Albion Hotel
Albion Street; off M2 & A299

Licensee: Roger Family
Tel: 0843 68071
Fax: 0843 61509

The Royal Albion is a handsome building with a commanding position on the cliffs of this fine old seaside resort made famous by Charles Dickens, who finished *Nicholas Nickleby* while staying there. The original Bleak House is nearby. The hotel began life as the Phoenix Inn in 1760 and by 1816 had changed its name to the Albion. Visits by several members of the royal family added the prefix. The hotel has been run by the Marchesi family for 12 years and they have owned the separate restaurant (open every day for lunch and dinner) for more than 100 years. Reasonably priced dishes include homemade soups, scallop and bacon salad, poached fillet of turbot, Dover sole, rack of lamb and vegetarian dish of the day. Bar food is also available but not from October to April. The Bradstow Bar was once a separate house and was where Dickens lived and worked for several years. The immaculate guest rooms all have en suite facilities, colour TVs and tea and coffee makers. The hotel can arrange day trips to France.

Beer: Shepherd Neame Master Brew Bitter on handpump.

Accommodation: 2 singles, 14 doubles, 2 family rooms. B&B £60 single, £35 double per person, £40 family room. No pets. Cards: Access, Amex, Diners, Visa.

CHIDDINGSTONE CAUSEWAY

Little Brown Jug
Opposite Penshurst BR station; B2027

Licensees: Mr C.R. & Mrs S. Cannon
Tel: 0892 870318

The Little Brown Jug was built some 120 years ago at the height of the railway boom, and its construction coincided with the arrival of the train service. It is a striking building with a tall and imposing chimney stack and a gabled and porched entrance. It is an excellent base for visiting Hever Castle, Penshurst Place and Chartwell. Chiddingstone village and its castle are two miles distant: they are owned by the National Trust. The pub has a large public bar, a saloon and a separate restaurant. Bar food is available lunchtime and evening, while the evening restaurant offers several menus that include roast poussin, lamb in filo pastry, roast loin of pork and fillet of beef in red wine sauce. The pub has open fires, a warm welcome and, among its ales, Larkin's bitter brewed in Chiddingstone on a hop farm.

Beer: Harvey Best Bitter, Larkins Traditional Bitter and two changing guest beers on handpumps.

Accommodation: 2 singles, 5 doubles, all with en suite facilities. B&B £29.50 single, £39.50 double. Cards: Access and Visa.

Chislehurst: see LONDON

EASTLING

Carpenters Arms
The Street. 4 miles from A2/M2, 4 miles from A20 at Lenham

Licensee: Tony O'Regan
Tel: 0795 89234

From the road the Carpenters Arms looks like a modern pub but the frontage has been added on to the 1380 original, best seen from the car park with its steeply tumbling roofs, dormer window and some half-timbers. The back room, now used as a restaurant, was once the bar and has an old baker's oven. The pub tells

you in no uncertain terms that you are in Kentish hop country, with friezes of hops above the bar and fascinating old photos of hop-picking in the 1930s. There are old church pews, cottage furniture and inglenook fireplaces. Bar food (not Sunday evening) includes soup, pizza, burgers, countryman lunch of spicy Kent sausage, Cheddar cheese, onion, lettuce, pickles and French bread, ham and eggs, ploughman's, sandwiches and toasties. The restaurant (not Sunday evening) offers among its menus a businessman's lunch and a roast Sunday lunch. Accommodation is in the adjoining Carpenters Lodge, a listed building.

Beer: Shepherd Neame Master Brew Bitter and Spitfire Ale on handpumps.

Accommodation: 4 singles, 4 doubles, 4 rooms with en suite facilities. B&B £30 single, £40 double. 10% reduction for 5 days or more. No pets. Cards: Access, Amex, Visa.

LAMBERHURST

George & Dragon Inn
School Hill, A21, 21 miles south of M25

Licensee: John N. Eaton
Tel: 0892 890277

The George & Dragon is a timbered inn in the picturesque village of Lamberhurst, famous for its vineyards. The inn dates back to the 15th century but was extensively modernized at the turn of the 20th. Hungers are dealt with from dawn until dusk as the inn serves breakfasts from 7.30am and also supplies bar meals and full restaurant meals at lunchtime and evening. There are two bars, a lounge with comfortable settees and log fires and a public bar with darts and pool. The guest rooms have colour TVs and tea and coffee making facilities. Places of interest in the area include the vineyards, Bewl Bridge Reservoir, Scotney Castle and Bayham Abbey trout fishery.

Beer: Draught Bass, Greene King IPA and Abbot Ale on handpumps.

Accommodation: 6 doubles, 2 family rooms, 4 rooms with en suite facilities. B&B from £25 single, £35 double, £47.50 en suite, £45 family room. Children's rates according to age. No pets. Cards: Access, Switch, Visa.

LENHAM

Dog & Bear Hotel
The Square. A20 near Maidstone; M20 exit 8

Licensees: Robert & Sheila Hedges
Tel: 0622 858219
Fax: 0622 859415

The Dog & Bear was built in 1602 at the height of the coaching period when the inn provided shelter for travellers, and refreshment for local market traders. It has a steeply tiled roof and an attractive claret and white fascia decked out with flowering tubs and hanging baskets. The first floor bears the bold coat of arms of Queen Anne who visited the inn in 1704. It is a good base for visiting Canterbury, while Leeds Castle is just 10 minutes away by car. Food – both bar meals and restaurant meals – is available lunchtime and evening. Food in the bar includes ploughman's, salads, sandwiches, homemade soup, chilli con carne, cottage pie, fillet of plaice, sausage, bacon and egg with fried potatoes and tomatoes, grilled gammon, and scampi. The guest rooms all have en suite bathrooms,

direct-dial phones, radios, TVs and tea and coffee making facilities. The inn also has a function room suitable for meetings and conferences.

Beer: Shepherd Neame Master Brew Bitter and Spitfire Ale on handpumps.

Accommodation: 4 singles, 13 doubles/twins, 3 family rooms. B&B £43.50 single, £56.50 double/twin, £66.75 family. Weekend Break £74 per person for 2 nights. Pets welcome. Cards: Access, Amex, Switch, Visa.

PLUCKLEY

Dering Arms
Station Road. At Charing (A20) take B2077 to Pluckley

Licensee: Jim Buss
Tel: 023 384 371

The Dering Arms is a striking 17th-century hunting lodge with a Dutch gabled roof and stone and wood bars. It stands in what was once the Dering estate. A member of the Dering family escaped through a window of the lodge when he was pursued by the Roundheads during the Civil War. Since then all the windows on the estate have been designed along similar lines and the style is now known as a Dering Window. The 30-seater restaurant specializes in fresh fish and local game, while in the bar you can choose from homemade soup, Sussex smokies, local trout, ploughman's, blacksmith's (ham), gamekeeper's (rabbit and pigeon) and squire's (Stilton) lunches. There are good puds, too: fruit crumble, banana pancake and orange in caramel. No food is served Sunday evenings. The guest rooms all have colour TVs and tea and coffee making facilities.

Pluckley is a good base for touring the county and taking in Canterbury, and Leeds and Bodiam castles.

Beer: Dering Ale is a house beer brewed by Goachers of Maidstone, with Goachers Dark and Old (winter only), Shepherd Neame Spitfire Ale and Youngs Special Bitter all on handpumps.

Accommodation: 3 doubles (double and single bed in each room: can be used as single; 1 can be twin or family). B&B £28 single, £36-£40 double room. Children welcome, rates depend on age. Pets welcome.

SANDWICH

Bell Hotel
The Quay. A257; off M2 & M20.

Licensee: M.I. Turner
Tel: 0304 613388
Fax: 0304 615308

The Bell is a grade two listed building dating from the 17th century, with carved brickwork and Flemish-style gables. It is based in the oldest of the ancient Cinque Ports that was the second most important port in England after London. The Quay is an historic street of timber-framed houses where Tom Paine, author of *The Rights of Man* and a major influence in the American and French revolutions, lived. One street in Sandwich is believed to be the longest continuous timber-framed thoroughfare in the country. The houses were built by Huguenot weavers who settled in England to escape repression on the continent. The Barbican Toll Gate dates from 1023 and dominates the eastern approaches to the town. Modern Sandwich is also the home of the Royal St George's golf club, where the British Open is played, and the

hotel organizes special golfing weekends. There are facilities for clay pigeon shooting nearby while Sandwich is a good base for visiting Canterbury, Dover, the castles at Deal and Walmer and local nature reserves. Magnums wine bar in the hotel has grills, pies and dishes of the day while the restaurant offers both table d'hôte and à la carte menus. All the guest rooms are decorated and furnished to a high standard and have en suite facilities.

Beer (in wine bar): Ruddles County and Websters Yorkshire Bitter on handpumps.

Accommodation: 8 singles, 20 doubles/twins, 1 family room, all en suite. B&B £60 single, £90 double and family room. Children free of charge sharing with 2 adults. Breaks Oct-March from £40 per person per night; April-Sept £50. Family lounge. Pets welcome. Cards: Access and Visa.

SHATTERLING

Green Man Inn
Nr Wingham, A2/A257, between Wingham and Ash

Licensees: P.J. Ferne & G.F.S & A. Greenwood
Tel: 0304 812525

The building dates from 1728 and was granted an ale licence in 1820. It has developed into a fully residential inn, with an à la carte restaurant and two bars where bar meals are served. It is situated among hop fields and orchards in the middle of the Thanet peninsula and is less than 30 minutes' drive from Dover and Ramsgate and 20 minutes from Kent International Airport. Seven golf courses, Howletts Zoo and Canterbury are close at hand.

Beer: Adnams Bitter, Youngs Bitter and Special Bitter on handpumps.

Accommodation: 3 doubles/twins, 1 family room, 1 room with en suite facilities. B&B £20 single, £32 double, £17.50 per person in family room, reductions for children under 14. Pets accepted. Cards: Access and Visa.

SHEERNESS

Seaview Hotel
Broadway. A249 Sheppey road

Licensee: Maurice Flynn
Tel: 0795 662003

The Seaview is a cheerful and friendly small hotel with a good pubby atmosphere that specializes in home-cooked food in the bar and separate restaurant. It has a large garden and two separate function rooms. All the guest rooms have colour TVs, tea and coffee makers and uninterrupted views of the Thames estuary. The Seaview is a good base for the Olau line ferry service to Holland.

Beer: Shepherd Neame Master Brew Bitter and Spitfire Ale on handpumps.

Accommodation: 1 single, 3 doubles, 7 twins, 1 family room, 2 rooms with private facilities. B&B £13.50 single, £32 double/twin, £15 per person for 4 adults in family room. Children under 5 free. En suite facilities £5 extra. Pets welcome.

SMARDEN

Bell
B2077, ¾ mile from the village, off A20

Licensee: Ian Turner
Tel: 023 377 283

A fine old Kentish inn in unspoilt countryside near Leeds and Sissinghurst castles, the Bell has three large bars with oak beams, candlelight, inglenooks with welcoming winter fires, flag-stoned floors and pews and chairs round wooden tables. It was built as a farmhouse during the reign of Henry VII, and was granted an ale and cider licence in 1630. Smarden stems from the Anglo-Saxon for a 'fat and wooded place'. The front bar of the Bell, popular with locals, offers pool, darts, shove ha'penny and dominoes. The tile-hung and rose-covered exterior is a summer delight when you can sit among the trees in the garden. Splendid bar food includes homemade soups, ploughman's, Greek-style shepherd's pie, sandwiches and toasties, steak and kidney pie, pizzas and homemade chocolate crunch cake and apple crumble. Bar meals are served every day. The guest rooms have colour TVs.

Beer: Brakspear Bitter, Flowers Original and Fremlins Bitter, Fullers London Pride, Goachers Maidstone Ale, Ringwood Old Thumper and Shepherd Neame Master Brew Bitter on handpumps.

Accommodation: 4 doubles. Bed and continental breakfast £18 single, £15 double per person. Children's room; children welcome, no reductions. Closed Xmas Day. Cards: Access and Visa.

WINGHAM

Anchor Inn
On A257

Licensees: Jez Gaiger & Paul Stevens
Tel: 0227 720229

The Anchor is a delightful old pub with tall chimneys on a rambling roof, close to Canterbury and its historic pleasures. The pub is a grade two listed building dating back to the 16th century, and has the ghost of a former landlord, Ernest Twiddy, who died when he fell down the stairs. Bar snacks and meals are available every day with a wide selection of pasta dishes, steaks, chicken chasseur, Kiev and cordon bleu, seafood, scampi, grilled trout, plaice and prawn meunière. Meals are served in the lounge and there is also a public bar and games room with bar billiards, pool and darts. The Anchor has a pleasant garden in summer and outdoor swimming pool, families are welcome and there are camping facilities. The accommodation is being extended and will eventually have three more rooms: two singles and one double.

Beer: Flowers Original and Fremlins Bitter on handpumps.

Accommodation: 3 singles, 2 doubles, 1 family room. B&B £20 single, £30 double, £35 family room. Children welcome. Dogs by arrangement.

WORTH

St Crispin Inn
The Street, main road between Sandwich and Deal

Licensees: Randolph Tillings & Jefferey Lenham
Tel: 0304 612081

St Crispin is a 16th-century inn in a pretty village, with a log fire in winter and fine gardens in summer. The inn began life in the 15th century as a mortuary, but it is very much alive today. It lies back from the road, with a free-standing inn sign, steeply pitched roof and two porched

entrances. Bar food is available every day, lunchtime and evening, and includes grills, steaks, fish, pies, a roast carvery and daily specials. There is a separate restaurant. Accommodation is split between the inn and an adjoining building. Worth is close to Sandwich and the other Cinque Ports and several championship golf courses.

Beer: Gales HSB, Marston Pedigree Bitter and Merry Monk, Shepherd Neame Master Brew Bitter and regular guest beers straight from the cask.

Accommodation: 3 twins, 4 family rooms, all en suite. B&B £30 single, £45 double, £45.50 family room. Children's rates by arrangement. Pets accepted. Cards: Access and Visa.

WYE

New Flying Horse Inn
Upper Bridge Street. Off A28, 4 miles from Ashford

Licensee: Norman Evans
Tel: 0233 812297

The New Flying Horse is a fine 17th-century inn, which probably replaced an old or original hostelry of the same name, in this historic town once famous for its smugglers who dealt in French brandy and lace. Wye College, founded in 1447, is now a famous agricultural college that specializes in developing new varieties of hops that are resistant to pests and fungal attack. The bar of the inn is a delight, with a fine old pub feel to it enhanced by beams, brasses, wooden pillars and an open fireplace. The Flying Horse is a good base for visiting Romney Marsh, Rye, Dover and Canterbury and for a trip on the Romney, Hythe and Dymchurch railway. Bar meals are available lunchtime and evening every day and include homemade soup, grills, omelettes, seafood platter, trout with prawns and almonds, steaks, sandwiches, toasties and ploughman's.

Beer: Shepherd Neame Master Brew Bitter, Best Bitter and Spitfire Ale on handpumps.

Accommodation: 7 doubles, 1 family room, 4 rooms en suite. B&B £31 single, £36 en suite, £41/£46 double. Weekend Breaks: £128 for 2 people sharing en suite room for any 2 nights, B&B plus dinner; £118 for room without bath. Children welcome, charged only for meals. Cards: Access, Amex, Diners, Visa.

LANCASHIRE, MANCHESTER & MERSEYSIDE

BLACKPOOL (LANCS)

Empress Hotel
59 Exchange Street, North Shore; off M6 & M55

Proprietors: Chris & Jean Murray
Tel: 0253 20413

The Empress is an imposing three-storey red brick Victorian hotel with a traditional vault (public bar to Southerners) and plush lounge; there is a full-size snooker table in the vault, welcome relief from the ubiquitous 'keg' pool table, and a concert room. The Empress, which boasts some of the most comfortable beds found anywhere in Britain, was built by the son of a local brick merchant in 1847 using handmade bricks. Some of the ceilings were sculpted by Venetian craftsmen. The roll call of stars of stage, screen and politics who have visited the Empress over the years includes Vesta Tilley, G.H. Elliott, Florrie Forde, Elizabeth Welch, Mae West, Johnny (Tarzan) Weissmuller, Sir Robin Day and Edward Heath. It remains a genuine local, though, and Blackpudlians put on their best bibs and tuckers for dancing there every weekend. In season all bars are open until 1am Friday and Saturday. The quality of the service can be gauged by the fact that Chris Murray has been judged Landlord of the Year in 1986 and 1987 while Jean has been nominated Landlady of the Year in 1982, 1983 and 1986. The Empress has been in every edition of the Good Beer Guide.

Beer: Thwaites Best Mild and Bitter on handpumps.

Accommodation: 1 single, 6 doubles, 4 twins, 3 family rooms. B&B £12.50 per person, £17 with evening meal. Blackpool Lights Weekend (2 nights) £35. Winter reductions, mini-breaks. 4 Day Xmas Special £145. Children welcome, reductions if sharing. 10% discount for CAMRA members. No pets.

Highlands Hotel
206 Queens Promenade, Bispham

Licensee: Kenneth Banks
Tel: 0253 54877

The Highlands is a large residential hotel on the sea front at Bispham, opposite a tram stop. Bar food includes homemade special dishes of the day, hot roast beef sandwiches and ploughman's.

Beer: Thwaites Mild and Bitter on handpumps.

Accommodation: 2 singles, 7 doubles/twins, 2 rooms with en suite facilities. B&B £15-£20. Children welcome. Special rates on application.

Ramsden Arms Hotel
204 Talbot Road, opposite railway station

Licensees: Christine & Albert Caffrey
Tel: 0253 23215

The Ramsden is an impressive Tudor-style pub on the edge of Blackpool town centre. It has a large oak-panelled lounge and a games room popular with darts, dominoes, pool and snooker players. Three blazing log fires help to brighten the coldest winter day. Bar lunches are served Monday to Saturday and include homemade pies, ham, roast beef, scampi and chilli. There is a residents' TV lounge and the guest rooms have central heating, colour TVs and tea and coffee making facilities. The pub is close to the bus and railway stations. The Ramsden Arms has been voted the local CAMRA Pub of the Year in both 1988 and 1989 and Mr Caffrey has been awarded the prestigious title of North-west Innkeeper of the Year in 1988 and 1989 by the British Institute of Innkeepers, and Master Cellarman of the Year 1990/91.

Beer: Cains Bitter, Thomas Greenalls Original Bitter, Hydes Anvil Bitter, Ind Coope Burton Ale, Jennings Bitter, Mitchells Bitter, Robinsons Best Bitter, Tetley Mild and Bitter, Whitbread Boddingtons Bitter on handpumps.

Accommodation: 3 twins. B&B £17.50 single, £22.50 with bath or shower, £30/£40 double/twin. Children under 10 £3 reduction. 3-day break from £60 per couple. Long stays: every 7th day free. No pets.

BOLTON (GREATER MANCHESTER)

Gilnow Arms
258 Deane Road. Off A666

Licensees: Sylvia & Trevor Crewe
Tel: 0204 25254

The Gilnow is a 19th-century public house that has been carefully modernized but which retains its old-world charm with original oak-beamed ceilings and friendly atmosphere. There is a wide range of traditional pub games for locals and visitors. Evening meals are available and guests can use both a TV lounge and a dining room.

Beer: Whitbread Boddingtons OB Mild and Bitter on handpumps.

Accommodation: 2 singles, 1 twin. B&B £12.50 per person.

BURSCOUGH (LANCS)

Martin Inn
Inn signposted on B5242, off A59 near Ormskirk. (OS 414127)

Licensee: John Mawdsley
Tel: 0704 892302/895788
Fax: 0704 895735

The Martin is a remote yet welcoming inn in the heart of the west Lancashire countryside on

Martin Mere, with a wildfowl trust, leisure lakes and riding schools. Boating, windsurfing and water-skiing are also available at Mere Brow. The inn serves snacks lunchtime and evening until 10pm and private parties are catered for in the Cottage Grill restaurant. Bar food includes soup, mushrooms with garlic dip, a range of sandwiches, steaks, chicken, plaice, homemade steak and mushroom pie, salads and children's meals. The guest rooms all have showers, colour TVs, tea and coffee making facilities and direct-dial phones. There are several first-class golf courses in the area and Burscough is a good base for Southport, Wigan, Liverpool and Manchester.

Beer: Courage Directors, John Smiths Bitter and guest beers on handpumps.

Accommodation: 4 singles, 8 doubles/twins. B&B from £22.50. Children's rates by negotiation. Pets accepted. Cards: Access, Amex, Visa.

ELSWICK (LANCS)

Boot & Shoe
Beech Road, in centre of village. Near Preston. Off B5269

Licensee: Hugh Dunn
Tel: 0995 70206

The Boot & Shoe is a welcome newcomer to the guide, as Mr Dunn has recently added accommodation to his modern and friendly village pub. It has a family room and large outdoor play area. The traditional pub food is home-cooked and there is a barbecue every Friday in summer.

Beer: Thwaites Best Mild and Bitter on handpumps.

Accommodation: 1 single, 1 double, 1 twin, all with en suite facilities. B&B from £12 per person. Children welcome.

ENTWISTLE (LANCS)

Strawbury Duck
Near Bolton. Off B6391, north of Chapeltown. (OS 726177)

Licensee: James Barry Speakman
Tel: 0204 852013

The oddly named Strawbury Duck, originally the more prosaic Station Hotel, is a fine half-timbered and remote inn tucked away down narrow lanes from Bolton. The cheery bar has a flag-stoned floor, rough stone walls, settees and pews, beams and old prints. The pub is Victorian and has been extended to include the adjacent Bridge Cottage, which is more than 300 years old. Bar food is available every day (not Monday lunch except Bank Holidays) and includes soup, garlic bread with cheese, corn on the cob, plaice or cod and chips, fisherman's pie, Aberdeen Angus steaks, chicken or beef curries, vegetable biriani, wheat casserole, vegetable lasagne or moussaka, filled jacket potatoes, steak and kidney pie, burgers and a children's menu. The tap room, also flag-stoned, has darts, dominoes and pool. In summer you can sit on tables overlooking the railway line that occasionally has trains from Bolton and Blackburn. The surrounding countryside is splendid for walking. Mr Speakman is a keen real ale connoisseur and seeks an enterprising range of guest beers.

Beer: Marston Pedigree Bitter, Timothy Taylor Best Bitter and Landlord, Whitbread Boddingtons Mild and Bitter and Flowers Original and up to three different guest beers every week, all on handpumps.

Accommodation: 1 twin, 4 four-poster rooms, all en suite. B&B £35 twin room (£28 single occupancy), £37 four-poster room (£32 single occupancy). Weekends £5 reduction on all rooms for stays of 2 nights or more.

GARSTANG (LANCS)

Royal Oak Hotel
Market Place. B6430, off A6

Licensee: J.M. Hewitson
Tel: 0995 603318

The Royal Oak is a 500-year-old coaching inn and is a listed building. It once stood on the main coaching route between London and Edinburgh. Garstang is still a small but thriving market town, and the Royal Oak continues to offer excellent ale and victuals to locals and visitors. It provides both hot and cold bar snacks. Major renovation work was underway when the guide went to press and there will be eight double guest rooms when the work is complete. Please enquire about rates when booking.

Beer: Robinson Best Mild and Best Bitter on handpumps.

Accommodation: 5 doubles, 2 rooms with private baths. B&B £15 per person, £16 en suite. Children and dogs by arrangement.

LEIGH (LANCS)

Three Crowns Hotel
188 Chapel Street. A580

Licensee: Bernard Reid
Tel: 0942 673552

The Three Crowns is one of the oldest pubs in Leigh. It was originally a farm and no one is certain when it obtained a liquor licence. Records date back to 1836 when a John Taylor was the landlord, and, by the 1890s, when John Benyon was the owner, the pub could stable five horses, feed 55 travellers and offer just one bed for all of them! Facilities are better today. The pub has been sensitively up-dated to retain its old atmosphere. Bar food is available all day, every day, and there is a separate restaurant. The vault has a wide range of pub games and there is a pleasant garden for the summer months.

Beer: Whitbread Boddingtons Mild and Bitter on handpumps.

Accommodation: 2 singles. B&B £12 per person. Children free under 5. No pets.

LITTLE ECCLESTON (LANCS)

Cartford Country Inn
Cartford Lane. Near Preston, ½ mile from A586

Licensees: Valerie Williams & Carol Mellowdew
Tel: 0995 70166

The inn is delightfully situated by the River Wyre and has its own fishing rights. The comprehensive menus include vegetarian dishes and children's choice.

Beer: Whitbread Boddingtons Bitter and guest beers on handpumps.

Accommodation: 6 doubles/twins, all en suite. B&B £24.50 per person, £37 double. 2 or more nights £22.50 per night. Children welcome.

LYTHAM (LANCS)

Queens Hotel
Central Beach, A584

Licensee: Mrs Shepherd
Tel: 0253 737316

The Queens is a popular and busy town pub overlooking the Ribble estuary, a windmill and a lifeboat station. It offers main meals and bar snacks, and there is also a separate restaurant; vegetarian options are available and there is a traditional Sunday lunch.

Beer: Theakstons Best Bitter, XB and Old Peculier on handpumps.

Accommodation: 1 single, 8 doubles/ twins, 4 family rooms, all en suite. B&B £20-£30 per person. Children welcome.

OLDHAM (GREATER MANCHESTER)

Park Hotel
159 Park Road. Off A62

Licensee: Edith Fairbrother
Tel: 061-624 5713

The Park is a cosy small hotel opposite Alexandra Park and just a

few minutes from the town centre. The atmosphere is friendly and relaxed and the hotel offers traditional pub games in the bar, a beer garden and live entertainment. Meals are served lunchtime and evening. The accommodation has been redecorated by the new licensee.

Beer: Whitbread Boddingtons OB Mild, OB Bitter and Bitter on handpumps.

Accommodation: 4 doubles, 1 family room. B&B £15 per person. Children welcome, terms negotiable. No pets.

SALFORD (GREATER MANCHESTER)

Prince of Wales Hotel
165 Oldfield Road; from end of M602 follow Salford signs and turn left at Sainsbury's

Licensees: D.A. & J.M. Brightman
Tel: 061-832 5716

The Prince of Wales was built in 1900 and has retained its traditional atmosphere with a central bar, a vault with an open fire, a lounge and a games room. The pub is host to three darts teams and a cricket team, and darts and dominoes are played in the vault. Meals and snacks are available every lunchtime and until 9pm in the evening. There is a residents' lounge and dining room with a TV. The accommodation has been refurbished and extended since the last edition of the guide. The hotel is close to Salford Quays, Manchester, Granada TV, the G-Mex Centre and is half a mile from the motorway network.

Beer: Marston Pedigree Bitter, Whitbread Boddingtons Bitter,

Castle Eden Ale, Chesters Best Mild and Flowers Original plus Shiners Bitter, a house beer, all on handpumps.

Accommodation: 2 singles, 2 twins, 1 family room. B&B £16.50 single, £30 twin, £45 family room (3 people). 2 nights or more £15/£27/£40. Pets by arrangement.

SOUTHPORT (MERSEYSIDE)

Herald Hotel
16 Portland Street. A565 & A570 lead to Lord Street; Portland Street is off Lord Street

Licensees: Derek & Jean Ditchfield
Tel: 0704 534424

The Herald is a smart and welcoming pub in this stately Victorian seaside town with its Parisian style boulevards and vast beaches. The hotel offers bar food lunchtime; evening meals by request. All the well-appointed guest rooms have colour TVs, telephones and tea and coffee making facilities. There is live entertainment in the lounge bar on at least three nights of the week. The full English breakfast, with a wide choice and special diets catered for, should satisfy even the heartiest of appetites. Nearby are Martin Mere Wildfowl Trust and the preserved village of Churchtown with its thatched cottages, two ancient pubs and botanical gardens and boating lake.

Beer: John Smiths Bitter and Magnet, Whitbread Boddingtons Bitter on handpumps.

Accommodation: 2 singles, 5 doubles, 4 twins, 1 family room, 6 rooms with

private baths. B&B £20 single, double/twin from £40. Children welcome, terms by agreement. Pets accepted.

STALMINE (LANCS)

Seven Stars
Hallgate Lane, A588

Licensee: Arnold Clayton
Tel: 0253 700207

The Seven Stars is a 16th-century family-run village pub, popular with locals and visitors but only now included in the guide due a switch to cask beer with the introduction of Greenall's new premium Original. The pub also now graces the Good Beer Guide. Mr Clayton has won a regional award in the Thomas Greenall first anniversary competition. Jean Clayton's menu ranges from sandwiches to steaks. The pub has a profusion of period furniture and old brasses and there are two bars: the games room used by locals and the lounge with a real fire. It is a good base for visiting the Fylde Coast and the Lakes.

Beer: Thomas Greenall Original Bitter, Stones Best Bitter on handpumps.

Accommodation: 1 single, 2 doubles, 3 twins, all rooms with bath or shower. B&B £14 per person. Children welcome.

WHITEWELL (LANCS)

Inn at Whitewell
Forest of Bowland, near Clitheroe, 9 miles from A59, off M6

Licensee: Richard Bowman
Tel: 02008 222

The inn is a superb whitewashed and mullioned building set in remote and lovely countryside. Parts date back to the 14th century, and it has Georgian and Victorian additions. It belongs to the Duchy of Lancaster and has extensive fishing rights on both banks of the river. Inside there are carved stone fireplaces, oak beams, wood panels and sonorously ticking antique clocks. The Hodder Bar has darts, dominoes and shove ha'penny. There is also an art gallery with work by artists from all over Britain and the inn acts as a wine merchant, which means there are exceptional vintages to enjoy if you prefer the grape to the grain. Home-cooked food includes soup, duck pâté, steak and kidney pie, fisherman's pie, seafood or savoury pancake, Cumberland sausage, courgette lasagne, Whitewell Trencher ploughman's (Stilton and Cheddar with apple, celery, pickled onion, hard-boiled egg and granary bread), Coniston cold smoked trout, and trout gravlax. Food is served as bar meals or in the restaurant. In warm weather you can sit on trestles in the garden and enjoy the splendour of the setting.

Beer: Moorhouse Premier Bitter and Pendle Witches Brew on handpumps.

Accommodation: 9 doubles: 6 can be let as family rooms and all as singles, all rooms with en suite or private facilities. B&B £38-£43 single, £39-£57 double. Children welcome, £9 in family room. Children welcome in public areas except pool room. Pets accepted. Cards: Access, Amex, Diners, Visa.

WIGAN (GREATER MANCHESTER)

Charles Dickens Hotel
Upper Dicconson Street, town centre

Licensee: G.E. Cowap
Tel: 0942 323263

The hotel has a splendid, traditional public bar that is justifiably popular with locals and visitors. Bar food is served lunchtime and evening and there is also a separate restaurant. A pianist adds to the lively bar atmosphere four nights a week.

Beer: Draught Bass, Marston Pedigree Bitter, Tetley Mild and Bitter, Whitbread Boddingtons Bitter and Flowers IPA on handpumps.

Accommodation: 9 singles, 5 doubles/twins. 2 family rooms, all rooms en suite. B&B £21 single, £30 double/twin, £37 family room. Pets welcome. Cards: Access and Visa.

LEICESTERSHIRE

ASHBY PARVA

Hollybush Inn
Main Street. Off M1 (Lutterworth exit 20) & A426; from north, exit 2 M6/M69/A5

Licensee: John Bayliss
Tel: 0455 209328
Fax: 0455 202588

John and Mary Bayliss have been running the Hollybush since 1979 and have carried out a great deal of careful renovation to introduce new bars and en suite guest rooms. The inn was previously known as the

Shoulder of Mutton. The building dates back to 1623 and has been a public house since 1879. Mr Bayliss lived in part of the property from six weeks of age until he was 23 and then returned in 1979 to buy the place. The Hollybush has a separate restaurant and a function room that caters for 80 people. Food is available lunchtime and evening and there is a traditional roast on Sunday (no restaurant meals Sunday evening). Ashby Parva is a charming and tranquil conservation village with riding stables; the local hunt often meets at the inn, which is a good base for the Midlands. Birmingham Airport and the NEC are 30 minutes away.

Beer: Marston Burton Bitter and Pedigree Bitter plus guest beers on handpumps.

Accommodation: 4 singles, 9 doubles/twins, 3 family rooms, 13 rooms with en suite facilities. Room prices: £20 single, £35 double/twin, £42 family. Breakfast £5.95 extra. Rates for children on request. Children's room. Cards: Access, Diners, Visa.

BELTON

George Hotel
17 Market Place. Off B5324 near Loughborough/M1 exits 23 & 24

Licensee: Hector Houston
Tel/fax: 0530 222426

The George is a large country inn dating from 1753, and noted for its excellent home-cooked food lunchtime and evening. It is next to an old church and has a maypole in the grounds. Guest rooms with en suite facilities also have TVs, telephones and tea and coffee makers. The hotel is handy for Donington Park race circuit and is close to the M1 and East Midlands airport.

Beer: Home Bitter, Younger Scotch and No 3 on handpumps.

Accommodation: 7 singles, 14 doubles, 2 family rooms, 17 rooms en suite. Room £23 single, £35 en suite, double £35/£45, family room £45/£55. Breakfast £3.75-£4.95. Children and dogs welcome. Cards: Access, Amex, Diners, Switch, Visa.

CLAYBROOKE MAGNA

Woodcutter Inn
Main Road. Junction of A5 & Fosse Way; 2 miles south of A5/M9 junction

Licensee: Malcolm Finch
Tel: 0455 209796

The Woodcutter is a 200-year-old pub in a small village where the A5 meets the Fosse Way. The cheery locals' bar has darts and table skittles while the wood-panelled lounge has a marble fireplace with an open log fire; the fireplace was obtained at the turn of the century from a local stately house. Food (lunchtime and evening) includes a traditional Sunday lunch and there are also steaks, duck and fish as well as vegetarian options.

Beer: Adnams Bitter, Marston Pedigree Bitter, Tetley Bitter and guest beers on handpumps.

Accommodation: 1 single, 2 doubles. B&B £16 single, £30 double. No pets. Cards: Access and Visa.

HINCKLEY

New Plough Hotel
24 Leicester Road, off A5 and M1

Licensee: Mary Swain
Tel: 0455 615037

There is a a warm and friendly welcome in the Plough with a real fire and wooden seats in the bar and a comfortable lounge. The locals call the pub the 'Vatican Arms' as there is a Roman Catholic church next door. Cheese table skittles are played in the pub, which has two ladies' teams. Guest rooms have TVs, tea and coffee makers and hot and cold water with a shared bathroom. Hinckley has a ruined castle.

Beer: Marston Burton Bitter and Pedigree Bitter on handpumps.

Accommodation: 1 single, 2 twins. B&B £17 per person.

LOUGHBOROUGH

Swan in the Rushes
21 The Rushes. A6, 5 minutes' walk from town centre

Manager: Rob Coupe
Tel: 0509 217014

The Swan is a fine example of a genuine and unspoilt town pub, with some fine exterior tile work. It was rebuilt in 1932 and was formerly the Charnwood until it was reopened as a free house in 1986. One of the two bars – the 'smart side' – has a parquet floor, and both bars have benches and stools and are served from a central bar. The plainer of the two bars has a juke box with classic pop hits, and a fruit machine; live blues are played at weekends. There is a separate room for breakfasts which can also be used by families at lunchtime and in the evening. Bar food is available lunchtime and evening (not Sunday evening) and is all home-cooked and comes chip-free; new cook Anna Cudbill has managed to improve on the previously high standard: a typical menu includes beef and mushrooms in Guinness, lamb

Madras, sausages and mash, avocado stuffed with tuna and egg mayonnaise, tuna and sweetcorn lasagne, vegetable goulash, spaghetti Bolognese and chilli con carne. The Swan is a good base for visiting Derby, Nottingham and the Peak District, and canal users can pull up just across the road. As well as impeccably kept cask beers, the Swan also has a splendid range of fine bottled beers, including Trappist beers from Belgium and such Czech delights as Pilsner Urquell and the genuine Budweiser Budvar.

Beer: Bateman XXXB, Marston Pedigree Bitter, Tetley Bitter and regular guest beers including one regular guest mild ale, all on handpumps.

Accommodation: 2 doubles/twins, 2 family rooms, 2 rooms en suite (all rooms no-smoking). B&B £20 single, £15 per person sharing, £25 single en suite, £17.50 double, £15 per person in family room. Discounts for group bookings, long stays and CAMRA members. Children's rates by negotiation. Pets welcome.

OAKHAM

Rutland Angler
6-8 Mill Street. Off A6

Licensees: John & Matthew Woods
Tel: 0572 755839

The Angler is a friendly and welcoming old Rutland pub, once Oakham's maternity hospital. Based in the historic market town, it is just 1½ miles from the vast man-made Rutland Water, with walks, bird-watching, sailing and fishing facilities. Satellite TV is available in the pub.

Beer: Marston Pedigree Bitter and Tolly Original on handpumps.

Accommodation: 4 singles, 3 twins, 1 double, 2 rooms with private baths. B&B £23.50 single, £39 double/twin, £46 with bath. Children welcome, terms by arrangement. Special rates for fishermen: £17 per night per person. No pets. Cards: Acces and Visa.

WHISSENDINE

White Lion
12 Main Street, 2 miles from Oakham-Melton Mowbray road (A6003)

Licensees: Steve Bebbington & Chris Hare
Tel: 0664 79233

The White Lion stands by the bridge over the Whissendine Brook. It has been an inn since the mid-1800s when the Earl of Harborough sold the building and the land. Whissendine is thought to come from the Anglo-Saxon 'whis' meaning tribe and 'dine', a narrow valley; the village was mentioned in the Domesday Book as Wichingdine. The pub is a cheery, friendly place with first-class food lunchtime and evening (no food Monday, or Sunday evening). Bar food includes soup, T-bone steak and vegetarian options; there is a separate restaurant. There is a strong emphasis on pub games: as well as darts and pool you can join in the rarer pub pastimes of Shut the Box and Devil Among the Tailors. There is a fine garden, where you can enjoy a drink and a meal in warm weather. The White Lion is well placed for Rutland Water and the lovely Vale of Belvoir.

Beer: Everard Tiger and Old Original on handpumps and regular guest beers.

Accommodation: 2 singles, 4 doubles, 1 family room. B&B £20 single,

White Lion, Whissendine

£30-£35 double, £35-£40 family. Children sharing parents' room £10 per night. Pets accepted. Cards: Access and Visa.

LINCOLNSHIRE

ASWARBY

Tally Ho
On A15 near Sleaford

Licensees: John Andrews & William Wood
Tel: 052 95 205

The Tally Ho is an 18th-century inn built of Ancaster stone and topped by a fine slate roof. It stands in fields and lovely parkland close to Sleaford. It is renowned for its lively and friendly atmosphere and the bar is the meeting and watering place of the local community. Traditional home-cooked food is served lunchtime and evening in the bar or separate restaurant. There are welcoming log fires in the winter and the guest rooms – in the tastefully modernized old stable block – have private baths, TVs and tea and coffee making facilities. It is a good base for visiting Stamford, Boston and Grantham.

Beer: Bateman XB and Marston Pedigree Bitter on handpumps and guest beers.

Accommodation: 6 doubles. B&B £28 single, £42 double. Weekend rates on request.

BOSTON

Carpenters Arms
Witham Street, off Wormgate

Licensee: R.K. Newberry
Tel: 0205 362840

The Carpenters is a lively, bustling pub hidden away in the small streets behind Boston Stump, the largest parish church in England with a tower that dominates the Fens and has acted as a navigation aid for sailors for centuries. The main bar of the pub is a meeting place for young and old, and there is imaginative lunchtime food – curries, pasta and vegetarian dishes. Evening food is by arrangement only. The four large guest rooms have brass bedsteads and pine furniture. Prices vary according to whether you want a full breakfast, continental or prefer to cook your own in the kitchen provided for early leavers. In Boston you can visit the church, the memorial to the Pilgrim Fathers, the Guildhall and the market place.

Beer: Bateman Mild, XB and XXXB on handpumps.

Accommodation: 4 doubles, including 2 family rooms. B&B from £15 per person. Half and full board available.

BURGH LE MARSH

White Hart Hotel
19-21 High Street. A158

Licensee: Karen Moody
Tel: 0754 810321

The White Hart is a comfortable and welcoming pub five miles from Skegness, a good base for touring the Lincolnshire coast and Tennyson region. The hotel has a pleasant lounge with a fine collection of

Crown Derby china, a lively public bar with games and juke box, and a separate restaurant called Harts; there are home-cooked meals in the bar and restaurant (no food Monday evenings). The charming guest rooms all offer tea and coffee making equipment.

Beer: Ansells Bitter, Bateman XB and XXXB and a guest beer on handpumps.

Accommodation: 6 doubles, 3 with en suite facilities. B&B £17.50 per person. Half and full board available. Cards: Access and Visa.

FREISTON

Castle Inn
Haltoft End. A52

Licensee: Mike Cassidy
Tel: 0205 760393

The Castle is an attractive inn four miles from Boston, with a comfortable and spacious bar with open fires in winter. This is a riproaring family pub with a superb adventure playground that includes an aerial runway and fishing boats. Bar food is served lunchtime and evening (not Sunday, or Tuesday evening); homemade steak and kidney pudding, rabbit and hare pies are pub specialities. The inn is well placed for visiting the Pilgrim Fathers' memorial near Fishtoft, and the Sibsey Traders Mill, a six-sailed windmill owned by English Heritage and open to the public.

Beer: Bateman Mild and XB, Draught Bass on handpumps.

Accommodation: 2 twins, 1 double with tea and coffee makers. B&B £27.50 per room. Reductions for more than 3 nights. Half board available. Dogs welcome.

SPILSBY

Red Lion Hotel
16 Market Street. A16, Grimsby to Boston road

Licensee: Wendy Cobb
Tel: 0790 53500

The Red Lion dates back to 1780 and has been thoroughly refurbished by the new owner, Mrs Cobb, who has sensitively kept and pointed-up many of the original features, such as brickwork and timbers and parts of the old reed ceiling. Bar food is available lunchtime. Live entertainment is a popular feature of the pub and a small dance floor has been installed. Darts, pool and dominoes are played, and the local cricket and football teams meet in the Red Lion. Spilsby is a busy market town on the edge of the Wolds. It is close to Somersby, Alfred Lord Tennyson's birthplace. The parish church of St James has a monument to Captain Sir John Franklin, the Arctic navigator who discovered the North-West Passage linking the Atlantic and the Pacific; there is a bronze statue of him in the market place. The great east coast seaside resort of Skegness is just 10 miles away.

Beer: Bateman XB and XXXB, John Smith's Bitter and Theakstons Best Bitter on handpumps.

Accommodation: 2 doubles/twins, 1 family room. B&B £18 per person. Pets welcome.

STAMFORD

Bull & Swan Inn
High Street, St Martins. B1081 south side of town, just off A1

Licensee: David J. Wood
Tel: 0780 63558

The Bull & Swan is a fine stone-built coaching inn in one of England's loveliest historic old towns. The inn has open fireplaces in each room of its three-level bar, low beams hung with copper kettles and comfortable plush seating. Bar food is served lunchtime and evening and includes such daily specials as avocado with prawns, homemade terrine of duck, devilled chicken liver and rice, moules marinière, salmon fishcakes in seafood sauce, lamb curry, Irish stew, vegetarian dishes on request, and homemade desserts. There is a separate restaurant (Thurs, Fri and Sat evenings and Sunday lunch). Stamford, the town of five steeples, has many quaint old passageways to wander through. Burghley House, famous for its horse trials, is just round the corner from the inn.

Beer: Cameron Strongarm and Tolly Original on handpumps (beer range liable to change).

Accommodation: 5 doubles, 2 family, 5 rooms en suite. B&B £28-£31 single, £32-£44 double, £51-£58 family room. Babies in cots £3. Winter Breaks Oct-Feb: weekend (Friday & Saturday or Saturday & Sunday) £98 for 2 B&B plus dinner. Lounge for families. Pets by prior arrangement. Cards: Access and Visa.

Daniel Lambert
20 St Leonard's Street. B1081 from A1, then A16 Spalding road

Licensee: Mrs Keithel H. White
Tel: 0780 55991

The Daniel Lambert is a listed Georgian building of pleasing mellow stone. It is named after the world's largest man; there is a model of him in the town's museum. Bar meals – rolls and toasted sandwiches – are served lunchtime and evening.

Bull & Swan Inn, Stamford

Beer: Timothy Taylor Best Bitter and Landlord on handpumps.

Accommodation: 3 twins. B&B £15 per person. Children 0-3 years free, 4-8 half price. Pets accepted.

WAINFLEET

Woolpack Hotel
39 High Street. A52

Licensee: Terry Chappell
Tel: 0754 880353

The Woolpack has been a licensed hostelry since the 18th century, though the building is older. Marked on the front of the hotel is one of the four measuring points for spring and winter tides to be found in the town. Home-cooked food, using locally grown fresh vegetables, is served every day (not Monday evenings) in either the lounge or the dining room and ranges from steak and kidney pie to steak and grills, with a traditional Sunday roast. Wainfleet is the home of Bateman's brewery, saved from extinction in the mid-1980s by George Bateman, his wife Pat and his son and daughter Stuart and Jackie, when other members of the family wanted to sell up and retire to the sun. The brewery's tasty, fruity mild and bitters have won several awards at CAMRA beer festivals.

Beer: Bateman Mild, XB and XXXB, Home Bitter on handpumps.

Accommodation: 2 doubles/twins, 3 family rooms. B&B £14 per person. Children half price sharing a family room. Baby-sitting service available. No dogs.

CHISLEHURST

Bulls Head Hotel
Royal Parade. From A20 take A222 to Chislehurst; turn left at crossroads by memorial; pub 250 yards on right

Licensee: Michael Chappell
Tel: 081-467 1727
Fax: 081-467 5931

Chislehurst, once of Kent, has been swallowed by the Great Wen of London. The Bulls Head is an 18th-century Georgian-style listed building opposite Scadbury Nature Reserve. The name of the hotel comes from the badge of the aristocratic Neville family who fought in the Wars of the Roses, while the address derives from the fact that the family of the deposed Nicholas III of France lived locally in the 1870s. Lunchtime bar food is served Monday to Saturday and a 60-seater restaurant is open lunchtime and evening.

Beer: Youngs Bitter, Special Bitter and Winter Warmer on handpumps.

Accommodation: 5 doubles, all en suite. B&B £68 single, £76 double. No pets. Cards: Access, Amex, Diners, Visa.

CLAPHAM SW4

Olde Windmill Inn
Clapham Common South Side, A24. Clapham Common Underground

Licensee: Richard Williamson
Tel: 081-673 4578

The Windmill is just a few yards from an old Roman road that has been carrying traffic for more than 19 centuries. An inn has stood on the site since 1665, and the mill from which it took its name was once the winning post for the Clapham Races.

The present building is largely Victorian in origin and the vast main bar has windmill pictures on the walls and seats and sofas round tables. Bar food includes ploughman's, chilli, curries and salads. There are terrace seats outside, and in good weather the crowds of drinkers spill out on to the common. Accommodation is in an adjoining house that was once the home of the founder of Young's brewery. There is a resident ghost known as Croaker.

Beer: Youngs Bitter, Special Bitter and Winter Warmer on handpumps.

Accommodation: 9 singles, 4 doubles, 1 room with private bath. B&B £33 single, £42 double. No pets. Cards: Access, Amex, Diners, Visa.

GREENFORD

Bridge Hotel
Western Avenue, A41. Greenford Underground

Manager: Natasha Parsons
Tel: 081-566 6246
Fax: 081-566 6140

The Bridge, a striking gabled building, has been carefully extended by Young's Brewery to offer top-quality accommodation. It has been a pub since 1932, and always in the hands of the Wandsworth brewery. The lounge and saloon bars have the original wood panelling and open fireplaces. Bar food is served every lunchtime except Sunday and the candle-lit and intimate restaurant is open lunchtime and evening. The guest rooms are on three floors and include no-smoking rooms and two rooms designed for disabled people.

Beer: Youngs Bitter and Special Bitter on handpumps.

Accommodation: 68 rooms, all en suite. B&B £80 single, £90 double. Children free if sharing with parents. Residents' lounge. Pets accepted. Cards: Access, Amex, Diners, Switch, Visa.

HOUNSLOW

Master Robert
Great West Road, A4. 5 minutes from Heathrow airport. Heathrow Underground; Hounslow BR and Underground; 1 mile from M4 exit 3; 3 miles from M25 exit 4A

Griffin Inns managed hotel
Tel: 081-570 6261
Fax: 081-569 4016

There was a pub called the Robert Inn on the site from 1845. It has been incorporated into the hotel, run by a subsidiary of Fuller's brewery, and renamed after the 1924 winner of the Grand National steeplechase. Additional rooms have been added in the past few years and the entire site is set in five acres of landscaped gardens. Hot and cold buffet meals are available lunchtimes Monday to Saturday, while a restaurant is open all day throughout the week, serving steaks, pies and two roasts from a carvery. Local places of interest include Syon Park, Kew Gardens, Hampton Court and Windsor Castle. Cask beers are served in the pub bar only.

Beer: Fullers Chiswick Bitter, London Pride and Mr Harry (winter), all on handpumps.

Accommodation: 10 singles, 70 doubles, 16 family rooms, all with en suite facilities. B&B £55 single, £65 double and family room. Children free when sharing with adults. Weekend £42 single, £55 double. Residents' lounge. Pets accepted. Cards: Access, Amex, Diners, Visa.

ATTLEBOROUGH

Griffin Hotel
Church Street. A11

Licensee: Richard Ashbourne
Tel: 0953 452149

The Griffin, a 16th-century coaching inn in the town centre, has been sensitively restored by the Ashbournes in the past two years. It has half timbers and a low-slung roof outside, and beams and open fires inside, and a fine welcome from staff and locals. The walls and fires are decorated with old shields, brass jugs, china and guns. There are excellent bar snacks, ranging from a three-course meal to a sandwich, and usually locally caught fresh fish, while the separate restaurant is open Monday to Saturday evenings, with a traditional roast lunch on Sundays. The guest rooms are centrally heated and are equipped with TVs. Attleborough is close to Snetterton race circuit and Sunday Market, and Banham Zoo.

Beer: Greene King Abbot Ale, Marston Pedigree Bitter, Whitbread Wethered Bitter on handpumps, with a weekly guest beer and local cider.

Accommodation: 1 single, 7 doubles. B&B £20 single, £40 double, £50 family room. 10% reduction for week's stay. Children welcome to stay, no reductions. Pets welcome.

BROCKDISH

Olde Kings Head
The Street. 5 miles east of Scole on A143

Licensees: David & Helen Dedman
Tel: 0379 75 8125

The Kings Head is a rambling

17th-century coaching inn with heavily beamed lounge bar and restaurant, a large open fire in the lounge, and a separate games room where darts and pool are played. Bar snacks such as ploughman's are served lunchtime and evening, including a children's menu. There is a separate restaurant menu and a traditional Sunday roast. The inn is situated in the picturesque Waveney valley, a fine base for touring East Anglia and close to the Otter Trust, Bressingham Gardens and Steam Museum and the Broads. David Dedman says his Adnams Bitter is 'better than the brewery can produce: they keep saying I put something in it, but I don't!'

Beer: Adnams Bitter and Broadside and guest beers on handpumps.

Accommodation: 6 doubles/twins, 1 family room, all with en suite facilities. B&B £19 single, £32 double, £32 family room plus £8 per child. Residents' family room. Pets welcome. Cards: Access and Visa.

CLEY-NEXT-THE-SEA

George & Dragon Hotel
High Street, A149 near Holt

Licensee: Rodney Sewell
Tel: 0263 740652

This historic building was rebuilt in 1897 but dates from the 17th century. It stands in one of the prettiest villages in North Norfolk in an area of bleak beauty by the salt marshes leading down to the sea. It is ideal bird-watching territory and the George & Dragon has a room dedicated to the Norfolk Naturalist Trust which was founded in the hotel in 1926. There are boat trips to see the seals on the point. The pub has many 'G&D' artefacts, including a stained glass window of England's patron saint slaying the mythical beast. Bar meals are served lunchtime and evening, and include local crab and lobster in season, mussels, venison, specialities from the village's own smoke house and pan haggerty – baked layers of cheese, onion and potato with three slices of bacon, two sausages and tomato. There is a large beer garden. Families are welcome and there is a newly created internal hide lounge for residents overlooking the hotel's own enlarged 'scrape' or shallow lake, an ideal hidey-hole for keen bird-watchers.

Beer: Greene King IPA and Abbot Ale on handpumps, with regular guest beers including Bateman's.

Accommodation: 8 doubles including 1 en suite family room, 4 doubles en suite, including a four-poster and twin-bedded room en suite. B&B £20-£35. Facilities for the disabled.

CROMER

Bath House
The Promenade. Off A149

Tel: 0263 514260
Licensees: Bertram & Barbara Wheston

The Bath House is a lovingly restored and elegant Regency inn on the promenade of this fine Victorian seaside resort, the county's most northerly coastal town, famous for its crab fishing, sea fret or mist and small lifeboat museum. The pub was built by Simeon Simon in 1822 as a bath house, and became so celebrated that it was frequented by the likes of Clement Scott and the poet Swinburne. It flourished until the turn of the century when it was converted to an inn with letting rooms. The guest rooms of the Bath House are on the first floor and most have views of the sea. All the rooms

Bath House, Cromer

are en suite and have central heating, colour TVs and tea and coffee makers. There is a residents' lounge, seats on the prom, and excellent lunches and evening meals (every day) including homemade soup, wings of fire, deep fried mushrooms with garlic dip, steak and Guinness pie, lasagne, prawn or chicken curry, cheese and potato bake, steaks, plaice or cod, mariner's fish bake, Cromer crab salad, ploughman's, and sweets. The inn is just a few yards from the beach, the pier and the crab landing area.

Beer: Greene King Abbot Ale, Sam Smith Old Brewery Bitter and Tolly Original plus such regular guest beers as Bateman's and Felinfoel Double Dragon, all on handpumps.

Accommodation: 4 doubles, 3 twins, all en suite. B&B £24.50 per person. Off-season 3-Day Bargain Breaks £88 dinner, B&B. No pets. Cards: Access, Amex, Visa.

Red Lion Hotel
Brook Street

Licensee: Miss V.E. Medler
Tel: 0263 514964

The Red Lion is a large and welcoming hotel with two bars, one with an interior flint wall, the second with wood and glass panels and two open fires, both linked by the long serving area. A third small bar adjoins Galliano's evening restaurant. Bar food, served lunchtime and evening, includes four special dishes of the day plus steaks, chicken, salads and sandwiches. The hotel has impressive views overlooking the promenade and the sea and is just a few yards from Cromer's fine flint-faced church. There is also a function room catering for up to 60 people.

Beer: Adnams Bitter, Draught Bass, Greene King Abbot Ale and one guest beer on handpumps.

Accommodation: 1 single, 11 doubles/twins, 1 family room, 12 rooms with en suite facilities. B&B £35 per person. Children 3 and over half price sharing with parents. Mon-Thurs only 2 or more nights £25 per person per night, £20 third night. Residents' area for children. No pets. Cards: Access, Amex, Visa.

DISS

Cock Inn
Fair Green. Off A1066

Licensee: Stevan Moyard
Tel: 0379 643633

The Cock is 300 years old and stands on the Thetford and Scole road, overlooking Fair Green. A few miles away at Redgrave two rivers, the Waveney and the Little Ouse, spring from the same well and flow in opposite directions. The inn's guest rooms include one four-poster; and bar snacks are available.

Beer: Adnams Mild and Bitter, Greene King XX Mild and IPA on handpumps.

Accommodation: 1 single, 1 double. B&B £20 single, £36 double.

DOWNHAM MARKET

Crown Hotel
Bridge Street, close to market square and town clock. Off A10

Proprietor: John Champion
Tel: 0366 382322

The Crown's small frontage on Bridge Street belies the scope of the old inn that lies down a long and narrow cobbled yard to the side. The earliest parts are thought to have been built on the site of a medieval monks' hospice. It was the headquarters of the Downham Cavalry in the early 19th century and became an important coaching inn on the London to King's Lynn, Norwich and Peterborough routes. Today it is listed as a building of historical and architectural interest and its rooms retain their old atmosphere with exposed beams, bare brick walls and, in the bar, two open fireplaces. The more recent history of the area is captured by many photos of air crews stationed nearby during the Second World War. Mr Champion is well named for he is indeed the champion of independent brewers in eastern England, and serves their ales in the bar, along with lunchtime bar meals ranging from rolls to hot dishes of the day. Lunch and dinner are served in the adjoining restaurant.

Beer: Bateman XB, Draught Bass, Greene King Abbot Ale, Woodforde Wherry Best Bitter and weekly guest beer, all on handpumps.

Accommodation: 1 single, 9 doubles/ twins, 7 rooms with en suite facilities. B&B £24 single, £32 en suite, £34 double room, £42 en suite. 2 interconnecting rooms can be arranged as a family room. Children's rates depend on age and sleeping arrangements. Weekend rates on application. Pets welcome. Cards: Access, Amex, Diners, Visa.

GREAT BIRCHAM

King's Head Hotel
Lynn Road. B1153 off A148

Licensee: I. Verrando
Tel: 048 523 265

The King's Head is a handsome

country inn with steeply sloping roofs, tall chimneys and dormer windows. It is close to Sandringham and the Peddars Way. There is a gracious lawn for warm weather eating and drinking. Bar meals are available lunchtime and evening and the candlelit restaurant uses local produce for its varied menu: it is renowned for the quality of its beef and shellfish dishes. There is a traditional roast at Sunday lunchtimes. The guest rooms all have baths or showers, TVs and tea and coffee making facilities.

Beer: Adnams Bitter, Draught Bass and Charrington IPA on handpumps.

Accommodation: 3 twins, 2 doubles. B&B £27.50 per person double occupancy. Cards: Access and Visa.

HOLKHAM

Victoria Hotel
On A149

Licensees: Mr & Mrs Victor Manning
Tel: 0328 710469

The Victoria is a late 19th-century brick and flint hotel on the North Norfolk coast road. It stands opposite the long drive that leads down to the great sweep of Holkham beach and wildlife reserve, one of the finest coastal stretches in eastern England. The bar enjoys darts, dominoes, crib and shove ha'penny, while the pleasant lounge has bay windows with fine views of the coast. There are tables in the old stableyard in summer. Bar meals include soups, ploughman's, sandwiches, salads, steaks and local fish and shellfish: new licensees are extending the range. There is a residents' TV lounge and the guest rooms have all been upgraded to en suite status and have colour TV and tea and coffee making facilities. Holkham Hall, open to the public, is close by.

Beer: Greene King IPA and Marston Pedigree Bitter on handpump.

Accommodation: 6 twins en suite. B&B £30 single, £55 twin. Children and pets welcome, children's rates on application. Cards: Access and Visa.

Near KING'S LYNN

Red Cat Hotel
Station Road, North Wootton. 1½ miles off A148 & A149

Licensee: Peter Irwin
Tel: 0553 631244

Peter Irwin is a former chairman of the local branch of CAMRA, so you can be assured of a good pint in his popular marshland real ale oasis near the Wash, close to the ancient monument at Castle Rising. The Red Cat is a two crown English Tourist Board hotel, faced with carrstone and dating back to the beginning of the last century. Good value bar snacks are available at all times and cooked evening meals are available in a fine beamed dining room. The comfortable guest rooms have tea and coffee making facilities and all have en suite showers or baths. The original red cat has pride of place in the bar and the pub named after it has a large garden, family room and open fires.

Beer: Red Cat Special Bitter is brewed for the pub by Woodforde, plus Adnams Bitter and Old (winter), Draught Bass and frequent guest beers on handpumps and seasonal old ales straight from the cask.

Accommodation: 3 singles, 2 doubles, 1 twin, 1 family room. B&B £31 single, £42-£45 double/twin, £50

family room. Children are included in family room price. *Beer, Bed and Breakfast* rates on request. Pets welcome. Cards: Access and Visa.

Farmers Arms (Knights Hill Hotel)
Knights Hill Village, South Wootton. Junction of A148 & A149

Licensees: H.J. Darking & M.J. Halls
Tel: 0553 675566
Fax: 0553 675568

The Farmers Arms is a pub in an eleven-acre farm complex that includes a hotel and restaurant. The pantiled and carstone buildings have been converted from old stables, byres and a grain store, and the pub has a wealth of exposed beams, open fireplaces and cobbled floors. Above the bar, the old grain store, the Hayloft, is used for entertainment. Food is served from 11am to 10pm and the same menu is used in the pub and the restaurant, ranging from homemade soup, farmhouse terrine or Farmers Boots (filled jacket potatoes) to lemon sole, gamekeeper's pie, baked lasagne, duck, grills, vegetarian pasta and vegeburger and a children's choice. The complex has facilities for conferences and many indoor sporting activities. All the guest rooms have en suite facilities, colour TVs, direct-dial phones and tea and coffee making equipment. The hotel is a good base for visiting Sandringham, Castle Rising, Holkham and Houghton Halls, and King's Lynn. There are superb golf courses in the area.

Beer: Adnams Bitter and Broadside, Draught Bass, Charrington IPA and Worthington Best Bitter, Ruddles County, Sam Smith Old Brewery Bitter and regular guest beers, all on handpumps.

Accommodation: 8 singles, 46 doubles/twins. Room from £58.50 single, £68.50 double or twin. Full breakfast £6.25 extra, continental £3.50. Children under 15 free when sharing with adults. Dogs allowed in restricted areas. Cards: Access, Amex, Diners, Visa.

MUNDESLEY

Royal Hotel
30 Paston Road. A1159

Licensee: Michael Fotis
Tel: 0263 720096

The Royal is a 300-year-old inn with superb views of the sea from Mundesley cliffs, with original beams and timbers and strong connections with Admiral Lord Nelson, who stayed at the inn while he attended Paston school in North Walsham. The pub was known as the New Inn in those days, and the change of name followed a visit by royalty in the late 18th century. The Nelson Bar of the hotel has splendid bar meals that feature locally caught fish and shellfish as well as cold meats and salads. The separate Buttery is open for lunch and dinner. The guest rooms all have private baths or showers, colour TVs, radios and tea and coffee making equipment. The hotel is a good base for visiting the many delights of North Norfolk, including the shrine to Our Lady of Walsingham, Blakeney, the pleasant seaside resort of Sheringham and its steam railway, and miles of unspoilt coast.

Beer: Adnams Bitter and Old, Greene King IPA and Abbot Ale, Sam Smith Old Brewery Bitter and guest beer on handpumps.

Accommodation: 26 singles/twins, 14 doubles. B&B £29.95 single, £45

double. Weekend (2 nights) £75 double, £79 four-poster. Children welcome, generous reductions. Cards: Access, Amex, Diners, Visa.

MUNDFORD

Crown Hotel
Near Thetford. Off A134 & A1065

Licensee: John A. Maling
Tel: 0842 878233

The Crown is a 17th-century coaching inn, a listed building in the centre of an old village overlooking the green. The hotel has a wealth of old beams and low ceilings and is a maze of different levels as it is set into the side of a hill. There is a patio garden. Food is served in the bars or restaurant, and à la carte or table d'hôte menus are available, based on fresh local vegetables and a wealth of local produce; there are vegetarian options. The guest rooms are all en suite and include a four-poster bed in one room.

Beer: Ruddles County and Websters Yorkshire Bitter, Woodforde Wherry Best Bitter and Nelson's Revenge on handpumps.

Accommodation: 2 singles, 2 twins, 2 doubles. B&B from £25 single, £45 double. Children under 12 half price. Residents' lounge. Pets welcome. Cards: Access, Amex, Diners, Visa.

NEATISHEAD

Barton Angler Country Inn
A1151 from Norwich through Wroxham; turn right to Barton Turf/Neatishead; in Neatishead village take road to Irstead, adjacent to Saddlery restaurant

Licensee: Tim King
Tel: 0692 630740

The Barton Angler is an elegant 400-year-old hotel on the banks of lovely Barton Broad, 280 acres of Anglian water where Nelson learnt to sail. The hotel can arrange for dinghy and boat hire. It has large, sweeping, flower-filled gardens. The Tangler Bar has a log fire and oak beams and offers home-cooked bar food, such as steak and ale pie and oxtail casserole, every lunchtime and evening. The restaurant, built over the hotel in Georgian times, is elegantly decorated with antiques and a Honduras mahogany bar; à la carte meals are served here Thursday to Saturday evenings, and include such specialities as devilled chicken and pork in cider.

Beer: Greene King IPA, Rayments Special Bitter and Abbot Ale on handpumps.

Accommodation: 3 singles, 4 doubles, 5 rooms with en suite facilities. B&B £20 single, £27.50 double. Prices include continental breakfast; full English breakfast £5 extra. Reduced prices for 2 and 7 night stays. Children's rates on request. No pets. Cards: Access, Amex, Visa.

ORMESBY ST MARGARET

Grange Hotel
Yarmouth Road, off A149 & B1159

Proprietors: Pearl & Roy Smith
Tel/fax: 0493 731877

The Grange is a former Georgian country house in two acres of grounds that include a children's log cabin, a pets' corner and an adventure playground. It is an ideal family pub with a room for children and parents inside, too. The bars offer excellent food while the guest rooms have colour TVs, phones and tea and coffee making facilities. There are also self-catering cottages. The Grange is a good base for visiting Caister Castle and car museum, Thrigby wildlife park and local beaches and golf courses.

Beer: Adnams Bitter, Bateman XXXB and Charrington IPA with one guest beer on handpumps.

Accommodation: Bed and continental breakfast: £30 single, £35 double en suite, £45 family room. Self-catering cottages £180 a week low season, £200 high season, up to 4 people sharing. Cards: Access and Visa.

SCOLE

Scole Inn
The Street. A140 midway between Norwich & Ipswich

Licensees: Phil & Jan Hills
Tel: 0379 740481
Fax: 0379 740762

The Scole is a famous old East of England 17th-century coaching inn and a grade one listed building. Its most famous claim to fame – its inn sign – no longer exists. When village carpenter John Fairchild was commissioned by a wealthy Norwich wool merchant, John Peck, to build the inn, he added a gallows sign that straddled the road and cost the astonishing sum for 1655 of £1,057. It included many mythical and classical figures, including Neptune rising from the waves, with pride of place going to a white hart, the inn's original name. It was demolished about 250 years later, but an engraving of it by Joshua Kirby hangs in the bar. The notorious highwayman John Belcher used the inn as his headquarters. The inn today retains many of its original features, with a wealth of beams, oak doors and inglenook fireplaces. There is both good bar food and a separate restaurant. Food in the bar is waitress-served and includes homemade soup, ploughman's, steaks, crab salad, steak and kidney pie, and such homemade pâtés as Stilton, celery and port or smoked salmon.

Beer: Adnams Bitter and Broadside, Draught Bass on handpumps.

Accommodation: 20 doubles, 3 family rooms, all with en suite facilities, 12 rooms in converted stable block. B&B £46-£51 single, £63.50-£71.75 double, £63.50 family room. Bargain Breaks from £66.50 per person sharing double room for any 2 nights B&B plus dinner. Pets accepted. Cards: Access, Amex, Diners, Visa.

THORNHAM

Lifeboat Inn
Ship Lane, ½ mile off A149; 4 miles north-east of Hunstanton

Licensees: Nicholas & Lynn Handley
Tel: 048 526 236/297
Fax: 048 526 323

You wake in the Lifeboat's large and comfortable rooms to the sound of the sea and both doves cooing and cows mooing across the road. It is a wonderful old pub on the edge of the vast salt flats that lead to the sea and across which smugglers struggled with their contraband centuries ago. The Lifeboat, a series of small rooms, has low beams, five crackling log fires in winter, oil and gas lamps, and pub games that include darts, shove ha'penny and a penny-in-the-hole bench. Although it can be cold outside in winter, the pub has a flourishing vine in a terrace at the

Scole Inn, Scole

back. There are a few seats at the front, and the back garden has seats among the trees, a climbing frame and toys for children, and a donkey. Splendid bar food (lunchtime and evening every day) concentrates on homemade dishes such as soups, ploughman's, pasta, cheese and onion quiche, potted shrimps, lamb stew, mussels, fresh local fried fish, game pie, steaks, sandwiches and homemade ice creams. The small candle-lit restaurant (evening every day) has à la carte meals that include local seafood and game. A fine place to stay, eat and drink. The accommodation has been extended considerably from the last issue of the guide, and all rooms have en suite facilities.

Beer: Adnams Bitter, Greene King IPA and Abbot Ale on handpumps and straight from the cask, plus such guest beers as Tetley and Woodforde.

Accommodation: 13 doubles/twins; 3 rooms can be used as family rooms with addition of single bed. B&B £35 single, £60 double, £70 family room with extra bed. £10 for children sharing; no charge for babies in travel cots; £2 for baby in pub cot. Pets accepted. Cards: Access, Amex, Diners, Visa.

WELLS-NEXT-THE-SEA

Crown Hotel
The Buttlands. Off A149

Licensee: Wilfred Foyers
Tel: 0328 710209

The Crown is charmingly placed by a large green in this picturesque old sea port that is these days also a good hunting ground for buyers of antique furniture and paintings. The old coaching inn has a popular bar with a

piano and good bar food that includes soup, ploughman's, omelettes, vegetarian tagliatelle, crab, steaks, and steak and kidney pie. There are separate dishes for children. The separate restaurant has no fewer than four chefs and offers acclaimed French and English cooking. There is a conservatory and also seats in a courtyard. Wells is a delightful town to stroll in, and is close to Blakeney, Holkham Hall, the North Norfolk Heritage Coast and Sandringham.

Beer: Adnams Bitter, Marston Pedigree Bitter and Tetley Bitter on handpumps.

Accommodation: 1 single, 12 doubles, 2 family rooms. 10 rooms with en suite facilities. B&B from £27 per person. Weekend from £75 for dinner B&B, Week from £262.50. Children's room; children welcome to stay, reductions on application. Cards: Access, Amex, Diners and Visa.

WOLTERTON

Saracen's Head
Off A140, 1½ miles from Erpingham

Licensees: Robert Dawson-Smith & Iain Bryson
Tel: 0263 768909

The Saracen's Head is of unusual design even by Norfolk standards. It is modelled on a Tuscan farmhouse and was built by Horace Walpole as a coaching inn for nearby Wolterton Hall. Bar food, available lunchtime and evening, includes soups, homemade pies, fried aubergines, seafood, steaks and rustic lunches. There is a separate restaurant for lunch and dinner. Throughout the year there are regular feasts for a minimum of 12 people, including seafood and game.

Beer: Adnams Bitter and Broadside and one weekly guest beer, all on handpumps.

Accommodation: 3 doubles, all en suite. B&B £25-£35. Children by arrangement. Pets welcome. Cards: Access, Amex, Visa.

NORTHAMPTONSHIRE

ASHBY ST LEDGERS

Olde Coach House Inn
Off A361 between Daventry & Rugby; 4 miles from M1 exit 18

Licensees: Brian & Philippa McCabe
Tel: 0788 890349
Fax: 0604 20818

Accommodation at the Olde Coach House includes stabling for horses,

recalling the time when the stone buildings were a farm with the front room set aside as a bar. Careful restoration in recent years has discovered wonderful old inglenooks and stone floors from the time a hundred years ago when it was first built as a rural pub. The many small rooms have settle chairs, farm kitchen tables, old harnesses and hunting prints. Table skittles, darts and dominoes are played in the front bar. The spacious garden has a climbing frame and swings for children and there are summer barbecues. Bar food includes such daily specials as game, steaks, fresh fish and homemade desserts, while regulars on the menu are Danish herring, mushrooms, chicken, sweet and sour pork, and bacon, lettuce and tomato on a French stick. There is a children's menu and a traditional roast lunch on Sundays. The lovely old village has stone and thatch cottages and the Gunpowder Plot was hatched in the

Olde Coach House Inn, Ashby St Ledgers

manor, Althorp Hall.

Beer: Everards Tiger and Old
Original, Whitbread Boddingtons
Bitter and Flowers Original and two
guest ales on handpumps.

Accommodation: 5 doubles/twins, 1
family room, all with en suite
facilities. B&B £38 single, £22.50 per
person double/twin, £22.50 per adult
(max 2) in family room, £10 extra
adult, £5 child under 12, £10 over 12.
Pets accepted. Cards: Access and
Visa.

BLAKESLEY

Bartholomew Arms
High Street, 4 miles off A5; 4 miles
off A43 at Silverstone

Licensee: Tony Hackett
Tel: 0327 860292

A cheerful village local with, says Mr
Hackett, no gimmicks – no pool, juke
box, space invaders or plastic food.
'We offer good beer and company.'
The beamed bars are packed with
cricketing memorabilia, nautical
artefacts, hams, guns and 96 malt
whiskies. Excellent bar food is served
at lunchtime, with a limited choice in
the evening. All the guest rooms have
colour TVs and central heating. The
pub is a good base for Towcester and
its race course and the Silverstone
motor racing circuit.

Beer: Marston Pedigree Bitter and
Ruddles County on handpump.

Accommodation: 1 single, 4 doubles,
1 room with en suite facilities. B&B
£18 per person. Full board available.
Children welcome, 40% reduction.
Pets accepted.

Near SILVERSTONE

Green Man Inn
Brackley Hatch. A45, 1 mile south of
Silverstone

Manager: Judy Webb
Tel: 0280 850209
Fax: 0280 850532

The Green Man is a remarkable pub,
a former 16th-century coaching inn
that still retains much of its old charm
and atmosphere inside with log fires
and original beams. It has been
developed brilliantly as a family pub
and the large landscaped gardens are a
paradise for children and tired
parents. There are swings and
climbing frames and a cabin when the
weather is not kind: special children's
menus are available there. The large,
airy conservatory is also used by
families. If you want to get away
from the kids for an hour or two, the
small restaurant at the far end of the
inn, away from the gardens, will
provide sanctuary. Food is served in
the bar and restaurant. The Green
Man is close to Silverstone motor
racing circuit and five miles from
Towcester racecourse.

Beer: Whitbread Boddingtons Bitter
on handpumps.

Accommodation: 9 doubles/twins, 4
with en suite facilities, 1 room with
sauna. B&B from £25 per person
sharing. Cards: Access, Amex,
Diners, Visa.

TOWCESTER

Sun Inn
36 Watling Street. A5, M1 junction
15

Licensee: E. Tomlin
Tel: 0327 50580

The Sun is one of the oldest pubs in Towcester and stands on the old Roman Watling Street. The exterior is striking, with bowed windows on the ground floor and a great dormer in the steeply sloping roof. The building dates from 1650 when it was a coaching inn. At one stage of its history it doubled as a mineral factory, using water from a natural well under the restaurant area. The home-cooked menu changes daily and may include chicken casserole, chilli, steak pie and cottage pie.

Beer: Bateman XB, Hook Norton Best Bitter and Old Hooky, Marston Pedigree Bitter and regular guest beer on handpumps.

Accommodation: 1 single, 4 doubles, 4 twins, all with private facilities. B&B £35 single, £40 double/twin, £45 family. Children and pets welcome. Cards: Access and Visa.

WEEDON

Globe Hotel
High Street. Junction of A45 & A5. 3 miles from M1 exit 16; 8 miles west of Northampton

Licensees: Peter & Penny Walton
Tel: 0327 40336
Fax: 0327 349058

The Globe is a modernized and extended early 19th-century posting house on the junction of the A45 and Watling Street. The Waltons have launched a programme of careful and tasteful refurbishment to the lovely old buildings in order to offer the best of both the old and the new worlds, along with first-class cuisine and guest rooms with en suite facilities. The Globe Pantry serves food all day and offers soup, smoked mackerel, meat and vegetable curries, beef in beer, fisherman's bake, grilled

trout, steaks, salads, vegetarian dishes of the day, and, for children, chicken nuggets, fish fingers or beefburgers. There is a separate lunch and evening à la carte restaurant. The Globe overlooks rolling countryside and is a good base for visiting the site of Naseby civil war battlefield, Sulgrave Manor, Althorp House, Banbury, Stratford, Warwick, Silverstone grand prix circuit and Milton Keynes.

Beer: Marston Pedigree Bitter, Ruddles County and a guest beer on handpumps.

Accommodation: 4 singles, 11 doubles, 3 family rooms, all en suite. B&B £40.50 single, £55 double. Weekend 2/3 nights £39.95 double per night. Children free under 8 sharing. Children's room. Pets welcome. Cards: Access, Amex, Diners, Visa.

NORTHUMBERLAND

ALLENDALE

Hare & Hounds
The Peth, just off Market Square towards River Allen. A6303, Alston road

Licensee: Alexander Fernyhough
Tel: 0434 683300

The Hare & Hounds is a fine old 18th-century coaching inn standing in beautiful countryside near the Cumbrian and Durham borders. It is a vigorously old-fashioned hostelry, with stone floors and open fires in the bar and lounge. It is a good base for touring the wild and unspoilt Northumberland moors and forests. Mr Fernyhough serves food lunchtime and evening, and there is a separate restaurant in the summer months. The bars are quiet and free from intrusive canned music.

Beer: Ruddles Best Bitter and County on handpumps.

Accommodation: 2 doubles, 1 family room, all rooms en suite. B&B £17.50 per person. Child sharing £5. No pets.

ALNMOUTH

Schooner Hotel
Northumberland Street. 5 miles off A1

Proprietor: G.T. Orde
Tel: 0665 830216

The Schooner is a beautifully restored Georgian coaching inn and has been the hub of local life for many years in this lovely seaside village of tumbling streets, bordered by water on three sides. John Wesley described Alnmouth in 1748 as 'a small seaport town famous for all kinds of wickedness', which must add to its attractions. The exterior of the Schooner is striking, with its many shuttered windows. It has two cheerful and welcoming bars and pool, darts and dominoes are played. Bar meals are available lunchtime and evening and include fresh local lemon sole, Northumbrian game pie and pan haggerty hot-pot. There is a choice of menus in the Malcolm Miller evening restaurant or the Mediterranean atmosphere of the Casa Edro Italian restaurant. All the guest rooms in the hotel have en suite facilities, colour TVs and in-house videos, phones and tea and coffee making equipment. The Schooner has a squash court and solarium and is close to a golf course. The resident ghost is said to be partial to Belhaven 90 shilling ale – a discriminating ghoul.

Beer: Belhaven 90 shilling, Ruddles County, Theakston XB and Old Peculier, Vaux ESB and Samson and a regular guest beer on handpumps.

Accommodation: 3 singles, 18 doubles/twins, 2 family rooms. B&B £30 single, £50 double, £60 family room. Children's rates depend on age. Discounts for 2/3 days' stay. Children's room. Pets welcome. Cards: Access, Amex, Diners, Visa.

ALNWICK

Oddfellows Arms
Narrowgate. Off A1

Licensee: Anthony Copeland
Tel: 0665 602695

The Oddfellows is a cheerful and welcoming pub by the castle in this cobbled and castellated historic town (pronounced 'Annick'), the centre of many long and bloody battles and sieges over the centuries. The Oddfellows offers coal fires, a public bar with darts and dominoes, 'but no pool', and a comfortable lounge. The inn is a haven of quiet, without juke boxes and other distractions, and has a pleasant beer garden for the summer months. Food is served lunchtime.

Beer: Vaux Samson on handpump.

Accommodation: 2 doubles, 1 family room. B&B £15 per person. Pets accepted.

BAMBURGH

Victoria Hotel
Front Street. B1341, 5 miles from A1; 45 miles north of Newcastle

Licensees: Mr & Mrs Robert Goodfellow
Tel: 066 84 431

The Victoria, as its name implies, is an impressive Victorian building rebuilt in 1893 on the site of an earlier inn. Both hostelries had associations with lifeboat heroine Grace Darling, who was born and died in the village. The friendly hotel is in the heart of Bamburgh village in one of the loveliest coastal areas of Britain. Bamburgh was once the capital of the ancient kingdom of Bernicia and is now designated an area of outstanding beauty, with the great castles of Bamburgh, Dunstanburgh and Lindisfarne nearby. Bamburgh remained a crown castle until the union of England and Scotland; Christianity was introduced to Northumbria in Bamburgh when King Oswald invited St Aidan from Iona to establish his church there. Aidan also founded the priory on Lindisfarne. The Victoria is a splendid base for touring the area, with the Farne Islands, Holy Island and the Grace Darling Museum. The hotel has a wide range of bar meals – toasties, ploughman's, homemade soups, fish and chips, burgers and children's portions – served lunchtime and evening, plus excellent meals in separate dining room and bistro. Breakfasts are superb and include locally cured kippers from Craster. There is a residents' lounge and all-day coffee shop. Real ale is served in the back bar and includes beer from the new Longstone brewery, based in Belford five miles away and the county's only brewery.

Beer: Longstone Bitter, Stones Best Bitter and Tetley Bitter on handpumps.

Accommodation: 5 singles, 14 doubles/twins, 4 family rooms, 16 rooms with private baths. B&B from £18.25-£25.30 per person depending on season. Children £5-£15 depending on age. Winter Breaks (Nov-April) £35-£40 per person per day B&B plus dinner. Small charge for dogs. Cards: Access, Amex, Diners, Visa.

CORBRIDGE

Wheatsheaf Hotel
St Helens Street. Off A69 & A68

Proprietor: Gordon Young
Tel: 0434 632020

The Wheatsheaf is a friendly inn in an ancient village with Roman connections, including the remains of a fort; Corbridge was a supply depot for Hadrian's troops and the fort includes a granary with an advanced system of grain ventilation. The granary certainly produced bread and may have supplied malt for brewing. The Wheatsheaf has a comfortable bar and lounge with live music at weekends and a darts and dominoes competition every Tuesday. The pub has a large conservatory dining room open every lunchtime and evening. Lunchtime bar meals include soup, farmhouse grill, chops and fish, sandwiches and children's meals. Full evening meals offer steaks, fish, homemade pies and a vegetarian dish. There is a large beer garden for the summer months.

Beer: Lorimer Scotch, Vaux ESB and Samson, Wards Sheffield Best Bitter on electric and handpumps.

Accommodation: 1 single, 2 doubles, 2 twins, 1 family room, all rooms with private bath, TVs, direct-dial phones and tea and coffee makers. B&B from £21 per person. Weekly discounts. Children welcome. No pets. Cards: Access, Amex, Visa.

FALSTONE

Blackcock Inn
Off A68; follow Kielder Water signs
N of Corbridge; 9 miles from
Bellingham

Licensees: Tom & Alex Richards
Tel: 0434 240200

The Blackcock, the last inn in
England, really has a warm welcome
with a collection of vintage coal fires.
The fireplace in the bar was made in
Newcastle at the turn of the century
and first fitted in a house in Hexham.
It is complete with oven and hot
water tank. The lounge has a small
stove made in Fife and called a
'Beatonette', in honour of Mrs
Beaton of Victorian home-hints fame.
The dining room has a large open fire
with a handsome black marble
surround, built for Allerwash Hall at
Newbrough. The village-centre inn is
more than 200 years old and was
originally a single-storey thatched
building, which has been extended
and modernized over the years
without losing its genuine character.
The residents' lounge includes a
grand piano and the dining room
seats 30. Food is available lunchtime
and evening and includes steak and
kidney pie, cod in batter, homemade
pizza, lasagne and giant Yorkshire
puddings with choice of fillings.
Falstone, from the Anglo-Saxon for
'stronghold', is on the banks of the
Tyne, close to Kielder Forest with the
largest man-made lake in Europe and
facilities for water sports, walking,
fishing and pony trekking.

Beer: Whitbread Boddingtons Bitter
and Castle Eden Ale on handpumps
plus a wide range of guest beers.

Accommodation: 1 single, 2 doubles,
all en suite. B&B £25 single, £20 per
person in double. Children welcome,
half price under 12. Pets welcome.

LOWICK

Black Bull Inn
4 Main Street. B6353

Licensee: Tom Grundy
Tel: 0289 88228

The Black Bull is a delightful old
village inn renowned for its welcome,
good ale and bar food, served
lunchtime and evening. There is a
separate restaurant with 68 covers.
The inn is a fine base for visiting the
Scottish borders, the Cheviots, the
great castles of north
Northumberland and the vast
stretches of unspoilt beaches. Lowick
is also handy for the main A1 to the
south.

Beer: McEwan 70 and 80 shilling,
Theakston Best Bitter on
handpumps.

Accommodation: in self-catering
cottage next to pub. Rates depend on
number of guests and time of year:
phone for details. Cards: Visa.

NEWBIGGIN-BY-THE-SEA

Old Ship Hotel
63 Front Street. Off A1189

Licensees: Keith & Jennie
Richmond
Tel: 0670 817212

The Old Ship is a coaching inn on the
seafront of this delightful fishing
village, once a major port in the 15th
century. Fishermen still put to sea in
their traditional 'cobbles' to catch
salmon and lobster. The hotel offers a
good welcome and good cheer, with
an extensive menu in a cosy evening
restaurant and bar snacks lunchtime
and evening. Wansbeck Riverside
Park and Woodhorn Lake are close to

Newbiggin. St Mary's Church in Woodhorn is the oldest church on the Northumbrian coast and is now a museum and cultural centre.

Beer: Vaux Samson on handpump.

Accommodation: 1 single, 4 doubles and 1 family room. B&B £13 per person. Children 2-7 years £6.50, 8-12 £9.50.

SEAHOUSES

White Swan Hotel
Main Street/Broad Road

Managers: John & Tina O'Donnell
Tel: 0665 720211

The White Swan, on the outskirts of Seahouses, has new American managers, thought to be a first for this guide. The hotel is half a mile from the harbour and close to fine sandy beaches. It is next to a riding school and surrounded by farms. There are views of Bamburgh Castle from some of the guest rooms, and the hotel has a spacious walled beer garden. Bar food, served lunchtime and evening, includes traditional Northumbrian dishes. A restaurant is open in the evening.

Beer: Constantly changing range that may include Belhaven 60, 70, 80 and 90 shilling, Longstone Bitter, Theakston Best Bitter, XB and Old Peculier, Vaux ESB and Wards Sheffield Best Bitter on handpumps.

Accommodation: 2 singles, 12 doubles/twins, 3 family rooms, all with en suite facilities. B&B £25-£35 single, £50-£60 double/twin, £50-£75 family room. Discounts for children sharing with parents. Special rates for groups and long stays. Children's room. Pets welcome. Cards: Access, Amex, Diners, Visa.

WOOLER

Anchor Inn
2 Cheviot Street. Off A697

Licensee: David Newton
Tel: 0668 81412

The Anchor is a striking two-storey building, decked out with hanging baskets and pots of flowers, in a pleasant old market town at the foot of the Cheviots in the Glendale Valley. The building has been an inn for at least 250 years and the first floor was used as the local court until 1878 when the local police station was enlarged. It is a genuine family pub and is popular with people on walking holidays or touring Northumberland. Berwick, Alnwick, Seahouses, Bamburgh, Craster and Kelso are close by. Bar meals are served at lunchtime; evening meals by request.

Beer: Lorimer Best Scotch and Vaux Samson on handpumps.

Accommodation: 1 twin, 1 double, 1 family room. All rooms have colour TVs and tea making facilities. B&B £16.50 per person. Week: 10% discount. Children half price if sharing. Pets by arrangement.

Ryecroft Hotel
On A697 on northern edge of town

Licensee: David McKechnie
Tel: 0668 81459

The Ryecroft is a friendly, family-run hotel with log fires, sited on the outskirts of the town. Pat McKechnie supervises the cooking and discriminating diners come from far afield for her meals that are based on local produce and include fruits of the sea, creamed mushrooms, cheese soup, pork steaks braised in cider, and smoked salmon quiche. The comfortable bar has strong local support for enthusiasts of darts, dominoes and quoits. The Ryecroft has a residents' lounge and all the guest rooms have en suite facilities. The hotel arranges special bird-watching and walking weekend holidays with guides, from March to May and in September and October.

Beer: Longstone Bitter, Tetley Bitter, Yates Bitter and guest beers on handpumps.

Accommodation: 1 single, 8 doubles. B&B £31 single, £62 double. 2 nights B&B plus dinner £66 Nov-Feb. Children half price for meals, no charge if sharing with parents. Pets welcome. Cards: Access, Diners, Visa.

NOTTINGHAMSHIRE

HAYTON

Boat Inn
Main Street. 1 mile off A620

Licensee: Anthony Ralton
Tel: 0777 700158

The delightful Boat is on the banks of the Chesterfield Canal, where it has its own moorings and is a popular stopping place for boating people. The inn has a large car park and spacious gardens that run down to the water's edge. The rooms are in converted cottages next to the pub. Carvery meals are served in a separate restaurant seven days a week, booking advisable. Bar meals are also served. There are facilities for camping, too.

Beer: Draught Bass and Stones Best

Bitter, Whitbread Castle Eden Ale and guest beer on handpumps.

Accommodation: 3 singles, 5 doubles, 2 family rooms, 5 rooms with private bath. B&B from £15 single. Children can stay in the family rooms.

KIMBERLEY

Nelson & Railway Inn
12 Station Road. Off A610

Licensees: Harry & Pat Burton
Tel: 0602 382177

If you wonder what connection there is between Lord Nelson and the railway, the answer is that the pub's original name was 'The Lord Nelson Railway Hotel'. Although Kimberley is just a village, at the height of the railway boom it boasted two competing railway stations, both a few yards from the pub. The stations still exist, as Kimberley Ex-Servicemen's Club and as the offices of a local timber firm. The inn is now the brewery tap, for Hardy (no connection with Nelson) and Hanson's large and imposing brewery dominates the village and looms over the pub. Both the lively bar and more sedate lounge offer a friendly welcome to visitors. There are gardens front and rear, with swings for children. The pub has darts and long alley skittles. Bar snacks are served lunchtime and early evening and include chip, bacon, sausage and fried egg butties, jacket potatoes with choice of filling, burgers, homemade quiche, cottage pie, chilli and lasagne, ploughman's, gammon, steaks, omelettes, and a children's menu. There is a roast Sunday lunch, too. Kimberley is close to Eastwood and the D.H. Lawrence museum.

Beer: Hardy & Hanson Kimberley

Best Mild, Best Bitter and Classic on electric and handpump.

Accommodation: 2 doubles. B&B £18 single, £31 double. Children welcome, £10 if sharing with 2 adults.

NOTTINGHAM

Queens Hotel
2 Arkwright Street, opposite railway station

Licensee: Stephen Webster
Tel: 0602 864685

The Queens is some 140 years old and has been refurbished to retain its character. It has a superb Victorian public bar and contrasting lounge. It is the ideal place for refreshment as you leave the railway station or head for Trent Bridge cricket and football grounds. Pub meals are all prepared on the premises. The pub is just half a mile from Nottingham's city centre and is a good base for visiting the castle and another splendid hostelry, the Trip to Jerusalem, England's oldest pub. The Queens has a meeting and function room for up to 30 people.

Beer: Thomas Greenall Original Bitter, Shipstone Mild and Bitter, Stones Best Bitter and Tetley Bitter plus guest beers on handpumps.

Accommodation: 1 single, 6 doubles, 2 family rooms. B&B £17 single, £30 double, £45 family rooms. No pets.

WALKERINGHAM

Brickmakers Arms
Fountain Hill Road, ½ mile off A161

Licensee: W. Tindall
Tel: 0427 890375

The Brickmakers is a traditional old-world pub with one bar and a restaurant with good value food and more than 90 dishes, with prices ranging from £1. There is also a varied restaurant menu including pheasant and duck. There are welcoming log fires in winter. The guest rooms have baths or showers, colour TVs and tea and coffee making equipment. Walkeringham is well placed for visiting Wesley's house at Epworth, Mattersley Priory, and the Old Hall at Gainsborough.

Beer: Draught Bass, Ruddles County and Websters Yorkshire Bitter on handpump.

Accommodation: 18 rooms including a bridal suite; all rooms with private facilities. 2 further rooms are planned. B&B £30 single, £40 double, £50 family room. Weekend: £28/£32/£38. 10% discounts 3-6 nights, 20% discounts 7-28 days, extra discounts for longer stays. Great Escape Weekend: room free of charge, £7.50 breakfast, £15 dinner. Children welcome, terms included in price of family room. Cards: Access, Amex, Visa.

OXFORDSHIRE

BICESTER

Plough Inn
63 North Street. A421 by Banbury-Buckingham roundabout

Licensees: Per & Tracy Egeberg
Tel: 0869 249083

The Plough is a delightful 400-year-old pub with oak beamed ceilings and large open fireplaces, and is a good base for visiting Stratford-upon-Avon, Woodstock, Blenheim Palace and Oxford, which is 12 miles away. Part of the Plough's horseshoe-shaped bar is set aside as a restaurant area that serves such homemade dishes as mushroom, onion and garlic soup, fillet of pork in cider sauce, sausage casserole, tandoori chicken, steak, mushroom and Guinness pie, steaks, lasagne, trout and scampi, followed by such homemade sweets as bread-and-butter pudding or fruit crumble. Rolls and sandwiches are also available. Food is served lunchtime and evening.

Beer: Morrells Best Bitter and Varsity on handpumps.

Accommodation: 3 twins, 2 family rooms, all with en suite facilities. B&B £20 single, £12.50 per person in twin, £12 in family room. Pets welcome.

BURFORD

Lamb Inn
Sheep Street. Off A361

Licensees: R.M. & C. de Wolf
Tel: 0993 823155

The Lamb is a 500 year-old mellow stone inn in the loveliest of the Cotswold towns. The bar has a flag-stoned floor and high-back settles, while the spacious, beautifully furnished lounge has beams, panelled walls, mullioned windows and old wooden armchairs. Log fires burn in the bar and lounges all winter, while in summer visitors can enjoy lunch in the flower-filled garden. The beer is dispensed for both bars from a remarkable old beer engine in a glass cabinet. Menus change daily but bar food may include homemade soups, jugged hare, venison casserole, steak and kidney pie, chicken and quail terrine, ploughman's and such

homemade desserts as chocolate roulade, rum and banana cheesecake or coffee and hazelnut gâteau. Bar food is served lunchtime while the restaurant is open in the evening.

Beer: Wadworth IPA and 6X on handpumps, Old Timer in winter from the cask.

Accommodation: 3 singles, 9 doubles, 3 family rooms, 12 rooms en suite. B&B £30 single, £32.50 double/family. Winter Weekend Break: from £90 per person for 2 nights, plus £17.50 dinner allowance. Midweek Breaks from £80 per person for 2 days including dinner allowance. Children welcome in lounge areas and parts of bar. Pets welcome. Cards: Access and Visa.

FRILFORD HEATH

Dog House Hotel
Off A34 & A338. From Wantage turn right at crossroads; or leave A34 at turning marked RAF Abingdon, follow signs to Frilford, take first right and continue for 2½ miles

Licensee: Clive E. Haggar
Tel: 0865 390830/390896

The Dog House is some 150 years old and used to house hounds reared for hunting; the Berkshire Hunt used to meet there. It has been thoroughly overhauled and renovated, and offers top-class service in beautiful surroundings with views of pasture land with grazing cows and the Vale of the White Horse. Frilford Heath golf club is just 300 yards away. Food is available lunchtime and evening every day, with daily specials chalked on a board.

Beer: Morland Bitter, Old Masters and Old Speckled Hen on handpumps.

Accommodation: 1 single, 16 doubles/twins, 2 family rooms, all with en suite facilities. B&B £57.50 single, £69.50 double. Weekend (2 nights) £30 single, £40 double. Children under 10 charged for breakfast only. Cards: Access, Amex, Diners, Visa.

GREAT TEW

Falkland Arms
Off B4022, 5 miles east of Chipping Norton

Licensees: John & Hazel Milligan
Tel: 060 883 653
Fax: 060 883 656

The Falkland Arms is one of the most popular entries in the guide and the Milligans' guest book confirms this with such superlatives as 'magical', 'superb', 'brilliant', 'delightful and charming' and 'not our first visit, nor our last'. It is a stunning old inn in one of the loveliest of Oxfordshire villages. It dates back to the 15th century and was originally named the Horse & Groom but was renamed in honour of the local lords of the manor. It has a partially thatched roof and vast overhanging tree. Inside there is a panelled bar with high-back settles, flagstones, oil lamps and an enormous collection of pots and tankards hanging from the beams. Lunchtime food (not Monday) makes use of the Milligans' own free-range chicken and duck eggs, and dishes include homemade seafood, cheese and ale, Stilton and cauliflower and carrot mint soups, lamb cobbler, Lancashire hot-pot, pork and Stilton pie, homemade fish cakes or faggots, spicy stuffed marrow and rabbit stew, with ploughman's and salads. The guest rooms have old iron bedsteads and pine furniture. A gallon of ale is offered to anyone who sees the ghost of Lord Falkland. The inn has a range

of 51 malt whiskies and 16 country wines.

Beer: Donnington BB, Hall & Woodhouse Tanglefoot, Hook Norton Best Bitter, Wadworth 6X and five guest beers on handpumps.

Accommodation: 4 doubles, 1 family room, 3 rooms with en suite facilities. B&B £25 single, £40-£45 double, £50 family room, 2 rooms with four-poster beds. No pets.

IFFLEY

Tree Hotel
Church Way, ½ mile from Oxford ring road, 1½ miles from Oxford city centre

Licensee: Mrs E. Bowman
Tel: 0865 775974

The Tree Hotel is based in the ancient village of Iffley, which was first recorded in AD 941 and was listed in the Domesday Book. The name stems from the Saxon 'giftelege', meaning a field of gifts. The small Victorian hotel, with a handsome exterior of bowed windows, is close to the village's Norman church, which is more than 800 years old, and the Isis river and Iffley lock are close by. The excellent bar food is based mainly on homemade dishes and there is a separate restaurant with a full à la carte menu. All the guest rooms are en suite and have colour TVs, phones and tea and coffee making facilities.

Beer: Morrells Bitter and Varsity on handpumps.

Accommodation: 7 rooms. B&B £50 single, £70 double, £80 family or executive room.

MOULSFORD-ON-THAMES

Beetle & Wedge Hotel
Ferry Lane. Off A329

Proprietors: Richard & Kate Smith
Tel: 0491 651381
Fax: 0491 651376

Beetles and wedges are the ancient tools used by boat builders and woodmen on this stretch of the Thames. The red-brick building dates from the early 18th century, while the adjacent cottage and the building that form the Boathouse Bar date from the 12th century. The hotel overlooks a gentle stretch of the Thames and featured as the 'Potwell Inn' in H.G. Wells's *History of Mr Polly*. Jerome K. Jerome, author of *Three Men in a Boat* lived in the adjacent cottage, while the area also appears in *Wind in the Willows*. All the guest rooms have been redecorated to a high standard and have colour TVs and tea and coffee making facilities. There are two restaurants, a dining room in the hotel and meals served in the Boathouse. Meals in the Boathouse Bar include homemade soup, mussels, grilled sardines, smoked sea trout, whole crab, avocado salad with smoked chicken and prawns, asparagus Hollandaise or vinaigrette, crispy duck, stuffed aubergine, steaks, grilled halibut, cold poached salmon, tagliatelle with seafood and chive sauce, and ploughman's. There is a garden menu in summer – booking advisable. Overnight mooring costs £15, refundable against dining room charges. A rowing boat comes with each booking.

Beer: Adnams Bitter, Hall & Woodhouse Tanglefoot and Wadworth 6X on handpumps.

Accommodation: B&B from £70 per person. Double £75-£95. Champagne Weekend including flowers in room and dinner – £175 per person for 2 nights. Cards: Access, Amex, Diners, JCB, Visa.

NEWBRIDGE

Rose Revived
A415, 7 miles south of Witney

Licensee: Andrew Dearie
Tel: 086731 221

The Rose Revived is set in lovely countryside at one of the oldest crossing points on the Thames. It dates back to the 14th century, and the bars have flag-stoned floors and open fires. There is a separate restaurant specializing in homemade dishes, and bar food is also available, including many homemade dishes. Food is served from noon to 10pm every day and includes cream teas. There is a children's menu and children are welcome in the non-bar area of the pub. In summer visitors can use the large riverside garden and patio. Some of the guest rooms have splendid views of the Thames; Oxford and Woodstock are close at hand. There are facilities for fishing and Frilford golf club is nearby.

Beer: Morland Bitter, Old Masters and Old Speckled Hen on handpumps.

Accommodation: 7 rooms, some with en suite facilities. B&B £40 single, £55 double en suite. Cards: Access, Amex, Visa.

OXFORD

Berkshire House
200 Abingdon Road. Off A4144, A34 & A423

Licensee: Catherine Coyle
Tel: 0865 242423

The Berkshire House, built in the 1930s, is a spacious hostelry close to Oxford city centre. It has three bars with one used mainly by parents and children; this bar has access to a garden where the ancient pub game of Aunt Sally is played in the summer. The pub has been thoroughly refurbished since the last edition of the guide. The main bar is comfortably carpeted while the third bar is used mainly by customers playing darts and pool.

Beer: Morrells Best Bitter on handpump.

Accommodation: 3 twins all with private showers. B&B £18 per person. No pets.

Globe Inn
59-60 Cranham Street, Jericho

Licensees: Mick & Sue Simmonds
Tel: 0865 57759

The Globe is a delightful, old-fashioned local with one large bar and homemade food. It is close to St Barnabas church, the John Radcliffe hospital and Port Meadow. Food is available from breakfast time and there is a daily lunchtime special and a roast on Sundays.

Beer: Morrells Bitter and Varsity on handpumps.

Accommodation: 1 single, 1 double, 2 family rooms, all centrally heated and with colour TVs. B&B £15 per person. No pets.

WITNEY

Red Lion Hotel
Corn Street, town centre. A40

Licensee: Ian Russell Payne
Tel: 0993 703149

The Red Lion was built as a coaching inn in the 17th century in an historic Cotswold village that is the home of the Witney blanket. The hotel has a welcoming lounge bar and a busy games room with a hexagonal pool table. Bar meals are available all day from 10am to 11pm (not Sunday afternoons). The delightful guest rooms have the air of a country cottage with attractive fabrics and furnishings.

Beer: Morrells Mild, Bitter, Graduate and Varsity on handpumps.

Accommodation: 1 single, 1 double, 2 twins, 2 rooms with en suite facilities. B&B £24.69 single, £29.38 en suite, £35.25/£39.95 double/ twin. Children's room. No pets. Cards: Access and Visa.

SHROPSHIRE

BISHOP'S CASTLE

Castle Hotel
Market Square. A488 from Shrewsbury

Licensees: David & Nicola Simpson
Tel: 0588 638403

The Castle, in the centre of this small, bustling Shropshire town, is a coaching inn dating back to 1709. The three bars have log fires and are cheerful and welcoming. Pub food (lunchtime and evening) is excellent and includes dishes for vegetarians. Dogs are welcome, there are baby-minding facilities and fishing is available nearby. Another pub worthy of note in the town is the Three Tuns, a famous home-brew inn with a small tower brewery in the backyard that produces excellent ales. There is a traction engine rally in the

town on August bank holiday. Little
remains of the castle that gave the
town its name but there is a profusion
of fascinating architectural styles,
with many half-timbered buildings of
which the best known is the House
on Crutches. Offa's Dyke and the
rock outcrops of Long Mynd and the
Stiperstones are nearby.

Beer: Draught Bass, Marston
Pedigree Bitter, Wadworth 6X,
Whitbread Boddingtons Bitter and
Woods Special Bitter on handpumps.

Accommodation: 1 single, 4 doubles,
3 family rooms, 2 rooms with en suite
facilities. B&B £22.60-£24.50 single,
£36-£41 double/family. Children free
if sharing with parents. Cards: Access
and Visa.

CLUN

Sun Inn
On B4368, west of A949 at Craven
Arms

Proprietors: Keith & Bunny Small
Tel: 05884 277

'The quietest place under the sun',
said A.E. Housman of Clun, but the
small town's history is anything but
quiet. It was the scene of protracted
battles between Britons and Romans.
Later skirmishes with the Welsh
forced King Offa to build his dyke to
contain them, and Clun Castle was
built in the 11th century in a further
effort to keep back the marauding
Welsh. The Sun Inn, dating from the
15th century, is a delightful place to
stay, and a good base for visiting the
Iron Age forts, Offa's dyke, the
medieval saddleback bridge over the
river Clun, the castle and the
fascinating museum in the town hall.

Sun Inn, Clun

The inn has a wealth of exposed beams, a vast fireplace in the bar, flagstones and settles. The restaurant offers exotic dishes from around the world based on local produce. There are always vegetarian dishes. Bar food includes homemade soup, garlic and herb mushrooms, Spanish butter bean stew (fabada), curries, vegetarian cassoulet, beef and cashew nuts, apple and cinnamon pie and cheesecake. The pub is a chip-free zone. Residents have the use of a comfortable lounge with an open fire, beamed ceiling and TV. Accommodation is in the converted old bakery and old stables attached to the inn.

Beer: Banks Mild and Bitter, Woods Special Bitter and guest beers in summer on handpumps.

Accommodation: 2 singles, 6 doubles, 1 family room, 4 with en suite facilities. B&B £18 single, £40 double en suite.

LUDLOW

Church Inn
Buttercross (town centre). Off A49 between Shrewsbury & Hereford

Licensee: Stuart Copland
Tel: 0584 872174

The Church is an extensively modernized inn, with a pleasantly painted Georgian pastel exterior. Church is the fifth name it has had in 500 years. There is a comfortable lounge bar and a separate restaurant. Bar food includes soups, steak and mushroom pie, trout, plaice, curries, steaks, fisherman's pancake and homemade sweets. The restaurant menu offers a three-course table d'hôte menu with six choices. The inn is close to the medieval castle where the unfortunate princes stayed before

leaving for London and dying at the hands of either Henry Tudor or Richard Plantagenet, depending on which conspiracy theory you prefer. Nearby is the parish church of St Laurence, burial place of the Shropshire poet A.E. Housman.

Beer: Ruddles County and Websters Yorkshire Bitter, Woods Special Bitter, a house beer, Bellringer Bitter, and regular guest beers on handpumps.

Accommodation: 9 doubles, all en suite, with TVs and tea and coffee making facilities. B&B £28 single, £40 double, family room £50. Children welcome. Cards: Access and Visa.

MARKET DRAYTON

Corbet Arms Hotel
High Street. From A41 head for town centre at junction of Shrewsbury road and High Street; hotel is next to Woolworth's

Licensee: Peter Stubbins
Tel/fax: 0630 652037

The Corbet Arms is a creeper-clad, 16th-century coaching inn in the centre of the fine old Shropshire market town, mentioned in the Domesday Book and scene of a major battle in the Wars of the Roses. Present-day attractions include a Safari Park, the Shropshire Union canal, fishing and horse riding. The hotel's accommodation has been refurbished since the last edition of the guide; it has a separate restaurant that seats 50 and has both à la carte and table d'hôte menus, including vegetarian dishes. Bar meals are available lunchtime and evening. The hotel has a 'friendly' lady ghost. The guest rooms are all en suite and have colour TVs, direct-dial phones and tea and coffee making facilities.

Beer: Whitbread Best Bitter, Boddingtons Bitter and Castle Eden ale on electric pumps.

Accommodation: 3 singles, 7 doubles, 1 family room. B&B £39.50 single, £49.50 double, £55 family room. Children charged £10. Special Breaks: 2 days B&B plus dinner £66.50 per person; Honeymoon Special £60 per person. Pets welcome. Cards: Access, Amex, Diners, Visa.

OSWESTRY

Olde Boote Inn
Whittington. Old A5

Licensee: K.H. Lawrenson
Tel: 0691 662250

The Olde Boote is an ancient inn in a suburb of Oswestry where Dick Whittington is said to have passed on his way to make his fortune in London. The inn has a panoramic view of the ruins of an old moated Norman castle. Inside the Olde Boote there are oak beams and many horse brasses. A golf course is nearby. Lunchtime bar snacks and daily specials plus an evening restaurant are available every day.

Beer: Robinson Best Mild and Best Bitter on electric pump.

Accommodation: 4 doubles/twins, 2 family rooms, all with en suite facilities, colour TVs and tea and coffee making facilities. B&B £23 single, £38 double/twin/family room. Children £5 sharing. No dogs. Cards: Access and Visa.

SHREWSBURY

Swan Inn
Frankwell. A458, north-west side of town

Proprietors: Don & Shirley Reynolds
Tel: 0743 364923

The small Georgian inn offering a cheery welcome is based in one of the oldest areas of Shrewsbury. Don Reynolds is a Burton Ale Mastercellarman, and takes great pride in serving cask beers in the Victoria Bar, where excellent home-cooked food is also available lunchtime and evening. The guest rooms have en suite facilities, colour TVs and tea and coffee makers as well as fine views over Shrewsbury. The Mount, just round the corner from the hotel, is the birthplace of Charles Darwin, and close by is the impressive medieval Fellmongers' Hall. A few minutes' walk across the Welsh Bridge brings you into the heart of old Shrewsbury with its half-timbered buildings and Georgian and Queen Anne architecture. Clive of India's house, now a museum, and the Rowley House museum tell the history of the town. Military history is on display in Shrewsbury Castle that guards the loop in the River Severn on which the old town is based. The abbey over the English Bridge is the inspiration for the Brother Caedfel detective stories of Ellis Peters.

Beer: Ansells Bitter, Ind Coope Burton Ale, Wadworth 6X and Woods Wonderful on handpumps.

Accommodation: 2 doubles, 2 family rooms. B&B £24 single, £35 double, £42 family room with 1 child, £48 with 2. Pets welcome. Cards: Access and Visa.

AXBRIDGE

Lamb inn
The Square, ½ mile from A371
Wells to Cheddar road

Licensee: Dave & Sue Williams
Tel: 0934 732253

The Lamb is a fascinating 15th-century coaching inn that has previously been named both the Holy Lamb and the Lamb & Flag. The Williams specialize in good plain cooking – 'anything from a steak to a sandwich', says Mr Williams – a sensible range of ale, and comfortable accommodation in rooms with TVs and tea and coffee making facilities. Homemade bar food includes soup, ploughman's, lasagne, steak in ale pie, sirloin steak, trout, plaice, prawn chowder, chicken pie, pancakes stuffed with chilli, and a children's menu; children can also choose smaller portions from the main menu; there is a Sunday roast lunch. Sue Williams is a vegetarian and makes sure there is a good selection of veggie dishes. No meals Sunday night, or Mondays in winter. The Lamb has a skittles alley, and customers can also play darts, table skittles and shove ha'penny. It has an unusual bar made of old beer bottles set in cement some 20 years ago. The inn, one of three pubs owned by Butcombe Brewery, stands in the square famous for St John's hunting lodge and Axbridge church. The handsome old town nestles on the southern slopes of the Mendips and is close to both Cheddar and its gorge and much abused cheese, and Wells with its magnificent cathedral.

Beer: Butcombe Bitter, Draught Bass, Wadworth 6X and Thatcher's farmhouse cider on handpumps.

Accommodation: 1 double with en suite bath, £45; 1 twin with own

bathroom next door, £35; 1 family room with en suite shower, £40. £10 for children sharing. All rooms have TVs and tea and coffee makers.

BATCOMBE

Three Horse Shoes Inn
1½ miles off A359, Bruton to Nunney road. Pub next to church

Licensee: Mrs J.S. Charlton
Tel: 074 985 359
Fax: 074 985 630

The Three Horse Shoes is a 600-year-old stone building that was originally a toll house. It is set in lovely countryside overlooking the Somerset Levels. The inn has old beams, copper and brass artefacts, three log fires and a minstrels' gallery. Home-cooked food in bar and restaurant includes smoked trout pâté, ploughman's, baked jacket potatoes with choice of fillings, salads, sandwiches, chicken tikka, prawn curry, steaks, duck, steak and kidney pie, mushroom and nut fettucini, broccoli bake, vegetable curry and a children's menu. The pub has a resident ghost named George. Local attractions include Cheddar, Wookey Hole, Glastonbury Tor, Stourhead and Longleat.

Beer: Marston Pedigree Bitter, Whitbread Boddingtons Bitter and Flowers Original on handpumps.

Accommodation: 2 singles, 2 doubles, 1 family room, 2 rooms with en suite facilities. B&B £22 single, £36 double, £44 family room. Pets accepted. Cards: Access, Amex, Diners, Visa.

BURNHAM-ON-SEA

Royal Clarence Hotel
31 Esplanade. 3 miles off M5 exit 22

Licensees: Dennis & Paul Davey
Tel: 0278 783138
Fax: 0278 792965

The Clarence is an old coaching inn with facilities that range from a skittles alley to a Regency suite. It has fine views over the beaches and sea, and it boasts its own miniature brewery where Clarence Bitter is brewed. There are good bar meals, while the elegant restaurant offers sole, rainbow trout, pork Normande in cream and cider, duck, carbonade of beef and a daily vegetarian dish.

Beer: Butcombe Bitter, Clarence Pride Bitter and Regent Bitter, Wadworth 6X and four guest beers on handpumps.

Accommodation: 3 singles, 13 doubles, 3 family rooms, 17 rooms en suite. B&B £28 single, £42 double, family room from £50. Children under 3 free, half price 3-11. Special Breaks: 2-6 days dinner, B&B £30 per person per day; 7 or more days £27. Residents' lounge for families. Dogs by arrangement. Cards: Access, Amex, Diners, Visa.

FROME

Sun Inn
6 Catherine Street. Off A361, A36 & M4

Licensee: D.J. Hands
Tel: 0373 473123

Not so much a pub, more a permanent beer festival with seven real ales always available. The Sun is an old coaching inn and listed building with a vast and impressive fireplace dominating the interior.

There is excellent pub grub every day and a Saturday roast lunch. The guest rooms all have colour TVs, and Mr Hands supplies friendly ghosts at no extra charge. Frome is four miles from Longleat and Bath is just 12 miles away.

Beer: (including) Butcombe Bitter, Courage Directors, Fullers London Pride, Marston Pedigree Bitter and Wadworth 6X all on handpumps.

Accommodation: 2 doubles, 2 family rooms. B&B £16.50 single, £25 twin, £33 family room. Children welcome, 20% reductions.

LUXBOROUGH

Royal Oak of Luxborough
Minor road off A39 at Washford; at Luxborough turn right over bridge (OS 984377)

Proprietors: Robin & Helen Stamp
Tel: 0984 40319

The Royal Oak is a rural pub of great charm and antiquity in Exmoor national park. The inn, known locally as the Blazing Stump, dates back to the 15th century and has stone-flagged and cobbled floors, inglenook fireplaces and a wealth of ancient beams. There are three bar areas and a charming garden. Quiz night is Tuesday and music night Friday. Fresh local produce is used for both bar snacks and food in the dining room and dishes include Royal Oak prawns, homemade soup, sandwiches, ploughman's, chilli, steaks, pasties, vegetarian dish, beef and Beamish pie, salads in season, with sweets and a children's menu of fish fingers or sausages. Mr Stamp claims that 'when you walk through the door you will think you have stepped back two centuries and you won't have changed your mind when

you leave'. Except for the prices, but
even they are extremely reasonable
by 20th-century standards. The
quality of the pub can be gauged by
the fact that it has been voted
CAMRA Somerset Pub of the Year
and South-West England Pub of the
Year in 1989/90 and 1990/91.

Beer: Cotleigh Tawny Bitter,
Eldridge Pope Royal Oak, Exmoor
Gold, Flowers IPA and guest beers
straight from the cask or on
handpumps.

Accommodation: 4 doubles. B&B £19
single occupancy, £26 double. Week
£150 (7 nights). Pets accepted.

MIDDLEZOY

George Inn
Main Road. ¼ mile off A372
between Bridgwater & Langport

Licensees: Keith & Maureen Waites
Tel: 0823 698215

The George is a 17th-century inn in a
fascinating village on the Somerset
Levels. The Wiltshire militia lodged
here during the battle of Sedgemoor
in 1685 and the inn was used by
'Hanging Judge' Jeffreys during the
subsequent trials. The inn has
retained a wealth of old beams,
flag-stoned floors and inglenook
fireplaces. Mrs Waites and her
daughter Hayley are the cooks, and
offer fresh local produce on the
menu, which includes fish from
Brixham, organic pork and
vegetables, and local beef and lamb.
Mr Waites stages twice-yearly real ale
festivals and has a vast range of ales
on offer in the course of a year. The
George won the CAMRA Best Pub
in South-West England award in
1991.

Beer: Cotleigh Tawny Bitter, Harrier

Bitter and six guest beers a week on
handpumps or straight from the cask
in the cellar.

Accommodation: 1 single, 3 doubles.
B&B £15 single, £27 double. No
children or pets.

MONTACUTE

Phelips Arms
The Borough. A303 to Cartgate
roundabout, 50 yards beyond
entrance to Montacute House

Licensee: Roger Killeen
Tel: 0935 822557

The Phelips Arms is named after the
family that built Montacute House.
The pub is constructed of local
hamstone and has an impressive
exterior with steeply sloping roofs,
hanging baskets and a porched
entrance. It dates back to the 17th
century when it was a posting inn. It
has been carefully renovated to
provide one large bar that leads to a
courtyard and a secluded walled
garden. Bar meals are served every
day, lunchtime and evening, with
daily specials chalked on a board that
may include sweet and sour squid,
smoked prawns, boozy beef,·
thatched pork casserole, Persian lamb
kebabs, Oriental beef, whole West
Bay plaice, red gurnard with peach
sauce and tuna in garlic. You can also
tuck into such regulars as homemade
soup, monkfish in batter, sirloin
steak, lasagne, Montezuma's Revenge
(a powerful chilli), spare ribs,
beefcakes and a range of vegetarian
dishes. The Phelips Arms is the ideal
base for visiting Forde Abbey,
Brympton d'Evercy and other local
historic houses.

Beer: Palmer Bridport Bitter, IPA
and Tally Ho on handpumps.

Accommodation: 2 doubles/twins, 1 family room, 2 rooms with en suite facilities. B&B £25 single, £36 double, £45 family room. Children's room. No pets. Cards: Access and Visa.

PRIDDY

New Inn
Priddy Green, near Wells. 3 miles west of A39 Bristol to Wells road

Licensees: Anne & Doug Weston
Tel: 0749 676465

The inn was originally a 15th-century farmhouse owned by local alehouse keepers, who moved their business to the present building to meet the demands of the hard-drinking lead miners in the area. The tavern remained largely unchanged until the 1970s when a lounge was added from existing outhouses, the bar replaced an old staircase and a skittles alley and guest rooms were developed. The Westons concentrate on good food and ale. Bar meals include specially prepared jacket potatoes mixed with cider with a wide choice of toppings, omelettes, home-made vegetarian dishes – Mendip hot-pot, cashew nut paella, genuine Indian recipe vegetable curry – oak-smoked gammon, and trout, and such old-fashioned puddings as jam roly-poly and bread and butter pudding. Priddy, at the heart of the Mendips, is an ideal base for walking, seeing local country crafts of cheese and cider making, and visiting Wells and its cathedral, Bath and Bristol.

Beer: Eldridge Pope Thomas Hardy Country Bitter, Marston Pedigree Bitter, Wadworth 6X on handpumps and Wilkins cider from the jug.

Accommodation: 5 doubles, 1 family room. B&B £29.50 double or twin, £18.50 single occupancy, family room £36. Children welcome. No pets.

SHEPTON MALLET

Kings Arms
Leg Square. Off A37

Licensee: Drew Foley
Tel: 0749 343781

The Kings Arms, a pub of great charm that covers three sides of a courtyard, was built in 1660 and has been a pub since 1680. Today it has a main bar, a heritage bar and a skittles alley. The patio is a popular drinking spot in the summer. Bar food is served lunchtime and evening every day except Saturday lunch. The guest rooms are all en suite and have colour TVs and tea and coffee makers.

Beer: Ansells Bitter, Ind Coope Burton Ale and Wadworth 6X on handpumps.

Accommodation: 3 doubles. B&B £25 single occupancy, £35 double. 10% discount for CAMRA members. No children or pets. Cards: Access and Visa.

STOGUMBER

White Horse Inn
Off A358, Minehead-Taunton road

Licensee: Peter Williamson
Tel: 0984 56277

The White Horse is a small white-painted inn opposite a 12th-century church in a delightful conservation village near the Quantocks and Brendon Hills. The main bar has a coal fire in winter and old settles. Skittles, darts, dominoes and shove ha'penny are played in a separate room. Bar food (lunchtime and evening) includes homemade vegetable soup, smoked mackerel pâté, steak and kidney pudding, lamb curry, three types of lasagne, trout with almonds, fish in a poke, fried cod, steaks, salads, omelettes, sandwiches and such tasty sweets as walnut tart and cream, apple crumble and homemade ice-creams. The separate restaurant is the village's old market house now joined to the inn, with the village 'reading room' on the top floor. There is a pleasant garden for sunny weather.

Beer: Cotleigh Tawny Bitter, Exmoor Ale on handpumps.

Accommodation: 1 double, 1 family room, both with en suite facilities, TVs and central heating. B&B £25 single, £35 double. Children welcome, terms according to age. No pets. Cards: Access and Visa.

TAUNTON

Masons Arms
Magdalene Street, town centre. Off M5 exit 25

Licensee: J.J. Leyton
Tel: 0823 288916

The elegant three-storey building stands in the shadow of the superb St Mary Magdalene church and in an area of considerable historical interest. At the turn of the 19th century the present broad street was a squalid alley called Blackboy Lane, named after an inn whose landlord was accused of murdering a soldier and throwing his body into the River Tone. Cursing and swearing often drowned the singing in the church. The authorities cleared this 'sink of iniquity' in 1864 and turned the hovels and tenements into Magdalene Street. The Masons Arms was formerly the house of the local rent collector and became a beer house in 1855. Today it offers a good selection of bar meals (lunch and evening) as well as fine ale. There is a wide range

of salads, plus turkey pie, savoury flans, Cornish pasties, steak and kidney pie, curry and jacket potatoes. The pub has a traditional skittles alley. Accommodation is in a self-catering flat with colour TV, kitchen and bathroom.

Beer: Draught Bass, Exmoor Ale and many guest beers, all on handpumps.

Accommodation: Self-service flat with 1 twin and 1 single room. £30 per night for the flat, minimum 3-4 nights. 8 or more nights 20% discount. Children 6 and over welcome.

Near TAUNTON

Rock Inn
Waterrow. 14 miles west of Taunton on B3227 (formerly A361); off A303 & M5

Licensee: B.R.P. Broughall
Tel: 0984 23293

The Rock is a 400-year-old inn beside the River Tone in a lovely village nestling beneath the steep wooded hills of the Tone valley. It is a splendid base for touring Exmoor and the north Devon coast. The inn has a large cosy bar, and both bar and restaurant meals are available lunchtime and evening, including grills, poultry, fish, and vegetarian dishes. All the guest rooms have private bathrooms, central heating, colour TVs and direct-dial phones. There is also a residents' lounge.

Beer: Cotleigh Tawny Bitter, Exmoor Gold and Ushers Best Bitter on handpumps.

Accommodation: 5 doubles, 1 family room, 5 rooms en suite. B&B £19 per person. Children's rates according to age. Winter Breaks: 2 days B&B plus dinner £47 Nov-March; April-Oct £48. Pets accepted. Cards: Access and Visa.

WEST PENNARD

Lion at Pennard
Newtown. A361 between
Glastonbury & Shepton Mallet

Proprietors: Bob Buskin & Lorraine Jessemey
Tel: 0458 32941

The Lion at Pennard, just three miles from Glastonbury, was built in 1678, probably as a farmhouse, and retains much of its old charm with flag-stoned floors, low beams and log fires in inglenooks. Snacks and full meals are available lunchtime and evening. Bar meals include curries, lasagne, ham, egg and chips, cod, and pizza. There is a roast lunch on Sundays and a separate evening restaurant (closed Wednesday). Accommodation is in a converted old barn and all the luxurious carpeted rooms have private baths, colour TVs, central heating, direct-dial telephones, and tea and coffee making facilities. The Lion is a good centre for walking and visiting Glastonbury Abbey, Wookey Hole, Cheddar, Bath, Longleat, the East Somerset steam railway and English wine makers at Wooton, Pilton Manor and Coxley.

Beer: Ash Vine Bitter, Benskins Best Bitter, Hall & Woodhouse Badger Best Bitter, Ind Coope Burton Ale, Oakhill Farmers Ale on handpumps.

Accommodation: 6 doubles/twins, 1 family room. B&B £35 single occupancy, £24.75 per person double or family. Children under 10 sharing free; over 10 £15. Weekend Breaks (Oct-March): 2 nights B&B, dinner and Sunday lunch £85 per person. No pets. Cards: Access, Amex, Diners, Visa.

WILLITON

Foresters Arms
Long Street, on A39 Bridgwater to Minehead road; off M5

Licensees: Sunny & Aidan Downing
Tel: 0984 32508

The Foresters is a 17th-century building, though some parts may be considerably older. Its first name as a licensed house was the Lamb, but this was changed to the Railway Hotel with the arrival of steam – the West Somerset railway is just five minutes away. It was renamed the Foresters Arms in 1984. The Downings have extended the quality of the welcome, the food, the ale and the accommodation. There is a children's room, and spacious gardens with ornamental pools and patios. The pub offers a fine range of lunchtime and evening bar and restaurant meals, with six to 10 homemade daily specials, including vegetarian dishes. There is also a lady ghost. Williton is well placed for touring the Quantocks and visiting the picturesque town of Watchet.

Beer: Cotleigh Tawny Bitter, Marston Pedigree Bitter, Wadworth 6X and weekly guest beer on handpumps.

Accommodation: 1 single, 5 doubles, 2 family rooms, 4 rooms en suite, all with colour TVs and tea and coffee making equipment. B&B £22 single, £40 double, £15 per person in family room; children under 14 £10. Full board available. Facilities for the disabled in pub and restaurant only. Pets accepted. Cards: Access and Visa.

WINSFORD

Royal Oak Inn
Exmoor National Park. Off A396
near Minehead; M5 exit 27

Licensee: Charles Steven
Tel: 064 385 455
Fax: 064 385 388

The Royal Oak is a 12th-century thatched inn in the heart of Exmoor. For many years it doubled as a farm as well as a licensed house. Members of the wool trade operated from the inn, working with both local wool and Irish yarn. Tom Faggus, a 17th-century highwayman, lived near the village and was a character in *Lorna Doone*. The inn today has cheery bars, a welcoming open fire, bar meals and an evening à la carte restaurant. Bar meals (lunchtime and evening) include homemade country soup, chicken liver or smoked fish pâté, baked jacket potatoes with choice of fillings, salads, sandwiches, roast of the day, fresh fish casserole, chicken and leek pie, steak and kidney pie, sirloin steak, homemade pasties and homemade sweets.

Beers: Flowers Original and IPA on handpumps.

Accommodation: 1 single, 5 doubles, 2 twins in the inn, all en suite, five doubles in courtyard complex, which also has a family cottage for 2 adults and 2 or 3 small children. Prices per person from £49.75 B&B, £69.75 with dinner. Midweek Breaks (Sunday to Thursday): 1 & 2 nights dinner, B&B from £54.50 per person per night. Single room occupancy of double room £15 supplement per night. Children in family cottage £15 per night B&B. Kennel for dogs. Cards: Access, Amex, Diners, Visa.

Royal Oak Inn, Winsford

ABBOTS BROMLEY

Coach & Horses
High Street. B5014 near Rugeley

Licensee: Carol Hood
Tel: 0283 840256

The Coach & Horses is an attractive 16th-century inn, with a comfortable lounge and a bar with inglenook fireplaces where dominoes, darts and bar billiards are played. There is a residents' dining room, large car park and beer garden. The guest rooms all have colour TVs and tea and coffee making facilities. The inn has a resident ghost and is a good base for visiting Alton Towers and Cannock Chase.

Beer: Ansells Bitter and Ind Coope Burton Ale on handpumps.

Accommodation: 3 twins. B&B £17.50 single, £28 double.

ALTON

Bull's Head Hotel
High Street. Off A52, A515 & B5417

Licensee: Brian Harvey
Tel: 0538 702307

The Bull's Head is a fine 18th-century village inn in the picturesque Churnet Valley conservation area. The village is crowned by fairytale Alton Castle, which gives it more the air of the Rhineland than the Staffordshire moors. Alton Towers fun park is close by. The beamed hotel has a 35-seater dining room that specializes in home-cooked food that includes imaginative use of local vegetables; there is always a daily vegetarian wholefood dish. Tempting desserts include a gâteau of meringue, rum, cassis and blackcurrants. Bar food is also available every lunchtime.

The guest rooms all have showers, toilets, colour TVs and tea and coffee making facilities.

Beer: Draught Bass and Tetley Bitter on handpumps.

Accommodation: 6 doubles/twins. B&B from £25 single, £15 per person in double or twin. Extra bed in room £8. No pets. Cards: Access and Visa.

BURTON UPON TRENT

Station Hotel
Borough Road, next to railway station

Licensee: Alex Hill
Tel: 0283 64955

The Station is a cheerful and welcoming pub five minutes' walk from the town centre. It has a lounge bar, pool room and railway memorabilia. Hot and cold food is served every lunchtime and evening. The bedrooms have tea and coffee making facilities and colour TVs. Burton is the historic centre of the British beer industry, its roots going back to monastic brewing. Bass, Allied's Ind Coope, Marston and Burton Bridge brew in the town, and both the Bass Museum and the Heritage Brewery Museum, in the former Everard's plant, have fascinating displays about the industry ancient and modern. Information about both museums is available in the hotel, where Alex Hill – a former brewer, member of both the Guild of Master Cellarmen and an Ansells Master of Ales – will be happy to debate the merits of different beers over a jar or two.

Beer: Ansells Bitter and Ind Coope Burton Ale on handpumps and a guest beer.

Accommodation: 1 double, 3 twins, 2 family rooms. B&B £16 per person.

BUTTERTON

Black Lion Inn
Near Leek. Off A52 & A523, between Onecote & Hartington

Licensee: Ronald Smith
Tel: 0538 304 232

The Black Lion is a characterful, stone-built 18th-century rural pub with several rooms off the main bar. Furnishings range from pretty sofas to settles and bar stools with back rests. There are beams, open fires, a kitchen range and a carefully restored dining room. Excellent bar food includes ploughman's, sandwiches, steak and kidney pie, lasagne, vegetarian lasagne, liver, bacon and onions, beef in red wine and daily specials such as chicken provençale. Games to play include darts, dominoes, pool and shove ha'penny. A pleasant terrace has tables and chairs for warmer weather and fine views of the hamlet of Butterton close to Dovedale and the Manifold Valley. At the Black Lion there is a residents' TV lounge, while the guest rooms, which have been refurbished since the last edition, all have en suite facilities, TVs and tea and coffee making equipment.

Beer: McEwan 70 shilling and 80 shilling, Theakston Best Bitter and Younger No 3 on handpumps.

Accommodation: 2 doubles, 1 family room. B&B £19 per person, £25 single occupancy. No pets.

HARTINGTON

Manifold Valley Hotel
Hulme End, B5054. Off A515 Burton-Ashbourne road

Proprietors: Todhunter & Milner families
Tel: 0298 84537

The hotel is a delightful old village inn in a hamlet in the north Staffordshire Peak District, close to the lovely Manifold Valley and the tourist centre of Hartington. The inn has one cheerful bar with an open fire. A large and varied menu, including vegetarian choices, is available seven days a week in the bar and dining room. There is a daily lunchtime special and a children's menu. Accommodation is in a converted blacksmith's forge next to the hotel; all rooms are en suite and have colour TVs and tea and coffee making facilities. One room is suitable for disabled people. There is a separate residents' lounge and there are camping facilities close by.

Beer: Darley Dark Mild, Thorne Bitter and Ward Sheffield Best Bitter on handpumps with guest beers every week in summer.

Accommodation: 1 single, 3 doubles, 1 twin. B&B £26 per person; 2 night summer break £24 per person per night. Small charge for children. No dogs. Cards: Access and Visa.

ALDEBURGH

Mill Inn
Market Cross Place. A1094, off A12

Licensees: John & Brenda Nash
Tel: 0728 452563

The Mill is an attractive old pub close to the sea front of this famous Suffolk resort with its powerful Benjamin Britten associations: Snape Maltings concert hall, founded by the composer, is just outside the town and *Peter Grimes* is based on a story about this part of the Suffolk coast. Opposite the Mill is the medieval Moot Hall or meeting place. The inn has a large public bar that attracts both local fishermen and the gentry, while the lounge is small, cosy and sedate: the two rooms are divided by an unusual fire raised above ground level and behind a glass front. A tiny snug room is a couple of steps down from the public bar. There are lunchtime and evening grills (not Wednesday or Sunday evening). The guest rooms have TVs and tea and coffee making facilities. Booking is advisable for summer and the Aldeburgh Festival.

Beer: Adnams Bitter, Broadside and Old (winter) on handpumps.

Accommodation: 1 single, 2 doubles, 1 twin. B&B £17.50 per person. No pets.

BARDWELL

Six Bells Inn
The Green. ½ mile off A143 Bury to Diss road

Licensees: Carol & Richard Salmon
Tel: 0359 50820

The Six Bells is a 16th-century inn with exposed beams and an inglenook fireplace. It is on an old coaching route and stands close to the village green and duck pond in an acre of land surrounded by farmland. Bury St Edmunds, Lavenham, Bressingham and Newmarket are close by. The restaurant of the Six Bells incorporates an old Suffolk range with its original oven and copper. The Salmons specialize in prime steaks, fresh fish and game in season, and the restaurant offers Stilton steak – fillet steak with gammon and mushrooms glazed in Stilton – salmon thermidor, scallop strudel, breast of chicken with apricots and brandy, and pheasant and port casserole. Bar meals include game pie, tipsy roast lamb in red wine and herbs, smoked breast of chicken salad, and grilled sardines. Not surprisingly, the Salmons have been regional finalists in the Pub Caterer awards for 1988, 1989 and 1990. Their food is available every day, lunchtime and evening; there is a roast lunch on Sunday. Accommodation is in a converted barn; all the rooms are en suite and have colour TVs, tea and coffee making facilities and direct-dial phones.

Beer: Adnams Bitter and Old (winter), Wadworth 6X and Whitbread Boddingtons Bitter on handpumps.

Accommodation: 2 singles, 4 doubles/ twins, 1 family room. B&B £28 single, £50 double/twin, £55 family room. Children £5 for second additional bed in room and breakfast. Special rates for 2 & 3 day breaks including dinner allowance. Children welcome in designated areas of inn. Pets accepted. Cards: Access and Visa.

BILDESTON

Crown Hotel
High Street. B1115 between Stowmarket and Hadleigh

Licensees: Edward & Dinah Henderson
Tel: 0449 740510

The Crown is timber-framed coaching inn built around 1500. It has a wealth of exposed beams and there are log fires in winter; it is close to the stunning medieval wool town of Lavenham and is also handy for Bury, Ipswich and Constable Country. Food is available in both the restaurant and bar and includes an à la carte menu and such bar meals as toasted sandwiches, ploughman's, omelettes, chicken and chips, clam fries and egg piperade.

Beer: Adnams Bitter, Mauldon Black Adder, Marston Pedigree Bitter and Nethergate Bitter on handpumps.

Accommodation: 15 doubles/twins, 2 family rooms, 11 with en suite facilities. B&B from £20 single, £30-£55 double. No dogs. Cards: Access and Visa.

BURY ST EDMUNDS

Bushel Hotel
St John's Street, town centre. Off A45

Licensees: Mr & Mrs E.V. Groves
Tel: 0284 754333

The Bushel, sandwiched between St John's Street and St Andrew's Street in the town centre, dates back to the 15th century and is an old coaching inn. It was sensitively refurbished in the late 1980s to bring out the true atmosphere of the old building. Bar meals and restaurant meals are available; the restaurant has a carvery and full à la carte menu. There are daily specials on the lunchtime menu. Food lunchtime and evening except Sunday evening. All rooms have colour TVs, hot and cold water and tea and coffee makers.

Beer: Greene King IPA, Rayments

Crown Hotel, Bildeston

Special Bitter and Abbot Ale on handpumps.

Accommodation: £20 single, £15 double per person. Cards: Access and Visa.

Dog & Partridge
29 Crown Street. A45, south of town, next to Greene King brewery

Licensee: C.A. Painter
Tel: 0284 764792

The Dog & Partridge is an inn of enormous antiquity, built in approximately 1689 and with many of its original features – beams, pillars and pews – left intact. It is a grade two listed building; it was first a private house, then became an inn called the Mermaid that specialized in rook pie, and later adopted the present name and, thankfully, phased out its bird dishes. Full meals and bar snacks are served at lunchtime. The bar at the rear has been fashioned from the inn's old stables. It is near the cathedral, Abbey Gardens and St Mary's Church.

Beer: Greene King IPA, Rayments Special Bitter and Abbot Ale on handpumps.

Accommodation: 2 doubles, 1 twin. B&B £32 per room. Shared bathroom and toilet. Children sharing with parents £8 including breakfast. No dogs.

CAVENDISH

George Inn
The Green. A1092

Licensee: J.E. Harwood
Tel: 0787 280248

The George is a 15th-century village pub overlooking the green in Cavendish. It has a tall, imposing chimney and a handsome bow-windowed frontage. Inside there is a cosy public bar and a spacious lounge; a home-cooked menu is available seven days a week, lunchtime and evening; in summer fresh fish is a speciality. This is Constable Country and the pub is a splendid base for visiting Flatford and Dedham. Closer to Cavendish are a vineyard, a working priory and the Sue Ryder Foundation headquarters.

Beer: Flowers IPA and Original, Tolly Mild and Bitter on handpumps.

Accommodation: 2 doubles, 1 twin; all rooms have hot and cold water, central heating, TVs and teasmades. B&B £17.50 single, £30 double. Dogs by arrangement. Cards: Access and Visa.

CHELSWORTH

Peacock Inn
The Street. B1115

Licensees: A.F. Marsh & L.R. Bulgin
Tel: 0449 740758

The Peacock is a superb country pub ten miles from the nearest market town and five miles from Lavenham, one of the finest examples of a preserved medieval town in England. The 14th-century inn, with oak timbers and inglenook fireplaces, is opposite a tiny bridge over the narrow River Brett. It has five small guest rooms, most with exposed beams. The horseshoe bar divides into a stand-and-chat bar, a snug with a blazing open fire and a smart lounge with a permanent art gallery. There is an extensive menu of homemade food (lunchtime and evening), including on Sundays roast beef cooked over a log fire. Special dishes include game pie in winter, seafood Mornay, pasta dishes, vegetarian quiche, steak, kidney amd mushroom pie, homemade soup, sweet and sour chicken, ploughman's and granary bread sandwiches. The saloon bar has a piano and there is live music, usually jazz, on Fridays.

Beer: Adnams Bitter, Greene King IPA and Abbot Ale, Mauldon Bitter on handpumps.

Accommodation: 1 single, 4 doubles/ twins. B&B £24 single, £42 double. No pets.

CLARE

Bell Hotel
Market Hill. Off A1092

Licensees: Brian & Gloria Miles
Tel: 0787 277741
Fax: 0787 278474

The Bell is an imposing 16th-century posting house with a half-timbered façade, a panelled and beamed bar with an open fire, and a wine bar with fascinating memorabilia connected with canal building. The splendid accommodation is furnished with period furniture and includes a four-poster bedroom. Bar food, seven days a week, includes soup, toasties, homemade lasagne and grills. There is a separate à la carte restaurant, too, and afternoon tea is served in the conservatory. Clare has the remains of a castle and priory and is the home of the small Nethergate Brewery: the Bell was the first outlet for its fruity ale.

Beer: Greene King IPA and Abbot Ale, Nethergate Bitter and Old Growler on handpumps.

Accommodation: 1 single, 20 doubles, 2 family rooms, all rooms with en

Peacock Inn, Chelsworth

suite facilities. B&B £49.95 single, £64.95 double, £84 family room. Bargain Break: £27.25 per person per night B&B, £43.20 with dinner. Children welcome, no reductions. Dogs by arrangement. Cards: Access, Amex, Diners, Visa.

DUNWICH

Ship Inn
St James Street. 2 miles off B1125

Licensees: Stephen & Annie Marshlain
Tel: 072 873 219

The nautical bar of the Ship is, rather suitably, slightly sunken, for the once great medieval city of Dunwich – the greatest in East Anglia and the seat of kings – lies beneath the North Sea and only the church bells can be heard tolling at night before a storm (or so legend, embellished by a few pints, claims). The bar of the Ship has a tiled floor, wood-burning stove and captain's chairs. Home-made bar food includes soup, locally caught fish with chips, cottage pie, salads, ploughman's and various puddings. The separate restaurant (open for lunch and dinner) has homemade boozy pâté, fresh fish dish of the day, chicken Kiev, vegetarian dish, ice creams and sorbets. There is a pleasant garden, terrace and conservatory, ideal for families. Children are allowed in all rooms except the bar.

Beer: Adnams Bitter and Old (winter), Greene King Abbot Ale on handpumps.

Accommodation: 1 single, 2 doubles, 1 twin, 1 family room. B&B £19 single, £38 double/twin. Children welcome, terms negotiable.

FELIXSTOWE

Fludyer Arms Hotel
Undercliff Road East. Off A45

Licensee: John Nash
Tel: 0394 283279
Fax: 0394 670754

The Fludyer Arms, close to the beach in old Felixstowe, is a large and impressive Victorian building with several splendid Dutch gables and a large conservatory with fine views of the sea. There are two bars and a children's room. Extensive bar food includes a special 'spud grub' section – baked jacket potatoes with a wide range of fillings, from baked beans to curry and prawns – plus homemade soup, whitebait, fillet of cod, steak and kidney pie, chicken curry, omelettes, ploughman's, sandwiches, burgers, and such sweets as apple pie and vanilla ice cream.

Beer: Tolly Bitter, Courage Directors on handpumps.

Accommodation: 2 singles, 5 doubles/ twins, 1 family room, 4 rooms with en suite facilities. B&B £18 single, £26 with shower, £32 double, £40 with shower, £50 family room. Pets welcome. Cards: Access and Visa.

Ordnance Hotel
1 Undercliff Road West

Licensee: Roger Cox
Tel: 0394 273427
Fax: 0394 277126

The Ordnance Arms Hotel, as it was first called, was built in 1854 close to the old coastal defence battery in Felixstowe, now a leisure centre. In the bicentary history of the Ipswich brewers, Cobbold, the hotel was described as the 'oldest hotel in Felixstowe, well known for its catering'. Today the hotel is set in large gardens close to the town centre and the beach, and handy for the port terminal. It has a bar and lounge. Bar snacks are available lunchtime and evening every day (lunch only at weekends) and there is an American-style diner menu offering starters such as chicken tikka, baked brie, loaded potato skins with cheese, bacon and sour cream, plus such main courses as salmon fillet, swordfish, and steaks. The guest rooms have been refurbished to a high standard since the last edition and most are now en suite.

Beer: Tolly Bitter on handpump.

Accommodation: 6 singles, 10 doubles/twins, 1 family room. B&B £25 single, £35 double, £45 twin. No dogs. Cards: Access and Visa.

FLEMPTON

Greyhound
The Green. A1101, behind village church, Bury St Edmunds-Mildenhall road

Licensee: David R Nunn
Tel: 0284 728400

The Greyhound is a large, lively and rambling local overlooking the green in this old Saxon village with its ancient forge. The Greyhound, which is featured on the pub weathervane, has a heavily windowed exterior and a charming, unspoilt interior with welcoming open fires. There is bar food lunchtime and evening, and a walled garden for the summer months. The pub is a good base for visiting the village, the local abbey gardens and Bury St Edmunds.

Beer: Greene King XX Mild, IPA, Rayments Special Bitter and Abbot Ale on handpumps.

Accommodation: 2 doubles, 1 family room. B&B £14 per person. No pets.

FRAMSDEN

Dobermann
The Street. Signposted from B1077 south of junction with A1120 Stowmarket to Earl Soham road

Licensee: Susan Frankland
Tel: 0473 890461

The Dobermann, despite its rather alarming name, is a gentle and welcoming old thatched pub tucked away down a lane. The owners raise the hounds and the lounge is decorated with the many rosettes they have won. Inside, the pub has been carefully rendered back to its original style, with bare brick walls, beams and wooden partitions. The plainer bar area and chintzy lounge are connected by a large see-through fireplace that is decorated with flowers in the summer. Imaginative bar food includes a daily vegetarian dish along with homemade rabbit pie and game pies, trout in wine and almonds, steak and kidney or chicken pie, scampi, Stilton ploughman's, and turkey fricassée. There is a charming garden to the side of the pub where boules is played and there are picnic tables and a summertime barbecue.

Beer: Adnams Bitter and Broadside, Draught Bass, Felinfoel Double Dragon, Wadworth 6X and regular guests such as Courage Directors and Robinsons Best Bitter, all on handpumps.

Accommodation: 1 double room, £15 per person.

GREAT GLEMHAM

Crown
1½ miles off A12 at Stratford St
Andrew

Licensee: Roger Mason
Tel: 072 878 693

The Crown is a wonderfully
welcoming pub with a massive,
dominating fireplace and a log fire in
winter. The comfortable lounge has
captain's chairs round kitchen tables,
and there are local paintings and
photographs decorating the white
walls. There are seats on the lawn in
spring and summer, and inside locals
play darts, dominoes and crib. New
licensee Roger Mason is a chef by
trade and has upgraded the menu and
increased the size of portions. His
comprehensive menu includes
starters of liver or smoked mackerel
pâté, soup and freshly baked roll,
salade niçoise, prawn cocktail,
homemade steak and kidney pie,
chilli, chicken parmigana, barbecued
half-chicken, American-style
burgers, salads with Suffolk ham,
roast beef or prawns, and such
vegetarian options as ratatouille and
tagliatelle. There are fish dishes, too.
The pub has a separate dining room
but customers can eat in any part of
the building. Families can use the
dining room at lunchtimes during the
week.

Beer: Adnams Bitter and Old
(winter), Greene King IPA and
Abbot Ale on handpumps.

Accommodation: 1 single, 1 double, 1
family room. B&B £17.50 per person.
Children £7 according to age.

IPSWICH

Lion's Head
213-215 Cauldwell Hall Road.
Ipswich East turn from A45 & A12

Licensees: Barry & Teresa French
Tel: 0473 727418

The Lion's Head is a turn-of-the-
century building on the east side of
Ipswich. It is decorated inside with a
plethora of plates, and there are good
value bar meals, from a sandwich to a
steak, served lunchtime and until 9 in
the evening (no food Sundays). A
large garden has a children's play
area.

Beer: Tolly Mild, Bitter and Old
Strong (winter) on handpumps.

Accommodation: 1 single, 3 twins.
B&B £15 per person. Children
welcome, no reductions. No pets.

LONG MELFORD

George & Dragon Inn
Hall Street, centre of town

Licensee: Peter Thorogood
Tel: 0787 71285

The George & Dragon is an ancient
coaching inn that was restored in
Victorian times. It is a typical Suffolk
pub with a large lounge bar and a
genuine locals' public bar with darts
and pool and regular folk and jazz
nights. Bar food is available
lunchtime and evening in the lounge
and traditional dishes range from
ploughman's to East Anglian topside
of beef. There are splendid breakfasts,
too.

Beer: Greene King IPA, Rayments
Special Bitter and Abbot Ale on
handpumps.

Accommodation: 3 singles, 4 doubles/ twins, 1 room with en suite facilities. B&B £15 per person. Children allowed in lounge bar. Pets welcome.

ORFORD

Jolly Sailor
Quay Street. B10884, off A12, 12 miles from Woodbridge

Licensees: Pat & June Buckner
Tel: 0394 450243

The sea has receded from Orford but has left this merry matelot behind as a reminder of the town's nautical days. Parts of the 16th-century inn are built from the timbers of old shipwrecked vessels.

Beer and food come from a central hatch that serves the bar, lounge and snug. Darts, dominoes, crib and shove ha'penny are played by locals and the bar is warmed by an old-fashioned stove. There is a spiral staircase and a collection of stuffed miniature dogs thought to come from Tudor times. Bar food (lunchtime and evening) includes hot daily specials, ploughman's, steaks (if ordered), sausages, goujons of plaice and salads. A large garden at the back has a children's play area. Orford has one of the finest castles in East Anglia and the renowned Butley Orford Oystery restaurant specializing in seafood.

Beer: Adnams Bitter and Old (winter) on handpumps.

Accommodation: 1 single, 3 doubles. B&B £16 per person. Children and small dogs welcome.

RICKINGHALL

Hamblyn House
The Street. On A143 Diss to Bury road, 4 miles from Diss

Licensees: Dave Robinson & George Wellings
Tel: 0379 898 292

James Hamblyn, who played an important role in the founding of Chicago, built his house 480 years ago. It has a striking and unusual Flemish exterior that spans two parishes: the lounge and bar are in Rickinghall Inferior while the restaurant, fittingly, is in Rickinghall Superior. Inside there is a huge stone fireplace, black timbers and copper and brassware. The en suite guest rooms are tucked away under the eaves. All food is homemade by an enthusiastic chef; steak pie and chicken pie are popular. Food is available in the bar and the separate restaurant seven days a week. Children are welcome in designated parts of the pub and in the restaurant. There is a sunken garden with swings.

Beer: Adnams Bitter and Old (winter), Greene King IPA and Abbot Ale on handpumps.

Accommodation: B&B £30 single, £40 double/twin with shared bath; £50 en suite, 4-poster en suite £60. Cards: Access and Visa.

SAXMUNDHAM

White Hart Hotel
High Street, B1121. 1½ miles off A12

Licensee: Malcolm Banks
Tel: 072860 2009

The White Hart is a 16th-century coaching inn in a small market town that stages twice-weekly auctions. The inn has two bars and a restaurant and open log fires. Bar food, available lunchtime and evening, offers sandwiches, roasts, salads and daily specials. The restaurant is open Wednesday to Sunday. The hotel was thoroughly renovated and refurbished in 1989, and is a good base for visiting Framlingham castle, Woodbridge, Bruisyard and Shawsgate vineyards, Minsmere bird sanctuary and Snape Maltings.

Beer: Courage Directors, Tolly Bitter, Original and Old Strong (winter) on handpumps.

Accommodation: 1 single, 3 doubles/ twins, 4 family rooms. 1 room en suite, all rooms have hot and cold water, colour TVs and tea making facilities. B&B £16.50 single, £33 double/twin, £45 family room. Children by arrangement. Pets welcome. Cards: Access, Amex, Visa.

SIBTON

Sibton White Horse
Halesworth Road. A1120, ½ mile from Peasenhalll

Licensees: Fay & Tony Waddingham
Tel: 072 879 337

The White Horse is a delightful 16th-century pub in 2½ acres of ground and surrounded by fields in a conservation area. Darts, cribbage, dominoes, shove ha'penny and petanque are available. There is a pleasant outside seating area on shingle at the front and a children's play area at the rear with more seating. Inside, the pub has a 20-seater beamed restaurant and a raised gallery area where children are welcome. Bar meals are available lunchtime and evening and always

include vegetarian dishes. Accommodation is in a separate building in the grounds; most of the rooms have en suite facilities.

Beer: Adnams Bitter and Broadside on handpumps.

Accommodation: 3 singles, 3 doubles, 3 twins, including 1 family suite with double and single beds and bathroom. B&B £15-£18 per person according to room and length of stay. Children's rates according to age. Pets welcome.

SOUTHWOLD

Crown Hotel
90 High Street. Off A12

Manager: Anne Simpson
Tel: 0502 722275

The green and cream Georgian hotel announces Adnams' dominant position in the town. The carefully extended brewery lies behind the Crown, which doubles as small town hotel-cum-pub and, upstairs, the brewery's fast expanding and much praised wine business. The food is outstanding and, like the accommodation, is surprisingly reasonably priced. Bar food may include smoked haddock bake, spiced baked vegetable Wellington, mixed seafood salad, North Sea fish gratin, escalope of turkey, pan-fried noisettes of lamb, homemade soup, melon and avocado, whole roast quail, smoked fillet of trout, Sole Bay seafood chowder, half roast guinea fowl and Malay spiced vegetable stir fry. Restaurant meals (lunch and dinner £12.75-£17.75) are accompanied by recommended glasses of wine for each course, the wines kept under nitrogen pressure in a Cruover machine: the only permitted form of gas pressure in the guide. Regular jazz and classical music evenings are staged. The Crown holds regular wine appreciation weekends: details and prices from Ms Simpson.

Beer: Adnams Bitter, Broadside and Old (winter) on handpumps.

Accommodation: 2 singles, 4 doubles, 5 twins, 1 family room, 9 rooms en suite. B&B £33 single, £52/twin double, £77 family room. Children welcome, half price plus food. Dogs by prior arrangement. Cards: Access, Amex, Visa.

Red Lion
2 South Green

Licensees: Mr N.J. & Mrs R.A. Sayers
Tel: 0502 722385

The Red Lion has one of the best positions in this delightful Victorian seaside town with roots dating back to the 15th century when it was granted a charter by Henry VII. The famous battle of Sole Bay was fought here in 1672, with the combined English and French fleets against the Dutch. The pub, with a striking figure of a red lion, welcomes you to the wide expanse of South Green, just a few yards from the sea and the wide shingle beach. Inside there is one long panelled bar with bench seats running round the walls below the windows and fascinating old photos of Southwold as it was before the Victorians discovered the place. To the left of the bar is a small family room, to the right a restaurant serving a full menu seven days a week, including locally caught seafood when available. There is a children's menu, too. Children are welcome in the family room. The Red Lion is renowned for its generous traditional breakfasts.

Beer: Adnams Bitter, Broadside and Old (winter) on handpumps.

Accommodation: 1 single, 1 twin, 2 doubles. B&B £15 single in winter, £17.50 summer, twin/double £30/£35, double en suite £35/£40.

STOKE BY NAYLAND

Angel Inn
On B1068 Sudbury to East Bergholt road, 5 miles off A12

Licensees: P.G. Smith & R.E. Wright
Tel: 0206 263245

The Angel is a 16th-century inn on the Essex border in the heart of Dedham Vale – Constable Country. The village was much loved by the painter who immortalized its cottages and river banks on canvas. The lively inn has a wood-burning stove, original timbers and beams. Bar food is available lunchtime and evening, is prepared only from fresh ingredients, and includes soups, ploughman's, asparagus, moussaka, homemade gravadlax, chicken and prawn brochette, and a plate of three fresh griddled fish. There is a separate restaurant for evening meals. The guest rooms all have en suite facilities, colour TVs, telephones and tea and coffee makers.

Beer: Adnams Bitter, Greene King IPA and Abbot Ale, Nethergate Bitter on handpumps.

Accommodation: 6 singles, 6 doubles, 1 family room. B&B £42 single, £55 double. No children under 10. No pets. Cards: Access, Amex, Diners, Visa.

STRADBROKE

Ivy House
Wilby Road. B1117; off A140

Licensee: John O'Brien
Tel: 0379 84634

The Ivy House is a charming
thatched pub close to Eye and Diss. It
has two bars, a lounge, dining room,
and a pleasant garden for families in
summer. Food is available lunchtime
and evening and ranges from three-
course meals to bar snacks. Daily
homemade specials, with fresh
vegetables, include beef and Guinness
casserole, pork braised in cider, and
steak and kidney pie. Wingfield
Castle is close by and it is a short
drive to the Otter Trust at Bungay,
Framlingham castle and Bressingham
steam museum and gardens.

Beer: Adnams Bitter, Marston
Pedigree Bitter and Flowers Original
on handpumps.

Accommodation: 1 single, 2 doubles/
twins. B&B £13.50 per person. No
pets. Cards: Access and Visa.

SUDBURY

White Horse
North Street. Off A134

Licensee: Anne Martin
Tel: 0787 71063

Sudbury was the home of Thomas
Gainsborough, once the greatest
portrait painter in England, and his
nephew was landlord of the White
Horse for a time. The pub is 500
years old, and many architectural
styles have been added to it over the
years but have not tampered with its
essential charm and cosiness. It has a
40-seater lounge restaurant serving a
wide range of home-cooked meals at
lunchtime. Bar meals are also
available. It is a fine base for touring
the Stour valley, Constable Country
and the old market towns of Clare
and Lavenham.

Beer: Greene King XX Mild, IPA,
Rayments Special Bitter and Abbot
Ale on handpumps.

Accommodation: 3 singles, 2 doubles.
B&B £17.50 single, £35 double. No
dogs.

WALBERSWICK

Bell Hotel
B1387, off A12. Go right through
village to green, turn right for pub

Licensee: Mark Stansall
Tel: 0502 723109

The Bell is an atmospheric old
fishermen's inn in a village that has no
truck with such modern refinements
as pavements or street lighting. The
inn is 600 years old and the passage of
feet has worn and bowed the old
stone floors. There are high-backed
settles in the main bar, photos of the
village and some of the local
characters in a smaller side bar and a
large room where shove ha'penny
and crib are played. A vast back
garden with hedges, trees and tables,
is ideal for summer Sundays when
crowds descend for Adnams' ale and
the Stansalls' buffet lunch of fresh
seafood and salads. There is an inside
dining room, too, for lunches and
dinner. Food includes homemade fish
pie, freshly caught fish, homemade
quiche, smoked mackerel, prawns
and crab, with additional hot dishes
in winter. The Bell is a genuine local,
with fishermen strolling up from the
mouth of the Blyth for a pint and a
crack. The ferryman will row you
across to the opposite bank from
where you can buy fresh fish and
crabs or walk into Southwold.

Beer: Adnams Bitter, Broadside, Extra and Old (winter) on handpumps.

Accommodation: 1 double, 2 twins, 2 en suite doubles. B&B £20 per person, £25 in en suite room.

WOOLPIT

Swan Inn
The Street. 1 mile from junction of A45 & A1088

Licensee: Joseph Thompson
Tel: 0359 40482

The Swan is a 400-year-old red brick former coaching inn in the centre of the village, with one large L-shaped bar which has a log fire in the winter. There are excellent lunchtime bar snacks (not Sundays) and hearty breakfasts. The guest rooms are in an annexe off the main building, and they all have colour TVs and tea and coffee making facilities. Children of all ages are welcome. Bury St Edmunds is just 10 minutes' drive and Felixstowe ferry port is 45 minutes.

Beer: Courage Directors and John Smith's Bitter on handpumps.

Accommodation: 1 single, 3 twins, 1 double, 1 double/family room en suite. B&B £17.50 single, £16 per person twin/double/family room. Children 13 and under £12.50

SURREY

BLETCHINGLEY

Whyte Harte Inn
11/21 High Street. A25, 2½ miles from M25 exit 6

Licensees: David & Miriam Yarwood
Tel: 0883 743231

The Whyte Harte is a 600-year-old inn, with low beams, wood floors, an inglenook fireplace with an ancient and sagging beam, and settles and stools to sit on. It was once owned by cousins of Sir Francis Drake; some of the inn's beams are old ships' timbers. The pleasant garden is bounded by a stone wall and old Tudor cottages and there are also seats at the front among flower tubs. Homemade pub fare (lunchtime and evening) in the bar and restaurant includes soup, smoked mackerel, potato skins, brie armandine, chilli con carne, homemade curries, steaks, steak and ale pie, fish platter, beef Stroganoff, swordfish and special vegetarian dishes of the day. Mr Yarwood is a member of the prestigious Guild of Master Cellarmen.

Beer: Friary Meux Best Bitter, Tetley Bitter and Ind Coope Burton Ale on handpumps.

Accommodation: 5 singles, 3 doubles, 4 twins, 9 rooms en suite. B&B £50 single, £65 double, £75 four-poster room. 20% weekend discounts. Travel cot supplied for babies; children up to 12 must share a room with parents. Children welcome in dining area. No pets. Cards: Access, Amex, Diners, Visa.

CHERTSEY

Crown
London Street. A3 exit 10 Wisley; M25 exit 11. Pub is by Old Town Hall

Licensee: Bill Peters
Tel: 0932 564657
Fax: 0932 570839

Chertsey was once a major coaching route, and the Crown hotel became an important staging post and watering hole for travellers. It was rebuilt at the end of the 19th century and was bought by Young's brewery in London. It is a striking and imposing three-storey building, with verandahs and dormer windows, a free-standing inn sign and a 'gallows' sign over a side entrance once used by coaches. The decline of pub accommodation in London and the surounding areas meant that the Crown had retreated to being just a pub, but Youngs restored the accommodation in 1990 with a substantial face-lift. The inn offers bar meals and full restaurant meals lunchtime and evening and there are barbecues in summer.

Beer: Youngs Bitter, Special Bitter and Winter Warmer on handpumps.

Accommodation: 26 doubles, 4 family rooms, 26 rooms with en suite facilities. B&B £75 single, £85 double. Children free under 12. Pets accepted. Cards: Access, Amex, Diners, Visa.

DORKING

Pilgrim
Station Road, off A24, next to Dorking West railway station

Licensee: Bob Waterton
Tel: 0306 889951

The Pilgrim is a cheerful old inn tucked away from the town centre and offering a traditional pub alternative to Dorking's many pricey hotels.
The handsome town is close to the well-known beauty spots of Leith Hill – at 1,000 feet the highest place in the south-east – and Box Hill. The North Downs run along the northern edge of the town. The Pilgrim has a garden and serves bar food lunchtime

and evening. There is a small dining room, where children are welcome; special meals are provided for residents on request.

Beer: Friary Meux Best Bitter, Tetley Bitter and Ind Coope Burton Ale on handpumps.

Accommodation: 5 doubles, 1 family room. B&B £25 single, £40 double, £55 family room. Cards: Access, Amex, Diners, Visa.

FELBRIDGE

Woodcock
Woodcock Hill, A22

Licensee: Valerie Jones
Tel: 0342 325859

The Woodcock is a wistaria-clad inn, some 400 to 500 years old, with leaded windows and old beams, furnished throughout with original Victorian items. There are two bars: a lounge where you can eat and a drinkers' bar. The lounge is comfortably furnished with chaises-longues and there is a separate dining room. Food comes in the form of bar meals and full restaurant meals; bar meals include fresh sardines in garlic sauce and such homemade pies as steak and mushroom cooked in Guinness. There is always a selection of fish dishes and vegetarian options, and Mrs Jones will cook a vegetarian dish to order using fresh vegetables and, given notice, prepare a three or four-course vegetarian dinner. The guest rooms have names including Stripes and Lace, and the Chinese and Pink suites.

Beer: Greene King Abbot Ale, Harvey Armada, Ringwood Old Thumper and Wadworth 6X on handpumps with Larkins Best Bitter and Pilgrim Surrey Bitter in summer.

Accommodation: 2 doubles, two suites. Doubles £35, suites £55-£65, all rooms with TVs, direct-dial phones and tea and coffee makers. Children welcome; cot available, nominal charge for small children. No dogs. Cards: Access and Visa.

GODSTONE

Bell Inn
128 High Street, B2236, just off village green; 1 mile south of M25 exit 6

Licensee: Eric A. Henderson
Tel: 0883 743133

The Bell is a splendid 600-year-old coaching inn with a large beamed bar with open log fires and a wealth of copper and brass. Traditional bar food is served lunchtime and evening, and there is also a separate à la carte restaurant. The Bell has a large garden with a children's play area; children have their own food menu, too. The inn is close to the village green and pond, and handy for visiting the North Downs, Penshurst Place, Hever Castle and Chartwell with its Winston Churchill connections. Guest rooms at the Bell include a four-poster bedroom and a family room.

Beer: Friary Meux Best Bitter, Ind Coope Burton Ale and Tetley Bitter on handpumps with such guest beers as Gales, King & Barnes, Wadworth and Youngs, all on handpumps.

Accommodation: 2 doubles, including a four-poster room, 1 twin. B&B £29-£39 single, £36-£46 double/twin. £50 for a family of 2 adults and 1 child up to 14 years. Pets welcome. Cards: Access and Visa.

HINDHEAD

Devil's Punchbowl Hotel
London Road, A3

Licensee: Mick Batterbee
Tel: 0428 606565
Fax: 0428 605713

The imposing hotel, with porches, dormers in the steeply sloping roof and a central tower, stands 900 feet above sea level with superb views of the Surrey Downs and the famous Devil's Punchbowl beauty spot from which it takes its name. The building was originally the country residence of the Hon Rollo Russell, son of Lord John Russell, the first Liberal Prime Minister. The present hotel retains a genuine pub atmosphere in a busy bar popular with locals. There is a lounge for morning coffee and afternoon tea, while Squire's restaurant offers a wide choice of à la carte meals. including steaks, lemon sole, rainbow trout, chicken Kiev, roast duckling and vegetarian lasagne. There are meals in the bar, too. All the beautifully appointed guest rooms have en suite facilities, colour TVs and tea and coffee making equipment.

Beer: Hall & Woodhouse Badger Best Bitter and Tanglefoot, Ruddles Best Bitter and County, Websters Yorkshire Bitter on handpumps.

Accommodation: 8 singles, 30 doubles/twins, 2 family rooms. B&B £55.50 single, £65.50 double/twin, family room £75. Children under 16 sharing with 2 adults free; 75% of tariff in own room. Weekend minimum 2 nights, £36.25 per person per night B&B plus dinner. Cards: Access, Amex, Diners, Visa.

OCKLEY

Kings Arms
Stane Street, A29

Licensees: David & Helen Smith
Tel: 0306 711224

The Kings Arms is an attractive old inn on an even older Roman road in a pleasant village with a large green. There is a separate restaurant with a full menu, and an emphasis on traditional homemade English dishes; no food Sunday and Monday evenings in winter. The pub has an outdoor drinking area for the warmer months and an indoor family area is being prepared by the new licensees. The Kings Arms is popular with people using Gatwick Airport and booking is therefore essential.

Beer: Courage Best Bitter, Exmoor Ale, Fullers London Pride and ESB Wadworth 6X and such guests as Ringwood, all on handpumps.

Accommodation: 3 doubles en suite, 2 family rooms; all rooms have colour TVs and tea and coffee makers. B&B £40 single, £55 double; family room from £35. Weekend rates on application. Cards: Access, Amex, Visa.

SUNBURY

Flower Pot Hotel
Thames Street, off A308 & M3

Licensee: Pat Spaven
Tel: 0932 780471

The hotel is one of the oldest licensed houses in Sunbury; it was first built alongside the Thames, and was moved to its present position in 1747. It was first piously named the Inn of the Annunciation but was changed to the Flower Pot in Cromwell's time.

(The puritans did away with any Popish associations, but the Flower Pot, with its links with the Virgin Mary, still subtly made its point; inns that bore the inscription 'God Encompasses Us' became, under Cromwell, the Goat and Compasses.) The Sunbury Flower Pot has ancient beams and doors with low entrances. There is one large bar with one end set aside for diners. Lunchtime snacks are served every day, there are evening bar meals and a Sunday lunch; all the food is home-cooked. In summer people flock to Flower Pot Green opposite the pub and overlooking the river.

Beer: Draught Bass, Brakspear XXX Mild and Bitter, Greene King IPA, Tetley Bitter, Youngs Special on handpumps.

Accommodation: 1 single, 4 twins, 4 doubles; 1 double en suite, can be used as a family room. B&B £47.40 per room; en suite £65; weekends £37.50. Children welcome. No dogs. Cards: Access, Switch, Visa.

ARDINGLY (WEST SUSSEX)

Ardingly Inn
Street Lane. Off B2028

Licensee: Amanda Buchanan-Munro
Tel: 0444 892214

The inn is a large village-centre pub with a spacious and comfortable lounge where meals are served lunchtime and evening. It has a real fire and a pleasant garden, and is close to Ardingly College, the South of England Showground and the

Bluebell Railway at Horsted Keynes. The inn's guest rooms all have colour TVs and tea and coffee making facilities. If you need to ask the way, the village is pronounced 'Arding-lie'.

Beer: Hall & Woodhouse Badger Best Bitter and Tanglefoot, Shepherd Neame Spitfire ale on handpumps.

Accommodation: 3 twins, 3 doubles, 3 with en suite facilities. B&B £37.50 double, £44 en suite. Cards: Access and Visa.

ARUNDEL (WEST SUSSEX)
The Swan
High Street. A27

Licensees: Diana & Ken Rowsell
Tel: 0903 882314
Fax: 0798 831716

The Swan, with a handsome façade, striking red window shades and a high dormer roof, is the oldest inn in this famous old Sussex town with its imposing castle. The Rowsells continue energetically to improve the facilities of the hotel and have added three extra guest rooms. The large L-shaped, partly timbered lounge serves good food based on local produce, including homemade soup, rolled smoked salmon and prawn, whitebait, a wide range of sandwiches and toasties, chicken and chips, burgers, grilled pork chop with apple sauce, fresh Sussex trout, steaks, salads, a daily vegetarian special, and filled jacket potatoes. There is an evening à la carte restaurant on Friday and Saturday and traditional Sunday roasts. All the guest rooms have en suite facilities, phones and tea and coffee making equipment.

Beer: Ballard Best Bitter, Courage Best Bitter and Directors, Hall &

Woodhouse Badger Best Bitter and Tanglefoot, Mitchells Bitter on handpumps.

Accommodation: 2 singles, 10 doubles, 1 family room. B&B £42.50 single, £55 double. Two-Day Breaks including dinner £94 single, £136 for 2. Off-Season Breaks £100 for 2 people for 2 nights dinner, B&B. Children welcome £10 per night, (extra bed available in 2 double rooms.) Cards: Access, Amex, Diners, Visa.

BURWASH (EAST SUSSEX)
Bell Inn
High Street. A21

Licensees: David & Annick Mizel
Tel: 0435 882304

The Bell is a 17th-century inn opposite the church, and has exposed beams and a sloping floor. Ale and wine are mulled on the open log fire and you can try your hand at ring the bull, one of the oldest pub games, toad-in-the-hole, darts and cribbage. The comfortable lounge has old photos of the area, which includes Batemans, not a brewery but the former home of Rudyard Kipling. Bar food includes sandwiches, jacket potatoes, pitta pockets; daily specials, chalked on a blackboard, may include fresh plaice, sole, skate, chicken Wellington, and venison with mushrooms. The inn provides daily newspapers for customers and there are seats at the front in good weather.

Beer: Harvey BB and XXXX (winter) on handpumps and regular guest beers such as Everards, Fullers and Thwaites.

Accommodation: 1 single, 4 doubles. B&B £25 single, £35 double. Pub has room where children can eat. No pets. Cards: Access and Via.

EDBURTON (WEST SUSSEX)

Tottington Manor Hotel

Nr Henfield. Take A281 from A23. At Henfield go left at mini-roundabout towards Woods Mill and Small Dole; approx 1 mile after Small Dole take left turn to Edburton

Proprietors: David & Kate Miller
Tel: 0903 815757
Fax: 0903 879331

The food at Tottington Manor is likely to be good even by the now high standards of many small hotels and pubs, for David Miller was head chef at the Ritz in London's Piccadilly, though you may find prices a shade cheaper here. The manor, mentioned in the Domesday Book and now grade two listed, was built around 1604 and is a handsome building set in its own spacious grounds, with lovely views of the surrounding countryside. It stands between Brighton and Worthing, and guests can enjoy horse-riding, walking, tennis, squash, swimming, fishing and hang-gliding close by. Bar food (lunchtime and evening, every day) includes sandwiches, toasties, ploughman's with Sussex Cheddar, Irish blue cheese and various meats, homemade soup, deepfried butterfly prawns, salmon mousse, Welsh rarebit with bacon and tomato, and such daily specials as cider-baked ham, homemade sausages with bubble and squeak, grilled pork chop and black pudding, burgers, homemade pie of the day with potatoes and vegetables, Southdown lamb cutlets, steaks, and vegetarian dishes. There is a special Sunday roast served in the bar, and a separate à la carte restaurant for lunch and dinner is available.

Beer: Adnams Bitter and Broadside, Bateman XXXB, Fullers London Pride and King & Barnes Sussex Bitter on handpumps.

Accommodation: 6 doubles, all en suite and with colour TVs and tea and coffee making facilities. B&B £40 single, from £60 double. Family room £10 extra per child over 3. 5 nights or more £35 single B&B per day, £50 double. Children's room. No pets. Cards: Access, Amex, Visa.

FOREST ROW

Ashdown Forest Hotel

Chapel Lane. From A22 at East Grinstead take B2110. Chapel Lane is fourth on right

Licensees: Robin Pratt & Alan Riddick
Tel: 0342 824866
Fax: 0342 824869

The hotel is an elegant Edwardian building with a creeper-clad and balconied exterior, standing in secluded grounds with its own 18-hole golf course. It has a bar, à la carte restaurant and a suite that holds up to 120 people. As well as golf, there are facilities close by for pony trekking and fishing. Bar food, lunchtime and evening, includes seafood platter, vegetable dips, sandwiches, a hot potato dish, salads, canapés and a carved buffet.

Beer: Harvey BB and a regular guest beer on handpumps.

Accommodation: 2 singles, 10 doubles/twins, 3 family rooms, 10 rooms with en suite facilities. B&B (including morning paper) £45 single, £60 double, £75 triple. Golfing holidays: prices on application. Children welcome, no reductions but most meals half price. No dogs. Cards: Access and Visa.

HASTINGS (EAST SUSSEX)

Crown Inn
66 All Saints Street. Off A259

Licensee: L.C. Nuttall
Tel: 0424 428308

The Crown is well-positioned in the old town section of Hastings, just 80 yards from the promenade. Mr Nuttall offers a warm welcome and will help point you in the direction of the Old Town Heritage Trail where you can discover 15th-century half-timbered houses with Georgian architecture. A miniature railway, boating lake and the historic fish market and harbour are close to the pub, which was rebuilt in the 1920s. There are homemade snacks and bar meals at lunchtime.

Beer: Harvey BB on handpump.

Accommodation: 1 single, 1 double, 2 twins; shared bathroom. B&B £14 per person per night. No dogs.

LEWES (EAST SUSSEX)

Dorset Arms
22 Malling Street. Off A27

Licensee: Chris Morley
Tel: 0273 477110

The Dorset Arms is an historic Lewes pub known as the Cats. Parts have been rebuilt but it retains its essential 17th-century character, with two bars with open fires and a separate restaurant called the Georgian Room. Food is available every lunchtime and Wednesday to Saturday evenings and ranges from local fish dishes to sirloin steaks. There is a patio for warmer weather. Lewes is close to Brighton and Eastbourne, and the town is steeped in history, with many old timbered buildings and cobbled streets. It is also the home of Harvey's brewery, a splendid example of a Victorian 'tower' system where the brewing process flows by gravity from one floor to another.

Beer: Harvey Pale Ale, BB (winter) and Armada on handpumps.

Accommodation: 1 single, 2 doubles, 2 en suite. B&B £17.50 single, £35 double. Children's room. No dogs. Cards: Access and Visa.

LITTLEHAMPTON (WEST SUSSEX)

New Inn
5 Norfolk Road. Just off sea front; from A259 follow signs to sea

Owners: Brian Griffith/Bob & Diana Witney
Tel: 0903 713112

The New Inn belies its name: it is a listed building dating from around 1760. There are two comfortable bars decorated in traditional style and a separate games room. There is a residents' lounge and a dining room for guests. The new owners have a vigorous cask ale policy, and featured more than 130 beers in 1991 alone. Hot and cold bar snacks are available until 10pm.

Beer: Bateman XB, Fullers ESB, Youngs Special Bitter and five guest beers on handpumps.

Accommodation: 5 doubles, 3 family rooms. B&B £14 single, £25 double, £35 family room; all prices reduced for period stays. Cards: Access and Visa.

MANNINGS HEATH (WEST SUSSEX)

Dun Horse
Brighton Road. A281 near Horsham

Licensee: N.N. Goodhew
Tel: 0403 65783

The Dun Horse is a homely pub south of Horsham, with comfortable bars and guest rooms and fine windows dating back to the days of the Rock brewery. The pub has open fires, a garden with children's play area, excellent pub grub lunchtime and evening with homemade dishes, daily specials of fresh fish, vegetarian options and children's meals. There are traditional games in the public bar. All the guest rooms have colour TVs. The Dun Horse is a good base for visiting Leonardslee and Nymans gardens; Gatwick Airport is close by, and Brighton is 20 miles away.

Beer: King & Barnes Sussex Bitter, Whitbread Boddingtons Bitter and Flowers Original on handpumps.

Accommodation: 2 singles, 1 double, 1 family room. B&B £18 per person. Children's rates by negotiation. Pets by prior arrangement.

MIDHURST (WEST SUSSEX)

Crown Inn
Edinburgh Square. Off A272 & A286

Licensee: Paul Norton Stevens
Tel: 0730 813462

The Crown is a 16th-century free house with cosy bars and a log fire and stove. There are indoor spit roasts on the first Sunday of the month. Accommodation is in the oldest part of the building, which dates from 1580. There is a small courtyard area that is popular in summer, and there is a newly refurbished function room where pool can be played. Bar meals are served Monday to Saturday lunchtime and evening; a separate restaurant is open lunchtime Thursday to Sunday and is also open Sunday evening. Children are allowed in the dining area. The inn usually has ten real ales on offer.

Beer: Fullers London Pride and ESB, Mitchells ESB, Ruddles Best Bitter, Shepherd Neame Master Brew Bitter, Theakstons Old Peculier, Websters Yorkshire Bitter, Whitbread Boddingtons Bitter and regular guest beers on handpumps and straight from the cask.

Accommodation: 1 single, 1 double, 1 twin. B&B £15 single, £12.50-£15 double/twin. Children's rates by negotiation. No pets.

PETWORTH (WEST SUSSEX)

White Horse Inn
The Street, Sutton, near Pulborough. From A29 4 miles south of Pulborough turn right at foot of Bury Hill to Sutton; A285 4 miles south of Petworth turn left at foot of Duncton Hill, road signposted Sutton 2 miles

Licensee: Howard Macnamara
Tel: 07987 221
Fax: 07987 291

The White Horse, smothered in creeper, dates from 1746 and was a malthouse as well as an inn and probably supplied a local brewer. It is a fiercely traditional place, with no canned music or video games: entertainment is supplied by the locals. It is one mile from the Roman Villa at Bignor; Arundel, Chichester and Goodwood racecourse are close at hand. Bar meals and full meals in the dining area are served lunchtime and evening every day, and use fresh vegetables grown by the landlord. Main meals may include roast duck, steaks, Wiener schnitzel, rack of lamb, and fresh fish; daily specials are shown on a blackboard.

Beer: Bateman XB, Fullers London Pride, Ruddles County and Youngs Bitter on handpumps.

Accommodation: 4 doubles, 1 family room, all with private bathrooms. B&B £38 single, £48 double, £58 family room (2 adults and 1 child). Breaks: any 2 nights B&B £80 for 2 people sharing; £65 for 1 person. No pets. Cards: Access and Visa.

BRIERLEY HILL (WEST MIDLANDS)

Saltwells Inn
Saltwells Road, Quarry Bank. Just off A4036. Head for Merry Hill shopping centre, take Coppice Lane, signposted Saltwells Nature Reserve

Tel: 0384 69224
Licensee: Gillian Stewart

The inn is in the Saltwells woods and nature reserve in the heart of the Black Country. It has a smart 1930s appearance from the outside, with tall chimneys placed unusually either side of the main entrance. The interior has been extensively redecorated in 'modern Tudor', with ceiling beams and many old photos and advertising prints on the walls. The Stewarts offer a genuinely hospitable welcome and good food at reasonable prices:

White Horse Inn, Petworth

there is bar food lunchtime and evening – steaks, scampi, plaice, pizzas, steak and kidney pie, burgers, a daily special, sandwiches, salads, pasties, plus a children's menu – and Sunday lunch. The large garden is surrounded by trees, has a children's amusement area, and is floodlit at night. There is a large family room with camera link, and all the guest rooms have colour TVs and tea and coffee making equipment. Brierley Hill is close to Dudley Zoo, the Black Country Museum, canals and the tunnels beneath Dudley and is the home of Batham's Brewery. The inn is open all day Mon-Sat.

Beer: Banks Mild and Bitter and Hanson Mild on electric pumps.

Accommodation: 8 singles, 6 doubles, 3 family rooms, 10 rooms with en suite facilities. B&B £16 single, £18 en suite, £32 double, £35 en suite, family room £15 per person, £16 en suite. No pets. Cards: Access and Visa.

DUDLEY (WEST MIDLANDS)

Station Hotel
Castle Hill, junction of Trindle Road, A461

Manager: Mr S.A. Dunn
Tel: 0384 53418

The hotel dates back to 1898 and was extensively rebuilt in the 1930s. It is stone-built and crescent-shaped and was once the haunt of theatre-goers to the Dudley Hippodrome in the heyday of regional theatre and music hall. It is close to Dudley Zoo and Castle, and to the Black Country Museum. The hotel has a traditional lounge bar where snacks are available; there is a restaurant serving an extensive and mixed menu, open

all week except Saturday lunch; children are welcome in the restaurant. A solarium and gym have been added, and other major improvements include bringing the restaurant down to the ground floor and installing a new lounge bar. All guest rooms have colour TVs, tea and coffee makers and direct-dial phones; all rooms have either bath or shower. Dudley is built on the highest hill in the Black Country and is surrounded by villages created by the Industrial Revolution.

Beer: Banks Mild and Bitter on electric pumps.

Accommodation: 14 singles, 15 doubles/twins, 6 family rooms, 3 executive suites with jacuzzis, many rooms with en suite facilities. B&B £47.50 single, £59.50 double/twin, £51.50 single occupancy, £12 extra for executive room; £47 family rooms (weekend rate). Young children sharing charged £6.25 for breakfast. Real Ale Weekends run with Dudley Leisure Services: £91.50 for 2 nights B&B, dinner and high tea. Cards: Access, Amex, Visa.

KENILWORTH (WARWICKSHIRE)

Clarendon House Hotel
Old High Street. Off A452

Licensee: Martyn Lea
Tel: 0926 57668

Kenilworth and the hotel are steeped in the history of the English Civil War. The hotel was once the Castle Tavern and was used by Cromwell's troops during the siege of the town. The present hotel has Cromwellian armour and other artefacts of the Civil War period. The original pub was built in 1538 around an old oak

174

tree that today still supports part of the main roof. There is a comfortable bar and a restaurant in the converted stables with a full à la carte restaurant. There are lunchtime bar snacks, too, and a Sunday roast. Four of the guest rooms have four-poster beds, one of which is some 400 years old. All rooms have bath or shower.

Beer: Flowers IPA and Original, Hook Norton Best Bitter and guest beers, all on handpumps.

Accommodation: 17 singles, 9 doubles/twins, 1 family room. B&B from £51.50 single, £77 double/twin, £82 with four-poster, family room £82. Leisure Breaks: £25 per person per night for B&B; £39.50 with dinner. Cards: Access and Visa.

KINGSWINFORD (WEST MIDLANDS)

Old Court House
High Street. A4101, ½ mile from A491

Licensee: Terence Cable
Tel: 0384 271887

The Old Court, with its attractive cream and green façade and red-tiled roof and porch, was built as a court building in 1790 and still stands on the village green in this pleasant hamlet near Dudley. There is a lounge bar and separate restaurant/ conservatory. Bar lunches are served daily and there are evening meals in the restaurant every day.

Beer: Banks Mild and Bitter and Hansons Bitter, Courage Directors on handpumps.

Accommodation: 2 doubles, 2 twins, all with en suite facilities. B&B £39 single occupancy, £45 double, £55

twin. Weekend: £25 single, £35 double/ twin. Children welcome: an extra bed can be supplied. Cards: Access, Amex, Diners, Visa.

LONG ITCHINGTON (WARWICKSHIRE)

Jolly Fisherman
The Green. A423, opposite village green

Tel: 092 681 2296
Licensee: Peter Hewitt

The Jolly Fisherman is a large pub set back from the road across from the village green and pond. It has a large public bar that sports a photo of the pub in 1903, and a comfortable lounge that stages live music on Fridays and Saturdays. A games room offers pool, Japanese 'noise boxes', darts and dominoes. Food, including bar snacks, is traditionally English in style; meals include steaks and homemade pies – steak and kidney, meat and potato. There are daily specials and also a pensioners' meal each weekday for £2.50. There is a large garden for sunny days.

Beer: Ansells Mild and Bitter and Tetley Bitter on handpumps plus Banks Bitter as a regular guest beer.

Accommodation: 1 double, 2 family rooms. B&B £15 per person. Half and full board available. Children's room; children welcome to stay, 30% reductions according to age.

SHIPSTON-ON-STOUR (WARWICKSHIRE)

Halford Bridge Inn
Fosseway. A429, 12 miles from Banbury; 6 miles from M40

Owners: Tony & Greta Westwood
Tel: 0789 740382

The Halford Bridge is a 16th-century Cotswold stone coaching inn with a 30-seater restaurant and comfortable lounge bar with log fires in winter. The kitchen is open seven days a week and there is a wide range of hot and cold food in the bar; home-cooking is the order of the day and fresh vegetables are used whenever possible, along with homemade sauces, pickles and pies. The inn is on the edge of the Cotswolds and Shakespeare country; there are many good walks nearby and trout fishing can be arranged in local lakes.

Beer: Theakston XB and Younger Scotch Bitter plus guest ales on handpumps.

Accommodation: 1 single, 3 doubles, 1 family room, 3 rooms with own showers, all with colour TVs and tea and coffee makers. B&B £17.50-£25 single, £35-£46 double, family room rates on application. Children from £5 according to age. No pets. Cards: Access and Visa.

WALL HEATH (WEST MIDLANDS)

Prince Albert Hotel
High Street. On A449 at village crossroads

Licensee: John Fereday
Tel: 0384 287411

The Prince Albert, built in the 1880s, is in the centre of an urban village at the edge of the Black Country and close to the Staffordshire countryside and Broadfield House glass museum. The lounge bar is decorated in mock-Tudor style. Roast lunches are served every day, along with daily specials and bar snacks; there is no evening food. The hotel has public and lounge bars and traditional games.

Beer: Hansons Mild and Banks Bitter on electric pumps.

Accommodation: 3 singles, 1 twin, 1 family room. B&B £17 single, £15 double.

WARWICK

Black Horse Inn
62-64 Saltisford. A41 Birmingham-Warwick road

Licensee: Mrs B. Sohal
Tel: 0926 403989

The Black Horse is a delightful 17th-century inn with mullioned windows, dormers in the eaves and a striking pub sign. Inside there are two cheerful and comfortable bars. There is one large bar with an area where pool is played, a lounge-cum-restaurant and a function room with its own bar. There are both bar and à la carte menus which include Indian meals and children's specials.

Beer: Draught Bass and M&B Brew XI, Stones Best Bitter and weekly guest beer on handpumps.

Accommodation: 12 rooms all en suite, with colour TVs. B&B £20 single, £30 double. Children welcome. Cards: Access and Visa.

Wheatsheaf Hotel
54 West Street, near town centre. A429

Licensees: Keith & Rachel Hinton
Tel: 0926 492817

The Wheatsheaf, near the centre of this fascinating and historic town with its castle, doll museum and medieval Shire Hall, has an attractive three-storey exterior with white-painted brickwork and striped awnings. Keith Hinton, a self-confessed 'amiable nutter', and his wife Rachel run a small dining room that serves lunch, dinner and a traditional Sunday roast, and a lounge bar where darts, dominoes and pool are played. The delightful guest rooms all have central heating, colour TVs and tea and coffee making facilities. Two rooms have four-poster beds.

Beer: Ansells Bitter, Tetley Bitter and Draught Bass on handpumps.

Accommodation: 8 rooms, optional occupancy, including 2 four-poster rooms with shower. B&B £25 single, £35 double, £45 family room, £40 four-poster. 10% discount for weekly stay. Children welcome, 10% reduction under 12 years. Cards: Access, Amex, Diners, Visa.

WOLVERHAMPTON (WEST MIDLANDS)

New Inn
Salop Street. Near ring road

Licensee: David Edward Watkin
Tel: 0902 23779

The New Inn is a cheerful market pub which has an all-day market licence and opens at 10am for breakfast. Cooked lunches are served, and rolls and sandwiches are available at all times. It is a good base for visiting the Black Country, Audley, Cannock Chase and Birmingham. The guest rooms are served by three bathrooms and each room has colour TV and tea and coffee making facilities.

Beer: Banks Mild and Bitter on electric pumps.

Accommodation: 2 singles, 2 doubles,

2 family rooms. B&B £14 per person. Children welcome, rates depend on age. Pets welcome.

Wheatsheaf Hotel
Market Street, town centre, next to police station & corner of Tower street

Licensees: Mr & Mrs B. Hall
Tel: 0902 24446

The Wheatsheaf is a busy town centre pub, near the bus and rail stations, with public and lounge bars and a beer garden. It gets busy at weekends but is quiet at other times. There is a residents' TV lounge. Breakfast is the only meal provided but there are rolls at lunchtime and many inexpensive restaurants close to the hotel.

Beer: Banks Mild and Bitter on electric pumps.

Accommodation: 7 singles, 4 twins. B&B £15 per person; 2 or more nights £13. Children under 12 £9 per night. No pets.

WILTSHIRE

AMESBURY

Antrobus Arms
15 Church Street. ½ mile off A303

Licensee: Mrs P.B. Stammers
Tel: 0980 623163

The Antrobus Arms is in the heart of Salisbury Plain, close to Stonehenge. The pub is beautifully furnished with fine antiques, the bar has a cheerful, friendly atmosphere and the restaurant has a deserved reputation for quality cooking; bar meals are served, too. The garden has a Victorian pond and fountain. The guest rooms have colour TVs, phones and tea and coffee making facilities.

Beer: Draught Bass, Wadworth 6X and guest beers on handpumps.

Accommodation: 8 singles, 12 doubles, 1 family room, 2 rooms with showers, 11 rooms with private bath. B&B £30 single, £50 double, £60 with bath. Children welcome, charged £10 for additional bed in room.

BROAD HINTON

Crown Inn
Village centre. Off A4631. At Swindon take the Devizes road; there are 3 turnings marked for Broad Hinton; M4 exit 16

Licensee: Bob Tidey
Tel: 0793 731302

The Crown is a 19th-century inn in a village at the foot of the Ridgeway Hills and close to Avebury and the historic town of Marlborough. A full range of bar food is served every day, lunchtime and evening, and there is a separate 30-seater restaurant (closed Monday evenings). Children have a play area.

Beer: Arkell Bitter, BBB and Kingsdown Ale on handpumps.

Accommodation: 2 doubles, 1 en suite. B&B £25-£35. Weekend: 2 nights for the price of 1. Cards: Access and Visa.

Near CHIPPENHAM

Plume of Feathers
Burton, on B4039, 1 mile from Castle Combe and 1 mile from Badminton

Licensees: June & Peter Bolin
Tel: 0454 218251

Plume of Feathers, near Chippenham

The Plume is a splendid 400-year-old listed building between Chippenham and Chipping Sodbury and close to Castle Combe and Badminton. The pub has a resident ghost, allegedly a young woman but, according to Mr Bolin, acts more like a young man 'with a racy sense of humour'. The Bolins offer a vast range of hot and cold food, bar snacks and full meals, seven days a week, supported by good ale and some fine Antipodean wines. Just a glimpse at the formidable menu finds Japanese prawns with chilli sauce, trout baked with wine sauce and grapes, homemade steak and kidney pie or lamb and mint pie, pork cordon bleu served with charcutière sauce, lasagne, moussaka, and such daily specials as liver and onions, sausages and mash, or faggots and mash. Twenty years of living in the Far East are reflected in an extensive Oriental menu featuring curries, Chinese dishes and, during the winter months, a Sunday lunch of Indonesian rijsttafel (rice table) – four meat curries and four vegetable ones – and 30 other dishes selected from every country in SE Asia, and served buffet style in the Indonesian manner.

Beer: Draught Bass, Benskins Best Bitter and Ind Coope Burton Ale on handpumps.

Accommodation: 2 doubles, both en suite. B&B £30 single, £38 double. Children sharing with parents charged £5 for breakfast. Long-term bookings are negotiable. Pets accepted. Cards: Access and Visa.

DOWNTON

Kings Arms
9 High Street. Next to church.
B3080, 1 mile off A338 Salisbury-Ringwood road

Licensees: Colin & Yvonne Ludwell
Tel: 0725 20446

The Kings Arms is a lively village pub near Salisbury and the New Forest. Parts of the building date back to the 14th century and there are beams and open fires. Darts and most other pub games are played indoors while an outdoor pétanque pitch brings a Gallic influence to the large garden. Fishing is available on local rivers and lakes. The Kings Arms enjoys a reputation for its splendid home-cooked bar snacks and full meals.

Beer: Gibbs Mew Salisbury Bitter and Wiltshire Bitter on handpumps.

Accommodation: 1 twin, 1 double, 1 family room. B&B £12.50 per person. Children welcome, one-third reductions.

EVERLEIGH

Crown at Everleigh
A342 between Andover and Devizes

Licensee: Mrs Jacki Chapman
Tel: 0264 850229
Fax: 0264 850864

The Crown is on the edge of Salisbury Plain, close to Stonehenge and Avebury. It was built in the early 17th century as a dower house to the local manor and became a coaching inn in the mid-18th century. The visitors' book includes such illustrious names as Rupert Brooke and John Maynard Keynes; William Cobbett in *Rural Rides* described the Crown as 'one of the finest inns in England'. The Garden Room, now used for business meetings and small private parties, served in the past as the local court house, and Hanging Judge Jeffreys is reputed to have administered 'justice' there. The inn now incorporates a 50-cover restaurant reached from the bar by a magnificent chandeliered mahogany staircase. The restaurant menu may include roast rack of lamb with port and redcurrant sauce, pork tenderloin with mushrooms and tarragon, grilled turbot or homemade game pie, while the lounge bar may offer the chef's renowned cheese herbies, avocado and smoked chicken toasties, faggots in onion gravy, and ploughman's with a large selection of cheeses. All meals are prepared using fresh produce only and menus change daily. The Crown has exceptionally deep cellars and electric pumps are needed to pull beer to the bar.

Beer: Draught Bass, John Smith's Bitter and Wadworth 6X on electric pumps.

Accommodation: 1 single, 2 doubles, all en suite. B&B £25 single, £50 double. Nov-March: 3 nights for the price of 2. Pets accepted. Cards: Access and Visa.

FONTHILL GIFFORD

Beckford Arms
Crossroads halfway between Tisbury and Hindon; 2 miles from A303, signposted Fonthill Bishop; 1 mile from B3089

Licensees: Bob Miles & Peter Harrison
Tel: 0747 870385
Fax: 0747 51496

The Beckford Arms is a rural 18th-century inn on a crossroads between the villages of Hindon and Tisbury in the middle of the former Beckford's Fonthill estate. The pub has a large garden and there are lakeside and woodlands walks to enjoy. The pub has two bars, both with log fires and high ceilings; traditional pub games are played in the lively public bar. A wide range of both bar and restaurant food is available seven days a week, using fresh local produce. Bar food includes

Beckford Arms, Fonthill Gifford

homemade soup, ploughman's, steak and kidney pie, chicken and mushroom pie, carbonnade of beef, game casserole, chilli con carne, lasagne al forno, quiche of the day, steaks, fisherman's pie, cod in batter, and spinach and mushroom lasagne and other vegetarian options.

Beer: Courage Best Bitter and Directors, Ruddles Best Bitter, Ushers Best Bitter and Wadworth 6X on handpumps.

Accommodation: 2 singles, 5 doubles, all with en suite facilities. B&B £29.50 single, £24.75 per person double, £27.25 in four-poster room. No charge for babies sharing with parents: cot supplied, bring own linen. Breaks: 2 days £29.75 per person B&B plus dinner (excluding Easter, Christmas and New Year). Well-behaved dogs by prior arrangement. Cards: Access and Amex.

FOVANT

Cross Keys
On A30, 10 miles from Salisbury towards Shaftesbury

Licensee: Mrs Pauline Story
Tel: 0722 70284

This fascinating old coaching inn was built in 1485 and nestles in the village beneath the Fovant Badges carved on a ridge of hills and depicting the emblems of British and ANZAC regiments in the First World War. The Cross Keys, once a haunt of highwaymen, is homely and welcoming, but people of average height have to watch their heads to avoid contact with the low beams. The inn is a warren of nooks and crannies, has old open fires, a garden, camping facilities and splendid bar food served both lunchtime and evening.

Beer: Adnams Bitter and Wadworth 6X on handpumps.

Accommodation: 1 single, 2 doubles, 1 family room. B&B £17.50 single, £35 double, £40 family room. No pets. Cards: Access and Visa.

HIGHWORTH

Saracen's Head Hotel
Market Place. North on A361 from Swindon. M4 exit 15

Licensee: R. Bennett
Tel: 0793 762064/762284
Fax: 0793 765575

The Saracen's Head is an old coaching inn in the centre of Highworth. It has a comfortable lounge bar (no torn jeans, singlets or sleeveless shirts here, says the landlord) and a dining room. Bar food is served lunchtime and evening while the restaurant is open Monday to Saturday evenings. The hotel is a good base for visiting Lechlade, the Cotswolds and Cheltenham and Newbury races.

Beer: Arkell Bitter and BBB on handpumps.

Accommodation: 5 singles, 7 doubles/twins, 2 family rooms, all en suite. B&B £41.50 single, £54 double/twin, £60 family room. Pets by prior arrangement. Cards: Access, Diners, Visa.

SALISBURY

Old Mill at Harnham
Town Path, Harnham, just off A3094

Licensees: Mr & Mrs R. Thwaites
Tel: 0722 327517/322364
Fax: 0722 333367

The Old Mill is a breathtakingly

ancient building dating back to 1135 and built from brick, flint and stone. It was built for ecclesiastical purposes and became Wiltshire's first paper-making mill in 1550, when water from the River Nadder was diverted through the building to drive three water wheels; the three races can still be seen today. The mill was used to store church documents when the cathedral was being moved from Old to New Sarum and has also served as a monks' hospice and a leper hospital. The hotel has 11 bedrooms all with en suite facilities, central heating, direct-dial phones, hairdryers and tea and coffee makers; there is a TV lounge for residents. The restaurant uses fresh local farm produce such as natural meat guaranteed free from chemicals, growth promoters and hormones. The menu may include South Coast fish and shellfish in bar and restaurant plus such varied dishes as steak and kidney pie, pea and ham soup, Wiltshire porkies, local ham, mussels, sea bass, lobster and crab. Food in bar and restaurant is available every day, lunchtime and evening.

Beer: Wadworth 6X, Whitbread Boddingtons Bitter and Flowers Original on handpumps.

Accommodation: 2 singles, 6 doubles/twins, 3 family rooms, all en suite. B&B £35 single, £32.50 double/twin per person, £25 family room per person. Children's rates by negotiation. 10% reductions for weekly stays in winter. No pets. Cards: Access, Amex, Visa.

Red Lion Hotel
Milford Street

Proprietor: Michael Maidment
Tel: 0722 323334
Fax: 0722 325756

The Red Lion is a superb 13th-century inn rooted in the history of this magnificent cathedral city. It became an extended coaching inn in the heyday of horse-drawn road travel but its earlier origins are evident from the wealth of exposed beams and wattle-and-daub, with hand-painted medieval plasterwork and brass and copper decorations. Among the many antiques is a remarkable skeleton organ clock in which the skeletal figures ring the hours: it is thought to have been carved by Spaniards taken prisoner after the defeat of the Armada in 1588. The half-timbered exterior is partially covered by a fine Virginia creeper. The dining room specializes in traditional English cooking and includes venison and jugged hare in season, local trout and roast beef. Light meals are served in the lounge; the restaurant is available for lunch and dinner all year. Sumptuous accommodation includes several four-poster bedrooms.

Beer: Draught Bass, Ushers Best Bitter and Wadworth 6X and guest beer on handpumps.

Accommodation: 11 singles, 41 doubles, 4 family rooms, all en suite. B&B £56 single, £86 double, £96 family room. Children free in parents' room. Weekend Breaks: £51 per person per night inclusive of table d'hôte dinner. No pets. Cards: Access, Amex, Diners, Visa.

TISBURY

South Western Hotel
Station Road. Off A30 & A303

Licensee: Mrs P.V. Evans
Tel: 0747 870160

The South Western is a large and imposing pub with one L-shaped bar and a small games area where darts, crib and pool are played. A small dining room seats 20. Bar food includes soup, homemade pâté, grills, Wiltshire ham, chilli, burgers and vegetarian dishes. Food is served lunchtime and evening every day except Thursday evening. The hotel has been recently refurbished, the guest rooms all have tea and coffee making facilities and a function room is available for hire.

Beer: Wiltshire Stonehenge Best Bitter, Olde Grumble Bitter, Old Devil Strong Ale, Ma Pardoe's Mild plus regular guest beers, all on handpumps.

Accommodation: 1 single, 1 double, 1 treble, 2 twins en suite. B&B £14.50 per person, £16.50 en suite. Children half price. No pets.

Near WARMINSTER

Bell Inn
High Street, Wylye. Junction of A306 & A36, midway between Salisbury and Warminster

Licensees: Steve & Anne Locke
Tel: 09856 338

The Bell is a delightful coaching inn built in 1373 and has a superb location in the centre of the village, next to a 14th-century church. The inn has a large inglenook fireplace, low beams and a warm and cosy atmosphere. There is a walled garden at the rear overlooking the church, and a patio garden to the side. Food is available lunchtime and evening; there are daily specials with the emphasis on fresh produce. The inn is a good base for visiting Stonehenge and Salisbury, there are lovely walks along the River Wylye and fishing can be arranged in local trout lakes.

Beer: Chudley Local Line, Hall &

Woodhouse Badger Best Bitter and Wadworth 6X plus a weekly guest beer on handpumps.

Accommodation: 2 doubles en suite, 3 twins. B&B £17 single, £32 twin, £43 en suite double. Children sharing 30% reduction. Pets welcome by arrangement.

WHITEPARISH

Fountain Inn
The Street. A27 between Romsey and Salisbury

Licensee: Steve Worpole
Tel: 0794 884266

The Fountain is a cheerful, 300-year-old inn with beamed bar and dining room. Locals mix happily with visitors. It is a splendid base for visiting Salisbury, the New Forest and Romsey with the home of the Mountbatten family. All the cottage-style guest rooms are en suite and have colour TVs and tea and coffee makers. There is a lunch menu and a full à la carte evening one, with homemade specials of the day chalked on a blackboard; food is served every lunchtime and Tuesday to Saturday evenings. Lunch may include farmhouse pâté, calamari, mushroom Stroganoff, homemade soup, Wiltshire ham, scampi, plaice, local trout and a late breakfast, plus a good range of vegetarian options, salads and sandwiches.

Beer: Wiltshire Stonehenge Best Bitter, Olde Grumble Bitter, Wiltshire's alcoholic ginger beer, plus a guest beer, all on handpumps.

Accommodation: 1 single, 2 twins, 3 doubles, all en suite. B&B £25 single, £40 double/twin. No pets. Cards: Access and Visa.

WROUGHTON

Fox & Hounds
1 Markham Road. On A361 Swindon
to Devizes road; south of M4
between exits 15 & 16

Licensee: Eddie Adams
Tel: 0793 812217

The Fox & Hounds was originally a
thatched farm cottage and was
granted a licence to brew and sell beer
in the mid-1700s. It was rebuilt in the
1860s following a fire, and was left
virtually unchanged until 1984 when
it was extensively altered and
refurbished, but the old cottage
atmosphere was retained. In 1989 a
motel was opened next to the pub.
The pub has a log fire in winter and a
pleasant beer garden in summer. The
motel rooms all have en suite
facilities, colour TVs, phones and tea
and coffee making equipment. Pub
food, available lunchtime and evening
every day, includes sandwiches,
burgers, steaks, grills, trout, seafood
platter, salads, pizzas and home-
cooked daily specials. Wroughton is a
good base for visiting the Ridgeway,
Marlborough, Cirencester, Avebury
and the Cotswolds.

Beer: Arkell Bitter, BBB and
Kingsdown Ale on handpumps.

Accommodation: 4 singles, 1 double,
3 twins. B&B £39.50 single, £49.50
double/twin. Children's rates on
application. Reduced rates for 2 and 3
nights stay. No pets. Cards: Access,
Amex, Visa.

ABERFORD (WEST YORKS)

Swan Hotel
Centre of village on old A1

Licensees: Otto & Ann Kreft
Tel: 0532 813205

The Swan is a 16th-century coaching
inn on the Great North Road in an
attractive village now by-passed by
the new A1. The hotel has some
interesting outbuildings that date
back to coaching days, while inside
the main building there are two bars
linked together, a games room and a
separate restaurant. Bar meals and full
meals are served lunchtime and
evening; there are 168 different bar
meals, while the Cygnet restaurant
serves nouvelle cuisine dishes in
Yorkshire-size portions. The guest
rooms all have colour TVs and tea
and coffee making facilities and the
double rooms have their own
showers. The Swan has a pleasant
garden to enjoy in good weather and
is a good base for visiting such
interesting local places as Hazlewood
Castle.

Beer: Tetley Bitter, Whitbread
Trophy Bitter and Castle Eden Ale
on handpumps.

Accommodation: 2 singles, 4 doubles,
3 rooms en suite. B&B £17 single, £34
double. Dogs by prior agreement.
Cards: Access, Amex, Diners, Visa.

APPLETREEWICK (N YORKS)

New Inn
2 miles off B6160 at Barden Tower
or Burnsall (OS 051601)

Licensee: John Pitchers
Tel: 0756 720252

The New Inn is a cheering sight from the riverside Dales Way footpath. It stands at the foot of the village street in an area of great historic and scenic beauty. The inn is a fine Dales pub with horseshoe chairs and benches outside to enjoy the view. Mr Pitchers wisely retains the inn as a genuine local not a tourist trap. As well as his good draught ale, he has a world-wide collection of bottled beers, including some bottle-conditioned Trappist monastery brews from Belgium; he is currently serving Liefmans Kriek, a cherry-flavoured beer from Belgium, on draught. There is good lunchtime bar food. Appletreewick and its environs are packed with interest: the Earls of Craven supplied a Lord Mayor of London in 1610, Mock Beggar Hall was a shelter for the homeless, while Percival Hall dates back to Tudor times.

Beer: John Smiths Bitter, Younger Scotch Bitter and No 3 on handpumps and Wilkins Farmhouse cider.

Accommodation: 1 single, 3 doubles. B&B £20 per person per night; more than 1 night £17.50. Children welcome in pub but not to stay; dogs welcome.

BOROUGHBRIDGE (N YORKS)

Three Horseshoes Hotel
Bridge Street. 1½ miles from A1

Proprietors: R.S. & B.S. Porter
Tel: 0423 322314

The Three Horseshoes is an impressive hotel rebuilt between the wars and retaining a homely, 1930s flavour. The lounge has an unusual tiled fireplace and a wealth of wood panels and leaded glass. There is a basic public bar, separate dining room, a lounge and function rooms. Bar food is served lunchtime, while the dining room has lunch, high tea and dinner; food is available every day except Christmas Day. Boroughbridge is an historic market town on the old A1, with leisurely boating trips on the River Ure and visits to the stately home of Newby Hall.

Beer: Theakston Best Bitter on handpump, Vaux Samson on electric pump.

Accommodation: 6 singles, 6 doubles/twins, 2 family rooms, 6 rooms with private baths. B&B £19.50 single, £39 double/twin and family rooms. Children welcome, terms according to age. Limited facilities for the disabled; easy access to pub. Pets accepted.

BRADFORD (W YORKS)

New Beehive Inn
117A Westgate, off B6144

Licensee: Mr Wagstaff
Tel: 0274 724781

The New Beehive was built in 1901 and still has the trappings of an Edwardian tavern, with a five-roomed gas-lit interior with coal fires in winter. There is regular jazz and other live music. The atmospheric pub is handy for the city centre. The guest rooms have recently been refurbished and most are en suite. Homemade bar food is available at all times.

Beer: Caledonian Golden Promise, Old Mill Bitter, Robinwood XB, Tetley Bitter, Timothy Taylor Golden Best and Landlord on handpumps.

Accommodation: 2 singles, 10 doubles, 2 family rooms. 9 rooms en suite. £17 single, £28 double/twin, £11 per person in family room; £4 extra for breakfast. Weekend Specials: rates on application.

Victoria
Bridge Street, opposite transport interchange

Licensee: John Wilkinson
Tel: 0274 728706
Fax: 0274 736358

The Victoria is a city centre three-star hotel in a good position for Bradford's growing tourist industry. It is an imposing stone building dating from 1880 and was originally named the Great Northern Hotel when it stood opposite the now defunct Exchange railway station. The Victoria has a quiet residents' lounge, meals lunchtime and evening, and colour TVs and tea and coffee making facilities in all the guest rooms. Bradford's Barber Shop Singers regularly sing for their suppers in the plush public bar. The Victoria is next door to St George's Hall, which holds concerts and many other events, and is close to the National Museum of Photography, Film and Television, and the revamped Alhambra theatre.

Beer: Draught Bass and Tetley Bitter on handpumps.

Accommodation: 29 singles, 30 doubles (doubles can be converted to family rooms), all rooms with private baths. B&B £60 per person midweek. Weekend £41 per night (minimum 2 nights stay), Week from £200. Children welcome, terms negotiable. Cards: Access, Amex, Diners, Visa.

Westleigh Hotel, Bradford

Westleigh Hotel
30 Easby Road. A647 towards
Halifax, ½ mile from city centre

Licensee: John Jowett
Tel: 0274 727089

The Westleigh is a spacious and
comfortable pub that was once three
separate Victorian houses. It has a
cheerful, comfortable bar with a pool
table, a separate residents' lounge,
and a wide selection of bar meals. The
guest rooms have colour TVs,
phones, tea and coffee making
facilities and central heating. The
hotel is handy for the city centre, the
university, National Museum of
Photography, the Alhambra theatre,
Bradford's famous curry houses and
pubs, and it is just a short journey to
Haworth with its Brontë connections
and steam railway centre.

Beer: Theakston Best Bitter, XB and
Old Peculier, Younger Scotch Bitter
and No 3 on handpumps.

Accommodation: 10 singles, 11 twins,
2 family rooms, 12 rooms with
private baths. B&B £24 single, £40
twin/double, £6 extra for bath.
Children welcome, £12 sharing
family room. Dogs allowed. Cards:
Access and Visa.

CROPTON
(N YORKS)

New Inn
Near Pickering. Off A170 Pickering
to Helmsley road

Owners: Michael & Sandra Lee
Tel: 07515 330

The New Inn is close to Cropton
Forest and the North Yorkshire
Moors National Park. The inn was
originally a grain store where
travellers used to barter for grain and

cattle. The present owners have
introduced a top class à la carte
restaurant and carvery in a
conservatory; bar food is served
lunchtime and evening every day,
while the restaurant is open for
dinner every day; there is also a
Sunday roast lunch. The public bar is
run on strictly traditional lines with
bar food and darts and pool. The
inn's own micro-brewery is attached,
and two of its beers are permanently
on sale, along with Scoresby Stout
which is named after the famous
whaler born in Cropton. The village
is handy for York, Scarborough and
the North Yorks Railway.

Beer: Cropton 2 pints Best Bitter,
Special Strong, Scoresby Stout,
Tetley Mild and Bitter on
handpumps.

Accommodation: 2 singles, 5 doubles,
2 family rooms, all en suite. B&B £22
single, £42 double, £45-£47 family
room, 3 or 4 people. Children's rates
negotiable if not sharing family room.
Pets accepted. Cards: Access and
Visa.

DALTON (N YORKS)

Jolly Farmers of Olden Times
Off A168, A19 & A1, 5 miles south of
Thirsk

Licensees: Norman & Patricia Clark
Tel: 0845 577359

This much-loved small country inn is
a long-standing favourite in the
guide: letters regularly praise the
welcome, the food, and the ale. It is
200 years old with some of the
original beams and a welcoming coal
fire, in the heart of Herriot country
and with the white horse of Kilburn
cut in the chalk of the Hambleton
Hills visible from the village. The
Clarks are enthusiasts – for the pub,

for real ale (they are CAMRA members) and for organizing rambles and long walks in the dales and on the moors. The inn offers a games room, bar and lounge, an enclosed area with trees, and a welcome for families. Local produce is used for bar meals and the restaurant. Food in the bar includes steak, chops, gammon, haddock and trout. Meals in the small dining room (lunch and dinner: advance booking essential) offer soup, ham cooked in wine, mushroom and cheese sauce, casserole supreme, and curried lamb; vegetarians can be catered for – advise when booking. There is a traditional Sunday roast lunch, too – good value at £5 per person, 1991 price. Bookings by early Thursday mornings. (The pub does not always open lunchtimes: please phone in advance to avoid disappointment.)

Beer: Websters Yorkshire Bitter and Choice on handpumps with regular guest beers (John Smith's Bitter may replace Websters Yorkshire).

Accommodation: 1 double, 1 family room. B&B £15.50 for one night, £14.50 per person for more than one night. Residents' children may use the bar. Pets accepted.

DANBY (N YORKS)

Duke of Wellington Inn
Centre of village. 2 miles off A171 Whitby to Guisborough road; the village is a stop on the Esk Valley railway

Licensee: Anthony J. Howat
Tel: 0287 660351

The Duke of Wellington is an 18th-century coaching inn and the Iron Duke is believed to have used the building as a recruiting centre to raise a local regiment before the battle

of Waterloo. The bars are cheerful and friendly with low beamed ceilings; the public bar is popular with locals who play darts, cards and dominoes. The homemade food (lunchtime and evening) includes an enormous mixed grill, kebabs, Whitby fresh fish, soup, omelettes, salads and ploughman's, and several vegetarian dishes. Children have their own menu. Most of the guest rooms have bathrooms en suite and have been recently refurbished to include hand-made furniture; all rooms have central heating, colour TVs and tea and coffee makers. There is a residents' lounge and separate entrance. Danby is a tranquil village in the heart of the North Yorkshire Moors national park and home of the Moors Centre, an historic building set in 13 acres of riverside pasture with information and advice, guided walks and other activities. There is a 12th-century castle, and trout and salmon fishing are available close by (day and season tickets available).

Beer: Cameron Traditional Bitter and Strongarm on electric and handpump.

Accommodation: 2 singles, 5 doubles, 2 family rooms (double and single beds in each room). 5 rooms en suite. B&B £17 single, £17 per person in double, £3 extra for en suite rooms. Children under 10 half price. 2 nights or more B&B plus dinner from £23 per person per night. Details of autumn and winter breaks on application. Pets welcome. Cards: Access, Amex, Visa.

EASINGWOLD (N YORKS)

George Hotel
Market Square. Off A19 York-Thirsk road

Licensee: J.S. Lawrence
Tel: 0347 21698
Fax: 0347 23448

The George, an 18th-century coaching inn in a cobbled market square, has handsome white-painted bow windows and porch, and shutters on the top storey. It has all modern amenities such as central heating, colour TVs and tea and coffee making facilities in the charming guest rooms, but retains its old charm with beams, open fires and wood panelling in the bar and candle-lit dining room. Lunchtime bar snacks include homemade steak and kidney pie, ham, chicken and mushroom pie, sandwiches and salads. The dining room offers an extensive à la carte menu in the evenings, and a traditional Sunday roast. The hotel is a splendid base for visiting York, the east coast and the moors. An 18-hole golf course is close at hand.

Beer: Theakston XB and Old Peculier, Younger Scotch Bitter and IPA on handpumps.

Accommodation: 1 single, 11 doubles, 2 family rooms, all en suite. B&B from £35 single, £46 double, £60 family room.. Off-season weekend £30 per person per night B&B plus dinner. Children welcome. Cards: Access and Visa.

HAWORTH (W YORKS)

Brontë Hotel
Lees Lane, near junction with A6033

Licensees: Geoff & Sheila Briggs
Tel: 0535 644112/646725

The hotel was built 10 years ago in the village heavy with Brontë connections. It is a mile from the Brontë parsonage (now a museum) where Anne, Charlotte and Emily penned, despite their genteel surroundings, novels of great power and passion such as *Wuthering*

Heights and *Jane Eyre*. The hotel, with two comfortably furnished lounge bars, has all the amenities of a modern hotel, with meals lunchtime and evening. It is also a handy base for visiting the moors and the Keighley and Worth Valley Light Railway (Haworth station).

Beer: Stones Best Bitter and Tetley Bitter on handpumps.

Accommodation: 1 single, 6 doubles, 4 rooms with en suite facilities. B&B £15-£28 per person. Half and full board available. No pets. Cards: Access and Visa.

HELMSLEY (N YORKS)

Crown Hotel
Market Square, A170; off A1 at Thirsk

Licensee: Mr B.J. Mander
Tel: 0439 70297

The Crown is a 16th-century coaching inn that dominates one side of the square of this picturesque old market town with its eerie and awesome castle ruins, fine parish church, a miniature Albert Memorial and, nearby, the ruins of the great monastery of Rievaulx. The hotel has a small bar with darts, and a cosy lounge bar with a blazing imitation log fire and comfortable bench seats. The pleasant Jacobean restaurant serves lunch, high tea and dinner (last orders 8pm) using traditional English cooking and fresh local produce. Some of the guest rooms in this listed building have exposed beams, and all have colour TVs, phones and tea and coffee making equipment. There are residents' lounges.

Beer: Cameron Best Bitter on handpump (beer liable to change).

Accommodation: 6 singles, 6 doubles/ twins, 2 family rooms, all rooms en suite. One ground floor room. B&B £28.60 single, £57.20 double/twin and family rooms. Half and full board available. Winter Break: £73.50 per person 2 nights B&B and dinner. Children welcome, child in cot charged £2 per day; if in separate bed in parents' room, 20% reduction. Dogs welcome. Cards: Access and Visa.

HUBBERHOLME (N YORKS)

George Inn
Off B6160, 1 mile from Buckden on Hawes road. (OS 926782)

Licensees: John Fredrick & Marjorie Forster
Tel: 0756 760223

There are many claims on the title, but the George is probably *the* Dales pub. It was J.B. Priestley's favourite pub, and he is buried in the local churchyard. The inn dates backs to at least the 18th century, was once the village vicarage, and has stone-flagged floors, low beams, mullioned windows and antique furniture. There are blazing fires in winter and on New Year's Day the local parliament of 'House of Lords' (vicar and churchwarden) and 'House of Commons' (local farmers) negotiate the letting of nearby pasture land in aid of poorer parishioners. The George has a separate dining room, while bar meals include steak and kidney pie, chicken and mushroom pie, ploughman's, and filled crusty rolls. The evening menu includes salmon, venison, chicken and Scotch sirloin steaks. There are seats outside with stunning views of the moors rising all around. The village is named after the Viking Hubba who settled there, and remains an attractive

huddle of church, bridge and inn with a few scattered farms and cottages. The road through the hamlet is the highest in Yorkshire, reaching 1,934 feet on its way to Hawes.

Beer: Younger Scotch Bitter and No 3 on handpumps.

Accommodation: 3 doubles/twins. B&B £18 per person. Week £107.50. Children over 8 welcome, no reductions.

HUGGATE (N YORKS)

Wolds Inn
Driffield Road. Signposted from A166 York to Driffield road

Licensees: Norris & Lynda Binner
Tel: 0377 88217

The inn dates back to the 16th century, and has a wood-panelled lounge and dining room. There is a separate bar for walkers and ramblers. Bar and restaurant meals are available lunchtime and evening, walkers can get snacks at all times, and there is a roast lunch on Sundays. The inn is the highest pub on the Wolds and the village is the heart of the local farming community, with one of the deepest wells in England and a fine church. The Wolds Inn was first called the Chase; drovers stayed and next day chased their animals to market.

Beer: John Smith's Bitter and Tetley Bitter on handpumps.

Accommodation: 5 doubles/twins, 1 family room, all en suite. B&B £18 single occupancy, £14.50 per person sharing. Children half price; babies small charge for cot. Pets welcome.

JACKSON BRIDGE (W YORKS)

Red Lion Inn
Sheffield Road. A616, 2½ miles from Holmfirth

Licensee: Stephen Oscroft
Tel: 0484 683499

This is *Last of the Summer Wine* territory, near Holmfirth, and the success of the TV series draws visitors but cannot detract from the outstanding and unspoilt character of the countryside and its small towns and villages. The Red Lion is a delightful old inn with a cosy bar and open fire and beer garden. Home-cooked food is served lunchtime (not Monday) and Monday to Friday evenings. The guest rooms all have colour TVs and tea and coffee making facilities. The Red Lion has a ghost named Chippy Brook, a former landlord of the inn.

Beer: Tetley Mild and Bitter and guest beers on handpumps.

Accommodation: 2 twins, 4 doubles, 3 en suite. B&B £22.50 single, £25 en suite, £34 double, £39 en suite. No pets.

White Horse
Scholes Road. Off A616 3 miles from Holmfirth; M11 exit 35A

Licensee: Ron Backhouse
Tel: 0484 683940

This is the heart of the *Summer Wine* saga, for this splendid old stone-built Yorkshire pub features prominently in the series and is adorned with a multitude of TV memorabilia. But it retains its character – and its genuine local characters, too. The pub is popular with walkers and offers open fires in winter, a large and attractive garden, a games room with darts and

Red Lion Inn, Jackson Bridge

dominoes, and pub food lunchtime and evening. The guest rooms have central heating, TVs, radios and tea and coffee making facilities.

Beer: Mansfield Ridings Bitter and Stones Best Bitter on handpumps.

Accommodation: 2 doubles, 3 family rooms, may be used as singles according to demand. B&B £17.50 single, £15.50 per person sharing. Children £7.50 up to 14 years. No pets.

KIRBY HILL (N YORKS)

Shoulder of Mutton
Nr Richmond. 2 miles from A66 north-west of Scotch Corner (A1)

Licensee: Geoffrey Gore
Tel: 0748 822772

The Shoulder of Mutton is a country inn in a superb hillside setting near Richmond, overlooking lower Teesdale and the ruins of Ravensworth Castle. It was built in 1800, possibly as a farmhouse, and converted to licensed premises some 50 years later. It is in a village of great antiquity. The church dates back to 1200 while the handful of cottages stem from the 15th century. The inn has two lounge bars and a separate restaurant. Bar food ranges from steak and mushroom pie to gammon and steaks, local trout, crispy roast duckling, lasagne and jacket potatoes with a choice of fillings. Monday evenings are popular with locals and guests when there are impromptu sing-a-longs. Most guest rooms have en suite showers and all have colour TVs and tea and coffee making facilities.

Beer: Ruddles County, John Smith's Bitter and Websters Yorkshire Bitter on handpumps.

Shoulder of Mutton, Kirby Hill

Accommodation: 1 twin, 3 doubles, 1 family room, 3 rooms with en suite showers. B&B £25 single, £33 double, £19.50 per person in family room, children sharing £12. 3 days or more: £18.50 per person in en suite room; £15.50 sharing bathroom. No pets.

MALTON (N YORKS)

Crown Hotel (Suddaby's)
Wheelgate, off A64

Proprietor: Neil Suddaby
Tel: 0653 692038

Five generations of Suddabys have run the Crown since 1879, hence its local name. It is Georgian-style, built in the early part of the 19th century, and is in the main shopping street of the historic small market town. The Malton Brewery is nearby and the Crown is the unofficial 'brewery tap', serving all four beers. The hotel has a real fire in winter in the public bar and there is a conservatory bar and restaurant where meals are served at lunchtime. There is traditional Yorkshire homemade food such as meat pies and Yorkshire puddings, with a strong bias towards vegetarian dishes such as chilli, macaroni, lasagne, and such wholesome soups as sweetcorn and potato, and spicy bean. There are Sunday lunches and afternoon teas. A children's room has a cot and a high chair. The guest rooms were due to be upgraded to en suite during 1992; there is also a residents' lounge with TV.

Beer: Malton Pale Ale, Double Chance, Pickwick Porter and Owd Bob with guest ales on Bank Holidays, all on handpumps.

Accommodation: 2 singles, 4 twins, 3 doubles including 1 family room. B&B £18 single, £16 per person

double/twin, £1 less for stays of 2 nights or more. Children up to 12 years £7; cot available £2.50. Dogs by prior arrangement £3.50. Cards: Access and Visa.

MASHAM (N YORKS)

Kings Head Hotel
Market Place. A6108 near Ripon; 10 mins (approx) from A1

Licensee: Colin Jones
Tel: 0765 689295

The Kings Head is a stately, three-storey stone coaching inn built in 1685 in the home town of Theakston's brewery. The hotel has a large marble fireplace, cast-iron tables and a mass of plants. Excellent lunchtime bar meals include soup, sandwiches, smoked meat platter, Old Peculier casserole and fresh local trout. The evening restaurant has a full à la carte menu. There are a few seats in a courtyard in good weather. Masham is a fine base for visiting the dales. Theakston's brewery has a visitors' centre, open May to October, which offers a visit to the cooper's shop and a video film of the history of the company.

Beer: Theakston Best Bitter, XB and Old Peculier on handpumps.

Accommodation: 2 singles, 7 doubles, 1 twin, all rooms en suite. B&B £42.50 single, £55 double/twin. Weekend Rates: £38.50 single per night.

MIDDLEHAM (N YORKS)

Black Bull Inn
East Witton Road. B6108, 2 miles from Leyburn

Licensees: Howard & Maisie Fricker
Tel: 0969 23669

The Black Bull is a small village local that serves racing folk and visitors alike. This is horse-training country and you can watch horses on their daily gallops. Middleham is in an attractive dales location and Herriot country is nearby, along with Richard III's castle. The inn serves meals at all reasonable times. Thursday night is curry night.

Beer: Theakston Best Bitter on handpump with guest beer during summer and occasionally during winter.

Accommodation: 2 doubles en suite. B&B £16.50 per person. Children half price under 12. Stays of 3 nights or more: rates on application. No pets.

MIRFIELD (W YORKS)

Black Bull Hotel
Market Square, 130 Huddersfield Road. A644

Licensees: Tony & Helen Woods
Tel: 0924 493180

The Black Bull was built in 1850 as a railway hotel – it is still handy for Mirfield BR – but it has come a long way since its inception. Mr Woods runs a lively regime with a disco and cabaret, yet it retains some of its true local character. It has bar meals lunchtime and restaurant meals in the evening.

Beer: Tetley Mild and Bitter with guest beers on handpumps.

Accommodation: 1 single, 5 doubles, 2 family rooms. B&B £23 single, £33 double/twin, £45 family room. Children under 10 free of charge. Discounts for long-term stays. Pets welcome. Cards: Access, Amex, Visa.

OAKENSHAW (W YORKS)

Richardsons Arms
Bradford Road. A638, ½ mile from M62 exit 26

Licensee: Tony Maskill
Tel: 0274 675722

Richardsons is a lively pub with a strong emphasis on entertainment, with live music on Friday to Sunday evenings. It has a single, open-plan lounge and serves bar meals lunchtime and evening. The well-appointed guest rooms all have TVs and tea and coffee making facilities. Oakenshaw is a village that is being subsumed into Bradford's outskirts and is close to the M62 and M606.

Beer: Whitbread Trophy Bitter on handpump.

Accommodation: 5 singles, 4 doubles. B&B £12.50 per person.

OSSETT (W YORKS)

Crown
20 Horbury Road. 1 mile south of town centre

Licensees: Mr & Mrs Mellor
Tel: 0924 272495

The Crown is a small, traditional stone-built pub with panelled rooms and a collection of dolls in a cabinet.

Pub games include darts, dominoes and ring the bull. There are two lounge bars where bar meals are served Monday to Friday. The speciality of the house is Yorkshire puddings with various fillings. The guest rooms are in an adjoining building with a separate entrance. Each room has colour TV and tea and coffee making facilities.

Beer: Tetley Mild and Bitter on handpumps.

Accommodation: 2 singles, 1 double, 1 twin. B&B £17.50 per person. Cot available; children's rates on application.

OSWALDKIRK (N YORKS)

Malt Shovel Inn
Off B1363 & B1257 south of Helmsley

Licensee: Neil Danford
Tel: 043 93 461

The Malt Shovel is a 17th-century listed coaching inn, formerly a manor house, in a village mentioned in the Domesday Book. The inn has imposing staircases, log fires in winter, and many fascinating old photos in the beamed bars. The busy main bar has a fine fireplace and many traditional pub games, including darts, dominoes and shove ha'penny. The inn has been sympathetically refurbished by Sam Smith to reveal even more of its old-world character such as York stone slabs. The Malt Shovel has a deserved reputation for serving large helpings of food, especially hot roast dinners with fresh vegetables. During the week you may find game pie or beef and ale pie; there are scallops with Stilton and garlic in a creamy sauce and other adventurous dishes at

the weekend; children are welcome to eat and there is a separate menu for them in summer.

Beer: Sam Smith's Old Brewery Bitter with Museum Ale in summer, both on handpumps.

Accommodation: 1 twin, 2 doubles. B&B £18.50 per person. No children under 12. No dogs.

PICKERING (N YORKS)

White Swan Hotel
Market Place. Just off A169 & A170

Owner: Mrs Deirdre Buchanan
Tel: 0751 72288

The White Swan is a superb 16th-century coaching inn, once a staging route on the Whitby run used by salt smugglers. It has a fine stone exterior with a bowed ground-floor window and several dormers. There is a beamed bar and lunchtime meals and early evening suppers are available there, including traditional Yorkshire puddings served as a separate course. A separate restaurant has a menu based on fresh local produce. The hotel guest rooms all have en suite bathrooms and direct-dial phones. Pickering has a ruined castle, the parish church with fine examples of medieval wall paintings, Castle Howard, Rievaulx Abbey and the North Yorkshire Moors railway. Facilities for golf, riding, pony-trekking and fishing are close by.

Beer: Cameron Traditional Bitter and Theakston Best Bitter on handpumps.

Accommodation: 13 doubles/twins. B&B £42 single occupancy, £33 per person sharing. Children £10 sharing. Dinner B&B minimum 4 nights £37.50 double, £47 single occupancy,

£50 in Ryedale Suite. Dogs welcome.
Cards: Access and Visa.

REDMIRE (N YORKS)

Bolton Arms
Nr Leyburn. From A1 at Leeming
follow A684; turn off at Wensley for 3
miles

Licensee: John Brennan
Tel: 0969 24336

The Bolton Arms is a stone-built
village inn, more than 200 years old
and recently renovated and
refurbished. It stands in a picturesque
and unspoilt village in the heart of
Wensleydale and Herriot Country.
Close to the village are waterfalls,
castles, abbeys and market towns and
some splendid walks. Bar food is
served every lunchtime and evening
in the pub and there is a roast lunch
on Sunday.

Beer: John Smith's Bitter, Theakston
XB and Younger Scotch Bitter on
handpumps.

Accommodation: Flat with twin beds
in bedroom and sofa bed in sitting
room; suitable for 2-4 people. B&B
£15 per person. Children usually free
but depending on age. No pets.

ROBIN HOOD'S BAY (N YORKS)

Victoria Hotel
Station Road. Off A171 Whitby to
Scarborough road

Licensees: Richard & Dorothy
Gibson
Tel: 0948 880205

The Victoria, as its name implies, is a
turn-of-the-century hotel. It has a
commanding position on the cliffs

with stunning views of the bay. It has
a cheerful bar where locals and
visitors mingle and a large restaurant.
Bar meals are served lunchtime and
evening; the restaurant is open for
table d'hôte and à la carte meals every
night in season; Friday and Saturday
the rest of the year. From the hotel
you can walk down the tumbling,
cobbled streets to the village and the
seafront, or use the Victoria as a base
for touring the heritage coast and the
moors.

Beer: Cameron Traditional Bitter and
Strongarm, wide range of guest beers
including Big End, Jennings, Malton,
Marston Moor and Timothy Taylor
on handpumps.

Accommodation: 2 singles, 9 doubles/
twins, 2 family rooms, 6 rooms en
suite. B&B £21 single, £17-£26
double, £21-£26 family room.
Children half price sharing.
Children's room. No dogs. Cards:
Access and Visa.

SHELLEY (W YORKS)

Three Acres Inn
Roydhouse. Off A637 & exit 38 of
M1 (OS 216125)

Partners: Neil Truelove & Brian
Orme
Tel: 0484 602606
Fax: 0484 608411

Three Acres is a substantial country
pub and restaurant beautifully
situated in the rolling scenery of
Emley Moor, close to the TV mast. It
has spectacular views of the moors,
yet is within easy reach of the
motorway, Huddersfield and the
Holmfirth area. It has a cheerful bar
with beams and brasses, and
restaurants concentrating on quality
English and Continental cuisine. Bar
food is available lunchtime except
weekends; restaurant meals are

served lunchtime and evening (not Saturday lunch). The inn offers facilities for families and disabled people. The splendid guest rooms all have private baths or showers, colour TVs, and tea and coffee making facilities.

Beer: Tetley Mild and Bitter, Theakston Best Bitter and Timothy Taylor Best Bitter on handpumps.

Accommodation: 7 singles, 2 twins, 6 doubles, 3 family rooms, all en suite. B&B £47.50 single, £57.50 double/ twin and family rooms. No charge for children sharing with parents. Weekend £50 single for 2 nights, £75 for 3, double £80 for 2 nights, £120 for 3. No pets. Cards: Access, Amex, Visa.

SLAITHWAITE (W YORKS)

White House
Holthead. 1 mile from Slaithwaite B6107 Meltham to Marsden road, 6 miles from Huddersfield

Licensee: Gillian Swift
Tel: 0484 842245

The White House's official address is Slaithwaite but it is actually in the tiny hamlet of Holthead near the open moors of the Pennines. The cheerful, spacious old rural pub has retained much of its original charm, with open fires, a bar, facilities for families, and bar food and full meals in the separate restaurant. There is an extensive Sunday family traditional roast lunch menu. The guest rooms all have en suite facilities and tea and coffee making equipment.

Beer: Tetley Mild and Bitter, Younger IPA on handpumps.

Accommodation: 1 single, 6 doubles,

1 twin. B&B £23 single, £33 double, £30 for single occupancy in double room. £30 double per night at weekends. Pets by arrangement. Cards: Access, Amex, Diners, Visa.

SLEIGHTS (N YORKS)

Plough
180 Coach Road. At bottom of Blue Bank, A169 between Pickering and Whitby

Licensee: Colin Buxton
Tel: 0947 810412

The Plough is a splendid old pub with a cottage-style exterior behind a walled garden. It is deceptively large, with a bar and lounge and a 22-seater restaurant. There are fine views over the tranquil Esk valley from the garden, and swings and other playthings keep children happy. Bar meals are available daily, with an à la carte menu seven days a week in the restaurant. The North Yorkshire Moors steam railway is just two miles away.

Beer: Cameron Traditional Bitter on handpump (liable to change).

Accommodation: 2 twins, 1 double. B&B £32 per room; phone to check summer rates. Children under 5 free. No dogs.

STARBOTTON (N YORKS)

Fox & Hounds
B6160. 2 miles north of Kettlewell

Licensees: James & Hilary McFadyen
Tel: 0756 760269

The Fox & Hounds is set in a lovely limestone village in Upper

Wharfedale, just off the Dales Way in picturesque walking country. The stone-built pub is some 160 years old, and has a large stone fireplace, beams, flag-stoned floors, with settles and other old and comfortable furniture. Food is served lunchtime and evening (not Sunday evening) and dishes include parsnip and chestnut pie, almond risotto with peanut sauce, and spicy lentil and peanut pâté. There are tables and benches outside in warm weather with stunning views of the hamlet and the hills.
Beer: Theakston Best Bitter, XB and Old Peculier and guest beers in season on handpumps.

Accommodation: 1 double, 1 twin, both en suite. B&B £23 per person. No dogs.

THORNTON WATLASS (N YORKS)

Buck Inn
Signposted from B6268 Bedale to Masham road; off A1 at Leeming Bar

Licensees: Michael & Margaret Fox
Tel: 0677 422461

The handsome old inn with shuttered windows, stands in spacious grounds opposite the cricket pitch on the village green. It is close to the superb countryside of Wensleydale and Swaledale and guided walking holidays are offered; the leisurely walks take in old drovers' roads, lead mines, pack horse bridges and Norman churches. At the inn there are extensive lunch and dinner menus, available seven days a week.

Beer: Hambleton Bitter, Tetley Bitter, Theakston Best Bitter and XB on handpumps.

Accommodation: 1 single, 3 doubles, 1 family room, all en suite. B&B £25 single, £40 double. Guided Walking Tours: rates on application. No pets. Cards: Access, Amex, Visa.

WASS (N YORKS)

Wombwell Arms
From A19 York to Thirsk road, take right turn to Coxwold and follow signs to Wass

Proprietors: Alan & Lynda Evans
Tel: 03476 280

The Wombwell Arms is a fine old country inn with a pub sign bearing the crest of the Wombwell family who have lived for generations at Newburgh Priory two miles away. The inn is also close to the famous Ampleforth School and the ruins of Byland Abbey; parts of the inn are thought to have once been a grain store for the abbey. Food is available lunchtime and evening Tuesday to Sunday. (The pub is closed Mondays except Bank Holidays.)

Beer: Cameron Traditional Bitter, Everards Old Original and guest beers on handpumps.

Accommodation: 3 doubles. B&B £19.50 per person. Children by arrangement. Mid-week winter rates available at certain times: ring for details. No pets. Cards: Access and Visa.

GLYNDYFRDWY

Berwyn Arms
A5 between Llangollen & Corwen

Licensee: Paul Gallagher
Tel: 049 083 210

The Berwyn Arms is a fine old coaching inn with welcoming open fires in winter, superb views of the Dee valley and 1¾ miles of salmon, trout and grayling fishing. Food is served lunchtime in the bar and there are evening restaurant facilities. The pub has a beer garden with a children's play area and there are seats on a patio overlooking the River Dee. Camping can be arranged in the village.

Beer: Burtonwood Bitter on handpump.

Accommodation: 1 single, 4 doubles, 2 family rooms, 4 rooms with private showers. B&B £12 per person single and double; family room £37.50; £13 extra for rooms with showers. Children under 10 half price. Winter Breaks: 2 nights or more Oct-March £15 per person per night B&B plus dinner. Pets accepted. Cards: Access and Visa.

HANMER

Hanmer Arms
A525 from Whitchurch, A539 signposted Overton & Llangollen, left into Hanmer (OS 459399)

Proprietors: Trevor & Lesley Hope
Tel: 094 874 532/640
Fax: 094 874 740

The Hanmer Arms is in superb border country between Wales and Shropshire and overlooks the lovely Hanmer Mere. The village is dominated by the ancient church of St Chad's, where Owain Glyndwr married Margaret Hanmer in the 14th century, while Chirk Castle is nearby. The heavily beamed pub dates back to the 16th century when it was called the Blue Lion; it was rebuilt by Sir John Hanmer in 1821 following a fire, and named in his honour. It has a bar used mainly by local people, a lounge with a brick fireplace and range, where hot and cold bar meals are served, plus a bistro bar and separate restaurant. Food ranges from burgers and sandwiches to soup, deep-fried cod, whitebait, spare ribs, curries, steaks, duck and Dover sole, with a good choice of vegetarian dishes such as vegetable pie, biriani, lasagne, moussaka and mushroom nut balls in a sherry sauce. Both the pub and the accommodation are in buildings converted from a former inn and farmhouse. The guest rooms have a British Tourist Board 4-crown rating and surround a cobbled courtyard; two rooms have been specially converted for use by disabled people. All the rooms have colour TVs, video programmes, baby listening and private baths. The Hanmer is a good base for visiting Whitchurch and the Saxon town of Ellesmere and its mere.

Beer: Ind Coope Burton Ale and Tetley Bitter on handpumps.

Accommodation: 1 single, 15 doubles, 2 family rooms. B&B £25-£45 per person, £22-£28 if sharing double. Weekend Break: 2 people 2 nights (Fri, Sat or Sun) £19.50 per person per night. Half and full board available. Cards: Access, Amex, Visa.

LLANBEDR-DYFFRYN-CLWYD

Griffin Inn
A494. 1½ miles from Ruthin on the Mold road

Licensee: Mrs Menai Edwards
Tel: 08242 2792

The Griffin is an old coaching inn built in 1726. It has an imposing exterior with a large porch supported by pillars, and latticed windows. A former toll cottage, where money was collected at the turnpike, adjoins the hotel, which stands at the foot of the Clwydian Hills, with Moel Fammau – the Mother Mountain – just three miles away. There are ample facilities for fishing in rivers and streams nearby, while walkers and ramblers can visit Offa's Dyke. The old market town of Ruthin has a castle and many half-timbered buildings. The Griffin offers a blazing log fire in winter, several bars and a lounge overlooking the attractive gardens. Bar food, lunchtime and evening, includes homemade soup, steak and kidney pie, plaice or cod, burgers, lasagne, beef curry, chilli con carne, homemade pizzas, ploughman's, filled jacket potatoes and children's meals. There is a separate evening restaurant (not Wednesday).

Beer: Hartley Fellrunners and XB, Robinson Best Bitter on handpumps.

Accommodation: 1 single, 1 double, 3 twins. B&B £20 single, £17.50 per person double/twin. No dogs. Cards: Access and Visa.

LLANGOLLEN

Bridge End Hotel
Abbey Road. A539, near Dee Bridge

Licensee: Mrs Linda Taylor
Tel: 0978 860634

The Bridge End is an extensively modernized, lively and welcoming hotel that is close to the canal and has fine views of Llangollen and the River Dee. Llangollen is in the heart of the Welsh mountains and has the remains of a medieval castle; steam enthusiasts will enjoy the Llangollen railway. Fishing can be arranged for anglers, while there are facilities for canoeing, angling, hang-gliding, walking, pony-trekking and golf in the area. Meals are available lunchtime and evening with an à la carte restaurant in high season.

Beer: Robinson Best Bitter on handpump.

Accommodation: 8 doubles, 1 family room, 6 rooms with en suite facilities. B&B £14 single, £26 en suite, £34 double, £45 en suite. Week £180 per person, £220 en suite. No pets. Cards: Access, Amex, Visa.

LLANSANNAN

Saracens Head Hotel
Nr Denbigh. From A55 at Abergele take A548 to Llanfair Talhaiarn, then A544 to Llansannan

Licensee: Mr J.W. O'Donnell
Tel: 074577 212

The Saracens Head is a 12th-century inn with a striking black and white exterior with a porched entrance. Inside, the lounge bar has old beams and is dominated by an imposing brick fireplace, with log fires in winter, and topped by a plethora of brasswork. It is adjoined by a restaurant and children's room. All the guest rooms have hot and cold water, central heating and tea and coffee making facilities, and there is a residents' TV lounge, too. The hotel's permanent resident is a ghost called the Grey Lady. It is a good base for visiting the Aled Valley and north Wales. Lunch is served every day, including Sunday, and there are evening meals in the restaurant; no food Sunday evening.

Beer: Robinson Best Mild and Best Bitter on electric pumps.

Accommodation: 1 single, 5 doubles/twins, 1 family room. B&B £14 per person per night. Children under 12 half price. Dogs by prior arrangement. Cards: applying for Access and Visa.

RUABON

Wynnstay Arms
High Street; end of Wrexham bypass (A483)

Licensees: Paul & Marie Skellon
Tel: 0978 822187

The Wynnstay is an imposing stone-brick and ivy-clad building with a wood-panelled lounge and popular back bar where darts and dominoes are played. It is an old coaching inn that has refound peace and tranquillity with the opening of a new bypass. It takes its name from the estate of Sir Watkin Williams Wynn: the houses of the estate workers flank the road past the hotel. Bar lunches and the restaurant concentrate on local produce, and meals may include coq au vin, duckling, Welsh lamb, steak and kidney pie, curries, poached salmon, choice of salads, and open sandwiches. The comfortable guest

Wynnstay Arms, Ruabon

rooms all have TVs and tea and coffee making facilities. Ruabon has an ancient church with wall paintings, and is a good base for visiting Llangollen, Chester and the Shropshire meres.

Beer: Robinson Best Mild and Best Bitter on electric pumps.

Accommodation: 1 single, 8 doubles, 3 with private baths. B&B £26 single, £32 en suite, £40 double, £46 en suite; family rates on request. Pets welcome. Cards: Access, Amex, Diners, Visa.

DYFED

Near
HAVERFORDWEST

Denant Mill Inn
From Haverfordwest take B4327 to Dale; 2½ miles from town watch for sign for Dreenhill; inn is signposted 300 yards on; turn left past farm to bottom of valley

Proprietors: Sidney & Marjorie Vincent
Tel/fax: 0437 766569

Denant Mill is a 400-year-old, purpose-built corn mill converted into an inn; the original mill wheel and gearing are still intact and form a major feature of the building. There are lunchtime bar snacks and a restaurant for lunch and dinner; dishes include crunchy mushrooms with garlic dip, smoked mussels, game pâté, beigos do mar – a Brazilian seafood dish – Moroccan spicy meals, steaks, and a gourmet vegetarian dish of the day. The surrounding area has 180 miles of

coastal walks, bird sanctuaries, sailing, surfing, diving, golf and horse-riding. The Vincents are real ale enthusiasts and have a vast and ever-changing range.

Beer: (from) Adnams Bitter, Archers Best Bitter, Belhaven 80 shilling, Brakspear Special Bitter, Exmoor Gold, Greene King Abbot Ale, Mauldon Black Adder, Reepham Rapier, Ringwood Fortyniner, Timothy Taylor Landlord, St Austell Hicks Special on handpumps or straight from the cask.

Accommodation: 2 twins, 5 doubles, 1 family room, 2 rooms with en suite facilities. B&B £17 single occupancy, £21 en suite; £32 double/twin, £36 en suite, £50 family room. Children under 12 sharing free. 7½% discount for 7 days' stay. Pets accepted.

LLANDYBIE

Red Lion
2 miles from Ammanford on A483; 7 miles from M4

Licensees: Sara & Timothy Priestland
Tel: 0269 851202

The Red Lion is more than 200 years old and was originally a drovers' inn. It has inglenook fireplaces and old stone walls, and is a grade two listed building. It was extensively refurbished in the late 1980s, and offers a bar for drinkers, two no-smoking rooms (one of which doubles as a family room) and a lounge where bar meals are served. There is a separate restaurant seating up to 50 people. Most of the food is made from home produce. The Red Lion is closed on Sunday evenings, but food is available during all other sessions and includes a traditional Sunday lunch.

Beer: Draught Bass, Marston Pedigree Bitter, Whitbread Boddingtons Bitter and Flowers Original on handpumps.

Accommodation: 2 singles, 1 double, 1 family room, all with en suite facilities. B&B £19.50 single, £35 double, £40 family room: up to 4 people; cot available. No pets. Cards: Access and Visa.

NEW QUAY

Seahorse Inn
Llandyssul, 3 miles from A487

Licensee: John Evans
Tel: 0545 560736

The pub is some 200 years old and is situated at the top of a fishing village, just two minutes' walk to the beach. It is a fine family holiday base, with safe swimming. Deep-sea fishing trips can be booked. From the village the coastal path has breathtaking views of Cardigan Bay. There are four pony-trekking centres in the area. The pub serves bar food.

Beer: Buckley Dark Mild and Rev James Best Bitter on handpumps.

Accommodation: 1 single, 1 double. B&B £12 per person. Pets accepted.

PEMBROKE

Old Kings Arms Hotel
Main Street, A40.

Licensee: Mrs G.A. Wheeler
Tel: 0646 683611

The hotel is an ancient coaching inn, 'modernized' in 1830 but retaining many old features such as heavily beamed ceilings and flag-stoned floors. It has a striking blue façade

with a bow window above the entrance. It has been in the same hands for more than 30 years. All the guest rooms have private bathrooms, colour TVs and phones. Pembroke has a castle where Henry VII was born in 1457, and the town has sandy beaches, a golf course and leisure park. Restaurant meals and bar snacks are available every day, lunch and evening, and the menu often features fresh fish from Milford Haven, game in season and vegetarian dishes.

Beer: Draught Bass on handpump.

Accommodation: 8 singles, 12 doubles. B&B £28-£35 single, £45 double. Children sharing with parents £10, cot £5. Residents' lounge.
Cards: Access, Amex, Visa.

TAL-Y-BONT

White Lion Hotel
A487, 11 miles from Aberystwyth

Licensee: John C. Davies
Tel: 0970 832245

The White Lion dates back to the 16th century and retains some original characteristics in spite of many alterations over the years. It has an impressive façade with dormers in the roof, a balcony above the porch and fine bay windows on the ground floor. The hotel has coal and log fires in winter, and a ghost. Darts, pool, dominoes and cribbage are played in the bar and bar meals are served lunchtime and evening. Food includes fresh poached salmon and local trout, home-cooked ham, salads, jacket potatoes, steaks, sandwiches, toasties, curries, and burgers and fish fingers for children, plus apple pie, trifle and raspberry or lemon torte. Guest rooms all have tea and coffee making facilities. The area offers sandy beaches and golf courses, and narrow gauge railways at Rheidol, Tal-y-Llyn and Ffestiniog. Tal-y-Bont is a keen sporting village with football, cricket, darts and pool teams, and Mr Davies is happy to arrange sporting weekends for visiting teams and clubs. Lake and river fishing is free to guests, and pony-trekking and hacking can be arranged.

Beer: Banks Mild and Bitter on electric pumps.

Accommodation: 1 single, 3 doubles, 1 family room, 3 rooms with showers. B&B £17 single, £32 double, £47 family room. Children's rates according to age. 4 nights or more 10% reduction. No pets. Cards: Access and Visa.

GLAMORGAN

COWBRIDGE (S GLAMORGAN)

Bear Hotel
High Street. Off A48

Tel: 0446 774814
Licensee: H.P. Lewis

The Bear is a cheery 12th-century inn with a ramble of small rooms and beamed ceilings, a flag-stoned public bar and carpeted lounge, plus a wine bar/bistro and up-market cocktail bar. Good value bar food includes lasagne, steak and kidney pie and ploughman's. There is a separate restaurant in an impressive vaulted room. Two of the attractive guest rooms have four-poster beds, and all the rooms have colour TVs and tea and coffee making facilities.

Beer: Draught Bass and Welsh Hancock's HB, Brains Bitter and SA, Buckley Best Bitter, Felinfoel Double Dragon, Flowers Original, Marston Pedigree Best Bitter and Wadworth 6X on handpumps.

Accommodation: 13 singles, 23 doubles, 1 family room, 34 rooms with private baths. B&B £35 single, £45 double. Children welcome.

MERTHYR TYDFIL (MID GLAMORGAN)

Tregenna Hotel
Park Terrace. A470 & A465

Licensees: Kathleen & Michael Hurley
Tel: 0685 723627
Fax: 0685 721951

The Tregenna is a family-run hotel close to railway and bus stations and five minutes' drive from the Brecon Beacons national park. The hotel's guest rooms all have en suite facilities, colour TVs, trouser presses, phones and tea and coffee makers. There is a lounge bar and a large restaurant. Meals are served in the bar as well as the restaurant, and food is available seven days a week, lunch, tea and dinner. The extensive menu has traditional dishes as well as Asian specialities.

Beer: Brain Bitter and SA on handpumps.

Accommodation: 4 singles, 13 doubles, 6 family rooms. B&B £37 single, £47 double, £50 family room. Children sharing half price. Weekend Break from £39 per person for 2 nights. Residents' lounge. Pets accepted. Cards: Access, Amex, Visa.

NOTTAGE (MID GLAMORGAN)

Rose & Crown
Heol-y-Capel. A4299, 2½ miles off
M4 exit 37

Manager: J.T. Williams
Tel: 065 6784850

The Rose & Crown is a white-painted hotel with a stone porch, hanging baskets and outdoor trestle tables, in a village near Porthcawl. The bar has some original beams and stone walls, a separate restaurant and beautifully appointed guest rooms with private bathrooms, tea and coffee trays and colour TVs. The restaurant offers pâté, smoked mackerel, roast beef and Yorkshire pudding, desserts and a children's menu. There are facilities for sea fishing, sailing and golf in the area.

Beer: Ruddles Best Bitter and County, Websters Yorkshire Bitter on handpumps.

Accommodation: 2 singles, 6 doubles/twins, 1 family room. B&B £43 single, £56 double/twin. Off-season weekends: reduced tariff on application. Babies free, children 3-12 sharing with parents £7 per night including breakfast. Cards: Access, Amex, Diners, Visa, Grand Met.

GWENT

ABERGAVENNY

Great Western Hotel
Station Road
Off A40; 50 yards from railway station, 1 mile from town centre

Licensees: Pete & Carolyn Hayhurst
Tel: 0873 853593

The Great Western dates from the great days of steam and was built at the height of the railway boom. It is an imposing stone-built, grade two listed building. The bar has a collection of railway memorabilia, and is the meeting place of the Abergavenny Steam Railway Society. Bar food is available lunchtime and evening and ranges from a sandwich to a steak. Abergavenny is a market town bordering the River Usk and is a fine base for touring the Brecon Beacons.

Beer: Draught Bass, Ruddles Best Bitter and occasional guest beer on handpumps.

Accommodation: 2 doubles, 1 family, 2 rooms en suite. B&B £16 single, £30 double, £42 family room (3 people). Children's rates negotiable. No pets. Cards: Access and Visa.

Llanwenarth Arms Hotel
Brecon Road. A40 midway between Abergavenny & Crickhowell

Licensee: D'Arcy McGregor
Tel: 0873 810550
Fax: 0873 811880

The Llanwenarth Arms is a combination of 16th-century inn and modern hotel on the banks of the River Usk, with hills and mountains forming a backdrop. The pub has a welcoming exterior with awnings over the windows, and tubs of flowers on the forecourt. Inside there are two superb bars with beamed ceilings and bar meals, while the dining room that overlooks the river has an à la carte menu. All the well-appointed guest rooms have baths and showers, colour TVs, and tea and coffee making facilities.

Beer: Draught Bass and Wadworth 6X on handpumps.

Accommodation: 18 doubles. B&B
£49 single, £59 double. Weekend
£24.75 per person per day for any 2
nights. Children welcome, half price.
Facilities for the disabled. Cards:
Access, Amex, Visa.

CHEPSTOW

Coach & Horses
Welsh Street. Off A48

Licensee: Lewis Bell
Tel: 0291 622626

The Coach & Horses is a one-bar,
split-level pub at the end – or the
beginning – of Offa's Dyke, with a
strong emphasis on sport. The pub
boasts three darts teams and a crib
team, and there are regular quiz
nights. The locals are friendly and
always keen to discuss Rugby on the
firm understanding that Wales has the
best national team – a difficult claim
to sustain at present. There are bar
snacks at lunchtime (Mon-Fri) and
many nearby restaurants offer
evening meals.

Beer: Draught Bass, Brains SA,
Morland Old Masters, Websters
Yorkshire Bitter on handpumps.

Accommodation: 2 singles, 2 doubles,
1 family room, 3 rooms with private
baths. B&B £22 single, £40 double/
family plus charge for children
according to age. Residents' lounge.
No pets.

ABERSOCH

St Tudwal's Hotel
Main Street. Off A499 main road
from Pwllheli

Licensee: Stewart Niblett
Tel: 075 881 2539

This pub, popular with locals and
tourists alike, has a smart and
comfortable lounge, a rear bar,
restaurant and a large patio. St
Tudwal's has open fires in winter, a
welcome for families, a garden, pub
games, and good food both lunchtime
and evening. Abersoch, on the Lleyn
peninsula, has a good harbour and
fine beaches, and is the home of the
South Caernarfonshire Yacht Club,
one of the biggest in Britain. All the
guest rooms have TVs, central
heating and tea and coffee making
facilities.

Beer: Robinson Best Mild, Best Bitter
and Old Tom (winter) on electric
pumps and straight from the cask.

Accommodation: 12 single, 1 twin
and 5 en suite doubles. B&B from
£17.50 per person. Pets welcome.
Cards: Access and Visa.

BEAUMARIS
(ANGLESEY)

Olde Bull's Head
Castle Street. Off A545

Proprietors: Keith Rothwell & David
Robertson
Tel: 0248 810329

You are in distinguished company
here, for those two itinerant travellers
and boozers, Dr Johnson and Charles
Dickens, stayed here in the original
posting house of the borough,
established in 1472 and rebuilt in
1617. It is a grade two listed building

and is packed with fascinating antiques including brass and copper ware, china, armour and weapons. There is a 17th-century water clock, and a high-backed chair in the beamed bar that used to be the town's ducking stool for law breakers. Access to the enclosed courtyard at the rear of the inn is through the original stage coach entrance, which has the largest single-hinged door in Britain. Bar food includes homemade soup, sandwiches, ploughman's, venison sausages, baked hake with Gruyère cheese, smoked duck, stir-fried vegetables with prawns, and such delicious homemade desserts as raspberry crumble and chocolate roulade. The guest rooms have been upgraded and have four crowns from the Wales Tourist Board.

Beer: Draught Bass on handpump.

Accommodation: 1 single, 5 doubles, 5 twins, all en suite. B&B £40 single,

£68 double. Children welcome; special bedroom for children adjoining parents' double: £15 per child. Cards: Access and Visa.

BEDDGELERT

Prince Llewelyn
By bridge over river in centre of village. Off A498 & B4085

Licensees: Eddie Blackburn & Jill Lomas
Tel: 0766 86242

The Prince Llewelyn is a fine old three-storey, brick-built inn in a wonderfully peaceful setting by a river in the Snowdon mountains, with rushing streams and quiet meadows. The spacious inn offers a genuinely warm welcome, with open fires, facilities for families and campers, and good bar meals lunchtime and evening. It is named in

Prince Llewelyn, Beddgelert

honour of the Welsh prince who, according to legend, slew his faithful hound, Gelert, when he thought the dog had killed his son. In fact, the dog had killed a wolf to protect the child. The anguished prince buried the dog in a spot close to the present hotel: the name of the village means Grave of Gelert. Close to the hotel there are facilities for fishing, climbing, walking, canoeing and pony-trekking.

Beer: Robinson Best Mild and Best Bitter on electric pumps.

Accommodation: 2 singles, 4 doubles, 2 twins, 2 family rooms, 4 rooms with en suite facilities. B&B £16 per person. Children up to 2 years free, half price up to 14. No pets. Cards: Access and Visa.

Tanronen Hotel

From the A5 at Capel Curig take the A498 for Beddgelert; turn left over the bridge and the hotel is on the left

Licensee: William Alun Hughes
Tel: 076686 347

The Tanronen is a small hotel in the centre of the Snowdonia national park, at the foot of Snowdon and seven miles from the coast. The grave of Gelert and the Sygun copper mine with its craft shops are close at hand. Bar meals and restaurant meals are available lunchtime and evening.

Beer: Robinson Best Mild and Best Bitter on electric pumps.

Accommodation: 4 twins, 4 doubles. B&B £18 per person. Children sharing with parents charged half price 12 years and under and 25% 13 to 16 years. Mini-Break 2 nights including evening meal £55 per person, 3 nights £80. No dogs. Cards: Access and Visa.

Crown Hotel, Bodedern

BODEDERN (ANGLESEY)

Crown Hotel
B5109. 1 mile off A5

Licensees: Reg & Candy Bryant
Tel: 0407 740734

The Crown is a fine example of a traditional village pub and is a good base for both the beaches of Anglesey and the port of Holyhead. It offers good and reasonably priced accommodation and food, with bar meals – home-baked pies, jacket potatoes and basket meals – available both lunchtime and evening. The bars have beamed ceilings and stone fireplaces, with darts and dominoes played in the public. There is a children's room and a separate small restaurant. The Crown offers plenty of live entertainment, with quizzes on Sunday nights and regular parties and fancy-dress and charity fund-raising events.

Beer: Burtonwood Bitter on handpump.

Accommodation: 1 single, 3 doubles, 2 family rooms, 1 room with shower. B&B from £14 per person. Children welcome, free under 3, half price under 11. Pets accepted.

BULL BAY (ANGLESEY)

Trecastell Hotel
On A5025 1 mile north of Amlwch

Licensee: Arthur Leese
Tel: 0407 830651
Fax: 0407 832114

The Trecastell Hotel, with a striking bow-windowed and tall-chimneyed exterior, overlooks the rocks at Bull Bay and has magnificent views over the Irish Sea. There is a comfortable lounge bar with sea views, a cocktail bar, games rooms and residents' lounge and restaurant. Food ranges from bar snacks to grills. Most of the guest rooms have private baths and tea makers and all have superb sea views. Bull Bay has a natural harbour, the coastline is lush with heather and alpine flowers, and there is a golf club next to the hotel.

Beer: Robinson Best Bitter on electric pump.

Accommodation: 9 doubles, 3 family rooms, doubles let as singles when available. B&B £24 single, £40 double. Off-Season Breaks: details on application. Children welcome, 25% reduction 10-15 years, half price 2-10.

Near CAERNARFON

St Beuno Coach Inn
Clynnog-Fawr. A499 between Caernarfon & Pwllheli

Licensee: Stephen P. Williams
Tel: 0286 86212

The St Beuno is a spacious and comfortable old country inn overlooking the sea on the edge of Snowdonia. It has log fires, large gardens and cosy lounge and bar areas. Food is available all day, and includes soup, homemade steak and kidney pie, beef or chicken curry, spaghetti bolognese, chilli con carne, seafood platter, plaice or cod, beefburger, pizza, steaks, ploughman's and a children's menu. Sports fanatics will enjoy facilities that include a full-size snooker table, three pool tables, table tennis, a skittle alley, bar billiards and shove ha'penny. Outdoors, you can play golf, go shooting, fishing or walking.

Beer: Marston Burton Bitter and Pedigree Bitter on handpumps.

Accommodation: 6 doubles, 3 family rooms, 2 en suite. B&B £16 single, £32 double, £45 family room. 3 nights B&B £50 per couple. Children and pets welcome. Cards: Access and Visa.

CAPEL CURIG

Bryn Tyrch Hotel
On A5, 5 miles from Betws-y-Coed

Licensee: Rita Davis
Tel: 06904 223

The cheerful hotel on the A5 has a comfortable lounge with superb views across the valley to Moel Siabod, and a small public bar where darts and pool are played. There is an enterprising range of bar food lunchtime and evening, with the emphasis on wholefoods and an extensive vegetarian and vegan menu, using herbs and spices; the menu changes frequently to make use of seasonal ingredients. Carnivores can enjoy steaks, chicken tikka or cacciatore, Welsh lamb cooked with apricots and almonds, beef goulash, fisherman's pie, trout; there are also filled jacket potatoes and the sweets include treacle tart, locally made ice creams plus herb teas. The hotel offers real fires in winter, a welcome for families, a garden and camping. There are superb walks, facilities for fishing and you can swim in the river when the weather is hot.
Beer: Marston Pedigree Bitter, Whitbread Castle Eden Ale and Flowers IPA on handpumps.

Accommodation: 6 en suite double rooms, all with tea and coffee making equipment. B&B from £15 per person, discounts for group bookings. Cards: Access and Visa.

Cobden's Hotel
On A5, 4 miles north of Betws-y-Coed

Licensee: Craig Goodall
Tel: 06904 243
Fax: 06904 354

Cobden's is a lively and welcoming smart country hotel with a comfortable lounge and a climbers' bar. It offers facilities for families, a garden and excellent bar food both lunchtime and evening. It is a popular resting place for visitors who enjoy the surrounding countryside or who energetically clamber up the encircling peaks.

Beer: Courage Directors and John Smith's Bitter on handpumps.

Accommodation: 4 singles, 12 doubles/twins, 2 family rooms, all rooms with en suite facilities and TVs. B&B £25 per person. Cards: Access and Visa.

Tyn-y-Coed
On A5, 1 mile east of village

Licensee: G.F. Wainwright
Tel: 06904 331

Thousands of visitors know the Tyn-y-Coed as the pub with the stage coach in the car park. The prominent landmark, more arresting than any pub sign, stands opposite the liveliest hotel in Capel. At weekends the bars are bursting with thirsty walkers and climbers, while residents can relax in more peaceful lounges and the restaurant. There are open fires in chilly weather, a garden and welcome for families, and good bar food and full meals lunchtime and evening. Pen-y-Pass and Nant Ffrancon, two landmarks of Snowdonia, are just a few miles away and there are gentler walks and climbs for the less energetic all around. The guest rooms in the hotel all have private baths or showers as well as tea and coffee making equipment.

Beer: Whitbread Boddingtons Bitter and Castle Eden Ale on handpumps.

Accommodation: 10 doubles, 4 family rooms. B&B £25 single, £44 double. Children free sharing with parents. Reductions for stays of more than 1 night. Pets accepted. Cards: Access and Visa.

DOLGELLAU

Royal Ship Hotel
Queen's Square. Off A487, A470 & A494

Licensee: Mrs M.D.B. Parry
Tel: 0341 422209

The Royal Ship has a superb exterior, a dark stone, creeper-clad building with a gable end, five dormer windows and a porch supported by pillars. It was built as a coaching inn in 1813 and has been extensively refurbished in recent years, with smart and comfortable bars, lounges and a restaurant. The beautifully appointed guest rooms have central heating and colour TVs. Bar food is available lunchtime and evening, while the restaurant serves evening meals and a Sunday roast. Dolgellau has opportunities for walking, fishing and pony-trekking, and there are several steam railways in the vicinity.

Beer: Robinson Best Bitter on electric pump.

Accommodation: 2 singles, 20 doubles/twins, 2 family rooms, 16 rooms with en suite facilities. B&B £18.80 per person, £31 en suite. Children's rates according to age, ranging from free to 25% reduction. Two-day Mini Break dinner, B&B en

suite £78 per person, 3 days £114 per person. Children's room. No dogs. Cards: Access and Visa.

LLANBEDR

Victoria Inn
On A496 south of Harlech

Licensee: Lawrence E. Barry
Tel: 034 123 213

The Victoria stands on the banks of the River Artro in the picturesque Llanbedr valley with mountains, valleys, lakes and beaches all around. The inn has a superb garden with tables, chairs and benches, as well as a Wendy House and slides and swings for children. Inside, the antiquity of the building is underscored by massive beams, a rare circular wooden settle, an ancient stove, stone-flagged floors and exposed timbers. Bar food is served lunchtime and evening, and the dining room serves evening meals and Sunday lunch. All the guest rooms are en suite and have colour TVs and tea and coffee making facilities.

Beer: Robinson Best Bitter on electric pump.

Accommodation: 2 singles, 3 doubles. B&B £22.50 per person. Children half price. Two-night Stay £40, 3 nights £59.50. Pets welcome. Cards: Access and Visa.

LLANBERIS

Padarn Lake Hotel
High Street. Off A4086

Licensee: T. Skilki
Tel: 0286 870260

The stone-built hotel overlooks Padarn Lake and has magnificent views of Snowdonia. There is a public bar with darts and pool, a lounge bar, and a cocktail bar next to the restaurant. There is a wide range of bar food lunchtime and evening and the restaurant menu includes local produce and game whenever possible. The excellent accommodation has lake and mountain views, private baths or showers, TVs, phones and tea and coffee making equipment. The hotel is a fine base for the Snowdon Mountain Railway, Llanberis Lake Railway, the Welsh Slate Museum and Padarn Country Park where you can fish, sail or row. Dinorwig Power Station, known as the 'Underground Giant' as it is contained within the heart of the mountain, is the largest pumped storage power station in Europe.

Beer: Marston Pedigree Bitter on handpump.

Accommodation: 21 doubles/twins, 4 family rooms. B&B £29 single, £49 double. Children up to 12 half price; babies free, charge for cot. Two-day break including dinner: £68 single, £63 per person double. Dogs by arrangement. Cards: Access, Amex, Diners, Visa.

LLANDUDNO

Sandringham Hotel
West Parade

Licensee: D. Kavanagh
Tel: 0492 876513

The Sandringham is a small, family-run hotel just 30 yards from the West Shore beaches. It is decorated with a naval theme, and there are many seascapes and sailors' hats. There is a garden with splendid views of Conwy Bay and Snowdonia, and bar meals are served lunchtime and evening. The well-furnished guest

rooms all have en suite baths or showers and tea and coffee making facilities, TVs and hairdryers. Food is based on homemade dishes.

Beer: Burtonwood Best Bitter and James Forshaw's Bitter, Greenall Original Bitter on handpumps.

Accommodation: 3 singles, 11 doubles/twins, 3 family rooms. B&B £15-£25 per person. Winter rate: £20 per person B&B plus dinner; summer £33 B&B plus dinner. Children's rates on application. No dogs. Cards: Access and Visa.

MENAI BRIDGE (ANGLESEY)

Anglesey Arms Hotel
On A5025

Licensee: John Darlington
Tel: 0248 712305

Cross the Menai Strait by Telford's famous suspension bridge and on the left at the far end you will find the Anglesey Arms. The Britannia Bridge is farther along the coast and the hotel has an interesting collection of photos showing the bridge in its various stages of construction. Although it is on the main road to Bangor, the white-painted hotel with dormer windows is set in lovely tree-guarded gardens with panoramic views of Snowdonia. There is an extensive bar snacks menu while the restaurant offers both table d'hôte and à la carte meals. The spacious and comfortable guest rooms all have private baths or showers, tea and coffee making facilities and colour TVs.

Beer: Lees Bitter on electric pump.

Accommodation: 4 singles, 4 doubles, 9 twins. B&B £38 single, £47 double. Half board available. Weekend £50 half board per person. Children welcome, terms depend on age. Cards: Access and Visa.

TRAWSFYNYDD

White Lion Hotel
Top of the hill in centre of village, off A470

Licensee: J.W. Gregory
Tel: 0766 87277

The White Lion is a homely, unspoilt moorland village inn with solid brick walls and three small rooms in a beautiful setting between Porthmadog and Dolgellau in the hills south of Snowdonia. It is just ten minutes' drive from Blaenau Ffestiniog and its steam railway and slate museum. The pub has brasses and fascinating old photos on the bar walls; darts, dominoes and cards are played by locals and visitors, and bar meals are available lunchtime and evening. Trawsfynydd is an old droving village and the White Lion was a drovers' inn; locals maintain the heritage of the inn by extending a warm welcome to visitors.

Beer: Burtonwood Dark Mild and Bitter on handpumps.

Accommodation: 3 doubles. B&B £12.50 per person. Children, rates according to age. Pets welcome.

POWYS

BRECON

Gremlin Hotel
The Watton, A40

Proprietors Stuart & Eleanor Harwood
Tel: 0874 623829

The Gremlin is just outside the centre of Brecon and is a fine base for visiting the national park where canoeing, sailboarding, pony-trekking, golf, fishing and canal boating are available. Parts of the building date back more than 400 years. It is a genuine, popular local with open fires, a garden, and a public bar where darts and quoits are played. The Gremlin is claimed to be haunted by a piano-playing ghost named Hilda. Snacks and bar meals are available every lunchtime and there are evening bar meals Tuesday to Saturday; roast lunches are served in the dining room on Sunday. There is a small TV lounge.

Beer: Brains Bitter and Draught Bass plus a regular guest beer on handpumps.

Accommodation: 2 singles, 1 double, 3 twins, 1 family room. B&B £14 per person. No pets. Cards: Access and Visa.

ERWOOD

Erwood Inn
A470

Licensee: P.J. Lewis
Tel: 0982 560218

The Erwood is a happy-go-lucky old coaching inn in a village on the Cardiff road in the Wye Valley between Brecon and Builth Wells. The writer Henry Mayhew fled here from his creditors and his scribblings in the inn formed the basis for *Punch* magazine, which he helped found. The pastel-coloured exterior is prettily decked out with hanging baskets and window boxes. There are a few seats and tables at the front and a patio garden at the side leading to a terraced garden with fine views of the valley where salmon and trout fishing are available. The inn has a lounge and public bar, a games room with pool, darts and quoits and a dining room. Food is served lunchtime and evening every day. The guest rooms have tea and coffee making facilities. Petrol and oil are available 24 hours a day on the forecourt.

Beer: Marston Pedigree Bitter and a guest beer on handpumps.

Accommodation: 2 singles, 2 doubles, 1 family room. B&B £13 per person. Half and full board available. Children welcome. Cards: Access and Visa.

GLASBURY-ON-WYE

Harp Inn
B4350, off A438

Licensees: David & Lynda White
Tel: 04974 373

The Post Office thinks the pub and Glasbury are in Herefordshire but they are firmly and geographically in Wales. The inn is a former 18th-century cider house, now with a full licence, in the beauty of the Wye Valley and the Black Mountains. In summer you can soak in the surroundings from the back terrace and lawn that slopes down to the Wye. Inside there is a strong emphasis on games with shove ha'penny, cribbage, cards, dominoes and pool played in a separate room that overlooks the river. The lounge has brick walls and a log fire in winter. Bar food (lunchtime and evening) includes homemade hot-pot, chicken curry, lasagne verdi, chilli con carne, steak and kidney pie, such vegetarian dishes as nut roast, vegetable curry, aubergine and mushroom lasagne, and vegetable pasty, plus ploughman's, sandwiches, jacket potatoes and burgers. The

Whites welcome children, and sensibly ask that parents as well as offspring are well-behaved. The inn is a splendid base for walking, fishing, riding, golfing and canoeing; Hay-on-Wye, with its famous second-hand book shops, is close by.

Beer: Robinson Best Bitter, Whitbread Boddingtons Bitter and Flowers Original on handpumps.

Accommodation: 4 doubles/twins, 2 rooms en suite. B&B £20 single, £30 double/twin. Children free up to 2 years, 2-10 £10. Pets accepted.

LLANDRINDOD WELLS

Llanerch
Off Waterloo Road, near BR station.
A483

Proprietors: John & Kenneth Leach
Tel: 0597 822086

The Llanerch is a fine old inn in the county town of Powys, and was once an important coaching inn in old Radnorshire. Llanerch is a shortened version of 'Llanerchderion' – 'resting place by the glade for coaches'. The inn was built in the 16th century and still has old beams, an inglenook fireplace and superb Jacobean staircase. It stands in spacious grounds with a beer garden, terrace and children's play area. Darts, dominoes, pool and boules are played, and golf, fishing and pony-trekking are available in the area. There is a residents' TV lounge. Food is available from the bar or in the brasserie and includes onion soup with croutons, steak, kidney and mushroom pie, curry, rainbow trout, vegetarian pancakes, grills, toasties, jacket spuds, fisherman's pie, lasagne, omelettes, and children's dishes. The inn is a splendid base for visiting the Elan Valley, Powis Castle, the Wye

Valley and the neighbouring English towns of Ludlow and Shrewsbury.

Beer: Draught Bass and Hancocks HB, Robinson Best Bitter on handpumps.

Accommodation: 3 singles, 7 doubles/ twins, 2 family rooms, 6 rooms en suite. B&B £18-£22 per person. Two-day Break from £50 includes dinner. Week from £110. Children welcome, terms negotiable. Pets by arrangement. Cards: Access and Visa.

LLANFAIR CAEREINION

Goat Hotel
High Street. A458 Welshpool road

Licensees: Richard & Alyson Argument
Tel: 0938 810428

The Goat is a handsome country inn in old Montgomeryshire near the town of Welshpool: Llanfair and Welshpool are linked by the narrow gauge steam railway that operates in the summer months. The inn offers old-fashioned comfort with crackling fires, polished brasses and deep armchairs, with central heating, tea makers and telephones in the guest rooms. Bar meals include soups, ploughman's, jacket potatoes, home-cooked ham pie, sausages, chicken, curry, fish, and beef and kidney pie. The menu offers grills and Welsh lamb cutlets. The area is rich in history and places of interest, including Powis Castle, St Mary's church and well in Llanfair, the working weaving mill at Dinas Mawddwy, and Montgomery Castle.

Beer: Felinfoel Double Dragon and Welsh Hancocks HB on handpumps.

Accommodation: 5 doubles, 1 family room, 4 rooms with en suite facilities. B&B £15-£19 per person. 10% discount if you carry a CAMRA guide. Children's room; children welcome to stay, half price.

LLANGADFAN

Cann Office Hotel
A458

Licensee: Glyn Lewis
Tel: 0938 88202

A large pub set back from the road and with trees and bushes guarding the entrance, the Cann Office dates from the 14th century and offers facilities for all ages. Food, mainly home-cooked, includes children's meals and vegetarian dishes. Welsh singing often breaks out spontaneously at weekends. Local activities include fishing, pony-trekking and bird watching.

Beer: Marston Burton Bitter and Pedigree Bitter (summer) on handpumps.

Accommodation: 2 singles, 3 doubles, 2 family rooms. B&B £16 single, £14 per person sharing. Children welcome, rates negotiable. No pets.

LLANGURIG

Blue Bell Inn
A44, near Llanidloes

Licensees: Bill & Diana Mills
Tel: 05515 254

The Blue Bell is a 16th-century inn – two buildings knocked into one with an impressive double-porch façade – a fine resting place for touring mid-Wales. The hotel will arrange for permits for fly fishing on the

Clywedog reservoir, and there are also facilities for golf, pony- trekking, bird watching and walking in the beautiful surrounding countryside. The Blue Bell has a welcome for families, open fires in winter, a public bar, full restaurant meals, hot and cold bar snacks and packed lunches if required. Llangurig is 1,000 feet above sea level and has a 14th-century monastic church and a craft centre. Five miles away is the historic market town Llanidloes at the confluence of the rivers Severn and Clywedog. The Plynlimon mountains, Elan Valley and Claerwen lakes are all within easy reach.

Beer: Whitbread Best Bitter and Flowers Original on handpumps.

Accommodation: 4 singles, 5 doubles, 1 family room, 1 en suite. B&B £14.50 per person. Children welcome.

LLANWRTYD WELLS

Neuadd Arms Hotel
The Square. A483

Proprietors: Gordon & Di Green
Tel: 05913 236

The Neuadd Arms is a splendid 19th-century hotel by the river in the smallest town in Britain. There is carefully restored Georgian and Victorian architecture, log fires, the obligatory ghost and good cooking. The traditional back bar, where quoits, darts and shove ha'penny are played, has a good local atmosphere. There is Welsh singing at weekends. Gordon Green is an enthusiastic CAMRA member and organizer of the Mid-Wales Beer Festival every November, and a Real Ale Ramble in the forests. The Greens will also attempt to order any guest beers that visitors request and will arrange visits to Buckley's and Felinfoel breweries

Blue Bell Inn, Llangurig

in Llanelli. For visitors of a less bibulous nature there are guided walks, pony-trekking, horse riding, fishing, mountain cycling, para-gliding and bird watching facilities all around.

Beer: Draught Bass and Worthington Dark Mild, Felinfoel Double Dragon and guest beers every week on handpumps.

Accommodation: 7 singles, 7 doubles, 1 family room, 7 en suite. B&B £18 per person. Weekend £52, Week £155 full board. Details of beer festival and other ale-activities on request. Children welcome, up to 50% reductions. Cards: Access and Visa.

MACHYNLLETH

Dyfi Forester Inn
4 Doll Street. A489

Licensees: Victor Watson & Lars Sorensen
Tel: 0654 702004

The inn is more than 100 years old and has been sensitively renovated by its owners. Regulars and visitors can take part in such traditional pub games as darts, dominoes and cribbage, which are enjoyed especially in the autumn and winter in front of a blazing open fire. Food is served in both the bar (lunchtime and evening) and the evening bistro restaurant. The bar menu includes homemade chilli con carne, curries and vegetarian dishes. The bistro is famous locally for its grills. There is a pleasant residents' TV lounge and the guest rooms have tea and coffee makers. Places of interest include the Centre for Alternative Energy and working slate mines; Machynlleth has a nine-hole golf course.

Beer: Marston Burton Bitter, Pedigree Bitter and Owd Rodger

(winter) on handpumps.

Accommodation: 1 single, 1 twin, 1 family room (3 beds). B&B £17 per person. Pets accepted.

PENYBONT

Severn Arms Hotel
Junction of A44 & A488

Proprietors: Geoff & Tessa Lloyd
Tel: 0597 851 224/344

The Severn Arms is a splendid old coaching inn with ancient roots and a more recent Georgian frontage: Penybont or Pont Rhyd-y-Cleifon as it was first known, dates from medieval times when it served as the fortification of Castle Cefn Llys. An inn by the bridge over the River Ithon has existed for centuries and was known as the Fleece or New Inn until 1814, when it became known as the Severn Arms. It was moved, lock, stock and barrels, to its present site in 1840 and retains a wealth of old beams and log fires, with a traditional bar and a residents' TV lounge. Residents can use the fishing rights on the river, and pony-trekking is available locally. The inn is in a superb location and a good base for border hopping between Wales and Shropshire. Bar meals (lunchtime and evening) include steaks, lasagne, fillet of plaice, trout, smoked salmon, fisherman's platter and steak and kidney pie. There are full evening meals in the beamed dining room. Concessionary rates are available on two local golf courses.

Beer: Draught Bass on handpump.

Accommodation: 4 doubles, 6 family rooms, doubles let as singles when available. All rooms en suite, with colour TVs, radios and phones. B&B

£27 single, £24 per person in double. Two-day break: £61 including dinner. Week: B&B plus dinner £195 single, £185 per person double/twin. Children welcome, up to half price depending on age. Cards: Access, Amex, Visa.

RHAYADER

Cornhill Inn
13 West Street, town centre; off A470

Licensee: Barbara Fraser
Tel: 0597 810869

The Cornhill is a 16th-century inn built of old stone and timber with a wealth of oak beams. The accommodation is in an old blacksmith's shop; the guest rooms all have hot and cold water, and there are showers adjacent. There is a TV lounge. The pub has open fires, no jukebox or pool tables. All the food is homemade by Mrs Fraser, and is served lunchtime and evening.

Beer: Cornhill Reserve house beer, Marston Pedigree Bitter, Mitchells ESB and Wye Valley Hereford Supreme Bitter plus one guest ale on handpumps.

Accommodation: 2 singles, 3 doubles,

1 family room. B&B £14 per person. Pets accepted.

TALGARTH

Tower Hotel
The Square. A479

Licensees: J. Poole & M. Barnes
Tel: 0874 711253

The Tower is in the centre of town and offers excellent family-run accommodation and food. The bar has a large log fire in winter, a pool table and homemade bar snacks lunchtime and evening. The lounge has a TV for residents and children, while the separate dining room is open seven days a week. The guest rooms have tea and coffee making facilities. The surrounding area offers gliding, hang-gliding, canoeing, sailing, fishing, hill wallking, pony-trekking and golf.

Beer: Draught Bass, Whitbread Boddingtons Bitter, Flowers Original and IPA on handpumps and regular guest beers.

Accommodation: 6 twins/doubles, 2 family rooms, 5 rooms with en suite facilities. B&B £18 single, £23 en suite, £30/£35 double/twin, £30 family room. Children £5 under 10. No pets. Cards: Access and Visa.

Scottish pub hours are standard: 11–2.30 and 5–11, Sunday 12.30–2.30 and 6.30–11. Many pubs have regular afternoon and evening extensions that allow them to open all day and often until midnight or later. Not all pubs open on Sunday but hotels serve drinks to residents.

BROUGHTON

Greenmantle Hotel
On A701, 26 miles north of Moffat

Licensees: Ken & Julie McFarlane
Tel: 08994 302

The Greenmantle takes its name from the novel by John Buchan who lived in the village. The ranch-style roadside hotel is in the middle of this pleasant Peeblesshire village near Biggar. It has a bar and lounge, two open fires in winter, and a sitting room for residents. Families are welcome and there is a children's play area in the extensive grounds. Food is available all day. Home-baked bread and free-range eggs help make up the dishes which include a 'just for the bairns' children's menu, and 'a dair ya!' 32oz T-bone steaks. Broughton is the home of the small independent brewery of the same name, set up in 1980 by a former Scottish & Newcastle executive with the splendid brewing name of David Younger. In a country dominated by two giant groups, he has had surprising but welcome success.

Beer: Broughton Greenmantle Ale on air pressure, Oatmeal Stout on handpump.

Accommodation: 2 doubles en suite, 7 twins, 1 en suite. All rooms have colour TVs. B&B from £23 single, £36 double/twin, extra charge of £4 for en suite room. Reductions of up to 75% for children according to age. Social weekends for parties of 16: £25 per person for 2 nights B&B. Pets accepted. Cards: Access and Visa.

CARLOPS

Alan Ramsey Hotel
On A702

Licensee: Anthony Swift
Tel: 0968 60258

The Alan Ramsey is a 200 year-old 'howff' with blazing log fires in winter, and stone-flagged floors. There is a bar, food lunchtime and evening, family facilities and an outdoor area for picnics and barbecues in warm weather. Carlops is a tiny Borders village in wonderful walking country.

Beer: Belhaven 70 and 80 shilling and a guest beer on handpumps.

Accommodation: 2 singles, 4 doubles. B&B £16 per person single/double, family £42. Pets accepted. Cards: Amex and Visa.

COLDSTREAM

Newcastle Arms
50 High Street. A697

Licensees: Linda & Walter Douglas
Tel: 0890 2376

Trip and you fall into England in this famous old Borders town with its strong military connections – there is even a Coldstream Guards Museum. The Newcastle Arms is family run and offers a warm welcome in its bars. There is a separate dining room that serves meals at most times of the day.
Beer: Theakston Best Bitter on handpump.

Accommodation: 1 single, 3 doubles, 1 family room. B&B £15 per person. Children welcome, half price.

INNERLEITHEN

Traquair Arms
Traquair Road, B709; off A72

Licensee: Hugh Anderson
Tel: 0896 830229
Fax: 0896 830260

The Traquair Arms is a comfortable
stone-built hotel in a quiet Borders
town that is popular with hill walkers
and anglers. It has open fires, a family
welcome, a garden and excellent food
lunchtime and evening: Mr Anderson
is a trained chef. Meals in the large
bar include homemade soup; pâté;
savoury tomatoes, Finnan savoury of
flaked smoked haddock with onions,
butter, cheese and double cream,
omelettes, jacket potatoes with a
range of fillings, and such vegetarian
dishes as rice and vegetable cutlets,
lentil moussaka, and Hungarian bean
goulash. Breakfasts are spectacular.
The hotel is close to Traquair House,
the stately home that keeps its main
gates shut until a Stuart returns to the
throne. To keep herself occupied
while awaiting this unlikely event, the
Lady of Traquair, Catherine
Maxwell-Stuart, brews the famous
strong bottle-fermented beer named
after the house and has added a
delectable draught beer, too. Brewing
is in an 18th-century brew house, and
the entire estate is open to visitors.
Fishing can be arranged for guests at
the hotel, and the area is excellent for
walkers and golfers. Mr Anderson
has a good selection of bottled beers
as well as draught, including
Greenmantle and Old Jock from
Broughton, Traquair House Ale
(naturally) and Caledonian 70 and 80
shilling.

Beer: Broughton Greenmantle Ale,
Traquair Bear Ale on handpumps.

Accommodation: 3 singles, 6 doubles,
1 family room, all en suite. B&B

£15-£35 per person. Half and full
board available. Off-peak and
weekend breaks: terms on
application. Dogs welcome. Cards:
Access and Visa.

KELSO

Black Swan
Horsemarket. A689

Licensees: Ian & Sandra Cassie
Tel: 0573 24563

The Black Swan is a cheerful old pub
in a typical small Borders town. It has
an atmospheric public bar and a
comfortable lounge, and serves
lunches and suppers based on quality
home-cooking that include soup,
roast beef and Yorkshire pudding,
chicken and mushroom pie, macaroni
cheese, lasagne verde and vegetable
lasagne, moussaka, chilli con carne,
burgers, curries, fish and chips and, in
the evening, duck à l'orange, venison
in red wine, steaks and lemon sole;
beefsteak pie is especially popular.
Darts and dominoes are played, but
there is no intrusive piped music.
There are some facilities for the
disabled, and camping can be
arranged nearby. The pub is open all
day Monday to Saturday and Sunday
afternoons.

Beer: Caledonian 80 shilling on
handpump.

Accommodation: 1 double, 2 family
rooms, all en suite with colour TVs
and tea and coffee making facilities.
B&B £20 single, £36 twin. Family
room rates on application. Cards:
Access and Visa.

MELROSE

Burts Hotel
Market Square. Off A7 & A68

Proprietor: Graham Henderson
Tel: 089 682 2285
Fax: 089 682 2870

Burts Hotel dates from 1772 and is a listed building that has retained its historic charm. There are bars, a residents' lounge, a snooker room, and a pleasant garden in summer. Both Scottish and French dishes are served in the elegant restaurant, while bar meals are available lunchtime and evening. Guests can enjoy walking, fishing, riding, shooting and golf, and can visit several old castles and stately houses in the area.

Beer: Belhaven 80 shilling on air pressure.

Accommodation: 8 singles, 13 doubles/twins, 3 family rooms. 21 rooms en suite. Cot available. B&B £39 single, £64 double, £74 family room. Children sharing £10, cot £2.50 per night. Breaks: minimum 2 nights £92 per night double/twin B&B and dinner; single £50. Children's room. Pets welcome. Cards: Access, Amex, Diners, Visa.

OXTON

Tower Hotel
Off A68 near Lauder

Licensee: Mr G. Brougham
Tel: 05785 235

The Tower is a picturesque old country inn with a striking black and white exterior, stained glass windows, public and lounge bars and a separate dining room. The public bar has a traditional gantry, and a blazing fire on cold days. It is a genuine local, with a strong emphasis on darts and dominoes. All the guest rooms have TVs and tea and coffee making facilities. Food ranges from bar snacks to full meals; all food is home-cooked and is served seven days a week; an à la carte menu is available in the evening until 9pm.

Beer: rotating cask ale includes Caledonian 70 shilling, Broughton Greenmantle Ale, Ind Coope Burton Ale and Jennings Bitter on handpump.

Accommodation: 1 double, 2 family rooms. B&B £18 single, £32 double, family room from £40. Dogs welcome.

PEEBLES

Kingsmuir Hotel
Springhill Road. Off A72

Proprietors: Elizabeth & Norman Kerr
Tel: 0721 20151

The Kingsmuir is a century-old stately house in leafy grounds on the south side of the Royal Burgh of Peebles. There is a pleasant parkland walk to the high street. The guest rooms in the hotel all have colour TVs, direct-dial phones, private bathrooms and tea makers. The popular bar is one of the busiest in town and has retained its original thick walls that stress the quality of 19th-century workmanship. The traditional Scottish food is served in the bar and the dining room, and its quality has won 'Taste of Scotland' awards in 1987-1991, many local awards, and an entry in CAMRA's *Good Pub Food* guide. Bar food (lunch and evening) includes cullen skink soup, steak pie, haggis, neeps and mashed tatties, mince with skirlie pudding, vegetarian casserole, and sandwiches. Dinner may offer such dishes as lentil soup, roasts of lamb, beef and venison, sea fish such as smoked haddock in Mornay sauce, and roast chicken with skirlie stuffing. Peebles is famous for its many tweed and woollen shops, and there is also an 18-hole golf course, pony- trekking and fishing.

Beer: Broughton Greenmantle Ale and Oatmeal Stout on handpumps.

Accommodation: 2 singles, 7 doubles, 1 family room, all en suite. B&B £39 single, £64 double, £75 family room. Children welcome, no charge under 6, £11 sharing family room. Breaks: rates approx 15% less. Dogs accepted. Cards: Access and Visa.

ST MARY'S LOCH

Tibbie Shiels Inn
A708 Moffat to Selkirk road

Licensees: Jack & Jill Brown
Tel: 0750 42231

Tibbie Shiels is an historic and remote inn on the shores of beautiful St Mary's Loch, one of the most tranquil spots in southern Scotland. Isabella – 'Tibbie' – Shiel was a widow with six children; her husband had worked for the local landlord, Lord Napier, who established her in the little cottage by the loch to run a hostelry for travellers in 1820. Tibbie was a friend of James Hogg, the shepherd poet of Ettrick, and she often played hostess to Hogg, Sir Walter Scott and the literary society of the day. The original old stone cottage is still in use as a bar and restaurant, while a modern extension has waitress service. There is a strong emphasis on home-cooking and local produce; food includes homemade soup, haddock, chips and peas, Yarrow trout, homemade chilli con

carne, ploughman's, burgers and sandwiches plus a daily vegetarian special such as bulghur wheat and walnut casserole. Evening meals are available and there is also a splendid afternoon high tea. The loch offers sailing and windsurfing, and the inn is a good base for visiting Grey Mare's Tale waterfall and Abbotsford, the former home of Sir Walter Scott.

Beer: Belhaven 80 shilling and Broughton Greenmantle Ale on handpumps.

Accommodation: 5 doubles, 1 family room. B&B £20 single, £32 double and family room. Children under 9 half price. Facilities for the disabled: 5 bedrooms on the ground floor with wheelchair access to bathrooms. No pets. Cards: Access and Visa.

SWINTON

Wheatsheaf Hotel
Main Street, B6471, 12 miles north of Berwick

Proprietors: Alan & Julie Reid
Tel: 089 086 257

The Wheatsheaf, which faces the village green in Swinton, has a spacious lounge with a long oak settle, a log fire and some agricultural prints on the wall. A smaller locals' bar has darts, dominoes and a pool table. Mr Reid is an accomplished chef and seafood is his speciality. Bar meals are available lunchtime and evening (not Monday), with specials chalked on a board. You may find homemade soup, smoked Tweed salmon, baked avocado with seafood, vegetarian fettuccine, steaks, smoked fish pancake, fillets of sole in a prawn and cream sauce, chicken or prawn curry, beef and real ale casserole, spinach pancake, Norwegian prawn and cheese salad, and sandwiches.

The hotel won the Scottish section in the 1991 Guinness Pub Food awards. Guest rooms all have colour TVs and tea and coffee making facilities. The Wheatsheaf has a large beer garden with children's play area and is a fine base for visiting Berwick.

Beer: Broughton Greenmantle Ale and Oatmeal Stout on air pressure and handpump.

Accommodation: 4 doubles/twins, 1 en suite. B&B £18 per person, £24 single occupancy. Children free under 5; over 5 £7 sharing. Children's room. Pets welcome but not in public rooms. Cards: Access and Visa.

TWEEDSMUIR

Crook Inn
A701 near Biggar & Moffat

Licensees: Stuart & Mary Reid
Tel: 089 97 272
Fax: 089 97 294

The Crook is a former drovers' halt and coaching inn. There has been an inn on the site since the 14th century and the present building dates from 1604 and is thought to be Scotland's oldest licensed premises. It was a clandestine meeting place for the outlawed 17th-century Covenanters and takes its name from a landlady named Jeannie o' the Crook who hid a fugitive from the dragoons in a peat stack. Robert Burns wrote his poem 'Willie Wastle's Wife' in the kitchen of the inn, a defamatory piece about the wife of a local worthy. The inn's bar has the original fireplace which was built of stone around a cartwheel that was then set alight to leave the circular hearth. A 20th-century extension has some superb Art Deco touches. Bar food is all homemade from local produce and includes soup, steak pie, ploughman's and

apple pie. Three-course meals are available, too. Darts, dominoes and crib are played in a separate room. There is a pleasant garden and children's play area.

Beer: Broughton Greenmantle Ale on handpump.

Accommodation: 1 single, 7 doubles, 6 rooms with private baths. B&B £26 single, £44 double. Children welcome, 20% reduction sharing with parents. Breaks: B&B plus dinner £66 per person for 2 nights. Pets accepted. Cards: Access and Visa.

YARROW VALLEY

Gordon Arms Hotel
Mountbenger, junction of A708 & B709

Licensee: Harry Mitchell
Tel: 0750 82222

The Gordon Arms is a delightful old inn by the bridge at Yarrow Water. It was an ale house for drovers and traders and later was the meeting place for such noted local writers as Sir Walter Scott and James Hogg, the Ettrick shepherd poet. It was granted a full licence when proposed by Hogg and granted by Scott the magistrate, perhaps not a good example of the even-handed nature of the law. The hotel today has a cheerful bar, lounge and dining room. Food ranges from bar snacks to high tea and full dinner. Bar meals, lunchtime and evening, include homemade soup, ploughman's, sandwiches, haddock, steak pie, salads, grills and a children's menu. Fresh trout is always available, and residents can enjoy fishing on the Yarrow and Ettrick rivers and nearby St Mary's Loch and Meggat reservoir. The hotel has an all-day licence seven days a week and there are regular folk evenings. The Yarrow Accordion and Fiddle Club meet in the hotel once a month.

Beer: Broughton Greenmantle Ale and Oatmeal Stout on air pressure.

Accommodation: 6 doubles. B&B £20 single, £36 double. Children welcome. Good access to the hotel for disabled people. Dogs accepted. A bunkhouse that sleeps 20 and has washrooms and showers provides low-cost accommodation for walkers and cyclists: £4.50 per night; own sleeping bag required.

CENTRAL

CALLANDER

Bridgend House Hotel
Bridge End, A81 Aberfoyle to Glasgow road

Proprietors: Sandy & Maria Park
Tel: 0877 30130

The Bridgend is a friendly, welcoming country hotel at the foot of Ben Ledi, the gateway to the Trossachs. The hotel dates back to the 17th century and has a Tudor façade and luxurious furnishings inside. The emphasis is on quality and tradition; most of the guest rooms have private baths and colour TVs, and there are some rooms with four-poster beds. An extensive menu offers Scotch smoked salmon, trout, duck, steaks and salads (including vegetarian), served until 9.30pm. The hotel is close to the banks of the River Teith and is handy for Stirling Castle, Rob Roy's grave and Loch Katrine.

Beer: McEwan 80 shilling on air pressure and Theakston Best Bitter on handpump.

Accommodation: 5 doubles, 1 family room, 5 with private bath. B&B £27.50 single, £35 double, family rates on application; £10 extra for room with bath. Children's rates on application. Pets welcome. Cards: Access, Amex, Visa.

DOLLAR

Strathallan Hotel
Chapel Place. A91; off M9

Proprietors: Jim & Pat Boyd
Tel: 0259 42205

The hotel has won a fistful of awards for its food, service and range of whiskies. It overlooks Castle Campbell and is handy for St Andrews golf course, and facilities for golf, fishing and hill-walking are available locally. Bar food and restaurant meals are served lunchtime and evening. Beer lovers will find that the hotel acts as the 'brewery tap' for the Harviestoun Brewery, based in Dollar.

Beer: Harviestoun 70, 80, 85 shilling and Old Manor on handpumps.

Accommodation: 3 singles, 2 doubles, 1 twin, 1 family room, 1 room en suite. B&B £30 single, £40 double/twin, £50 family room. Children under 5 free, under 14 years £18. Pets accepted. Cards: Access, Amex, Visa.

DUMFRIES & GALLOWAY

CANONBIE

Riverside Inn
Signposted from A7; 14 miles north of Carlisle

Licensees: Robert & Susan Phillips
Tel: 03873 71512/71295

The Riverside is a lovely old inn in beautiful wooded countryside by the River Esk. There is an old beamed bar reached through an archway from the lounge, cheerful open fires in winter, old pictures of the area on the walls, stuffed wildlife, a long-case clock and comfortable seats. Food in the bars and dining room is imaginative and widely praised: sample homemade beef or lentil broth, quiches, including vegetarian, fresh salmon with spring onion and ginger sauce, selection of salads, steaks, and delicious sweets including date pudding and butterscotch meringue. There is a splendid range of local fish in the restaurant. Visitors praise the breakfasts, too.

Beer: Yates Bitter and a guest beer on handpumps.

Accommodation: 4 twins, 2 doubles, rooms can be let as singles; all rooms en suite. B&B from £20 per person. Winter Breaks: rates on application. No pets. Cards: Access and Visa.

GRETNA

Solway Lodge Hotel
97-99 Annan Road. Off A74(M) & A75

Licensee: John G. Welsh
Tel: 0461 38266
Fax: 0461 37791

The Solway Lodge, as its name implies, is close to the Solway Firth and the English border; the nearest town is Carlisle. The hotel has a cream-painted exterior with two large porches. Inside there is a comfortable lounge bar and restaurant; bar food is available lunchtime and evening and the restaurant is open for dinner. All the guest rooms have private facilities, TVs, phones and tea and coffee makers. Gretna is a good base for touring the border area.

Beer: Broughton Special Bitter and Tetley Bitter on handpumps.

Accommodation: 10 doubles/twins, all en suite. B&B £35 single, £24-£37.50 sharing. Children's rates according to age. Cards: Access, Amex, Diners, Visa.

LOCKERBIE

Kings Arms Hotel
29 High Street, town centre, ½ mile off A74

Proprietors: Ian & Wallace Guthrie
Tel: 05762 2410

The Kings Arms is a welcoming 17th-century coaching inn in the heart of Burns country – 'bonny, bonny Galloway' as he described the magnificent scenery. Both Prince Charles Edward Stuart and Sir Walter Scott stayed in the hotel. It offers substantial good value bar snacks and restaurant meals and is the ideal base for coarse fishing on the river or loch; and there are no fewer than six golf courses within a half-hour's drive.

Beer: McEwan 80 shilling on air pressure.

Accommodation: 1 single, 3 doubles, 7 twins, 1 family room. B&B £16 single, £30 double. Children welcome, up to 50% reduction; under 5 free.

Somerton House Hotel
35 Carlisle Road. From A74 take slip road into Lockerbie; the hotel is 1 mile from town centre

Proprietors: Mr & Mrs S. Ferguson
Tel: 05762 2583/2384

Somerton House is a stately Victorian

building made from local red sandstone. It is a listed building and has an ornate plaster cornice and unusual Kauri timber panelling imported from New Zealand at the turn of the century. All the guest rooms have en suite facilities, colour TVs, hairdryers and tea and coffee trays. Bar food, lunchtime and evening every day, includes homemade soup, deep fried mushrooms in garlic butter, plaice or haddock, curried chicken, minced beef cobbler, ploughman's and sandwiches. The separate restaurant has a 'Taste of Scotland' menu specializing in local fish, meat and game. There is a chef's special and vegetarian special every day. Guests can enjoy fishing, golf and walks in lovely countryside, and there are many old castles in the area. The hotel received the highest AA rating for any Scottish hotel in 1992. It has a sun lounge where children are welcome.

Beer: Ind Coope Burton Ale and Tetley Bitter on electric pumps.

Accommodation: 1 single, 4 doubles/ twins, 2 family rooms. B&B £36 single (£41 single occupancy of double room), £51.50 double/twin, £56.50 family room. Dogs by arrangement. Cards: Access, Amex, Visa.

MOFFAT

Balmoral Hotel
High Street. From A74 take A702

Licensees: J. Graham & C. Bingham
Tel: 0683 20288

The Balmoral is a friendly and family-owned hotel, more than 200 years old, and set in the picturesque Annan valley. Bar meals, served lunchtime and evening, include homemade steak and kidney pie,

Balmoral Hotel, Moffat

DUMFRIES & GALLOWAY

DUMFRIES & GALLOWAY

Madras curry, chilli con carne, deep
fried haddock, lamb chops, haggis,
lasagne, rainbow trout, Solway
salmon in season, salads, sandwiches
and a daily vegetarian dish. The
evening restaurant specializes in fish
and game, including tuna, shark and
swordfish steaks. (Restaurant closed
Oct-Feb but many items are
transferred to the bar menu.) Moffat,
once a spa town and centre of the
Scottish woollen trade, is now best
known as a small country town in
superb countryside, with facilities for
fishing, golf, riding, stalking and
walking. It is in the heart of Burns
Country and some claim that the poet
drank in the Balmoral – but then, in
common with Dickens and Johnson
in London, he seems rarely to have
passed a hostelry by!

Beer: Broughton Greenmantle Ale on
handpump.

Accommodation: 3 singles, 13
doubles/twins, 1 family room, 6
rooms with en suite facilities. B&B
£28 single, £35 en suite, £24 per
person in double, £28 en suite, £50
family room. Children under 6 free.
Discounts for 3 and 7 night stays.
Pets welcome. Cards: Access and
Visa.

Black Bull
1 Churchgate. 1 mile off A74

Licensee: Jim Hughes
Tel: 0683 20206
Fax: 0683 20483

The Black Bull is a splendid 16th-
century inn but its roots go back
much further. There was monastery
on the site and a papal bull or bulla
gave the monks permission to build
an ale and rest house for pilgrims.
The tiled lounge bar of the inn today
has old coaching notices and prints,
while the bar across a courtyard has

memorabilia of the more recent age of
steam: the defunct Caledonian
Railway ran close to the inn. Between
1682 and 1685 the inn was the
headquarters of Graham of
Claverhouse ('Bonnie Dundee'): his
dragoons ruthlessly put down
religious rebels in the area. Robert
Burns was a frequent visitor to the
Black Bull and scratched his 'Epigram
to a Scrimpit Nature' on a window
pane (it is now in a museum in
Moscow). Excellent bar food (lunch
and evening) offers homemade soup,
shepherd's pie, haggis, quiche, steaks
and salads. There is a restaurant, too.

Beer: McEwan 80 shilling, Theakston
Best Bitter and Old Peculier on air
pressure and handpumps.

Accommodation: 3 singles, 3 doubles,
2 family rooms; 1 room en suite, all
with TVs and tea and coffee makers.
B&B £24 single, £36 double, £42
family room. Children welcome,
price included in family room. No
pets. Cards: Access and Visa.

FIFE

ST ANDREWS

Russell Hotel
26, The Scores. Off A91

Proprietor: Gordon de Vries
Tel: 0334 73447
Fax: 0334 78279

The Russell is a small, friendly
family-run hotel overlooking St
Andrews Bay and close to the Old
Course of the Royal and Ancient golf
club. The hotel's cosy Victorian Bar
has a unique atmosphere in which
locals, undergraduates, young and
old mix freely. The hotel is renowned

locally for its splendid bar lunches, while the evening restaurant serves fresh local produce, including seafood, game and Aberdeen Angus beef. The hotel is a fine base for the golf course, the castle, medieval cathedral and town centre.

Beer: Caledonian 80 shilling and Broughton Greenmantle Ale on handpumps.

Accommodation: 2 twins, 2 doubles, 2 family rooms, all with en suite facilities. B&B £35 single, £50 double/twin/family room. Off-season Weekends available: terms on application. Children welcome, free under 12 if sharing, £12.50 up to 18. Pets accepted. Cards: Access and Visa.

GRAMPIAN

ABERDEEN

Brentwood Hotel
101 Crown Street, few minutes from Union Street (city centre). Off A92 & A93

Licensee: Jim Byers
Tel: 0224 595440
Fax: 0224 571593

The Brentwood is a stylish modern hotel in the centre of the magnificent granite city of the north. The emphasis is on quality and individual attention. Carriages Brasserie is designed as a traditional eating and drinking place with a good choice of food and ale. It is open seven days a week, lunchtime and evening, and children are welcome. Food includes homemade soup, smoked salmon, lasagne, lemon scampi, homemade steak and kidney pie, pork satay,

vegetarian dish of the day, roast breast of duck, steaks, salads and grills. Jim Byers is a devoted supporter of real ale and supplies a wide range from the Whitbread stable; he also serves the delicious Belgian speciality on draught, Liefmans Kriek (cherry) beer. The guest rooms are large and beautifully appointed, and excellent breakfasts include local kippers.

Beer: Whitbread Boddingtons Bitter, Castle Eden Ale, Flowers IPA and Wethered Bitter on handpumps plus two regular guest beers.

Accommodation: 30 singles, 34 doubles, 1 family room, 1 suite, all with private baths or showers. B&B £53.50 single, £65 double Monday-Thursday, £30 single, £40 double at weekends. Children welcome, terms by arrangement. Cards: Access, Diners, Switch, Visa.

Ferryhill House
Bon Accord Street

Licensee: Douglas Snowie
Tel: 0224 590867

The Ferryhill is a small, cheerful and attractive Georgian hotel with a large choice of cask beers for the area, some served by traditional tall founts. The other main plus point is that the hotel has no juke box or pool table: 'It is a pub where the art of conversation has not died,' according to one enthusiast. The main bar has large bow windows that overlook the hotel's spacious grounds. There is a hall with more seating and a plush cocktail bar. Bar food includes a wide range of ploughman's lunches, jacket potatoes with a choice of fillings and a large and varied menu in the separate restaurant. In warm weather there are tables and chairs on a patio.

Beer: Broughton Greenmantle Ale,
McEwan 80 shilling, Theakston Best
Bitter and Younger No 3, Orkney
Raven Ale, Timothy Taylor Best
Bitter on handpumps and air
pressure.

Accommodation: 4 singles, 6 doubles,
all rooms en suite with TVs, phones
and tea and coffee makers. B&B £46
single, £65 double.

FINDHORN

Crown & Anchor Inn
Off A96, 6 miles from Forres

Proprietor: George Burrell
Tel: 0309 690243

The Crown & Anchor is an 18th-
century inn on the edge of Findhorn
bay and jetty. The bar is packed with
old photos and prints of the area,
darts, dominoes, cribbage and
backgammon are played, and there is
a large fireplace with welcoming fires
in winter. There are more pictures in
the comfortable lounge which also
stages folk music on Sunday
evenings. Food is served all day –
anything from a jumbo sausage to a
T-bone steak, according to Mr
Burrell; the menu also includes local
fresh trout, Aberdeen Angus steaks,
and steak and kidney pie made with a
pint of real ale; children's portions
available. Residents have the use of
the inn's boats on the sandy beach.
As well as the excellent draught beers,
there is a collection of more than 100
international beers and 100 or so
different whiskies.

Beer: Courage Directors, Draught
Bass, Whitbread Boddingtons Bitter
on handpumps plus 4 regular guest
beers on handpumps.

Accommodation: 2 twins, 3 doubles,
1 family room, all with shower and
tea and coffee makers; TV available

on request. B&B £16 per person.
Children welcome, half price sharing.
Dogs accepted.

FORRES

Red Lion Hotel
2 Tolbooth Street. A96, 26 miles
east of Inverness

Licensees: Robbie & Carol
Sutherland
Tel: 0309 72716

The Red Lion, known locally as the
'Red Beastie', is an old hotel rebuilt in
1838, with small cosy bedrooms,
including attic rooms. The public bar
of the hotel has darts, dominoes and
cribbage, and there is a quieter,
wood-panelled lounge bar and a rare
example of a Campbell's Brewery
mirror. Forres is a delightful town
that takes a vigorous part in the
annual 'Britain in Bloom'
competition, and is a good base for
taking the Whisky Trail or visiting
Loch Ness. The town is known as the
Riviera of the North as a result of its
mild climate, and has a first-class golf
course.

Beer: McEwan 80 shilling and
Younger No 3 on air pressure.

Accommodation: 2 singles, 2 doubles.
B&B £12 per person.

INVERURIE

Thainstone House Hotel
2 miles outside town on A96

Proprietor: Edith Lovie
Tel: 0467 21643
Fax: 0467 25084

Thainstone House is a palladian
mansion in meadows and woodlands
of old Aberdeenshire's Don Valley.

The house was designed by the famous local architect Archibald Simpson as a medieval manor house; it was rebuilt in 1820 after a disastrous fire. It was once the ancestral home of James Wilson, a signatory to the American Declaration of Independence. Close by are the ruins of the fortifications where Robert the Bruce's troops rested before the Battle of Barra in 1308. The interior of the hotel is sumptuous, with elegant dining room, lounges, and beautifully appointed guest rooms, including two four-posters, all with private baths, TVs and tea and coffee making facilities. The bar menu offers soup, marinated Orkney herring, baked avocado and bacon hot-pot, roast sirloin of Aberdeen Angus beef, supreme of chicken in garlic, fresh Don salmon, haddock, escalope of pork Rob Roy filled with haggis, and vegetarian curry. There is a separate restaurant; both bar food and restaurant are open for lunch and dinner.

Beer: constantly changing range including Broughton Greenmantle Ale, Orkney Raven Ale, Tetley Bitter and Timothy Taylor Landlord on handpumps.

Accommodation: 13 singles, 29 doubles, 8 family rooms. B&B £65 single, £90 double and family room. Weekend £110 single, £140 double. Children welcome, charged for meals only if sharing. Residents' lounge. Pets welcome. Cards: Access, Amex, Diners, Switch, Visa.

KINCARDINE O'NEIL

Gordon Arms Hotel
North Deeside Road. A93

Licensee: Bryn Wayte
Tel: 03398 84236

The Gordon Arms is an hospitable old inn built around 1810 in one of the oldest villages in Royal Deeside, close to Balmoral Castle. Outside there are impressive chimneys and steeply sloping tiled roofs, inside carefully restored lounges and guest rooms with hand-picked antique furniture that reflects the inn's early 19th-century origins. Food is based on local produce and home cooking and includes inexpensive bar suppers. Vegetarians are catered for with a full menu. The village has a 13th-century church, there are many castles in the area, plus golf, fishing, shooting, pony-trekking, gliding and water skiing.

Beer: Theakston Best Bitter and Younger No 3 on handpumps with a regular guest beer.

Accommodation: 1 single, 4 doubles, 2 family rooms, 3 en suite. B&B from £16 per person. Apply for details of mini-breaks. Children and pets welcome.

STONEHAVEN

Marine Hotel
9/10 Shorehead. Off A92

Licensees: Mr & Mrs Philip Duncan
Tel: 0569 62155
Fax: 0569 66691

The Marine is a popular harbour hotel where you can sit outside in summer and watch the boats and the impressive mountainous backdrop while you eat and drink. The hotel is more than 100 years old and most of the guest rooms overlook the harbour. There is a games room with a pool table and a traditional red phone box. There are also a lounge bar and dining room. The hotel uses fresh local produce and offers morning coffee, lunch, high tea and evening meals. Fresh fish and seafood are the highspots of the menus. There is no specific children's room but they are welcome in the dining room.

Beer: McEwan 80 shilling and Timothy Taylor Landlord on handpumps.

Accommodation: 1 single, 6 doubles, 2 family rooms. B&B £25 single, £30 double. Children welcome, half price (some of the doubles also used as family rooms). Cards: Access, Amex, Visa.

HIGHLAND

FORT WILLIAM

Nevis Bank Hotel
Belford Road. A82, outskirts of town at junction to Glen Nevis

Licensee: Jim Lee
Tel: 0397 705721
Fax: 0397 706275

Nevis Bank is a cheerful and welcoming hotel on the outskirts of Fort William, a braw, sea-swept and historic old Highlands town. The hotel is conveniently placed at the start of the road up Ben Nevis and on the Road to the Isles. The hotel has two bars, offering a wide range of bar snacks, lunches and suppers. The separate Country Kitchen restaurant offers soup, country pâté, local salmon, Scottish lamb, Aberdeen Angus steaks, salads, and a local delicacy called Cranachan – raspberries blended with oatmeal, cream and malt whisky. The Ceildh Bar has weekend live Scottish and Country and Western music. The guest rooms have private baths, colour TVs and tea and coffee makers.

Beer: McEwan 80 shilling and Younger No 3 on air pressure.

Accommodation: 6 singles, 23 doubles, 2 family rooms. B&B £42 single, £52 double, £60 family room. Children free sharing. Various breaks and package deals: rates on request. Pets accepted. Cards: Access, Amex, Diners, Visa.

GLENCOE

Clachaig Inn
Off A82 on old riverside Glencoe road; near Ballachulish

Proprietor: Peter Daynes
Tel: 08552 252

The Clachaig Inn has one of the most spectacular settings in Britain – in the heart of Glencoe, scene of the massacre of the MacDonald clan by the combined forces of the Campbells and English troops in 1692: the inn once bore the sign 'Nae Campbells'. Wooded hillsides give way to the bare, bleak and awesome peak of Aonach Dubh. The inn has stood in its remote setting for some 300 years, but the Daynes have carefully modernized it, and the accommodation is of a high standard and there is a self-catering lodge as well as the guest rooms in the inn. The dining room seats 50 and serves good Scottish home-cooked food including homemade soup, pâté with oatcakes, sweet herring, vegetarian dish of the day, deep-fried scampi, the Clachaig Sizzler – 8oz rump steak cooked on a cast-iron platter – and a special children's menu. There are two bars, and the lounge has fine views of the west face of the mountain. The Clachaig is open all year and has folk music every Saturday night. The inn is the ideal base for climbing and walking, and there are also seasonal opportunities for fishing and skiing. There is a permanent beer festival during the winter months with cask beers from England and Scotland.

Beer: Arrols 80 shilling, Younger No 3 on handpump and air pressure and up to six guest beers.

Accommodation: 2 singles, 17 doubles/twins/family rooms, 16 rooms with private bath or shower. B&B from £22 per person, £16.50 per person in double/twin/family, £22-£24 en suite. Children half price under 12. Self-catering chalets: rates on request. Pets accepted. Cards: Access, Switch, Visa.

INVERNESS

Lochardhil House Hotel
Stratherrick Road, 1½ miles from town centre

Licensee: Richard Green
Tel: 0463 235995

Lochardhil House, on the outskirts of Inverness, is a splendid old mansion house set in five acres of grounds with a sunken garden. It has a partly castellated frontage, sweeping staircases, a quiet cocktail lounge and a genuine locals' bar in the courtyard. The dining room has Gobelin tapestries depicting the biblical story of Esther. Good pub food is available daily, along with a full à la carte restaurant; the frequently changing menu includes salmon, pheasant in season, and Black Isle beef. The hotel has one of the new Scottish children's certificates, which means children are allowed in the cocktail lounge until 8pm. The delightful guest rooms all have colour TVs, videos and satellite programmes, and tea and coffee making equipment.

Beer: Younger IPA on air pressure.

Accommodation: 3 singles, 5 doubles, 3 family rooms, all en suite. B&B £50-£65 single, £65-£85 double. Family room rates negotiable. Children welcome. Cards: Access, Amex, Diners, Visa.

LOTHIAN

DIRLETON

Castle Inn
½ mile off A198

Licensee: Douglas Stewart
Tel: 062 085 221

The Castle Inn was once an important coaching stop on the old Dunbar road to Edinburgh. Now it stands in a quiet old East Lothian village, still offering good ale and victuals to travellers. It has a long, low stucco frontage with tall chimneys and little windowless dormers, like raised eyebrows above the first-storey windows. There is a free standing inn sign and two porches. The inn looks across the village green to the castle, built in 1225, the scene of a major battle during the Civil War, when it was taken by Cromwell's forces. The village grew around the castle in the 17th century, when the sea engulfed the area of the original village and the people moved towards the safety of the battlements. The Castle Inn offers two bars – a public one with fine engraved mirrors and an open fire, and a comfortable lounge with another blazing welcome on chilly days. There is lunchtime food and service every day, including Sunday afternoons. The main building contains four guest rooms looking out over the green, and a further four are available in the converted stable block. There is also a charming cottage, designated as being of historic interest, which can be let to larger parties.

Beer: Caledonian 70 shilling and McEwan 80 shilling on air pressure.

Accommodation: 2 singles, 6 doubles, 4 rooms en suite. B&B from £21 per person. Children half price sharing. The cottage has 2 double rooms, kitchen, bathroom and living/dining room with open fire, rates on request. Cards: Access and Amex.

EDINBURGH

Navaar House Hotel
12 Mayfield Gardens. A7, 1 mile from city centre

Proprietor: A.S. Thomson
Tel: 031-667 2828

Mayfield is a late 19th-century suburb in the south of Edinburgh. Its houses are big, stately and elegant, and many on the main road have been converted into hotels. The Navaar has plasterwork in many of the rooms that suggests how ornate the interior must have been originally, before it was modernized into a comfortable, urbane roadside hotel. It is conveniently placed for the centre of Old Reekie, with its snooty elegance, magnificent buildings and some of the finest and most ornate bars in Britain. The bars in the Navaar House are popular with local amateur football, hockey and even cricket teams, and there is live jazz every Tuesday. The bars are open every day and all day until midnight, and food is served both lunchtime and evening. Guest rooms are all en suite and have TVs and tea and coffee makers.

Beer: Caledonian 80 shilling, McEwan 80 shilling and guest beers on air pressure and handpump and a regular guest beer.

Accommodation: 6 doubles. B&B from £22.50 per person. Half and full board available. Children welcome, half price. Cards: Access, Amex, Diners, Visa.

STRATHCLYDE

AYR

Chestnuts Hotel
52 Racecourse Hotel. A179 ½ mile south of town centre

Licensee: Mrs C. Bender
Tel/fax: 0292 264393

This elegant building was constructed in the late 19th century and was extended towards the end of 1890s by a Captain Reginald Hunter-Blair of the Gordon Highlanders; the ghost of a child seen in the kitchen is thought to have been one of his offspring. The house was converted to a hotel in 1937, and it offered hospitality for Jewish servicemen stationed in the area during the Second World War. In 1955 the hotel was sold to the Hebrew Society of Ayr and what is now the restaurant became a synagogue. It reverted to a hotel – for people of all denominations – in the 1970s. There are lunches and suppers in the bar and restaurant.

Beer: Caledonian Robert Deuchars IPA, Draught Bass, Greenmantle Broughton Special Bitter and a guest beer on handpumps.

Accommodation: 6 singles, 5 doubles, 2 family rooms, 11 rooms en suite.

B&B £29 single, £28.25 per person double/family room. Children half price. Weekend 2 nights B&B plus dinner £67.50 single, £126 double. Week £215 single, £420 double. Pets accepted. Cards: Access, Amex, Visa.

BRODICK (ISLE OF ARRAN)

Ormidale Hotel
Knowe Road; first left past Brodick church

Licensee: Tommy Gilmore
Tel: 0770 2293

The hotel is a fine Victorian building with superb views over Brodick Bay to the Sleeping Warrior crowned by Goatfell, 2,866 feet above sea level. The Ormidale has a large licensed conservatory with handsome brass beer founts. Summer entertainment includes folk nights, discos and quiz nights. The hotel is the focal point of the island's folk festival, held annually in early June. Good bar meals, with local seafood as a speciality, are served lunchtime and evening between Easter and September. There is a children's menu and a large beer garden with a play area. The island is a delight, with deer roaming through the heather and opportunities for fishing, walking, pony-trekking and golf: there are seven courses on the island and the first tee of one is just a few yards from the Ormidale. There are car ferries from Ardrossan to Brodick (booking essential in summer) and a smaller car ferry in summer only between Kintyre and Lochranza in the north of the island.

Beer: McEwan 70 shilling on air pressure.

Accommodation: (Easter-September only; bar open all year) 4 singles, 3 doubles, 1 family room. All rooms equipped with colour TVs. B&B £18 per person. Children welcome, half price. Pets accepted.

CUMBERNAULD

Castlecary House Hotel
Main Street. A80, off M73

Licensee: M. Johnston
Tel: 0324 840233
Fax: 0324 841608

Castlecary House is a small village hotel close to Glasgow, with a quiet lounge, busy bar and snugs, and a range of cask beers that constitutes a mini beer festival. It is open all day, including Sundays, and serves both lunch and evening bar meals. Food includes lentil and potato soup, grills, salads, trout, homemade steak and kidney pie, and haddock in beer batter. Accommodation includes rooms in the hotel and cottages, with twin and double rooms.

Beer: Belhaven 80 shilling, Broughton Greenmantle Ale, Jennings Bitter, Maclays 80 shilling on handpumps and air pressure.

Accommodation: 4 singles, 23 doubles/twins, 1 family room, all with en suite facilities. B&B £15-£25 single, £41-£56 double, terms depend on type of room and facilities: cottage accommodation includes private lounge and own TV and tea and coffee makers. Weekend: doubles/ twins charged at single rate. Pets accepted. Cards: Access, Amex, Diners, Switch, Visa.

COYLTON BY AYR

Finlayson Arms Hotel
On main road (A70) at east end of
village opposite church

Owners: Mr & Mrs M. Munro
Tel: 0292 570298

The Finlayson Arms is a 19th-
century village inn with modern en
suite guest rooms which all have TVs,
phones and tea makers. There are
open fires in both lounge and public
bar. Both bar food and an à la carte
menu are served lunchtime and
evening. The inn is well-placed for
exploring Burns country, with many
castles and country parks of historic
interest. The Munros will arrange
golfing holidays for guests with
tee-off times for most courses in
Ayrshire free of charge.

Beer: Broughton Greenmantle
Special Bitter and one guest beer on
handpumps.

Accommodation: 9 doubles. B&B £29
single, £48 double. Children under 10
free when sharing. 10% discount for
parties of 12 or more or for full 7 day
stay. Pets accepted. Cards: Access,
Amex, Diners, Visa.

EAGLESHAM

Eglinton Arms Hotel
Gilmour Street. Off A77

Licensee: Trevor Paterson
Tel: 03553 2631
Fax: 03553 2955

The Eglinton Arms is a popular
village local in old Renfrewshire. It
dates back to the 16th century when
it was an important coaching inn.
There are reminders of the past in the
Stables Bar and the Postilion
Restaurant. Darts and dominoes are

played in the snug, which has a
cheery fire in winter. Good bar food
includes homemade soups and pâté,
grills, chicken, seafood and poached
cod. Cask beer in the lounge bar
only.

Beer: Younger No 3 on air pressure.

Accommodation: 6 singles, 3 doubles,
5 twins, all with private baths. B&B
£51 single, £61 double/twin.
Weekend £27.50 single, £37.50
double/twin per day.

GLASGOW

Babbity Bowster
16-18 Blackfriars Street, east of the
city centre

Proprietor: Fraser Laurie
Tel: 041-552 5055
Fax: 041-552 5215

Fraser Laurie's brilliant creation
epitomizes the regeneration of
Glasgow as a major cultural centre in
Scotland. Babbity Bowster is bar, café
and restaurant rolled into one in an
elegant Robert Adam town house on
the site of an ancient monastery. The
fine recreation of a medieval inn sign
is repeated inside as a wall plaque.
There are tall windows, pastel walls, a
mass of drawings and photographs of
Glasgow and Glaswegians, and a
restaurant that also doubles as an art
gallery for Glasgow painters. Food
ranges from light snacks to full meals,
starts with breakfast and goes on until
the wee small hours. Try soup,
haggis, neeps and tatties, chicken,
mushroom or spicy vegetable pies,
fresh mussels in wine, filled jacket
potatoes, stovies, dish of the day, and
freshly baked bread, rolls, croissants,
sweets and fruit tarts. There are open
fires, outside seating in pleasant
weather and live music, including
traditional fiddlers. The enterprise is
named after a Scots kissing dance.

Beer: Maclay 70 shilling, 80 shilling and Porter plus one guest beer on air pressure.

Accommodation: 1 single, 1 double, 4 twins, all en suite. B&B £36 single, £56 double/twin. Children welcome to stay. Cards: Access, Amex, Visa.

GOUROCK

Spinnaker Hotel
121 Albert Road. A78, south of town

Licensee: Ann McCartney
Tel: 0475 33107

The Spinnaker is a friendly family-run hotel on the sea front with sweeping views over the Clyde to Dunoon and the distant Highlands. The hotel is a haven of peace with no juke boxes or gambling machines. There is a downstairs bar and dining room, and a cocktail bar on the first floor. A wide range of bar meals are served lunchtime and evening, all day at weekends; there are daily specials. Sailing, fishing, hill climbing and golf are all available in the area.

Beer: Belhaven 80 shilling on air pressure.

Accommodation: 2 singles, 1 double, 1 twin. B&B £17 single, £29 double, £40 twin en suite. Children welcome.

HOUSTON

Houston Inn
North Street. Off A761

Licensee: Thomas McKean
Tel: 0505 614315

The inn is the oldest pub in Houston and offers a warm welcome in the centre of a village near the Clyde, that is just ten minutes from Glasgow

airport and 15 minutes from Loch Lomond. There is a pleasant garden for warm weather, a residents' lounge for families, and lunchtime snacks. It is a good base for walking in the lovely countryside and for visiting Glasgow.

Beer: McEwan 80 shilling on air pressure.

Accommodation: 2 singles, 2 family rooms. B&B £21 single, £21 per person in family room. Children under 12 £15.50. Weekends £19 per person per night. Cards: Amex.

INVERBEG

Inverbeg Inn
On A82 near Luss, by Loch Lomond

Licensee: Jack Bisset
Tel: 043 686 678
Fax: 043 686 645

The inn, once known as the Ferry, stands in breathtaking countryside on the west bank of the loch opposite the great craggy slopes of Ben Lomond. The loch ferry calls at the inn's own jetty three times a day in summer. The Inverbeg was once a drovers' ale house and is still a genuine local with shepherds and fishermen playing dominoes and cribbage in the bar. The lounge bar has sofas and armchairs and a host of prints and original paintings. There is a non-smoking lounge and log fires in winter. Bar meals are served lunchtime and evening and include homemade soups, meat and fish grills, jacket spuds with choice of fillings, ploughman's, pizzas, quiche, vegetarian options, sandwiches, toasties, and salads. A children's menu includes hoops, bangers, beans, and fish fingers and chips.

Beer: Caledonian 80 shilling on air pressure.

Accommodation: 2 singles, 11 doubles, 1 family room, 7 rooms with private baths. B&B £30 single, £25-£35 double, family room from £15 per person. Reductions for children sharing. Limited facilities for the disabled. Pets with responsible owners welcome. Cards: Access, Amex, Visa.

KILMUN

Coylet Inn
Loch Eck. 9 miles from Dunoon on A819 going south

Licensee: Richard Addis
Tel: 036 984 426

The Coylet is a small roadside hotel with imposing dormer windows and superb views of the loch amid the lovely forests of Argyll and the idyllic Cowal peninsula. The Coylet was formerly a coaching inn and parts of the building date back to the 18th century. It offers excellent hospitality with open log fires in winter, a bar, and food lunchtime and evening, and it is a good base for fishing, walking or visiting nearby Dunoon. There are boats and motor boats for hire on the loch.

Beer: McEwan 80 shilling and Younger No 3 on air pressure.

Accommodation: 1 twin, 2 doubles. B&B £18 per person. Children welcome, half price under 12.

UPLAWMOOR

Uplawmoor Hotel
66 Neilston Road. From Glasgow M8 exit 24; A736

Owners: Reg & Pam Smith
Tel: 050 585 565/566

The hotel is an 18th-century coaching inn set in a tranquil village 11 miles from Glasgow, on the edge of Ayrshire and Burns country. Bar meals are served daily, lunchtime and evening, and there is an evening restaurant. The hotel stages a mini beer festival in February with up to nine real ales.

Beer: Theakston Best Bitter and Younger No 3 on handpumps.

Accommodation: 13 rooms let as singles or doubles, all en suite. B&B £50 single, £60 double. Children's rates by arrangement, normally charged only for breakfast. Weekend rates on request. Pets by arrangement. Cards: Amex and Visa.

WHITING BAY (ISLE OF ARRAN)

Cameronia Hotel
Shore Road. A841

Licensee: William Collingwood
Tel: 0770 7254

The Cameronia is a small and lively family-run hotel overlooking Holy Isle and close to Brodick Castle. There is a comfortable snug, and a steak and wine bar, with a high priority placed on home cooking for both bar and restaurant meals. The hotel is the home of the Cameronia darts team. Morning coffee is served in the bar, with bar meals at lunchtime. A full table d'hôte and à la carte menu is available in the evening. A large residents' lounge overlooks the sea. All guest rooms have en suite facilities. In winter there are wine and malt whisky tastings.

Beer: Broughton Greenmantle Ale on handpump

Accommodation: 1 single, 2 twins, 2

family double rooms. B&B £21 per person, £28 with evening meal. Winter Breaks: rates on request. Children welcome, under 11 years half price, 11-16 75%. Golf parties welcome.

TAYSIDE

CARNOUSTIE

Morven Hotel
28 West Path, off A92 Dundee to Arbroath road

Licensee: David Ireland
Tel/fax: 0241 52385

The Morven Hotel is a traditional Georgian manor house set in two acres of grounds. It was built in the early 1880s for a Captain Borrie, and inscriptions on the perimeter wall refer to 'Borrie's Bray' – the hill on which the building stands. Many of the original internal features have been retained, including a fine example of ornate plasterwork in the restaurant. The hotel commands magnificent views of the famous Carnoustie championship golf course; passes and individual tee-times can be arranged. Crombie and Monikie country parks are close by, and there are facilities for trout fishing, sailing and visiting the local fishing town of Arbroath, famous for the local delicacy, the Arbroath Smokie, which features on the hotel menu. The whisky trail includes Edradour and Blair Athol distilleries, and brewery tours can also be arranged. The hotel stages an annual beer festival during the last weekend in June, with jazz bands and marquees. Bar food is served in the hotel lunchtime and evening and there is an evening restaurant.

Beer: Belhaven 80 shilling, Draught Bass, Theakston XB on handpumps.

Accommodation: 6 doubles, 1 family room, 5 rooms with en suite facilities. B&B £17 single, £22 en suite; £30/£40 double, £40/£50 family room. Children sharing £10 per night. No pets. Cards: Access and Visa.

The Maps

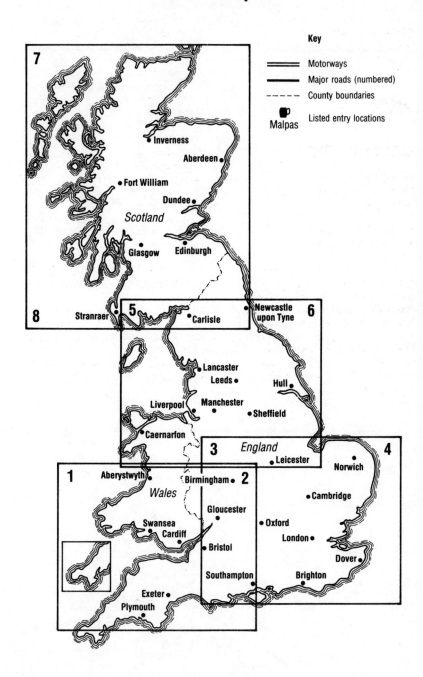

Key

≡≡≡	Motorways
▬▬	Major roads (numbered)
- - -	County boundaries
☕ Malpas	Listed entry locations

7

8

5

6

Inverness

Aberdeen

Fort William

Dundee

Scotland

Glasgow

Edinburgh

Stranraer

Carlisle

Newcastle upon Tyne

Lancaster

Leeds

Hull

Liverpool

Manchester

Sheffield

Caernarfon

3 *England* **4**

Leicester

Norwich

1

Aberystwyth

Birmingham **2**

Wales

Cambridge

Gloucester

Oxford

Swansea

Cardiff

London

Bristol

Dover

Southampton

Brighton

Exeter

Plymouth

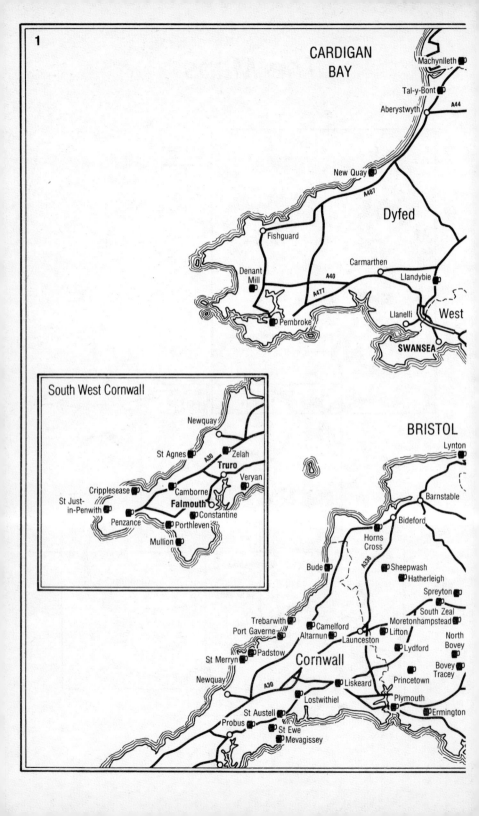

1

CARDIGAN BAY

Machynlleth

Tal-y-Bont

Aberystwyth   A44

New Quay

A487

Dyfed

Fishguard

Carmarthen

Denant
Mill   A40   Llandybie

A477

Pembroke   Llanelli   West

SWANSEA

South West Cornwall

Newquay

St Agnes   Zelah
        A30
                    Truro
Cripplesease   Veryan

St Just-   Camborne
in-Penwith   Falmouth

Penzance   Constantine
        Porthleven

Mullion

BRISTOL

Lynton

Barnstable

Bideford

Horns
Cross

Bude   Sheepwash
        A338   Hatherleigh

Spreyton

South Zeal

Trebarwith   Moretonhampstead
Port Gaverne   Camelford   Lifton   North
        Altarnun   Bovey
St Merryn   Launceston   Lydford
        Padstow
Cornwall   Bovey
        Tracey

Newquay   Princetown

        A30   Liskeard
                    Plymouth
        Lostwithiel   Ermington

St Austell
Probus   St Ewe
        Mevagissey

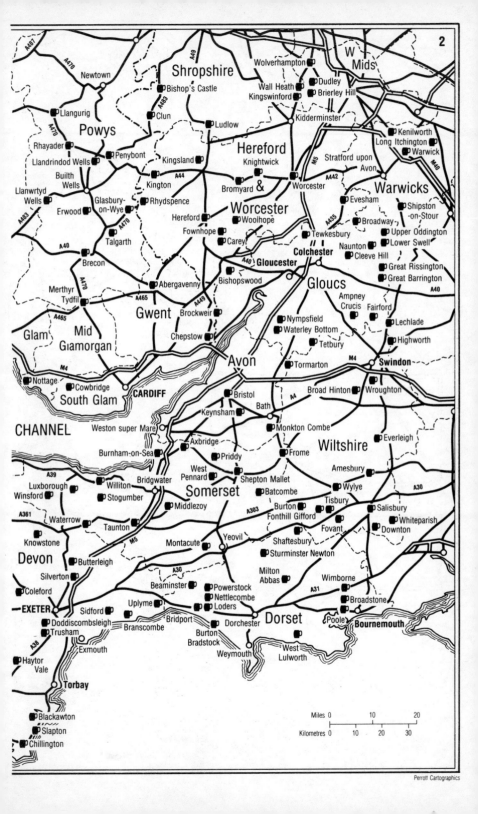

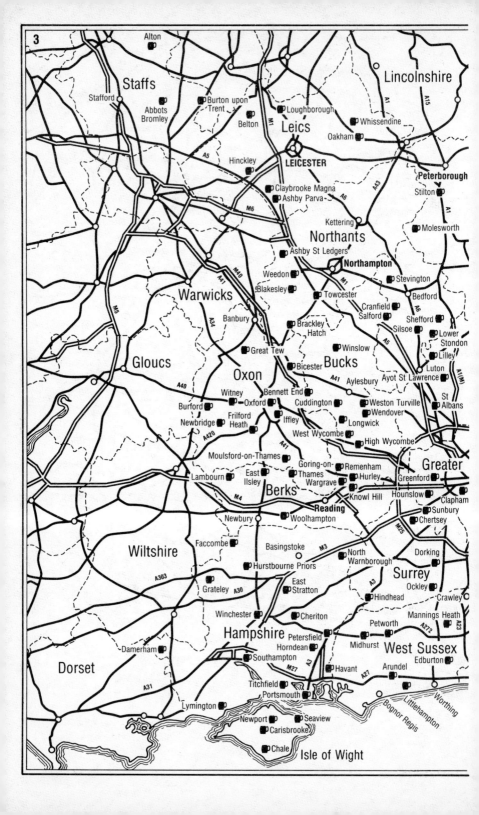

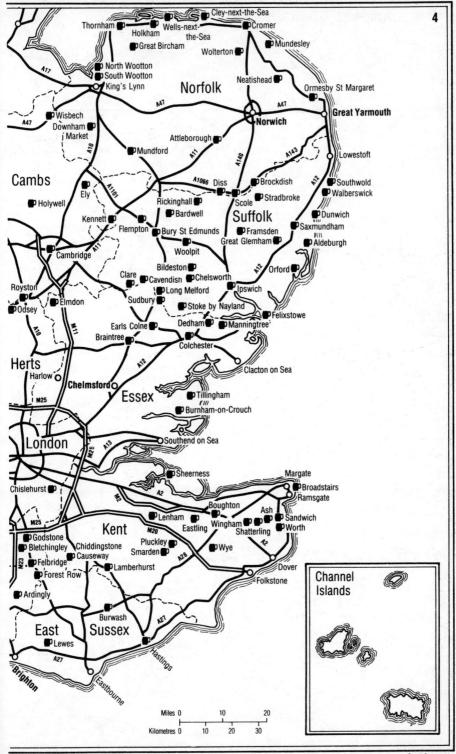

4

Cley-next-the-Sea
Thornham Holkham Wells-next- Cromer
the-Sea
Great Bircham Mundesley
Wolterton

North Wootton Neatishead Ormesby St Margaret
South Wootton
King's Lynn **Great Yarmouth**

Norfolk

Wisbech A47 Norwich A47
Downham Lowestoft
Market Attleborough
A10 A11 A143
Mundford A140 Southwold
Cambs A1066 Diss Brockdish Walberswick
Ely A1101 Rickinghall Scole Stradbroke
Holywell Bardwell Dunwich
Kennett Suffolk Saxmundham
Flempton Bury St Edmunds Framsden Aldeburgh
Woolpit Great Glemham
Cambridge A11 Bildeston Orford
Clare Chelsworth A12
Royston Cavendish Ipswich
Odsey Elmdon Long Melford
Sudbury Stoke by Nayland Felixstowe
Earls Colne Dedham Manningtree
Braintree Colchester
Herts A12 Clacton on Sea
Harlow Chelmsford
Essex Tillingham
Burnham-on-Crouch

London Southend on Sea

Sheerness Margate
Chislehurst Broadstairs
Ramsgate
Boughton Ash Sandwich
Lenham Wingham Worth
Godstone Eastling Shatterling
Bletchingley Chiddingstone Pluckley Wye
Felbridge Causeway Smarden
Forest Row Lamberhurst Dover
Ardingly Folkstone

Burwash
East Sussex
Lewes Hastings
Brighton Eastbourne

Channel
Islands

Miles 0   10   20
Kilometres 0 10 20 30

Perrott Cartographics

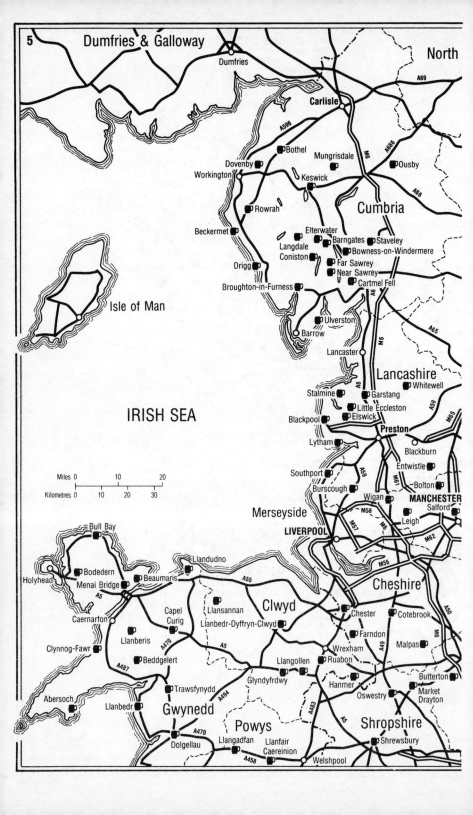

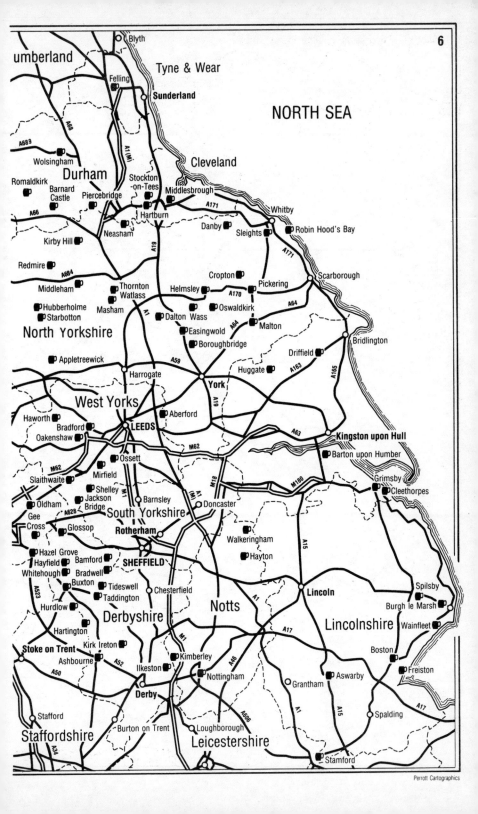

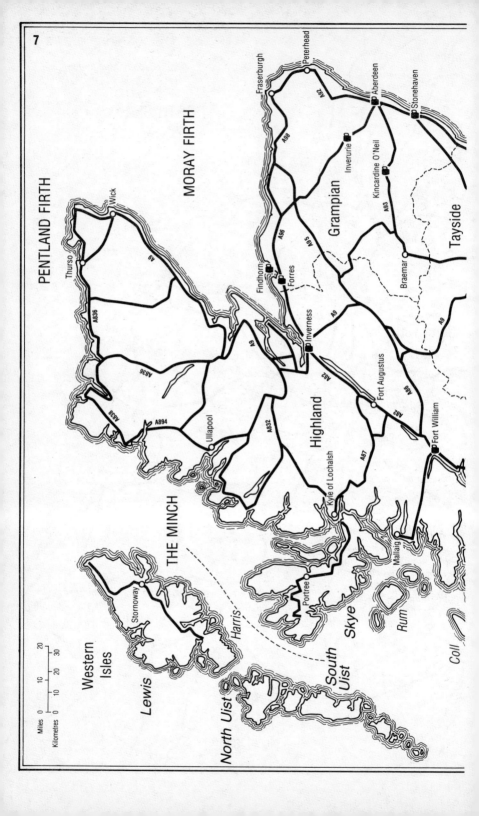

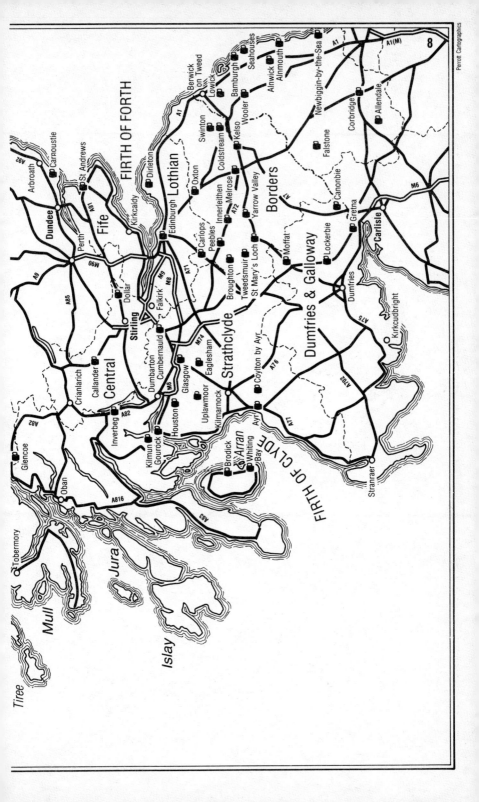

BOOKS FOR BEER AND PUB LOVERS

CAMRA have a growing list of titles that should be on every pubgoers' bookshelf.

The 1992 *Good Beer Guide*, edited by Jeff Evans, lists more than 5,000 pubs throughout the British Isles that sell real ale. Complete with a detailed brewery section, £7.99.

CAMRA *Guide to Good Pub Food* by Susan Nowak dispels the myth that pub food is no more than microwaved misery or curly cheese sandwiches. This best selling guide lists pubs throughout Britain serving fresh, imaginative and good-value food, £7.99.

The following well-designed and fully-mapped regional guides are now available:

Best Pubs in London by Roger Protz, £4.95.
Best Pubs in Lakeland by Mike Dunn, £3.95.
Best Pubs in Devon and Cornwall by Tim Webb, £4.95.
Best Pubs in East Anglia by Roger Protz, £4.95.
Best Pubs in North Wales by Mike Dunn, £4.95.
Best Pubs in Yorkshire by Barrie Pepper, £4.95.

If you enjoy going to pubs but don't want to leave the children at home or eat in fast-food burger joints, then you need *Best Pubs for Families* by Jill Adam, some 500 pubs nationwide that offer children's menus, family rooms, gardens and changing facilities for babies, £4.95.

And if you enjoy a good drop as well as real ale then don't miss David Kitton's definitive *Good Cider Guide*, which lists hundreds of pubs, clubs and off-licences that serve the fermented juice of the apple, £5.95.

The Real Ale Drinker's Almanac by Roger Protz (Lochar, £5.95) is a handsome pocket book that gives details of all cask-conditioned beers brewed in Britain, including recipes, ingredients and detailed tasting notes.

Available from all good bookshops or direct from CAMRA, 34 Alma Road, St Albans, Herts AL1 3BW. Add £1 post and packing per volume. Three books or more post free.

REPORT FORM

County _____

Town or village _____

Name of pub/hotel _____

Address _____

Location (A or B road) _____

Tel no _____ Name of licensee _____

Description of pub (including bars, food, guest rooms and any special facilities) _____

_____

_____

_____

Draught beers (including method of dispense) _____

_____

_____

Accommodation:

No of single rooms _____ doubles/twins _____ family rooms _____

Cost of B & B per person per day _____ cost for double/twin if price based on room _____ cost for family room _____

No of rooms with en suite baths or showers _____

Can children stay ☐ yes ☐ no Children's reductions _____

Cost of any special 'breaks', eg off-season, weekend, mid-week _____

Date of Stay _____

Name and address of person recommending _____

_____

_____

Send to
Roger Protz, CAMRA, 34 Alma Road, St Albans, Herts AL1 3BW

DELETION FORM

County _____

Town or village _____

Name of pub/hotel _____

Address _____

_____

_____

The entry should be deleted for the following reasons:

_____

_____

_____

_____

_____

_____

_____

Date of stay _____

Name and address of person recommending deletion

_____

_____

_____

Send to
Roger Protz, CAMRA, 34 Alma Road, St Albans, Herts AL1 3BW